Labor Unions and Democratic Unrest in North Africa

The political upheavals witnessed in North Africa during the 2011 Arab uprisings brought renewed attention to the region. This book focuses on the inconspicuous yet critical role of labor unions in shaping protest success (and failure) during this period. Drawing on a comparison between Tunisia and Morocco, Ashley Anderson connects the divergent protest strategies of each country to the varying levels of institutional incorporation and organizational cohesion developed by labor unions under authoritarian rule. Using material drawn from English, Arabic, and French news sources, archives, and extensive interviews, Anderson demonstrates how Tunisia's exclusionary corporatist system enabled the Tunisian General Labour Union (UGTT) to emerge as a powerful political actor, while Moroccan unions struggled to extract minimal concessions from the incumbent regime. By highlighting the interplay between authoritarian institutions, labor activism, and political reforms, this book sheds light on the challenges that labor organizations face in transforming their countries' political and economic future.

ASHLEY ANDERSON is Assistant Professor at the University of North Carolina – Chapel Hill. Her research and teaching interests are in comparative politics, with a focus on authoritarian regimes, Middle Eastern political development, and contentious politics. Anderson has previously published research with Cambridge University Press, and in journals such as *Political Research Quarterly*, *Social Science and Medicine*, and *POMEPS Studies*.

THE GLOBAL MIDDLE EAST

The Global Middle East series seeks to broaden and deconstruct the geographical boundaries of the "Middle East" as a concept to include North Africa, Central and South Asia, and diaspora communities in Western Europe and North America. The series features fresh scholarship that employs theoretically rigorous and innovative methodological frameworks resonating across relevant disciplines in the humanities and the social sciences. In particular, the general editors welcome approaches that focus on mobility, the erosion of nation-state structures, travelling ideas and theories, transcendental techno-politics, the decentralization of grand narratives, and the dislocation of ideologies inspired by popular movements. The series will also consider translations of works by authors in these regions whose ideas are salient to global scholarly trends but have yet to be introduced to the Anglophone academy.

OTHER BOOKS IN THE SERIES:

1. *Transnationalism in Iranian Political Thought: The Life and Times of Ahmad Fardid*, Ali Mirsepassi
2. *Psycho-nationalism: Global Thought, Iranian Imaginations*, Arshin Adib-Moghaddam
3. *Iranian Cosmopolitanism: A Cinematic History*, Golbarg Rekabtalaei
4. *Money, Markets and Monarchies: The Gulf Cooperation Council and the Political Economy of the Contemporary Middle East*, Adam Hanieh
5. *Iran's Troubled Modernity: Debating Ahmad Fardid's Legacy*, Ali Mirsepassi
6. *Foreign Policy as Nation Making: Turkey and Egypt in the Cold War*, Reem Abou-El-Fadl
7. *Revolution and its Discontents: Political Thought and Reform in Iran*, Eskandar Sadeghi-Boroujerdi

8. *Creating the Modern Iranian Woman: Popular Culture between Two Revolutions*, Liora Hendelman-Baavur
9. *Iran's Quiet Revolution: The Downfall of the Pahlavi State*, Ali Mirsepassi
10. *Reversing the Colonial Gaze: Persian Travelers Abroad*, Hamid Dabashi
11. *Israel's Jewish Identity Crisis: State and Politics in the Middle East*, Yaacov Yadgar
12. *Temporary Marriage in Iran: Gender and Body Politics in Modern Persian Film and Literature*, Claudia Yaghoobi
13. *Cosmopolitan Radicalism: The Visual Politics of Beirut's Global Sixties*, Zeina Maasri
14. *Anticolonial Afterlives in Egypt: The Politics of Hegemony*, Sara Salem
15. *What is Iran? Domestic Politics and International Relations*, Arshin Adib-Moghaddam
16. *Art and the Arab Spring: Aesthetics of Revolution and Resistance in Tunisia and Beyond*, Siobhán Shilton
17. *Tunisia's Modern Woman: Nation-Building and State Feminism in the Global 1960s*, Amy Aisen Kallander
18. *Global 1979: Geographies and Histories of the Iranian Revolution*, Arang Keshavarzian and Ali Mirsepassi
19. *Fixing Stories: Local Newsmaking and International Media in Turkey and Syria*, Noah Amir Arjomand
20. *Schooling the Nation: Education and Everyday Politics in Egypt*, Hania Sobhy
21. *Violence and Representation in the Arab Uprisings*, Benoît Challand
22. *A Social History of Modern Tehran: Space, Power, and the City*, Ashkan Rezvani Naraghi
23. *An Iranian Childhood: Rethinking History and Memory*, Hamid Dabashi
24. *Heroes to Hostages: America and Iran, 1800–1988*, Firoozeh Kashani-Sabet
25. *The Making of Persianate Modernity: Language and Literary History between Iran and India*, Alexander Jabbari
26. *Mandatory Madness: Colonial Psychiatry and Mental Illness in British Mandate Palestine*, Chris Sandal-Wilson
27. *Polluted Politics: The Development of an Israeli-Palestinian E-Waste Economy*, John-Michael Davis and Yaacov Garb
28. *The Cultural Politics of Art in Iran: Modernism, Exhibitions, and Art Production*, Katrin Nahidi
29. *Millennial Dreams in Oil Economies: Job Seeking and the Global Political Economy of Labour in Oman*, Crystal A. Ennis
30. *Civic Death in Contemporary Turkey: Mass Surveillance and the Authoritarian State*, Seçkin Sertdemir
31. *The Intellectual Thought of Al-Ghazālī: The Alchemy of Happiness and other Persian Writing*, Ali Mirsepassi and Tadd Graham Fernée

Labor Unions and Democratic Unrest in North Africa

Protest and Resistance in Tunisia and Morocco

ASHLEY ANDERSON
University of North Carolina, Chapel Hill

CAMBRIDGE
UNIVERSITY PRESS

CAMBRIDGE
UNIVERSITY PRESS

Shaftesbury Road, Cambridge CB2 8EA, United Kingdom

One Liberty Plaza, 20th Floor, New York, NY 10006, USA

477 Williamstown Road, Port Melbourne, VIC 3207, Australia

314–321, 3rd Floor, Plot 3, Splendor Forum, Jasola District Centre, New Delhi – 110025, India

103 Penang Road, #05–06/07, Visioncrest Commercial, Singapore 238467

Cambridge University Press is part of Cambridge University Press & Assessment, a department of the University of Cambridge.

We share the University's mission to contribute to society through the pursuit of education, learning and research at the highest international levels of excellence.

www.cambridge.org
Information on this title: www.cambridge.org/9781009634939

DOI: 10.1017/9781009634915

When citing this work, please include a reference to the DOI 10.1017/9781009634915

First published 2025

Cover image: May Day Rally in Tunisia, 2016 / Amine Landoulsi / Anadolu Agency / Getty Images

A catalogue record for this publication is available from the British Library

A Cataloging-in-Publication data record for this book is available from the Library of Congress

ISBN 978-1-009-63493-9 Hardback

To my family, who always said I could

Contents

Figures

Tables

Abbreviations

AMDH	Moroccan Association for Human Rights (*Association marocaine des droits humains*)
ANDCM	National Association of Unemployed Graduates (*Association nationale des diplômés chômeurs du Maroc*)
CCC	Collective agreement framework (*Convention collective cadre*)
CDT	Democratic Confederation of Labor (*Confédération Démocratique du Travail*)
CGT	General Confederation of Labor (*Confédération Générale du Travail*)
CGTT	General Confederation of Tunisian Workers (*Confédération Générale des Travailleurs Tunisiens*)
CGTT	General Confederation of Tunisian Labor (*Confédération Générale du Travail*)
CNCA	Civil National Constituent Assembly (*Assemblée Nationale Constituante Civil*)
CNSS	National Social Security Fund (*Caisse Nationale de Sécurité Sociale*)
CPC	Joint consultative committees (*Commissions paritaires consultatives*)
CSR	Committee for the Protection of the Revolution (*Comité pour la Sauveguarder de la Révolution*)
FDT	Democratic Federation of Labor (*Fédération Démocratique du Travail*)
FNTR	National Federation of Road Transport (*Fédération Nationale du Transport Routier*)
HoC	House of Councillors (*Chambre des Conseillers*)
ISROR	High Commission for the Protection of the Revolution (*Haute Instance pour la Réalisation des Objectifs de la Révolution, de la Réforme Politique et de la Transition Démocratique*)

LP	League for the Protection of the Revolution (*Ligue pour la Protection de la Révolution*)
LTDH	Tunisian League of Human Rights (*Ligue Tunisienne des Droits de l'Homme*)
MDS	Movement of Socialist Democrats (*Mouvement des Démocrates Socialistes*)
NCA	National Constituent Assembly *(Assemblée Nationale Constituante*)
OAT	Tunisian Order of Lawyers (*Ordre National des Avocats de Tunisie*)
ODT	Democratic Labor Organization (*Organisation Démocratique du Travail*)
PDJ	Justice and Development Party (*Parti du Justice et Développement*)
PPS	Party of Progress and Socialism (*Parti du Progrès et du Socialisme*)
PSD	Socialist Destourian Party (*Parti Socialiste Destourien*)
RCD	Democratic Constitutional Rally (*Rassemblement Constitutionnel Démocratique*)
SGERS	General Syndicate of Higher Education and Scientific Research (*Syndicat Général de l'Enseignement Supérieur et de la Recherche Scientifique*)
SNC	National Railworker's Union (*Syndicat National des Cheminots*)
UGTM	General Union of Moroccan Workers (*Union Générale des Travailleurs Marocains*)
UGTT	Tunisian General Labor Union (*Union Générale Tunisienne du Travail*)
UMT	Moroccan Labor Union (*Union Marocain du Travail*)
UNTM	National Union of Labor in Morocco (*Union Nationale du Travail au Maroc*)
UNFP	National Union of Popular Forces (*Union Nationale des Forces Populaires*)
USFP	Socialist Union of Popular Forces (*Union Socialiste des Forces Populaires*)
UTICA	Tunisian Union of Industry, Trade and Handicrafts (*Union Tunisienne de l'Industrie, du Commerce et de l'Artisanat*)
UTT	Union of Tunisian Workers (*Union des Travailleurs de Tunisie*)

Acknowledgments

This book is a testament to the benefits of perseverance. I have stuck with this project for probably far too long, but in that time I encountered so many people who made the work better with their feedback, research assistance, insights, and unwavering support. I thank all of them now, knowing that without their help there is no way this book would be what it is today.

First, I would like to thank my intellectual communities at Stanford and Harvard University, who inspired me to pursue a PhD and guided me through the process. A special thanks goes to my graduate advisors, Grzegorz Ekiert, Steve Levitsky, Melani Cammett, and Arthur Spirling; in some way, works by each of you have been an inspiration for my own.

I am also grateful to the many mentors, advisors, and assistants that I encountered while conducting this research. The greatest thanks goes to my three research assistants, Yosra Kaarani and Asma Riahi, and Luke Eggleston, who worked tirelessly to help in the collection of the data presented here. I also must thank the various institutions that provided funding for my fieldwork: the National Science Foundation, the Weatherhead Center, the Institute for Quantitative Social Science, and the Project on Middle East Political Science. For helping navigate the research terrain abroad, I thank the Centre des Etudes Maghrebines à Tunis and the Moroccan-American Commission for Educational and Cultural Exchange. Additionally, the following were very generous in allowing me access to their archives: the National Archives of Tunisia, the National Archives of Morocco, the Union Générale Tunisienne du Travail, *Echaab*, and *Libération*. Finally, this project would not have been possible without the help and knowledge gained from so many politicians, activists, and trade unionists who, at times, exposed themselves to great risk in order to serve as my interview subjects. Although their names are purposefully kept anonymous to protect them from reprisals, I remember each one and thank them from the bottom of my heart.

I am also grateful to the community of colleagues and mentors that I have cultivated at the University of North Carolina. So many people from senior colleagues to graduate students have helped in the refinement of this project. I thank you for pushing me intellectually, for giving necessary guidance, and for constantly reminding me to "get the damn thing sent."

Lastly, I am unspeakably grateful to my friends and family, who saw me through this project at my worst moments, and encouraged me to keep going when I wanted to quit. There are too many of you to name but know that I appreciated all of the late-night writing sessions, the accountability check-ins, the cupcakes, and the tacit support. And to the eight people that I call home, I owe you everything. Nothing I am, and nothing I do, would be possible without you cheering me on.

1 *Introduction*

By most accounts, 2011 was a watershed moment in the history of Tunisian politics. That year against a backdrop of high unemployment and rising costs, President Zine El Abidine Ben Ali found himself under intense pressure from a coalition of lawyers, students, and workers in the nation's interior. Galvanized by the self-immolation of Mohammed Bouazizi, demonstrators poured onto the streets, demanding an end to economic injustice and sweeping political reforms. To make matters worse, on January 4th, the nation's largest labor union – the Tunisian General Labor Union (*Union Générale Tunisienne du Travail*, UGTT) – abandoned its initial reluctance to join the protests and issued a statement of solidarity with the demonstrators.

By January 14th, labor-backed protests had spread from small towns in the nation's interior to major commercial centers, culminating in a two-hour general strike in the capital city. In less than a month, what began as local opposition to poor economic conditions had transformed into a nationwide movement against authoritarian rule. Later that day, labor opposition culminated in a suprising victory when Ben Ali fled the country, transferring power to an interim government. After nearly sixty years, Tunisia's once-durable dictatorship had come to an end.

Months later, in Morocco, labor unions faced a strikingly similar situation. As in Tunisia, Moroccan workers confronted a daunting set of circumstances – after a decade of neoliberal reforms, unemployment was at an all-time high, inflation was rising, and the minimum wage had remained stagnant for nearly three years. Yet despite substantial grievances, labor protests in Morocco remained comparatively mild. Although the nation's five main labor unions united in a call for a joint demonstration on May 1st, a mere 15,000 workers appeared in Casablanca's main square, with only two unions – the Moroccan Labor Union (*Union Marocain du Travail*, UMT) and the Democratic Confederation of Labor

(*Confédération Démocratique du Travail*, CDT) – explicitly supporting wage demands. Moreover, in stark contrast to Tunisia, labor protests in Morocco focused primarily on economic concerns. Despite active participation from the February 20th movement, which advocated for radical political reforms, union leaders made it a point to emphasize the apolitical nature of their demands. As one unionist commented, "We are marching because we want to push for a social agenda that has nothing to do with the political agenda of the February 20th movement" (Karam, May 1, 2011).

These contrasting vignettes pose a significant puzzle for the field of labor politics: despite facing similar socio-economic challenges, trajectories of labor opposition in Tunisia and Morocco varied. While trade unions in Tunisia successfully translated economic demands into a political movement for regime change, Moroccan unions vainly lobbied for economic concessions and limited policy reforms. These anecdotes reflect a general pattern of dissemblance between labor protests in Tunisia and Morocco; as Figure 1.1 shows, Tunisian unions routinely advance political demands during strikes, while Moroccan unions limit their claims to more narrow workplace and economic concerns. Tunisian unions are also more restive than those in Morocco – both the aggregate number of protests and the number of workdays

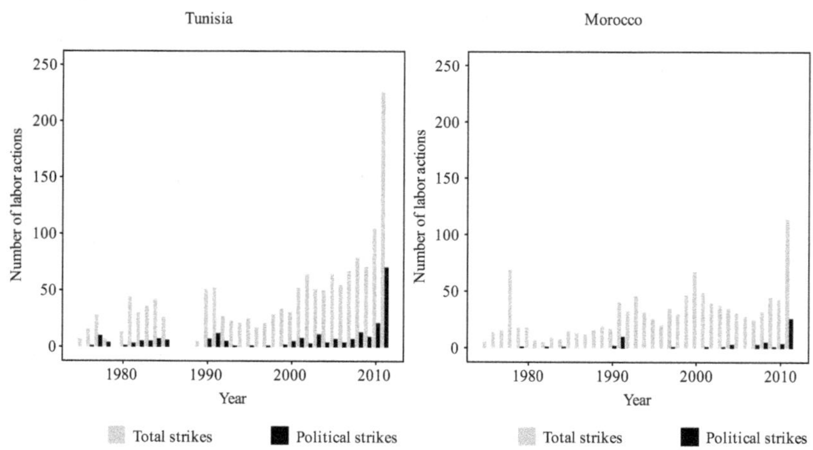

Source: MENALC Database
Note: Years 1979, 1986–1989 missing for Echaab

Source: MENALC Database
Note: 1982–1988 missing for Liberation

Figure 1.1 Strikes and political strikes in Tunisia and Morocco (1975–2011)

lost due to strikes attest to a higher level of militancy among Tunisian workers, as compared to their Moroccan counterparts (ILO, 2016).

If national trends in labor politics can be reduced to the dominance of one type of protest over another, Tunisian unions can be described militant, confrontational, and political, while Moroccan unions are moderate, law-abiding, and "*khubziste*" (i.e., preoccupied with bread-and-butter concerns) (Benhilal, 1984; Catusse, 2001; Menouni, 1979). Such divergent patterns of labor opposition raise the central question of this book: "Why, in authoritarian regimes, do some unions choose to engage in political mobilization while others do not?"

Astounded by the role that labor mobilization has played in crippling authoritarian regimes in Latin America, Asia, and Eastern Europe during the Third Wave, scholars have researched and written much about unions' political behavior. Existing scholarship has offered three main variables – structural-economic conditions, organizational traits, and political institutions – as core determinants of labor militancy. However, these studies, while contributing to our general knowledge about the causes of labor opposition, have been limited in three respects. First, existing research has focused on labor mobilization in single cases, obscuring significant cross-national variation in the modes of labor protest. Second, the bulk of scholarship has been geographically bounded to areas where labor mobilization coincided with democratization, leaving labor protests in more durable authoritarian regimes understudied. Finally, the theoretical frameworks employed by most studies conceive of labor opposition in a uni-dimensional fashion, driven either by top-down structural processes or bottom-up features of unions' internal organization. This work stands against newer, more integrative approaches in the social sciences that have identified a synthesis between unions' external and internal politics and consider the unique ways in which these distinct triggers of protest may come to interact.

Argument

In view of these deficiencies, this book presents an alternative account of labor protest that emphasizes the role that political institutions, particularly those that govern labor organization and interest representation under authoritarian rule, play in shaping unions' decision to engage in political protests. As the opening vignette suggests, the central question of this study is, "why do Tunisian unions engage in politicized, militant protests while their Moroccan counterparts pursue economic agendas through moderate tactics like negotiation and reform?" I argue that differences in unions' protest behavior stem from variation in the institutional structures that govern unions' relationship with the state and with their own internal members. Whereas the availability of formal channels for labor representation in the state shapes unions' willingness to engage in protest, their ability to *sustain* militant protest depends on their internal governance structures and the extent to which these enable union elites to develop robust coalitions with the rank-and-file.

In developing this argument, I connect unions' external political environment and their internal organization to their ultimate modes of protest in the following sequence. First, autocrats' labor control policies shape unions' institutional environment, biasing their initial preferences and capacities for collective action in unique ways. In this study, unions' mobilization strategies are conceptualized dichotomously as militant unionism (involving frequent strikes and demonstrations, often with direct political demands against the government) and moderate unionism (employing moderate, apolitical tactics aimed at lobbying the government within legal limits). In countries where labor is formally incorporated into the regime, as in Morocco, the availability of official channels for demand-making moderates union behavior by institutionalizing state-labor relations and strengthening coalitions between labor leaders and partisan elites. By contrast, where unions are excluded from formal politics, as in Tunisia, unions develop as political outsiders, leading organized labor to project a more militant and radical form of labor politics.

However, institutional exclusion alone is not sufficient to generate lasting labor militancy. If unions' initial willingness to engage in militant protest is influenced by their external environment, their ability to *sustain* radical protest campaigns is determined by the institutions that govern their internal organization and shape union leaders' relationships with the rank-and-file. I argue that democratic unions with inclusive governing structures are more likely to sustain militant protests than those without. Democratic unions decentralize decision-making, enable members to hold leaders accountable through (reasonably) competitive elections, and provide various mechanisms for rank-and-file workers to participate in union affairs. These institutions facilitate labor opposition by increasing vertical accountability between members and union elites and reducing the threat of co-optation known to imperil oligarchic labor unions (McAdam, 1982; Tilly, 1978). Moreover, by encouraging membership engagement in union affairs, democratic organizations strengthen intra-union solidarity, providing unions with the capacity needed to sustain militant protest campaigns.

Critically, I link the type of organization that unions form to the institutional conditions they face at their founding – only unions that are excluded from the formal political system are expected to establish democratic governance. This is because labor unions with limited state access and few influential allies have no choice but to wed themselves to the rank-and-file and undertake the laborious, costly, and autonomy-reducing work of crating democratic institutions. The effects of institutionalizing democracy on union behavior are expected to be "sticky"; once unions create democratic organizations, institutions such as elections or participatory decision-making may make it difficult for leaders to divorce themselves from the rank-and-file entirely. Conversely, unions that eschew accountable governance may have trouble mobilizing their membership during moments of crisis.

At the heart of the book's argument, then, lies a paradox: exclusionary policies meant to weaken and depoliticize unions are precisely those that engender political militancy. By casting unions into the institutional wilderness, autocrats who rely on exclusionary policies unintentionally arm their opponents, giving them the autonomy, incentive, and organizational capacity necessary to successfully challenge authoritarian rule.

Figure 1.2 outlines the preceding argument schematically, identifying the major actors, variables, and outcomes that I discuss in subsequent chapters. In the next section, I briefly discuss these dynamics in the cases of Tunisia and Morocco, highlighting the ways in which authoritarian institutions shaped unions' organization and protest trajectories.

Cases

The theory's predictions are borne out in the cases of Tunisia and Morocco. In the vast literature on North African politics, Morocco

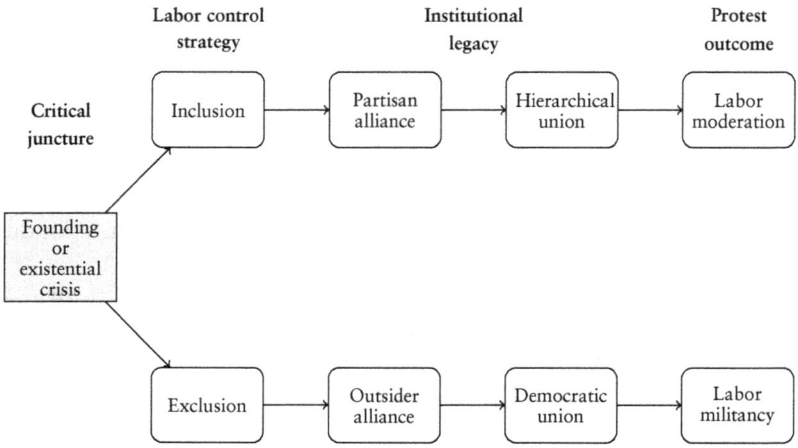

Figure 1.2 Schematic depiction of the book's argument

and Tunisia frequently team up as the most comparable pair (Cammett, 2007; Daadaoui, 2023; Dalmasso and Cavatorta, 2013; White, 2001; Willis, 2012). Both countries share a history of French colonialism, in which traditions of labor organizing and national labor confederations – derived from the French General Confederation of Labor (*Confédération Générale du Travail*, CGT) – were born. Additionally, in both countries relatively brief anti-colonial struggles were bolstered by working-class participation, earning unions nationalist credentials and substantial political legitimacy following independence. As a consequence, when autocrats moved to consolidate their power in the postindependence period, labor unions quickly became focal points for the regime, which mixed material inducements and constraints to eliminate potential opposition. In recent years, unions in both countries have faced significant economic and organizational challenges that fostered labor militancy and complicated unions' efforts to mobilize. For example, economic crises and reforms enacted in the 1970s and 1980s have impacted labor especially hard – in the face of declining budgets, workers have seen marked decreases in their purchasing power and employment prospects. While this has certainly provided an impetus for protest, it has simultaneously frustrated union organization. As a result of structural adjustment, both Tunisian and Moroccan unions witnessed cutbacks in key sectors and a decline in union membership.

These twin developments make Tunisia and Morocco ideal comparanda for a study on labor politics. Yet, underscoring the importance of an institutional explanation for labor protest, Tunisian and Moroccan protest patterns differed despite these countries' shared history. In Tunisia, authoritarian exclusion and the subsequent lack of institutional channels to express labor demands generated militant and political unions. In the postindependence era, early political challenges led President Habib Bourguiba to pursue dual strategies of co-optation and repression to contain labor militancy. While repressive periods were occasionally punctuated by attempts at conciliation – resulting in a "checkered alliance" between labor and the state (Bellin, 2002) – attempts to depoliticize unions alienated workers from the regime, creating a new class of unionists with a more radical and antagonistic approach to labor politics. In the 1970s, this radicalization was evident among labor elites, who, forced from their positions within the ruling coalition, joined with rank-and-file workers in their protests against the regime. At the height of labor confrontation, the UGTT used its scope of autonomy to expand worker participation in decision-making, democratize its internal bureaucracy, and lend support to regional/local affiliates undertaking contentious activity. Simultaneously, the closure of institutional channels to political opposition drove leftist parties to seek refuge within the UGTT, enabling the union to project a more politicized version of labor militancy.

Even following the ouster of Bourguiba and the inauguration of a program of political "*changement*" under Ben Ali, organized labor continued to exist on the margins of formal politics. While a brief period of liberalization in the early 1990s pacified relations between the regime and UGTT, its effects on the overall character of state–labor relations were short-lived. Attempts to co-opt the union's leadership were sporadic and confined to a small body of elites, failing to create a cohesive labor movement aligned with regime interests. Additionally, limited inclusion of opposition parties was complemented by harsh repression of excluded groups, reinforcing ties between labor and radical political actors.

Thus, in the mid-2000s, organized labor resumed its pattern of political confrontation with the regime. Although in specific instances, rivalries between co-opted union elites and workers inhibited labor militancy, more frequently, rank-and-file mobilization was endorsed by union officials, leading to a rise in political protests. Moreover, the persistent threat of institutional marginalization compelled UGTT leaders to enhance the union's internal democracy and strengthen its ties to the grassroots. As a result, when protests erupted in early 2011 over workers' economic grievances, the UGTT was poised to capitalize on these events and orchestrate a nationwide political campaign against the Ben Ali regime. In the subsequent political transition, the UGTT would emerge as a pivotal actor, leveraging its organizational capacity and social networks to influence the direction of Tunisia's democratic development.

The trajectory of labor politics in Morocco offers a contrasting narrative. As in Tunisia, postindependence competition for power led King Mohammed V to adopt dual strategies of repression and co-optation to mitigate threats from the dominant party (*Istiqlal)* and its union affiliate (the UMT). However, unlike Bourguiba, Mohammed V pursued a more inclusionary approach, aiming to fragment opposition elites while incorporating them as political clients of the state. In the early 1960s, the king established Morocco as a "democratic, constitutional monarchy," and created a bicameral parliament in which opposition elites, professional associations, and labor unions could compete for power. While this institution was explicitly designed to perpetuate authoritarian control, it also created a more open political arena in which unions had access to various channels for interest representation.

Ultimately, the incorporation of unions into formal politics had two complementary effects on labor militancy. First, by allowing labor representatives to serve in parliament, it created a cadre of union elites whose financial and symbolic status relied on state support. Second, competitive elections incentivized political parties to forge "organic links" with unions, creating clientelistic relations between union and partisan elites. With union leaders reliant on political affiliations for success, they had little incentive to heed rank-and-file demands or build robust connections to the grassroots. Consequently, in the early 1970s and 1980s, labor mobilization in Morocco became bifurcated along two lines: while union elites promoted a policy of apolitical moderation, rank-and-file workers resorted to spontaneous, wildcat demonstrations to make their demands heard.

Indeed, it was only during periods of significant repression marked by the near exclusion of unions from policy-making that labor mobilization appeared remotely political. During this period, opposition parties leveraged historical ties with labor unions to bolster their electoral campaigns with strikes, which took on an implicit political character. However, with the ascension of King Mohammed VI and the creation of new inclusive institutions that reinstated labor elites to positions of power in the late 1990s, the impetus for political militancy among unions waned. By the end of the decade, Moroccan unions had reverted to familiar patterns, engaging in fragmented, apolitical mobilization that reinforced the regime's hold on power.

Thus, when popular discontent fueled pro-democratic protests during the 2011 Arab uprisings, Moroccan unions remained weak and politically quiescent. Despite calls for militancy from informal workers and rank-and-file members, union leaders chose to pursue labor demands through moderate tactics like elite bargaining and negotiation. These strategies secured selective benefits for specific groups of workers and strengthened union representation in state institutions but failed to deliver lasting benefits for the working class. Consequently, in the post-Arab Spring era, labor politics in Morocco have been marked by passivity and heightened division between a politically captive elite and an increasingly demobilized base.

Methodology and Data Sources

To evidence these arguments, this book employs multiple forms of analysis and empirical material. The primary method is a comparative case study, through which I inductively build a theory of how political institutions affect labor mobilization in Tunisia and Morocco over fifty-five years (1956–2011). While case studies have been criticized for their lack of generalizability and difficulty in identifying causal effects (Campbell, 1963, 6–7,17; Dogan and Pèlassy, 1990, 121), they offer distinct advantages for theory-building and specifying causal processes (Eckstein et al., 2000; George and Bennett, 2005, 20–21; Gerring, 2006). For example, a detailed examination of individual cases is necessary for establishing causal relationships across lengthy periods, permitting researchers to identify the specific sequence in which variables must occur to influence an outcome of interest (McKeown, 2004). Additionally, focused comparison between cases facilitates the discovery of how variation in key explanatory variables leads to change, both across cases and over time (George and Bennett, 2005).

To maximize analytical leverage, I combine cross-case comparisons with longitudinal analyses of protest behavior within each case. The Tunisia–Morocco comparison approximates a "most-similar" case study design: while the two are not perfectly alike, they are arguably more similar than any other two cases in North Africa with respect to the variables treated as important in studies of labor politics – colonial history, industrial policy, state sector presence, and integration into the global market. These similarities allow me to "control" for competing explanations and assess my argument against reasonable counterfactuals. The analysis of four additional cases in the book's conclusion enhances generalizability and allows me to apply my theory to a broader range of authoritarian regimes.

The longitudinal analysis is structured around three periods corresponding to moments of significant economic and institutional change: the early-liberalization phase (1975–1985), structural adjustment (1985–1999), and the post-adjustment period (2000–2011). Given that economic shifts are (roughly) similar across both cases, while institutional designs vary, this periodization allows me to better isolate the effects of institutional arrangements on labor behavior.

Quantitative Data

The sources used to evidence my argument are varied. To track the evolution of labor protest, I use the Labor Conflict in the Middle East and North Africa Database (MENALC), an original dataset that contains geo-referenced information on over 2,000 protest events from 1975 to 2011. In addition to standard features like duration and attendance, it offers specialized information on protests like event type (i.e., strike, sit-in, hunger strike) actors, targets, and demands, enabling analyses along multiple dimensions. Additionally, drawing from a wide variety of international, regional, and local news sources (e.g., foreign news wires, state-owned media, opposition dailies, union press), MENALC is one of the most extensive databases on labor protest in North Africa to date.

A key advantage of the MENALC database is its ability to differentiate between economic and political forms of labor protest based on type of demand. For the purposes of this study, I define *political* protests in line with Lambert and Webster as collective action "that attempts to link production with wider political issues"

(Lambert and Webster, 1988, 1929). Unlike economic protests, which concentrate exclusively on workplace issues (i.e., wages and working conditions) and relegate workers' political concerns to the domain of parties and NGOs, political protests "link factory-based unions and communities," creating "challenges to states as well as individual employers" (Seidman, 1994, 3). Protest demands were collected from close reading of articles by trained research assistants and were classified as economic or political based on the type of demand. A complete listing of these demands, as well as the coding procedures and sources used to compile the dataset, is provided in Appendix A.

Despite the analytical benefits that such detailed protest data provides, it is important to recognize the limits of media-based data, including under-reporting, imprecise estimates, and potential censorship. MENALC contains several "missing" entries – in some periods for many months or years – and lacks precision on event duration and participation figures. Moreover, the data is deliberately a random sample of protest events and therefore can only approximate the total number of protests in a given year to an order of magnitude. Nonetheless, the breadth of the data gives me confidence in its ability to detect aggregate trends in protest behavior. When possible, I supplement MENALC data with statistics collected by the International Labor Organization (ILO) or national labor ministries to provide a more complete picture of labor opposition.

Qualitative Data

To gain insight into how political institutions shaped patterns of labor behavior, I rely on two sources of evidence: interviews and archival data. Over two years of fieldwork (2012–2014), I conducted more than 80 interviews with labor activists, civil society leaders, public officials, and academics. Interviews were conducted in two stages, each involving different methodologies and serving different analytical aims. The first round of interviews, held from June 2012 to January 2013, was comprised of unstructured discussions to gather detailed information on strike activity and union organization beyond what was available in secondary sources. Participants were selected nonrandomly, based on their union affiliations or knowledge of labor politics in their respective countries. The informal nature of these discussions allowed me to inductively gain insight into labor politics and refine my research questions for future inquiries.

The second round of interviews, which took place from August 2013 to May 2014, was designed to test hypotheses uncovered in these initial conversations and explore causal mechanisms. These interviews followed a semi-structured format with open-ended questions centered around consistent themes. Interviews were conducted in English, French, Spanish, and Arabic, depending on the interviewee's language preference, and lasted approximately an hour on average. Again, interviewees were selected on a nonrandom basis, with additional participants identified through a "snowballing method" based on recommendations from previous interviewees.

Finally, I utilize historical data from union and government archives in Tunis, Casablanca, and Rabat to examine the relationship between labor incorporation and union democracy. Most helpful in this regard were the UGTT archives, which contained detailed information on union elections at the national, regional, and local levels going back to the organization's founding in 1946. These records enabled me to assess the quality of the UGTT's internal democracy as well as trace its bureaucratic evolution over time. When possible, these data are compared with similar statistics on union elections in Morocco, though the data from Moroccan unions is notably more sparse. In addition, legislative, administrative, and ministerial data help me to assess the level of unions' embeddedness with the state's institutional apparatus. These data were collected from the Tunisian and Moroccan National Archives, and were supplemented with reports available in the *Annuaire de l'Afrique du Nord* (1952–2003) and local press outlets.

Theoretical Implications

Shifting the Focus of Labor Politics

The analysis presented in this book builds upon and nuances important research in political science and sociology. For scholarship on labor politics, it shifts the research agenda to under-explored empirical terrain. While the literature on industrial conflict is extensive, most insights have been derived from the study of advanced industrial democracies or developing countries with robust, independent labor movements such as Poland or Brazil (Ekiert and Kubik, 2001; Seidman, 1994) What is less well-understood, however, is how protest functions in autocracies where controlled or state-dependent unions are the norm (but see for important exceptions Bellin, 2002; Beinin, 2015; Bishara, 2018; Feltrin, 2019; Hartshorn, 2019; Robertson, 2010).

A brief examination of organizational life in these settings suggests that existing models of strike behavior may not be suitable for understanding labor opposition in authoritarian regimes. For example, reasonable protections for the free exercise of dissent are often absent or restricted under autocratic rule. As such, the decision to engage in protest is much more contingent: while opposition may risk the loss of organizational privileges and repression, compromise under state control can lead to the emasculation of the labor movement and the loss of potential gains in wages and rights (Bellin, 2002). These tensions, often absent in most democracies, complicate unions' decision-making and affect patterns of labor militancy in unique and theoretically significant ways.

Exploring labor mobilization under authoritarianism illuminates these dynamics and reveals substantial variation in labor protest across autocracies. Indeed, a central contribution of this study is to show that protest behavior may differ even when subjected to common conditions of authoritarian rule. As the case of Tunisia demonstrates, a legacy of political repression needn't prevent labor unions from engaging in militant protest or launching an effective challenge to the regime. Similarly, the case of Morocco reveals that pluralism and political incorporation, frequently thought to benefit unions in autocracies (Caraway, 2006; LeBas, 2011; Nelson, 1991), may undermine labor's strength and viability over the long term.

In making this point, I am not arguing that authoritarianism per se is more conducive to labor mobilization than democracy. In contrast, I emphasize that the label "authoritarian" does not tell us much about what levels of labor militancy to expect. Instead, I argue that the critical factor influencing labor opposition is the character of authoritarian institutions and their effects on union organization. Some regimes are so repressive that they prohibit labor organizing and make even clandestine mobilization virtually impossible (Franceschini and Nesossi, 2018; Fu, 2017b). Others provide unions with so many privileges that they become loyal allies of the state (Bellin, 2002; Bishara, 2018; Middlebrook, 1995). My work reveals that the relationship between political opportunities and protest is not linear: protest does not simply increase as we move from closed to more open regimes. Instead, labor militancy is most likely to occur under adverse conditions. When unions are born under conditions of institutional exclusion – provided that repression is not too extreme – they are more likely to develop the autonomy and organizational capacity to sustain political protest. In contrast, when unions are incorporated into formal politics, co-option and moderation are more likely to result. Although these insights arise from the study of labor unions in North Africa, they should have applications to social movements more broadly and in different geographic settings.

Moving beyond Authoritarian Stability

Additionally, for students of authoritarian politics, this study provides insights into the "politics of everyday resistance" and challenges existing narratives about the durability of authoritarian regimes. Traditionally, research on autocracies has emphasized their extraordinary stability; only recently have studies focused on understanding their weaknesses. In scholarship on North Africa and the Middle East, persistence narratives have become so common that experts emphasize the "robustness of authoritarianism" and invoke terms like "Middle East" or "Arab exceptionalism" when discussing the region's prospects for democracy (Bellin, 2004; Fish, 2002; Lakoff, 2004; Stepan and Robertson, 2003, 2004). In this context, studies have focused on the role that authoritarian institutions play in underpinning regime survival, enabling autocrats to weaken civil society organizations (Bellin, 2000), co-opt their opponents (Lust-Okar, 2005), distribute patronage within their ruling coalition (Blaydes, 2010), and effectively manage internal threats (Brownlee, 2007).

Yet, the problem with existing studies is that they obscure incremental processes that can contribute to political transformation in authoritarian regimes. This creates a falsely "invincible" image of autocracy, one in which dictators are assumed to select optimal strategies to preserve their rule, or where everyday citizens have little agency to work against elite designs. However, the wave of popular mobilization that shook the Middle East in 2011 has forced a reconsideration of these assumptions, spawning a broad literature on the sites of political resistance *within* autocratic regimes (Bishara,

2018; Fu, 2018; Ketchley, 2017; Robertson, 2010). By turning the spotlight onto somewhat unusual political actors – workers and unions – I contribute to this scholarship, highlighting how change within autocracies can be driven by ordinary people.

In doing so, I provide a new perspective that shifts the conventional wisdom on authoritarian politics in three key ways. First, by focusing attention on the political behavior of subordinate actors, I challenge existing narratives about the passivity of civil society in authoritarian regimes. While previous analyses have portrayed unions as weak in the face of corporatist controls (Bellin, 2002), I show that this image is misleading; workers do not merely obey the dictates of authoritarian regimes, nor do they passively accept the limitations placed upon them by corporatist institutions. Instead, in line with newer scholarship (Bishara, 2018), I show that unions actively challenge government maneuvers and creatively mobilize around institutional controls. As the case of Tunisia shows, although governments may limit opposition to specific fora, motivated groups can transform these institutions into staging grounds for political protest. In these settings, corporatism need not automatically produce labor quiescence; on the contrary, it may provoke a counter-reaction that results in more virulent and political opposition. This dynamic interplay between labor and the state, available only when we shift the focus to "ordinary" political actors, illuminates the possibility for social groups to exercise agency within authoritarian constraints. It also shows how everyday resistance can affect change in even the most durable of autocratic regimes.

Second, by drawing attention to the organizational roots of protest, this book demonstrates how inconspicuous, incremental behaviors can have profound political consequences. An analysis of unions' internal politics reveals that political resistance extends beyond overt collective action; equally important is what occurs within organizations to make such protests possible. When unions are able to create "pockets" of democracy within authoritarian regimes, they can socialize citizens into the political behaviors that induce broader democratization. Conversely, when unions reject member participation in union affairs, they generate tensions within the labor movement that make division and disaffection more likely (see also Bishara, 2018). An examination of what happens inside a movement, therefore, is critical to understanding its long-term political consequences. This insight offers a timely update to the prevailing literature on social movements, which tends to focus on the external manifestations of movement success and views several transition processes as occurring "out of nowhere" (Kuran, 1991; Kurzman, 2004).

Finally, my work provides a fresh perspective on the relationship between political institutions and protest in authoritarian regimes and raises some new potential paradoxes. I show that unions' external political environment and protest behavior are intimately connected, but in ways that scholars have tended to overlook. On the one hand, political institutions exert a known, direct effect on protest by "shaping the political arena" in which labor can make its demands (Collier and Collier, 1991). For example, formal rules encouraging alliances between unions and parties tend to negatively affect labor militancy by co-opting the interests of labor elites (Burgess, 1999; Levitsky and Way, 1998; Murillo, 2001; Robertson, 2004). However, political institutions also *indirectly* affect labor protest by shaping the types of alliances and organizations that labor unions ultimately develop.

The indirect effects of political institutions are likely to be unintentional and affect political outcomes in unexpected ways (Hall and Taylor, 1996; Pierson, 2004). At the core of my argument is a paradox: when autocrats create institutions meant to marginalize and depoliticize labor, they encourage exactly the types of mobilization they aim to prevent. This is because the effects of institutions on protest do not just depend on the rules themselves but also on the ways in which they affect the organizations working within or around them. When autocrats limit space for political opposition, they reduce incentives for unions to work within the system and increase the likelihood of mobilizing outside of formal politics. Additionally, by excluding unions from the political system, they inadvertently endow them with a wealth of organizational resources – autonomy, solidarity, cohesion – that can be used to effectively challenge the regime.

Labor Protest and Regime Change

Finally, my analysis adds to the growing literature on political transition and regime change. Whether lauded as the "key to labor revitalization" or criticized as a gross abandonment of unions' role as representatives of the working class, it is clear that unions' political behavior is highly consequential. As cases such as Brazil, Poland, and South Africa show, where labor is at the forefront of anti-regime protests, its actions can shift government policies and, at the most extreme, cause long-standing authoritarian regimes to fall. While this study does not assume that labor mobilization is *necessarily* pro-democratic, it highlights the varied implications of labor opposition for the stability of authoritarian regimes. On the one hand, where unions become directly involved in political protests, their actions can contribute to a climate of ungovernability that spurs the disintegration of existing authoritarian regimes. In these cases, autocracies are more likely to collapse and, to the extent that it can capitalize on its political influence, labor may continue to play a role in directing the subsequent political transition. On the other, where organized labor pursues more indirect opposition – combining limited street demonstrations with institutional strategies like negotiation and compromise – incumbent elites tend to dominate the process of political reform. In these cases, liberalization is likely to be more limited and authoritarian leaders typically survive.

A theory that explains variation in unions' protest behavior, therefore, is of critical importance to scholars trying to "make sense" of political transitions in authoritarian regimes. Understanding the factors that motivate some unions, but not others, to take political action against the regime can aid scholars in identifying where antiauthoritarian mobilization is likely to initiate a true political opening and where pro-democracy efforts are likely to stall. Still, even when labor opposition is not explicitly directed toward political aims, labor militancy may hasten the decline of autocracy by undermining traditional sources of legitimacy for the regime. Due to their capacity to disrupt economic activity, labor protests can facilitate economic crises, which weaken the structural power of populist authoritarian rule (Collier and Mahoney, 1997; Huntington, 1991; Tilly, 2004). Additionally, labor unrest can provoke splits within the ruling coalition that lead to preemptive democratization as a means of consolidating political support (Adler and Webster, 1995; Bunce, 2003; Wood, 2001). In this way, labor protests, even when nondemocratic, exert significant political leverage in shaping the fate of authoritarian regimes.

Organization of the Book

Following this introduction, this book is organized into seven main chapters. Chapter 2 begins with an elaboration of the central puzzle of my research – why are Tunisian unions militant and politicized while Moroccan unions are apolitical and moderate? I discuss how existing scholarship might answer this question based on the current literature on labor politics within democratic and authoritarian regimes. I review three main classes of arguments – focusing on structural–economic conditions, organizational structure, and political institutions, respectively – and evaluate their utility for understanding the Tunisia/Morocco comparison using comparative statistics. Finding these explanations wanting, I offer an original theory of labor protest, which highlights the role that labor incorporation policies play in shaping the preferences and organizational capacity of unions to engage in militant protest. This theoretical discussion provides the foundation for my empirical analysis in the forthcoming chapters, which examines the catalysts of political militancy in Tunisia and those of business unionism in Morocco.

In Chapter 3, I spell out the initial conditions of my theory, discussing how authoritarian labor control policies differed in Tunisia and Morocco. I show how exclusive labor policies adopted by the Bourguiba regime endowed the UGTT with a measure of autonomy from and enmity toward the authoritarian regime. In Morocco, I show how inclusionary policies meant to incorporate unions fully within the political sphere undermined labor's capacity for mobilization by fostering close linkages with parties and fractionalizing the labor movement into competing factions. I find that these differences had important consequences for how unions viewed their interests and capacities as they entered the neoliberal period: while the UGTT emerged as a cohesive, autonomous organization with an antagonistic vision of its relationship with the state, unions in Morocco developed as organizationally weak, politically co-opted actors that sought to exercise influence within the confines of the authoritarian regime.

Chapters 4–6 form the main empirical chapters of the book and analyze, in greater detail, the trajectories of Tunisian and Moroccan labor mobilization in three key periods of economic change. Chapter 4 begins the inquiry by examining labor opposition during the early years of economic reform (1975–1985). I show that despite adopting similar economic policies, leaders faced different levels of protest threat from organized labor (political militancy in Tunisia and apolitical protest in Morocco). I trace these differences to divergence in authoritarian leaders' strategies for incorporating labor into their regimes. While Tunisia's exclusionary corporatist institutions alienated key segments of the labor movement and political elite, producing widespread antagonism toward the Bourguiba government, the Moroccan monarchy's effort to expand labor representation inhibited political militancy by dividing and co-opting different sectors of the working class.

In Chapter 5, I continue the investigation of labor politics in Tunisia and Morocco by exploring how the mechanisms in my argument function in the context of institutional change. Focusing on labor mobilization during the structural adjustment period (roughly 1986–1997), I show that changes to the institutional structures governing labor representation triggered a surprising reversal in protest patterns in Tunisia and Morocco. In Tunisia, I demonstrate how changes to the corporatist bargaining and political system provided new channels for the expression of labor interests, quieting most sources of opposition to the regime. In Morocco, I show how institutions for labor representation interacted with declining economic conditions to produce new uncertainties for workers and union leaders, generating incentives for militant strikes.

In Chapter 6, I focus on the path-dependent effects of early institutional choices by examining how organized labor returned to its previous patterns of political militancy in Tunisia and business unionism in Morocco. I demonstrate the ways in which institutional reforms undertaken in the late 1990s reconfigured political coalitions in support of militancy and moderation. I also evidence new parts of my theory by focusing on the internal governance of labor unions and how relationships between union elites and rank-and-file members shaped their capacity for militant protest. I show how democratic organization facilitated radical opposition in Tunisia by increasing accountability between union leaders and the rank-and-file, allowing local demands to "scale up" through the union hierarchy and increasing solidarity between labor and pro-democratic elites. Conversely, I show how the absence of union democracy in Morocco left labor movements weak and divided, forcing labor unions to resolve their grievances through institutional channels and limited demands for reform.

Finally, in the last two chapters, I extend the study to the post-transition period (2011–2014) and to four additional cases: Bahrain, South Africa, Mexico, and Egypt. In Chapter 7, discuss how authoritarian legacies have shaped labor politics in liberalizing North African regimes, producing divergent reform outcomes in Tunisia and Morocco. The additional case studies discussed in Chapter 8 highlight the external validity of the argument and allow me to further test my explanation against existing alternatives. I conclude by considering the implications of the study for contentious politics, historical institutionalism, and the study of authoritarian regimes.

2 *Labor Protest in North Africa: Expectations and Realities*

This chapter begins the exploration of varying labor protest in Tunisia and Morocco by placing this puzzle in a broader theoretical context. To explain why unions in Tunisia are more militant and political than their Moroccan counterparts, I begin by reviewing existing scholarship on labor protest and analyzing its findings in relation to these two cases. This discussion serves two purposes: first, it familiarizes readers with key theories in labor politics, and, second, it assesses these theories empirically using quantitative data. This sets the stage for my original theory of labor protest, which highlights the importance of adopting an institutional approach for explaining protest patterns in authoritarian regimes.

I argue that labor mobilization cannot be understood without sufficient attention to political institutions. Differences in unions' protest behavior stem from variation in the institutional structures available for labor under authoritarian rule and the way in which these shape unions' internal governance. First, unions' willingness to engage in militant protest is determined by their level of incorporation into the political organs of the state. When unions are integrated into formal institutions, coalition-building between union and partisan elites moderates labor behavior by directing workers' demands into the formal political process. Conversely, when unions are alienated from formal politics, the absence of regular access to political elites radicalizes unions' agendas, necessitating a reliance on confrontational tactics to give voice to labor concerns.

Yet unions' motivation for political militancy is only part of the story; it is also necessary to examine whether they can *sustain* militant opposition by garnering membership support. I argue that this depends heavily on unions' internal politics, namely the ways in which their internal governance structure shapes the relationship between union leaders and the rank-and-file. Unions with democratic governance – where leaders are regularly elected, decision-making is decentralized, and members can challenge leaders, decisions – foster strong networks of accountability, providing unions with the capacity necessary to sustain radical protest campaigns. In contrast, hierarchically organized unions fall vulnerable to internal divisions that hinder militant mobilization.

Crucially, I link the types of organizational structures that unions form to the political conditions they face at their founding. Only unions that are excluded from the formal political system, are expected to establish democratic governance. This is because internal democracy is costly, time-consuming, and, for union leaders, autonomy-reducing; elites will only invest in democratic organization if they cannot influence politics through other means. Thus, a key implication of this theory is that when authoritarian regimes pursue policies that isolate and depoliticize labor, they may unintentionally create an opposition of their own making. By forcing labor leaders to seek unconventional allies, strengthen grassroots relationships, and democratize their organizations, exclusionary policies can inadvertently empower union leaders to challenge the state.

The chapter is organized as follows. The first section situates the argument within the broader literature on labor militancy and subjects existing theories to empirical scrutiny. This sets the stage for the second section, where I highlight the importance of institutional incorporation in shaping labor's protest trajectories. I discuss how inclusionary and exclusionary labor policies affect unions' strategies, alliances, and internal organization, leading to unions with different capacities for militant action. Although this discussion is framed broadly to apply across various authoritarian regimes, the conclusion connects the argument to the specific cases of Tunisia and Morocco, offering initial predictions for labor behavior in these countries. These predictions are then systematically examined in subsequent chapters (Chapters 4–6), which track labor protests during three key periods of economic decline.

Labor Militancy in Authoritarian Regimes: Clarifying the Terrain

Why are Tunisian unions regularly confrontational, radical, and militant while Moroccan unions are partisan, apolitical, and moderate? While comparative analyses of labor protest in the Middle East/North

Africa are scarce,[1] theories generated from a broader literature on labor politics provide a useful point of departure for understanding protest patterns in these two cases. Extant scholarship offers three distinct perspectives – focusing on the structural-economic conditions of the working class, the organizational traits of labor unions, and the institutional relationship between labor and the state – to account for variation in labor militancy within autocratic regimes. In the section that follows, I review these approaches before proposing an original theory that more fully explains differences in Tunisian and Moroccan unions' protest behavior.

Economic Explanations

In the political economy literature, where labor is usually studied, economic conditions are seen as the core determinant of unions' political behavior. While an earlier literature on strikes in Western Europe highlighted the inherent militancy of the working class (Bendix, 1964; Marshall, 1950; Therborn, 1977; see also Acemoglu and Robinson, 2006; Boix, 2003), newer scholarship suggests that labor's political mobilization is contingent upon the economic conditions workers face (Bellin, 2002; Ruschemeyer et al., 1992; Seidman, 1994). Four conditions shape labor behavior: changes in the business cycle, labor's structural position in the economy, the state's development strategy, and the nature of the moral economy. While each offers a partial explanation of labor militancy, none provides a sufficient explanation for the divergence in protest patterns witnessed in Tunisia and Morocco.

Economic Business Cycles

A lengthy tradition of political–economic research links strike activity to fluctuations in the business cycle. Across several cases, comparative research has shown that labor militancy tends to follow the growth and decline of the national economy, particularly changes in wages and unemployment (Ashenfelter and Johnson, 1969; Franzosi, 1995; Rees, 1952; Rist, 1907; Shalev, 1983). These analyses view strikes as strategic actions taken by labor unions to improve their bargaining position

[1] See for notable exceptions Beinin, 2015; Bishara, 2018; Feltrin, 2019; Hartshorn, 2019.

in economic disputes. This leads to two contrasting predictions – on the one hand, strikes may increase with economic prosperity as rising wages and low unemployment place workers in an advantageous position vis-à-vis their employers (Ashenfelter and Johnson, 1969; Franzosi, 1989; Levitt, 1953; Rees, 1952). On the other, economic declines may motivate strikes, as workers desperate to improve their situation turn to militant behavior as a last resort (Berger and Spoerer, 2001; Gurr, 1970; Nam, 2007; Parvin, 1973; Stein, 1990).

In the Middle East/North Africa, scholars have only limitedly employed business cycle theories due to the difficulty in acquiring cross-national data on wages and unemployment. Nonetheless, the general consensus is that labor militancy follows economic decline – as workers' material conditions decrease relative to the past, the accumulation of grievances provides novel incentives for workers to strike (Costello et al., 2015; Gunning and Baron, 2014; Salih, 2014; Walton and Seddon, 1994). Empirical support for this relationship abounds; the 1978 Tunisian general strike; the "bread riots" in Morocco, Egypt, and Jordan; and the 2008 textile strike in Mahalla El-Kobra, Egypt, were all initiated in response to economic crises (Beinin, 2009; Disney, 1978; Seddon, 1984). Similarly, the 2011 Arab uprisings were rooted in issues of economic concern. In nearly all of the cases where mass protests broke out, citizens' original demands were for secure employment, better wages, and social justice (Costello et al., 2015; Dahi, 2011; Lanchovichina, 2017).

Yet, while a focus on economic conditions provides a general explanation for labor behavior in the region, it performs less well in accounting for differences in strike activity among specific cases in the Middle East. For example, Morocco and Tunisia display varying patterns of labor militancy despite broad similarities in the rigidity of their labor markets. According to data from the ILO, in 2010, unemployment in Morocco was 9 percent, just 4 percentage points below that in Tunisia (ILO, 2016). Official figures also mask broad similarities in the precariousness of work in both cases, since 23.5 percent of Morocco's "employed" population fell within its "unpaid employed" category (Feltrin, 2019).

In a similar vein, economic arguments have trouble explaining historical differences between countries and within single countries over time. A focus on the business cycle, for example, cannot adequately explain why Tunisian and Moroccan workers, who faced similarly loose labor markets in the 1990s (~16 percent unemployment) displayed different patterns of labor protest. Nor can it sufficiently explain the timing of protest cycles; for example, why did Tunisian unions increase their militancy in the late 1970s, when workers faced better wage and employment prospects than they did in the previous decade?[2]

Labor Power

A second set of economic arguments focuses on the structural power of the working class. In this view, organized labor derives its mobilizing capacity from workers' structural position in the economy – the scarcity/abundance of excess labor, the skill level of the workforce, its concentration, etc. Where labor power is high, unions are expected to be more militant because workers face less fear of replacement during strikes. Conversely, where workers are weak vis-à-vis their employers, unions are expected to take a more cautious approach to the bargaining process and moderate their behavior.

Attention to structural factors sheds light on important elements of labor's capacity for collective action. Numerous studies confirm the relationship between excess labor and strikes, pointing to the crippling effect that the "reserve army of the unemployed" has on labor militancy (Edwards, 1975; Marx, 1976; Soskice, 1978). Research shows that the precariousness of low-skilled work makes opposition among such workers more risky and, thus, less likely to occur (Ashenfelter and Johnson, 1969; Franzosi, 1989; Rudra, 2005; Shalev, 1992). For example, Selwyn's (2007; 2011) studies of Brazilian fruit pickers demonstrate that differences in strike activity between domestic and export farms are closely linked to the skill level of their employees: in contrast to workers on farms producing grapes for domestic consumption, those working on high-quality export farms can leverage their expertise to pressure employers to accede to their demands. Finally, a high concentration of workers in large, industrial enterprises is said to "manufacture militance," given the facility with which these workers can organize disruptive action in the market (Seidman, 1994).

[2] According to data from the ILO, only fifty-nine strikes were held from 1960 to 1969 (ILO, 1970).

However, structural variables have limited explanatory power when applied to Tunisia and Morocco due to the similarity of economic conditions in these two states. Table 2.1 presents basic indicators of these economies over the period 1970–2010. As is evident, the principal difference between the two is one of size – Morocco's labor force is roughly three times that of Tunisia. However, this difference reflects broader disparities in their populace; as a percentage of the total population, labor force participation rates in the countries are roughly similar.

Total employment is also similar between the two cases, casting doubt on the sufficiency of arguments that cast excess labor as a threat to labor militancy. Remaining differences in the sectoral composition and concentration of the workforce lead to variable predictions about labor mobilization. On the one hand, the larger share of Tunisian workers in industry seems to favor more militancy in Tunisia relative to Morocco. Yet, the greater concentration of Moroccan workers outside of small and medium enterprises offers the exact opposite prediction.

Ultimately, the lack of disparity between Tunisia and Morocco suggests that structural factors alone cannot account for differences in their strike behavior. This is not to deny the role that alternative socio-economic conditions such as literacy and human development have on mobilization but rather to confirm the common structural bases of labor militancy in these two cases. In both countries, workers have been concentrated in small-to-medium firms with few employment protections.[3] Additionally, differences in the composition of the labor force fail to cleanly predict patterns of labor militancy, even within single cases. For instance, despite the large concentration of industrial workers in Tunisia, public sector unions have been mainly responsible for labor militancy throughout the country's history.

Development Strategy

A third class of economic explanations links labor's capacity for collective action to the state's choice of development strategy. Export-oriented development, for example, is said to inhibit labor militancy because it expands the "reserve army" of workers to a global scale

[3] See Cammett and Posusney (2010) for a review of labor legislation and flexibility standards in Morocco and Tunisia, as well as the wider Middle East.

Table 2.1. *Basic economic indicators, Tunisia and Morocco (1970–2010)*

Tunisia							
Year	Population	Labor force	Labor force participation rate (%)	Agriculture, forestry, fishing (%)	Mining, industry (%)	Services (%)	Employment in 100+ firms (%)
1971	5.18 m	1.39 m	48.8	41.0[1]	11.7[1]	19.5[1]	–
1980	6.37 m	1.81 m	48.7	30.5	19.1	–	–
1990	8.43 m	2.58 m	48.4	22.1	20.8	24.8	–
2000	9.71 m	3.25 m	47.5	20.3	20.1	24.0	–
2010	10.64 m	3.82 m	46.9	17.1	19.1	22.9	56.0[2]
Morocco							
Year	Population	Labor force	Labor force participation rate (%)	Agriculture, forestry, fishing (%)	Mining, industry (%)	Services (%)	Employment in 100+ firms (%)
1971	15.15 m	3.98 m	46.3	50.0	10.4	12.6	–
1982	20.25 m	5.99 m	49.8	39.2	16.6	16.6	–
1991	25.26 m	7.84 m	51.0	47.0	13.8	14.2	–
2000	28.79 m	9.85 m	51.4	45.5	13.1	14.4	–
2010	32.34 m	11.47 m	49.6	40.6	11.6	14.2	50.0[3]

Sources: ILOSTAT, UNPD, European Commission, Institut National des Statisques
[1]Statistics refer to 1966, [2]Statistics refer to 2005, [3]Statistics refer to 2008.

(Deyo, 1984; Foster and McChesney, 2017; Jonna and Foster, 2016; Kopinak, 1996). Development models that emphasize the production of agricultural goods are also thought to constrain labor mobilization because of their historical reliance on low-skilled and vulnerable work (Adams, 1997; Jenkins, 1985).

In Tunisia, the "democratic diffidence" of organized labor in the 1960s has been attributed to the onset of state-led industrialization and autocrats' subsequent sponsorship of the working class (Bellin, 2002). Under state-led development, the government forms the nexus of the labor market: state-owned industries employ the largest share of workers, state-directed institutions produce labor laws, and state-governed labor boards rule on the fairness of employment contracts and adjudicate labor disputes. Because unions under these conditions are heavily reliant on the state for their survival, they are expected to eschew militant mobilization and instead preserve their privileges by maintaining the status quo. Similar dynamics have been used to explain the weakness of labor mobilization and democracy in the Global South. In late developing countries where working class interests were shepherded by benevolent autocrats – such as Argentina under Perón, or Mexico under the Institutional Revolutionary Party (PRI) – it was the middle class, rather than organized labor, that led the charge for democratization (Ruschemeyer et al., 1992).

In many respects, a "late development" perspective accounts for important trends in Tunisia and Morocco, offering a significant improvement over alternative theories. A focus on state sponsorship, for instance, is useful for explaining the relative inactivity of the UGTT during the early years of the Bourguiba regime. As the government shifted from a capitalist to a socialist model of development, its sponsorship of labor through public sector employment and increased wages quieted most sources of labor opposition (Bellin, 2002). Conversely, the erosion of state support following "corporatist collapse" in the 1990s set the stage for a resurgence of labor protest during the late 2000s (Hartshorn, 2019).

Yet, while this explanation captures part of the story, it does not sufficiently explain why Tunisian unions, in the face of such privileges, were able to launch militant political protests against the regime in the 1970s, nor why Moroccan unions were unable to do the same. A comparison of economic policies in Tunisia and Morocco reveals that both countries implemented similar state-led

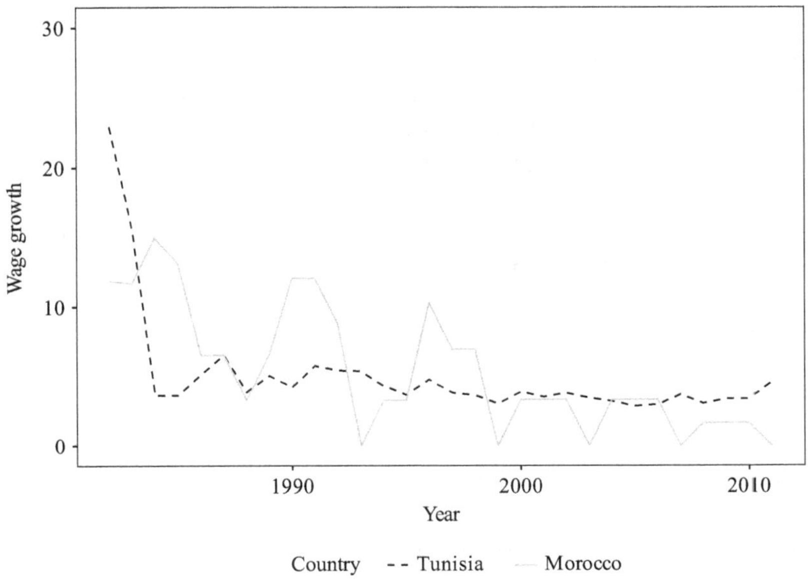

Source: Institut National de la Statistique (Tunisia), Haut Commissariat au Plan (Morocco)
Note: Wage growth expressed as a three-year moving average

Figure 2.1 Average growth in minimum wage (SMIG) in Tunisia and Morocco, 1980–2011

development programs at roughly the same time. While Morocco initially pursued more liberal development policies, by 1977 it had fully embraced state capitalism, with the monarchy owning most national enterprises, taking an interventionist role in commercial and labor markets, and fueling industrial development (Findlay, 1984). By 1985, the state-owned sector in Morocco accounted for 682 firms and 17 percent of employment (Saulniers, 1993a, 293), rivaling the size of the Tunisian public sector (Saghir, 1993, 7; Page, 2001, 68). Moreover, a comparison of minimum wage growth (an alternative indicator of state dependence, Figure 2.1) in Tunisia and Morocco demonstrates that Tunisian workers enjoyed greater privileges than their Moroccan counterparts.

Even within the Tunisian case, a focus on state dependence fails to account for temporal variation in labor protest. As Bellin notes, wage increases announced in the late 1970s and early 1980s did nothing to stem the tide of labor militancy in Tunisia, with two of its most important periods of political activism – "Black Thursday" and the protest wave of 1980–1984 – occurring after the government announced significant wage concessions to Tunisian workers (Bellin, 2002, 104–107; 109–111). Additionally, a focus on state sponsorship cannot explain why organized labor remained passive in the 1990s, despite significant reduction in state support. As Alexander (1996a) notes, even as the government abandoned its role in the public sector, the UGTT remained quiescent about Tunisia's regression to hegemonic authoritarian rule, going so far as to support the regime in its suppression of alternative political groups.

Moral Economy

Finally, a fourth, and theoretically distinct, class of arguments focuses on the role of the moral economy in influencing labor behavior. In this view, economic activity is embedded within a moral universe guided by norms of reciprocity, justice, fairness, and equality (Polanyi, 1957, 1977; Sayer, 2006; Scott, 1976). Consequently, it is this moral universe, and the rights and responsibilities embedded within it, that determines labor's behavior and its relationship with political elites. In the labor market, egalitarian beliefs lead workers to prioritize distributional equality over individual gains (Posusney, 1997; Sabel, 1982; Swenson, 1989; Thompson, 1971). Additionally, norms of justice and reciprocity govern workers' relationship with the state, creating a system of mutual obligations that must not be violated.

Within a moral economy, labor mobilization is expected to follow a "stability-disruption-protest" pattern, occurring when elites violate established norms (Posusney, 1993, 85). Collective action seeks to restore previous agreements and maintain economic stability, rather than disrupting production or seeking new collective rights (Kopstein, 1996, 394–395; Posusney, 1997, 15–16). Thus, labor mobilization is expected to be restorative rather than revolutionary – instead of constituting a new political order, militancy aims to reinstate the terms of the patron–client relationship previously established with political elites.

Viewing labor mobilization through the lens of a moral economy offers some analytical purchase in explaining protest patterns in Tunisia and Morocco. Supporting the theory that labor militancy occurs in reaction to violated expectations, protests in the early 1980s coincided with policies that inflated the prices of basic goods, leading unions to appeal to the state for price reductions to restore workers' purchasing power (Clement and Paul, 1984; Seddon, 1984). Additionally, the "Arab Spring" uprisings were rooted in moral economic concerns – declining wages, rising food prices, unemployment, and the loss of social mobility for recent graduates (Costello et al., 2015; Dahi, 2011; Lanchovichina, 2017). Notions of fairness were also influential. In both Morocco and Tunisia, perceived inequality between interior and coastal regions and working-class citizens and "corrupt" business elites fueled demands for social and political change (Bashir, 2018; Bergh and Rossi-Doria, 2018).

However, the moral economy approach also has several theoretical and empirical shortcomings that cast doubt on its sufficiency for explaining protest patterns in Tunisia and Morocco. Comparing wage and labor productivity growth in these two countries – one proxy for adherence to a "fair work, fair pay" ethos (Figure 2.2) – demonstrates that both countries witnessed similar decreases in real wages; yet only in Tunisia did unions use this grievance to justify political militancy. Violations of the patron–client relationship, such as increases in labor

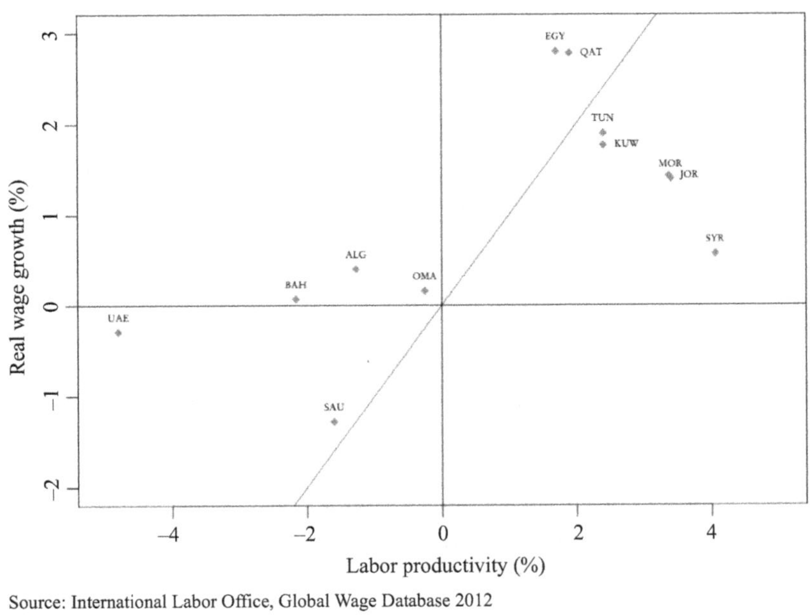

Source: International Labor Office, Global Wage Database 2012

Figure 2.2 Growth in wages and labor productivity in the MENA region, 1999–2011 (%)

flexibility and employment insecurity, were also concerns in both countries from the 1980s onward. Structural adjustment programs generated cuts in the public sector, increasing economic vulnerability for government employees and university-educated youth (Posusney, 1993). Similarly, labor code reforms in the 1990s and 2000s increased job insecurity by easing restrictions on firing permanent workers and hiring temporary replacements, resulting in significant downsizing in the private sector and expansion of the informal working class (Alexander, 2001; Denoeux, 2001).

Beyond this, a moral economy perspective struggles to answer this study's central question: why do some labor unions shift their agendas and conduct politically motivated strikes? In a moral economy, labor protests aim to restore, rather than upend, the status quo. Therefore, if labor truly operated within a moral economy, we would not expect to see political militancy at all. More broadly, focusing on the economic roots of labor protest oversimplifies unions' interests, reducing workers' preferences to narrow material terms. While concerns over fiscal well-being are important in unions' decision-making, the interests and strengths of labor organizations cannot be reduced to material grievances or perceptions of a "just economy." Indeed, as a growing body of scholarship shows, union behavior is influenced by various factors, including ideational motivations and organizational constraints. It is to this set of factors, and the theories associated with them, that I now turn.

Organizational Explanations

An alternative approach to analyzing labor protest emphasizes the organizational roots of labor militancy. Grounded in the sociological literature on resource mobilization, this approach views the organizational features of labor unions as key determinants of their resources and behaviors (Gamson, 1975; Oberschall, 1973; Olson, 1965; Tilly, 1978). Existing research highlights the pacifying effects of corporatism, emphasizing four main features: high union density, centralization of the bargaining process, union hierarchy, and the concentration of labor unions into a few peak organizations (Calmfors and Driffill, 1988; Cameron, 1984; Feltrin, 2019; Golden, 1993; Golden et al., 1999). An analysis of these factors in Tunisia and

Morocco leads to variable predictions regarding the likelihood of labor militancy and political protest.

Union Density and Sectoral Composition

Much of the comparative literature on labor politics focuses on union density – that is the percentage of the labor force that are union members – as a key indicator of labor strength. Low union density has been linked to limited strike activity, due to the necessity to attain a basic level of membership to mobilize collective protests (Feltrin, 2019; Olson, 1965; Tilly, 1978; Trejo, 2009). Labor unions with high density are also argued to lack motivation to strike because their size makes preemptive negotiations with employers more likely (Cameron, 1984; Hibbs, 1978; Korpi and Shalev, 1979). Thus, strikes should be most prevalent in countries with moderately sized unions, where the true strength of organized labor is harder to assess (Calmfors and Driffill, 1988; Lindvall, 2013; Piazza, 2005; Tsbelis and Lange, 1995).

In research on the Middle East, scholars adopting this approach have highlighted union weakness as a common explanation for the dearth of labor militancy (Bayat, 2002; Hibou, 2011; Yom, 2005). To begin, the dual legacies of repression and state corporatism are said to have undermined unions' capacity to mobilize. Because freedom of association is restricted within these regimes, unions face difficulty organizing independently from the state, resulting in low levels of union density (Bellin, 2004, 139; Yom, 2005, 19). Additionally, the prevalence of self-employed workers and micro-enterprises has contributed to a growing informal sector, further undermining unionization efforts (Aita, 2008; Feltrin, 2019; Heintz and Chang, 2007). Finally, increased privatization has undercut the primary source of union strength, leaving unions less capable of mobilizing collective action than in previous periods. As Bayat notes, "the economic restructuring of the 1980s has further undermined organized labor, as the public sector, the core of trade unionism, is shrinking because of closures, downsizing, and early retirements" (Bayat, 2002, 7).

However, despite its frequent invocation in the literature on labor politics, union density (or the lack thereof) cannot fully explain variation in protest patterns witnessed in Tunisia and Morocco. A comparison of union membership rates in both countries – 10–15 percent in Tunisia and 6–10 percent in Morocco – reveals labor movements with similarly weak organizational bases (Harper, 2006).

Despite this, Tunisia's UGTT has been able to mobilize periodic political campaigns against the regime, defying scholarly expectations. Additionally, alternative measures of unions' strength such as their sectoral composition[4] are roughly similar across both countries. According to data from *Trade Unions in the World*, the majority of union membership in both Tunisia and Morocco comes from the public sector, with the highest unionization rates found in traditionally militant sectors such as education, health, and local administration (Harper, 2006). In the private sector, unions draw significant membership from transportation, phosphate mining, and manufacturing, with an increasing percentage of workers being qualified as semi-skilled. One notable difference is the greater share of unionization in the agricultural sector in Morocco; however, while agricultural unions are generally seen as weak due to their reliance on low-skilled work, in Morocco, these unions are some of the most radical and militant (Appendix B: MS-4, 2/9/2014; MU-33, 5/15/2014). Thus, in many respects, Tunisian and Moroccan unions look more alike than different, necessitating a continued search for explanations of their divergent protest trajectories.

Union Centralization and Hierarchy

The centralization of the labor movement is another key factor conditioning labor's protest behavior. Centralization can refer to either the level at which unions are organized for collective bargaining *or* the extent of authority that peak labor unions exercise over their members. Unions with centralized bargaining structures are considered to be "encompassing" and have an interest in restricting labor militancy to reap the benefits of economic growth (Golden et al., 1999). In corporatist contexts, encompassing unions have been shown to be less likely to engage in protest than their decentralized counterparts, due to the latter's preoccupation with more limited, parochial goals (Cameron, 1984; Crouch, 1993; Korpi and Shalev, 1979).

[4] As Valenzuela highlights, sectoral unionization may be even more telling of mobilizing capacity than overall density because unionization in key industries, such as manufacturing or essential services, can increase the relative leverage of organized labor vis-à-vis the state (Alutto and Belasco, 1974; Seidman, 1994; Valenzuela, 1989).

Comparing Tunisian and Moroccan unions on this dimension, organized labor in Tunisia is much more encompassing than that of Morocco. Since the signing of the *convention collective cadre* in 1973, wage bargaining in Tunisia has been conducted at the national level, with tripartite negotiations serving as a general framework for wage agreements in individual sectors and plants. While in specific periods, negotiations have included representatives from various levels of the union hierarchy, bargaining has mainly been limited to a few peak leaders, reflecting the centralization of Tunisia's corporate structure (Alexander, 1996a, 201). By contrast in Morocco, legislation permits wage negotiation at all levels of union hierarchy: national, sectoral, and enterprise. Consequently, collective bargaining coverage, another factor influencing union militancy,[5] is more fragmented and less prevalent in Morocco than in Tunisia. According to the most recent (pre-2011) statistics, approximately 45 percent of Tunisian workers are covered by collective bargaining agreements as compared to fewer than 15 percent of Moroccan employees (ILO, 2008).

Measures of internal union centralization also fail to account for notable differences in protest behavior. According to Roomkin (1976), trade unions with a centralized authority structure – where national federations exert control over subordinate branches – are less likely to mobilize strikes due to the ability of peak union leaders to suppress rank-and-file militancy. An analysis of the organizational structure of Tunisian and Moroccan unions, however, reveals that the two share more similarities than differences. Owing to their common origins within the French CGT, unions in both countries are organized hierarchically, with vertical ties between national, regional, and local syndicates and horizontal linkages at the regional and sectoral levels. At the base of the union, rank-and-file members are organized in enterprise unions (*syndicats du base*), which are then aggregated at the industrial and regional levels in federal (*fédérations générales* and *syndicats nationaux*) and regional unions (*unions régionales*). At the top of the hierarchy are national bodies such as the Congress, Administrative Commission, and National Council, which exercise decision-making authority and control over union affairs. Although, as is argued in later chapters, informal relationships between national and

[5] Following Ashenfelter and Johnson (1969), several studies have shown that countries with more centralized bargaining are less likely to strike.

subnational branches vary across unions in Tunisia and Morocco, formal organization remains consistent, with the most important matters of union policy – agenda-setting, financial allocations, and matters of internal union policy – determined at the national level (Bellin, 2002; Appendix B: TU-11, 10/17/2013; MU-14, 3/31/2014). Lastly, both labor movements stem from a leftist tradition, which, in the developed West, has been shown to increase union centralization, density, and willingness to engage in collective bargaining (Blais et al., 1993; Wallerstein, 1989; Western, 1991, but see Hamann et al., 2013; Isitt, 2011; and Schipani, 2022 for contemporary evidence of the opposite).

Union Competition

Finally, the level of competition within the labor movement critically shapes unions' capacity for collective action. In much of the literature, union pluralism is viewed as a double-edged sword. On the one hand, multiple competing unions may undermine labor militancy by increasing divisions within the labor movement (Akkerman et al., 1995; Avdagic, 2005; Golden, 1993; Murillo, 2001). On the other, it may promote militant behavior by encouraging unions to strike as a means of drawing new members away from their rivals (Akkerman, 2008; Clegg, 1976; Kaufman, 1981; Ross and Irwin, 1951).

In Tunisia and Morocco, the extent of union pluralism marks a significant difference between the two cases (Table 2.2). While organized labor in Tunisia is concentrated within a single, national confederation, Moroccan workers are dispersed among numerous federations, with five unions comprising the majority of the workforce.[6] During periods of confrontation, the monopolization of the labor force by Tunisia's UGTT has strengthened its organizational capacity and its willingness to oppose authoritarian elites. Speaking on the UGTT's success in organizing anti-regime protests during the 2011 Jasmine Revolution, members of the executive bureau confirmed the "power in maintaining a unified labor movement in the face of internal tensions," particularly as a means of counteracting the "divide-and-rule tactics which have been used to undermine social movements in the past"

[6] These are the UMT, the General Union of Moroccan Workers (*Union Générale des Travailleurs Marocains*, UGTM), the CDT, the Democratic Federation of Labor (*Fédération Démocratique du Travail*, FDT), and the National Union of Labor in Morocco (*Union Nationale du Travail au Maroc*, UNTM).

(Appendix B: TU-5, 10/3/2013; TU-32, 11/21/2013; TU-44, 1/8/2014; see also Bishara and Grewal, 2022).

By contrast, Moroccan unions are notably weakened by their dispersal. With approximately thirty-four registered labor organizations, and five major national federations, the Moroccan labor movement is extremely diffuse, often to the detriment of its ability to mobilize. According to one union activist, "With three to four unions we might be fine, but with thirty plus ... we cannot present a united force" (Appendix B: MA-12, 3/25/2014). Even more troubling, the majority of registered unions are "*fantoches*": comprising no official membership, these organizations are simply creations of government elites, designed to bolster support for the monarchy rather than represent the interests of the working class. Therefore, union competition in Morocco has undermined the militancy of the labor movement by fragmenting the working class along political and ideological divides.

Although the difference in competition among Tunisian and Moroccan unions appears to lend credence to organizational theories of labor protest, this dissimilarity underscores the importance of adopting an institutional approach for explaining divergent protest patterns in these two cases. Indeed, the fact that unions in Tunisia are concentrated while those in Morocco are dispersed is a direct consequence of these unions' embeddedness within specific institutional structures. While neither government legally sanctions union pluralism, the Moroccan monarchy's endorsement of political pluralism in conjunction with its decision to incorporate unions into parliament induced the division of the labor movement along partisan lines. As will be discussed in more detail in the following chapter, this created strong incentives for parties to develop affiliate unions in order to capture more seats in policy-making bodies. Consequently, the once-unified Moroccan labor movement became increasingly fractionalized, as parties cannibalized Morocco's main trade union, the UMT, to create their own labor constituencies. Thus, a focus on union competition, while important, is insufficient for explaining differences in labor opposition because it downplays the extent to which divisions within the labor movement are endogenous to broader political designs.

Institutional Explanations

Finally, a third perspective on labor mobilization, and the one closest to the argument advanced in this study, emphasizes the importance

Table 2.2. ***Union organization in Tunisia and Morocco***

	Tunisia			Morocco		
Union density	10–15%			6–10%		
Union centralization	Centralized			Centralized		
Collective bargaining	National, sectoral			National, sectoral enterprise		
Union competition	Low (3 federations)			High (34 federations)		
Union autonomy	Moderate			Low		
Labor rights	High			High		
Sectoral composition	UGTT	UMT	UGTM	CDT	FDT	UNTM
	All sectors	Agriculture, banking, textiles, construction,	Agriculture, health, education, water	Education, health, civil service, petrol	Education, health, transport	Education, health, construction, textiles

of political institutions in analyzing labor protest. Within this view – exemplified by the works of the "new institutionalist" school – unions are viewed as social actors who engage and interact with the political environments in which they are embedded (Candland and Sil, 2001; Collier and Collier, 1991; Lee, 2011; Levitsky and Mainwaring, 2006; Lipset, 1983; Valenzuela, 1989).

The importance of institutions for understanding labor behavior has been especially pronounced in the literature on labor unions in authoritarian regimes, where unions have been placed under the direct influence – and oftentimes, control – of the authoritarian state. One key insight from this literature is that under state control labor politics becomes inseparable from its political surroundings, as this shapes the institutional setting in which labor is required to operate. As Collier and Collier highlight in their study of political development in Latin America, the genesis of labor unions within authoritarian regimes was often dictated by the political whims of the state, which used incorporation dually as a means of depoliticizing organized labor and co-opting working-class support for the regime (Collier and Collier, 1991, 8). Moreover, the formation of party-union linkages in several regimes effectively wed labor interests to those of the state through mutually beneficial systems of exchange, creating alliances that have continued to shape labor politics to the present day (Burgess, 1999; LeBas, 2011; Lee, 2011; Murillo, 2001).

In regimes where autocrats employ nominally democratic institutions to incorporate labor, the provision of regular opportunities to acquire benefits and negotiate demands has been shown to moderate labor behavior, leading to higher levels of overall labor peace (Kim and Gandhi, 2010). Even in regimes with a tradition of independent labor organizing – that is, autonomous unions that garner support outside of the conventional structures of the state – the influence of politics remains pervasive, as unions remain subject to the laws and restrictions on collective organizing developed by the autocratic state (Kwon and O'Donnell, 1999; Marks, 1989).

In the Middle East and North Africa, prominent institutionalist works have placed state corporatism as a central explanatory variable in accounting for unions' reluctance to oppose authoritarian regimes (Aidi, 2008; Bellin, 2002; Bianchi, 1989; Hartshorn, 2019; Posusney, 1997). A common perspective asserts that the legacy of state corporatism in North Africa has prevented labor militancy by giving the state control over the legal context in which unions operate, thus constraining their ability to carry out strikes (Alexander, 2001; Cammett and Posusney, 2010). Where the state sought to co-opt labor and limit its political strength, extensive entitlements were combined with severe de jure and de facto restrictions on organizing, resulting in relatively weak labor protections for unions and formal sector workers (Cammett and Posusney, 2010). Equally important in these analyses is the extent to which state corporatism inhibits labor autonomy. By serving as a means through which governments can channel specialized benefits to workers, corporatist institutions foster dependency relations between states and organized labor, which unions have little opportunity to disavow (Bellin, 2000, 2002; Bianchi, 1989; Hartshorn, 2019). Thus, given the relative weakness of labor unions under conditions of corporatist control, we should expect unions that are subject to the strictures of state corporatism to be less militant than those that are not.

The characterization of North African political regimes as state corporatist has been useful in distinguishing them from more labor-friendly, corporatist regimes in the developed West. Unlike in the societal corporatist states of Western Europe, corporatist institutions in North Africa and the Middle East have been explicitly designed to depoliticize and demobilize unions, cultivating a weaker tradition of labor organizing in this region (Bayat, 2002; Galenson, 2022; Hinnebusch, 2010; Yom, 2005). Yet, this explanation performs less well in accounting for differences in Tunisia and Morocco. Indeed, of our two cases, Tunisia is most commonly associated with state corporatism, given its monopoly over representation and its direct sponsorship by the state, whereas Morocco is more commonly identified with a pluralist labor tradition (Caraway, 2006), or "unruly corporatism" at worst (Alexander, 1996b, 82).

Moreover, an examination of labor provisions in both countries displays striking similarities. Comparing Tunisia and Morocco in terms of their freedom of association and collective bargaining (FACB) rights reveals that unions in both countries operate under relatively favorable conditions. According to data by Cammett and Posusney (2010), Morocco and Tunisia rank similarly on the strength of their de jure labor provisions, with Morocco placing first among North African countries (85.0 out of a possible 100) and Tunisia placing a close second (84.3). Even when disparities between de jure and de

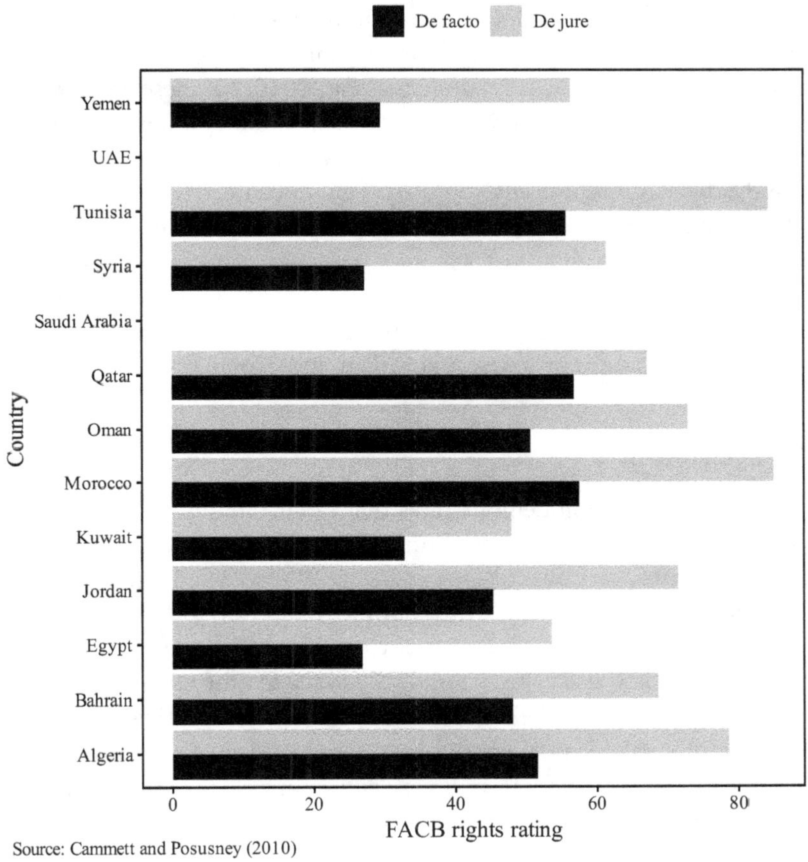

Figure 2.3 De jure and de facto labor rights in the MENA region, 2006

facto labor provisions are taken into account, Morocco and Tunisia have comparably robust labor protections, ranking as the second- and third-most liberal labor regimes in the MENA region, respectively (Figure 2.3).

Finally, institutionalist arguments (as they are currently conceived) have difficulty explaining moments of change. Most analyses have been devoted to identifying different types of corporatism or otherwise understanding the stability of labor behavior under corporatist regimes. However, corporatism is neither a "steady state" nor a structural impediment to alternative forms of labor politics. While leaders may design corporatist institutions to limit and control labor, unions can, and often do, work around these structures, exit them completely, or subvert them from within (Bishara, 2018; Burgess, 2004; Cook, 1996; Fu, 2017a; Robertson, 2010). In these cases, what must be explained is not why corporatism inhibits labor organizing but how unions mobilize in spite of corporatist restrictions and what conditions within these environments facilitate effective protest. Thus, the existing literature on state corporatism is limiting because it overstates the durability of state control over organized labor, both during periods of stability and change. This is especially salient in places like Tunisia and Morocco, where labor mobilization, despite the enduring nature of state corporatism, has evolved.

The Argument

The above discussion demonstrates that labor militancy is not simply a consequence of unions' structural-economic conditions, organizational features, or political environment. While each of these factors shed light on how unions form grievances and develop capacities for collective action, they alone cannot explain why some unions choose to express their grievances politically or why they employ varied strategies to achieve their goals. Adopting an integrative approach, I argue that labor mobilization is a consequence of the interaction between unions' external political environment and their internal organization, particularly the types of internal governance institutions that they adopt. Whereas the availability of formal channels for labor representation shapes unions' willingness to engage in protest, their ability to sustain militant protest campaigns depends on their internal governance structures and the extent to which these incentivize union leaders to develop robust coalitions with the rank-and-file.

This argument aligns with theoretical works emphasizing the importance of political institutions for understanding labor mobilization, while stressing the significance of unions' organizational life. In authoritarian regimes, different methods of labor incorporation provide unions with varying resources and mobilizing structures, biasing some towards opposition and others toward passive, party-mediated politics. Yet, maintaining militant mobilization also requires capable organizations that can bind movement participants together and maneuver creatively within the institutional structures in which they are placed. Here, unions' internal organization becomes paramount.

Democratic unions support labor militancy by strengthening accountability between labor elites and the rank-and-file, making defection by union leaders and activists more costly. Conversely, oligarchic unions are vulnerable to the twin dangers of co-optation and loss of member support, undermining their capacity for militant protest.

In developing this argument, I build upon institutionalist scholarship and sociological theories of the organization, modifying and extending them to explore how organizations with different types of governance institutions come about. In doing so, I link unions' external political environment to their internal organizational structure. I argue that unions will only establish democratic governance institutions when they are alienated from the formal political process. While unions with access to government institutions can use this as a substitute for robust internal organization, unions denied such access must turn inward to garner support, developing democratic institutions to strengthen their relationship with the rank-and-file. This, in turn, provides a useful resource for future militancy. With greater internal cohesion, unions are better equipped to sustain radical protest campaigns that pit organized labor against the state.

In what follows, I elaborate the logic of my argument. I begin by discussing the ways in which the state's choice of labor containment strategy impacts unions' institutional environment and mobilizing structures, influencing their initial decision of how best to mobilize. Next, I turn to the long-term effects of this institutional choice on unions' alliances and internal organization, linking these to their overall propensity to engage in political mobilization. I then consider how these relationships might shift in response to changes in the political environment (e.g., political crises, elite splits, leadership changes). Finally, I conclude with a discussion of how I expect this logic to unfold in Tunisia and Morocco, anticipating a pattern of politically militant protest in the former (based on its legacy of exclusionary corporatism) and moderate, institutionalized labor politics in the latter.

Labor Incorporation and Authoritarian Control

I begin my argument at the moment of state formation. During this period, the typical rules regarding representation fall into flux, as political groups jockey for influence and newly established dictators struggle to consolidate control. In these periods of extreme uncertainty, authoritarian leaders have out-sized ability to redesign institutions and forge alliances with powerful elites. Crucially, for organized labor, it is here that autocrats must first confront the "labor question," that is, how to regulate unions to ensure economic progress while containing the threat of an empowered, organized working class.

I argue that autocrats face a basic choice between two distinct labor containment strategies. At one extreme, dictators may attempt to control the labor movement through its complete incorporation – that is, integrating unions into the political system by providing formal channels for the articulation of workers' interests. Here, the aim is to preempt labor activism by linking unions to the state and channeling workers' demands into the formal political arena. As Collier and Collier aptly note, by providing institutional structures for the expression of dissent, autocrats hope to "take the labor question out of the street," thus allowing for the peaceful resolution of labor disputes (1991, 7).

At the other extreme, autocrats may adopt a containment policy that entails the suppression and marginalization of the working class. Here, the goal is to prevent labor activism, but the method is isolationist rather than incorporative. By excluding unions from the public sphere, autocrats hope to limit their political strength, disempowering organized labor as a source of potential opposition to the regime (Stepan, 1978). At the same time, by subordinating unions to government control, dictators aim to create a weakened, demobilized labor movement that can easily be controlled by the state (Kaufman, 1977, 12; see also Gerschewski, 2023, for a broader elaboration of this logic in authoritarian regimes).

It is important to note that the above strategies, while opposite, are not mutually exclusive. Dictators may vacillate between different methods or pursue hybrid strategies that combine both isolationist and inclusionary aims. When multiple unions exist, they may offer a mix of carrots and sticks, repressing some unions and incorporating others. Alternatively, periods of suppression may be punctuated by moments of openness in which labor is permitted to participate in some arenas of decision-making and control. However, for heuristic purposes, it is useful to conceive of containment strategies as divided into two ideal types: inclusionary (associated with labor incorporation) and exclusionary (associated with labor marginalization).

In this study, I conceptualize the difference between labor inclusion and exclusion by focusing on a number of institutions through which workers' interests can be expressed. First, I call attention to the host of corporatist institutions that govern industrial relations – labor laws, work councils, labor-related committees, negotiation boards, and tripartite bargaining arrangements. Second, I focus on the political institutions through which labor unions may be co-opted, such as executive cabinets, legislative bodies, and general government institutions. Throughout the book, I quantify labor's level of incorporation by offering statistics on the extent to which labor representatives are included within the aforementioned bodies. Generally, it is assumed that labor unions with access to fewer of these institutional channels are operating under conditions of state exclusion.

By selecting between inclusionary and exclusionary containment strategies, political leaders set into motion key transformations in the structure of industrial relations and the political opportunities available for labor representation and dissent under authoritarian rule. Inclusionary strategies facilitate the creation of meaningful channels to express labor interests, actively encouraging union participation in the formal politics of the state. In contrast, exclusionary strategies foreclose opportunities for labor representation, forcing unions to exist on the periphery of institutionalized politics. This choice has significant consequences for unions' mobilization strategies, alliances, and internal organization, which I describe below.

Immediate Effects: Strategies of Contention

The immediate effects of labor containment policies on labor mobilization are evident in the strategies, whether militant or moderate, that unions adopt to advance their demands. To recall the definitions presented in Chapter 1, militant protest refers to the use of "noisy" actions, such as strikes, that disrupt production lines or governance, while moderate protest refers to the use of "quiet" strategies like negotiation and intra-elite bargaining. When autocrats provide meaningful channels for the representation of labor interests, unions are expected to integrate into formal politics and moderate their behavior over time. In contrast, when autocrats exclude labor from formal institutions, they will remain as political outsiders and utilize militant tactics to articulate their demands.

This expectation is rooted in the strategic nature of contention. When faced with opportunities for collective action, organizations calculate the costs and benefits of different strategies, selecting the one that maximizes the returns to mobilization while minimizing risks (Olson, 1965). For labor unions incorporated into formal politics, the optimal strategy is to work within existing institutions to make demands, given the low cost of "within-system" opposition relative to popular protest (Lust-Okar, 2005). Within formal institutions, union leaders can glean the government's intentions and receive concessions without having to sustain the physical and material costs of mobilizing the rank-and-file. Moreover, adhering to institutional norms set by the regime enables workers to avoid the kinds of repression and punishment associated with independent action (Kim and Gandhi, 2010; Robertson, 2010). Finally, participating in formal institutions enables unions to secure credible commitments from authoritarian elites. Because institutions allow the opposition to monitor regime behavior and punish defection, they disincentivize autocrats from reneging on agreements, making it more likely that demand-making is successful (Boix and Svolik, 2013).

Even when institutions lack sufficient punishment power, the ability to "make demands legally" may provide union elites useful opportunities for future bargaining (Lust-Okar, 2005). As a broad literature on authoritarian institutions shows, formal institutions such as parties and legislatures can reduce long-term uncertainty over whether the opposition will be included in future negotiations, for the simple reason that overriding or closing these institutions can be costly for the regime (Acemoglu and Robinson, 2006; Gandhi, 2008; Gandhi and Przeworski, 2007).

Less-formalized institutions, such as ad hoc negotiations or party-directed labor committees, can serve similar functions but may not be sufficient to moderate labor protest for at least two reasons. First, the ad hoc nature of informal institutions reduces their credibility, making them less effective channels for promoting change. Repeated interactions within formal institutions extend actors' time horizons, making it less likely that short-term dissatisfaction will lead to institutional collapse (Gandhi and Przeworski, 2007; Persson and Tabellini, 1994; Soskice et al., 1992). With the prospect of continued participation, disaffected elites may be more willing to trade present-day quiescence for the promise of future benefits. At the same time, formal institutions provide "collective security" about future compromises, incentivizing elites to continue working within the system as the surest way of achieving their demands (North and Weingast, 1989; North, 1993).

Second, unlike formal institutions, ad hoc arrangements have fewer stable mechanisms to resolve internal disputes. A major benefit of parties and legislatures is that they offer a sustainable mechanism for balancing multiple, competing interests (Gandhi, 2008). In such fora, "even rival projects pushed by leaders with conflicting constituencies (for example capitalists favoring privatization against civil servants tied to bloated bureaucracies) may be accommodated" (Brownlee, 2007, 39). Anchored in an institutional setting in which clear rules govern decision-making, opposition elites can more readily arrive at "collective choices" that supersede individual preferences and are acceptable to most, if not all, parties (Aldrich, 1995). Consequently, formal institutions are more effective at securing compromise by resolving intra-elite conflicts and binding political actors to the regime.

Conversely, where institutional channels for organized labor are limited, unions operate as political outsiders and employ more confrontational methods of dissent. Here, labor militancy emerges not as an optimal strategy but as a last resort – when institutional avenues for demand-making are absent, unions must rely on costly, extra-institutional methods to communicate their interests to the state. The lack of access to the political system also radicalizes unions' behavior by intensifying labor demands. As Valenzuela highlights, syndically harsh environments "generate a greater accumulation of pent-up resentments and demands among workers, which can lead ... to a singularly strong wave of strikes and demonstrations" (1989, 458).

In extreme cases, the absence of institutional channels to mediate labor conflicts can motivate workers to embrace revolutionary aims. Without regularized opportunities to advance their interests, potential allies of the regime may seek its overthrow rather than languish in a system with no chance for compromise (Marks, 1989; Lipset, 1983). Thus, paradoxically, exclusionary authoritarian regimes breed the exact types of mobilization they are designed to prevent. By narrowing the space for organized labor to express its interests, exclusionary policies lead unions to pursue more revolutionary forms of protest *because* they lack the institutional access necessary to make their demands heard peacefully.

Medium-term Effects: Political Coalitions

The differences in labor containment policies that shape unions' strategies also affect another key aspect of their development – the coalitions they build with external political actors. Coalition-building is a crucial component of labor mobilization, positively influencing unions' strength in organizing (Frege and Kelly, 2003), success in collective bargaining (Nissen, 2000, 2003, 2004), and achievements in labor-reform negotiations (Lee, 2011). External alliances can increase unions' financial resources, provide influence and expertise, and furnish new bases of support for labor demands (Frege et al., 2004). Moreover, by aligning labor agendas with those of external actors, coalitions create change within unions themselves, serving as a site for the reconstitution of workers' interests and preferences (Tattersall, 2005).

Investigating labor's alliances, then, constitutes an essential step in analyzing unions' protest behavior. However, coalitions do not develop *ex nihilo*, rather, they are conditioned by the institutional setting in which they are embedded. Different institutions provide varying opportunities for coalition-building between labor and political actors, facilitating some coalitions and impeding others. From the patterns of labor control discussed above, we can identify two main types of coalition formation in labor politics: party-union alliances and outsider alliances.

In the first type, occurring when labor is incorporated into formal institutions, unions develop alliances with institutionalized political actors such as recognized parties and regime elites. Within legislatures, the exigencies of electoral politics drive parties to seek alliances with union leaders, upon whom they depend to deliver support from the working-class (Collier and Collier, 1991; Levitsky and Mainwaring, 2006; Murillo, 2001; Robertson, 2004). Similarly, unions may seek partisan alliances to extract greater concessions from the regime, as larger, more stable coalitions stand a better chance of challenging ruling elites (Gandhi, 2008; Gandhi and Reuter, 2016).

However, once formed, these coalitions moderate labor behavior, leading unions to pursue less radical demands. As the historical experiences of labor unions in Latin America, Eastern Europe, and Southeast Asia show, party-union alliances typically suppress labor militancy and push unions to moderate their agendas for reform

(Avdagic, 2005; Burgess, 2004; Etchemendy, 2004; Lee, 2011; Levitsky and Way, 1998; Murillo, 2001; Robertson, 2004). In mass unions, partisan ties may fragment the labor movement, creating ideological conflicts that precipitate membership defection (Bishara and Grewal, 2022; Caraway et al., 2015; Hartshorn and Sil, 2019). In addition, clientelistic exchanges between unions and parties can constrain labor autonomy, making unions more reluctant to engage in protests. As the principal agents that aggregate, represent, and articulate public interests to the state, parties can leverage their influence to secure more favorable labor laws and policies for unions in exchange for their quiescence and support (Levitsky and Mainwaring, 2006; Murillo, 2001; Valenzuela, 1992). Over time, these exchanges create bonds of loyalty between unions and partisan elites, enabling parties to leverage the delivery of current benefits to ensure moderation over the long term (Burgess, 2004).

Even when parties are too weak to significantly influence policy, partisan alliances can still moderate labor demands by co-opting the interests of union leaders. In addition to policy concessions, parties can offer selective inducements such as political appointments, sinecures, and financial perks to labor elites (Levitsky and Mainwaring, 2006; Robertson, 2004). These resources reduce leaders' uncertainty about their personal welfare, leading them to rely more heavily on partisan ties than policy gains to secure their well-being. This, in turn, incentivizes union leaders to restrict political militancy, as elite dependency on party-directed benefits creates a vested interest in maintaining the status quo. As McAdam confirms, political activism by incorporated elites reflects an "abiding conservatism" which encourages co-opted members to "resist changes which would threaten the current realization of their interests even more than they seek changes that would enhance their interests" (Tilly quoted in McAdam, 1999, 38). Thus, unions with partisan alliances are expected to exhibit low levels of militancy as partisan linkages discourage union elites from pursuing demands that could jeopardize the regime.

In contrast, where organized labor is alienated from formal politics, unions struggle to form alliances with influential elites. Absent opportunities to connect with regime insiders, unions must turn inward to their constituents, or to other marginalized social groups, to gain political support (Lee, 2011; Valenzuela, 1989; see also Brownlee, 2007, for how this works in the partisan context).

These "outsider alliances" encourage unions to adopt more militant and politicized forms of protest in two ways. First, outsider coalitions radicalize labor unions by enabling social movement elites to direct union agendas toward more revanchist, political demands. As Tattersall (2020) emphasizes, within coalitions, alliance partners exchange not only resources but also strategies, decision-making processes, and organizational structures. Consequently, when unions ally with excluded social groups, opposition elites gain significant discretion over unions' agendas and policy decisions. Moreover, because institutional channels for voicing dissent are limited, excluded political actors may use unions as a platform to vent their frustrations, deploying attendant protests to exert political pressure on the regime (Valenzuela, 1989).

Second, and more indirectly, outsider coalitions encourage political militancy by facilitating issue bridging between labor organizations and marginalized groups. Frequent interaction between unions and opposition groups initiates a process of "cognitive liberation,"[7] where workers come to perceive their grievances as part of a broader political struggle. In part, this is aided by the pervasiveness of political exclusion that characterizes closed regimes – as Lenin observed in Czarist Russia, "the yoke of autocracy appears to obliterate all distinctions between [an opposition movement] and trade unions because *all* workers' associations and *all* circles are prohibited" (1935, 179, emphasis original). By creating a sense of shared victimization, political exclusion reduces ideological differences between unions and marginalized groups, uniting them in a common desire to reconfigure the status quo (Yashar, 2005). Consequently, the modification of labor agendas to include revanchist political demands appears less co-optive of unions' goals and more consistent with their self-interested aims. Thus, cognitive liberation encourages the politicization of labor protest by enabling union actors to view their grievances in a broader political context (Lipset, 1983; Marks, 1989).

[7] According to McAdam, cognitive liberation refers to the process by which members of an aggrieved group fashion shared understandings that undergird collective action. In particular, he argues that "before collective [action] ... can get under way, people must collectively define their situations as unjust and subject to change through group action" (McAdam, 1982, 51).

Long-term Effects: Internal Organization

Finally, autocrats' mode of labor control – whether inclusive or exclusive – has enduring effects on unions' internal organization, influencing the types of relationships that develop between union members and elites. The critical role of unions' internal politics in shaping their protest behavior is well-established in the industrial relations literature. Beginning with Shorter and Tilly's (1974) study of political strikes in France, scholars have highlighted the importance of organizational factors for fueling labor activism, emphasizing traits such as leadership, membership commitment, and internal bureaucracy (Ahlquist and Levi, 2013; Frege, 2002; Gordon et al., 1980; Klandermans, 1986). Similarly, studies of labor opposition in authoritarian regimes have shown that internal organization helps to explain the presence of labor activism in hostile environments. For instance, Cook's (1996) study of teachers' unions in Mexico demonstrates how internal democracy bolstered labor protests by enhancing intra-union solidarity and helping union elites resist state co-optation.

What is less appreciated, however, is how unions' internal dynamics are influenced by their external political environment and how this interaction shapes their ultimate modes of mobilization. I argue that unions' external political conditions and internal organization are interlinked. Whereas unions incorporated into political institutions are expected to develop oligarchic organizations, which reduce their effectiveness in protest mobilization, unions excluded from formal politics are more likely to establish democratic unions, which facilitate political militancy.

The varying effects of labor containment policies on unions' internal development stem from the ways political institutions structure elite incentives in labor politics. By providing union leaders with mechanisms to express their interests, participation in formal institutions bureaucratizes union elites, moderating their demands and reducing their support for political mobilization. Additionally, by creating clientelistic relationships between labor and the state, institutional incorporation also reduces elite incentives to invest in internal organization. As McAdam notes, a "special danger" of external alliances is their likelihood of diverting attention away from internal networks of support, which can "serve as a hedge against the vagaries of elite sponsorship" (1982, 28).

I argue that institutional incorporation poses three interrelated dangers to labor organizations. The first is oligarchization – that is, the concentration of power within the union elite. According to Tilly, political incorporation drives elites to "fight tenaciously against the loss of power ... [and] work against the admission of contenders [who] would challenge the system in some serious way" (Tilly, 1978, 135). Thus, unions incorporated into the regime often restrict access to leadership positions, creating barriers to maintain incumbency advantage and protect their privileges. These barriers can range in severity and include measures like restricting member representation in governing bodies, modifying union administration, and delaying union congresses. Regardless of the measure chosen, the end result is to weaken vertical accountability between union elites and members, disempowering the rank-and-file (Bishara, 2018; Levitsky and Mainwaring, 2006; Korkut, 2006).

The second danger, co-optation, has been treated previously and warrants little elaboration here. However, one key insight bears repeating: by creating cliency networks between unions and government elites, labor incorporation may induce union leaders to deviate from the preferences of their members (Burgess, 1999). While union elections typically resolve internal conflicts by allowing members to punish deviant behavior, the danger of oligarchization prevents this kind of corrective retribution (Burgess, 2004; Levitsky and Way, 1998; Murillo, 2001; Valenzuela, 1992). With little accountability, union elites can enact self-serving policies with relative impunity. Consequently, the combination of oligarchy and co-optation undermines union militancy by preventing unions from creating precisely the types of institutions (i.e., competitive elections) that would allow rank-and-file members to remove ineffective elites.

The final danger to union organization – the dissolution of indigenous membership – emerges as a natural consequence of the first two. Disaffected by their lack of voice within union bureaucracy and inability to change the system from within, rank-and-file workers rationally pursue options for exit (Bishara, 2018; Hirschman, 1970; Klandermans, 1986). While disaffected workers may later pursue alternative forms of protest, such as wildcat strikes or creating independent unions (Bishara, 2018), in the short term, such defection limits the union's capacity to mobilize. Moreover, as labor's capacity for collective action decreases, union leaders depend more heavily on external linkages for support, since they can no longer exert the necessary organizational muscle to secure concessions from the government. Thus, the defection of indigenous members completes the vicious cycle whereby institutional incorporation inhibits labor militancy. In the absence of robust membership, unions must rely on institutional channels governed by the state, rather than protest politics to gain influence under authoritarian rule.

In contrast, where labor is excluded from formal politics, the absence of influential allies incentivizes union leaders to rely more heavily on grassroots networks for survival and support. Elites' incentives to invest in internal organization stem from the recognition that, under conditions of exclusion, they cannot depend upon external resources to secure their well-being. While "outsider alliances" can provide limited material resources, the marginality of actors within these coalitions prevents them from being a consistent source of support or from sustaining leaders' welfare over the long term (Cook, 1996; Tattersall, 2005). Therefore, to reliably obtain influence in the political system, union elites must turn inward, using rank-and-file support to bolster their positions vis-à-vis regime elites.

Like external alliances, the development of internal linkages between union members and elites critically affects unions' organization, impacting their ability to engage in labor militancy. However, unlike partisan ties that generate oligarchic unions, the development of internal support networks lays the foundation for a distinct form of organization – internal democracy. As Moody notes, "the activation of union members ... is interwoven with the question of union democracy and leadership accountability" (Moody, 1997, 277). To convince rank-and-file members to support union goals, elites must provide a measure of constituent influence over labor agendas, both at the bargaining and broader social level. This means that union leaders must establish procedures allowing members to exercise their decision-making power, such as proposing candidates for union leadership, voting regularly in union elections, and holding unsatisfactory leaders accountable through institutional constraints on union elites.

However, to be truly effective, elite efforts to engage the rank-and-file must go beyond procedural mechanisms of democratic accountability. For such procedures to function properly, they must be supported by an organizational culture that encourages active member participation and emphasizes rank-and-file voice and rights (Jarley et al., 2000; Levi et al., 2009; Strauss, 1991). Therefore, democratic unions must cultivate behavioral aspects of democracy, such as fostering internal opposition, soliciting member feedback, and increasing member participation in union activities. Additionally, democratic unions may implement more participatory forms of organization by granting autonomy to local and regional offices, including union members in policy debates, and creating channels of communication between union leaders and their constituent base (Levi et al., 2009).

By creating participatory structures that link union elites to the rank-and-file, internal democracy facilitates unions' political mobilization in three key ways. First, democratic organization enhances accountability between union members and elites, increasing the likelihood that unions pursue more radical, transformative goals. When rank-and-file members exhibit stronger preferences for political militancy than their leaders, democratic procedures bring political issues to the fore by allowing members control over union decision-making and goals. As the early works on union democracy discern, a key barrier to protest militancy is the absence of membership control over labor agendas. Where workers exert decision-making power, unions exhibit higher propensities to strike (Adler and Webster, 1995; Parnes, 1995; Yates, 1990), greater intransigence in bargaining (Wolfe, 1985), and more subversive, anti-capitalist agendas (Stepan-Norris and Zeitlin, 1995). Similarly, when intermediate bodies, such as union locals, act as a countervailing force against the national leadership, local political issues are more likely to be brought to the fore (Jones, 1998, 331).

Even when rank-and-file militants hold more moderate preferences than their leaders, democratic organization may still make the adoption of political agendas feasible. According to Levi (1997), procedural fairness can convince members whose political preferences diverge from the leadership to participate in protests. Because developing accountable governance institutions is costly, leaders who subject themselves to greater monitoring, and possibly punishment, for political action can induce greater commitment from their followers (Ahlquist and Levi, 2013). Furthermore, participatory democratic practices assist union organizing by reducing the "big union image" that leadership requires members to go along with decisions they don't like (Kochan, 1979; Maranto and Fiorito, 1987).

Second, internal democracy may also support unions' political militancy by helping unions safeguard against state domination. Oligarchic unions face serious co-optation concerns – without effective mechanisms of vertical accountability, union leaders may pursue moderate agendas driven by external sponsors rather than the wishes of the rank-and-file. In democratic unions, however, members' punishing power disincentivizes union elites from deviating from workers' demands, reducing the temptation to succumb to external pressures (Hirschsohn, 2007; Levi et al., 2009; Murillo, 2001; Scopes, 1992; Voss and Sherman, 2000). As Wolfe (1985) highlights, where participatory democratic structures are in place, union leaders are less able to exercise social control over their members, leading to the adoption of more radical demands.

Finally, internal democracy facilitates political militancy by strengthening labor solidarity, providing unions with the internal cohesion and capacity necessary to maintain radical protest campaigns. Democratic unions forge closer ties between union elites and rank-and-file members through institutions such as voting or open policy debates, reducing the "vertical social distance" between these groups (Lipset et al., 1956, 260; Mannheim, 1956, 180–181). Through repeated interactions, union members develop a stronger sense of identification with union leadership, creating a common political consciousness that can be activated to promote radical protest (Stepan-Norris and Zeitlin, 1995). Most important, encouraging membership engagement in union affairs fosters a stronger sense of dedication to the union, increasing labor solidarity and internal cohesion. As Lévesque et al. (2005) note, active participation in union administration generates greater commitment to union goals, in part because such agendas are perceived as products of members' own choosing. Participatory democratic structures also help rank-and-file militants overcome free rider instincts, creating an atmosphere where workers are willing to make necessary sacrifices to support protest action (Strauss, 1991). Thus, unions that establish democratic practices are more likely to engage in militant protest, as these unions possess the levels of worker consciousness and organizational solidarity necessary to sustain anti-regime opposition.

Mechanisms of Institutional Stability and Change

In short, labor's interests and behaviors cannot be fully understood without a systematic analysis of institutions. Different methods of labor incorporation set into motion contrasting developments in unions' strategies, alliances, and organization, culminating in vastly different trajectories of labor protest. Labor inclusion undermines union militancy by 1) channeling labor demands into formal institutions, 2) fostering coalitions between parties and union elites, and 3) diminishing vertical accountability between union leaders and the rank-and-file. In contrast, exclusion from formal politics radicalizes labor agendas by allowing unions to develop autonomous bases of support and increasing their capacity for collective action.

Like many path-dependent processes, the effects of labor incorporation policies are expected to be "sticky" and persist long past their initial creation. For example, the establishment of party-union alliances can divide the labor movement into multiple, competing organizations, which may be difficult to later reunite. Conversely, unions that develop democratic governance structures may find it hard to dismantle these institutions entirely or modify the "habits of mind" that workers develop when socialized into participatory, democratic environments (Lipset, 1959). For this reason, even if autocratic leaders attempt to change course and pursue a new method of labor control, it may not be feasible to durably alter pre-established patterns of opposition.

However, given the political logic detailed above, institutional choices do not determine patterns of labor politics indefinitely. To remain effective, political institutions must include mechanisms of reproduction, which bind coalitions of interest together and convince powerful actors to continue supporting the status quo (Mahoney, 2000; Thelen, 1999). If mechanisms of reproduction weaken, support for existing institutions can decline, offering new opportunities for innovation and behavioral change. For example, shifts in the economic environment may alter the functioning of bargaining institutions in ways that make rents more difficult to distribute and union elites harder to co-opt (Hartshorn, 2019). Similarly, opportunistic leaders may displace existing institutions in response to political crises, especially new or emergent threats to their rule (Waldner, 1999).

At such moments, the resulting contest for power makes outcomes less constrained by existing arrangements and more susceptible to change. Consequently, protest patterns may shift as unions respond to new political conditions and reassess the strategies that serve their best interests (Caraway, 2006). Particularly when declines in corporatist arrangements undermine elite privileges, either by limiting access to decision-making or slowing the flow of regime-directed benefits, loyal labor unions may begin to adopt militant tactics and contest the status quo (Hartshorn, 2019; Levitsky and Mainwaring, 2006). The extent to which these shifts will be lasting, however, depends on two key factors: 1) the ability of autocrats to quickly redesign institutions to reanimate elite support and 2) the ability of unions to sustain militant protest by implementing democratic practices and fostering linkages with the grassroots.

Conclusion

Based on the above discussion, Table 2.3 outlines the expectations for protest patterns in Tunisia and Morocco. I separate the predictions into three main periods, which correspond to different labor containment strategies and periods of economic change. While Tunisia is mainly characterized by exclusive labor control policies that predominated in the 1980s and 2000s, it witnessed a brief period of labor inclusion in the 1990s following the inauguration of President Ben Ali. Similarly, Morocco is dominated by a pattern of inclusive state-labor relations throughout most of its history, save a brief period of exclusion in the mid-1980s and early 1990s. Thus, we should expect to see greater prevalence of labor militancy in Tunisia during the first and third periods of economic reforms, and moderation during the early years of Ben Ali's rule. In Morocco, the inverse should be true: unions should moderate their behaviors in the 1980s and 2000s, and should engage in more militant behavior in the intervening period.

In short, the central argument of this book is that labor behavior cannot be adequately understood without attention to political institutions. Although macro-level economic conditions and organizational features are critical for gauging unions' capacity and interest in collective action, ultimately this potential is realized within an institutional environment, which provides important constraints on and opportunities for labor militancy. Like organizational perks and material benefits, institutions can serve as powerful mechanisms of co-optation, inducing unions to support the political status quo despite declines in

Table 2.3. *Theoretical predictions*

Incorporation policy	Political alliance	Internal organization	Nature of contention	Cases
Inclusion	Partisan alliance	Hierarchical	Elite moderation, rank-and-file militancy, apolitical demands	Morocco (1975–1986) Morocco (1996–2011) Tunisia (1989–1999)
Exclusion	Partisan alliance	Hierarchical	Elite-driven militancy, political demands	Morocco (1987–1995)
Exclusion	Outsider alliance	Democratic	Elite and rank-and-file militancy, political demands	Tunisia (1975–1985) Tunisia (2000–2011)

workers' economic conditions. Additionally, the institutional environment significantly influences unions' internal organization, providing additional possibilities for their trajectory between militancy and moderation. Thus, an appreciation of unions' institutional environment is necessary to develop an explanation for their protest behavior. Without disclosing the interactions between organized labor and its broader political context, we cannot fully grasp the causal paths that lead to national variations in labor mobilization.

3 Labor Control Regimes and Initial Conditions: Comparing Morocco and Tunisia

This chapter begins the empirical investigation into divergent protest patterns in Tunisia and Morocco by examining the political conditions faced by labor unions before the adoption of neoliberal reforms. Among cases for comparison, Morocco and Tunisia constitute a rare set of countries that share several similarities in their political and economic history. Both countries spent the majority of the twentieth century under colonial rule and inherited many of their institutional structures, including their traditions of labor organizing, from the French. In 1956, after brief independence struggles led by native intellectuals, petite bourgeoisie, and the working class, dictators rose to power and began initiating vast reforms to exert their control over the state. Given the organizational strength of unions and their rise to prominence during anti-colonial struggles, leaders swiftly targeted organized labor as a source of support for authoritarian regimes.

Beneath these similarities, however, important differences distinguished how these transitions developed in both countries. While leaders in Tunisia and Morocco initially adopted similar strategies to incorporate labor movements into their regimes – establishing inclusive, corporatist systems to restrain labor militancy – by the late 1960s, Habib Bourguiba and Hassan II relied on varying methods to contain labor unrest. In Tunisia, the failure of incorporative policies led Bourguiba to pursue exclusionary strategies predicated on heavy repression and gradual exclusion of labor elites. Conversely, in Morocco, tensions between unions and the monarchy spawned a brief crackdown, followed by the adoption of an inclusive, pluralist system aimed at integrating union leaders into key government institutions.

This chapter elaborates these different labor control strategies, analyzing how they shaped the institutional context in which unions mobilized. In the language of historical institutionalism, I consider the postindependence period to be a "critical juncture" – a moment of heightened contingency in which leaders wielded significant agency in shaping institutional arrangements and subsequent political events. In both countries, independence marked a period of radical change, permitting autocratic leaders substantial latitude to reconfigure political systems and forge alliances with elites and mass organizations. The different patterns of state–labor relations developed created distinct trajectories for labor organizations, biasing Tunisian unions toward coordinated opposition and Moroccan unions toward more fragmented, party-mediated politics.

This chapter thus highlights the role of contingency in determining trajectories of labor politics. I argue that labor control policies were the outcome of *strategic decision-making* by incumbent elites, not simply a reflection of pre-existing historical or social conditions. In both cases, leaders faced similar challenges from well-organized, historically rooted labor unions and, with their selection of labor control policies, aimed to pacify labor unrest. Moreover, in neither case did domestic political conditions preclude the adoption of an inclusionary or exclusionary strategy. President Bourguiba and Hassan II initially used very similar strategies of rule, and it was only in the late 1960s that their policies began to diverge. Consequently, it is not fixed coalitional structures that determine labor control strategies; it is leaders' selection of control strategies that influence which coalitions are allowed to form and what types of behaviors become politically feasible.

The remainder of this chapter proceeds as follows. In the first section (devoted to a discussion of Tunisia and Morocco, respectively), I outline labor unions' pre-independence origins, their development during French colonial rule, and their organizational and political endowments leading into the independence period. Following this, I discuss the dilemmas faced by dictators in consolidating control over their newly independent states and the varying strategies used to contain opposition from political and economic challengers. Here, the analytical focus is organized around three main themes: 1) an overview of authoritarians' labor control strategies, 2) an analysis of these strategies' impact on unions' relationship with the state and other political actors (parties and social movements), and 3) an examination of how the political coalitions developed between organized labor and these groups affected unions' perceptions and capacities for mobilization. Ultimately, the chapter illustrates how autocrats' strategies to contain labor unrest produced divergent possibilities and limitations for labor organizations as they entered the period of neoliberal reform.

Organized Labor Prior to Independence

Divergence in the postcolonial development of Tunisian and Moroccan labor unions belies numerous similarities in their earlier history. In both cases, labor unions predated the modern state, with labor organizations tracing their roots to the establishment of the French General Confederation of Labor (*Confédération Générale du Travail*, CGT). Under French tutelage (1890s–1940s), indigenous workers gained an appreciation for the benefits of labor mobilization, an aptitude for militancy, and a sense of national consciousness that would permeate unions' development for years to come. Additionally, with the creation of autonomous unions in the postwar period, labor confederations in both countries acquired a broad support base that would place them in a kingmaker role in impending nationalist struggles.

These twin developments set the stage for labor control policies enacted during the postindependence period. As influential actors with robust organizations and sterling nationalist credentials, unions made attractive partners for autocrats hoping to mobilize the masses behind their newly established regimes. However, their political influence also made them prime targets for state control once authoritarian rule was consolidated. As I show below, the methods through which this control was exerted would leave a lasting imprint on labor unions and their internal politics for years to come.

Tunisia

In contrast to most labor movements in the Middle East, the origins of Tunisian unionism can be traced back to the nineteenth century, shortly after the establishment of the French protectorate. Prior to this, most indigenous workers were embedded in artisanal modes of production, with only a small portion of the population (fewer than 10 percent) working outside of agriculture and handicrafts (Bellin, 2002, 89). However, with the arrival of foreign capital, Tunisia's labor force quickly coalesced into a wage-earning class that would prove ripe for formal organization. As European investment into mines, ports and commercial infrastructure grew, so too did the size of the working class – according to estimates, by 1926, the indigenous labor force comprised roughly 65,000 employees,[1] over half of which were concentrated in manufacturing sectors such as mining, fishing and transportation (Hermassi, 1966, 15).

Moreover, it was under the influence of French and Italian workers that Tunisians were first introduced to labor organizing. In many respects, the presence of European settlers proved a boon to Tunisian unionism, as expatriate workers brought with them traditions of union organizing and demands for the legal protections they enjoyed at home (Bellin, 2002). Although official legislation guaranteeing labor rights was not passed until 1932, by 1919 Europeans had established the first trade union federation on Tunisian soil, the General Confederation of Labor in Tunisia (*Confédération Générale du Travail en Tunisie*, CGT-T). Additionally, in a series of strikes, they secured a number of important concessions, including an eight-hour workday, the right to strike, and the application of numerous collective conventions (Boubaker, 1983). Through these activities, Tunisian workers gained a sense of class consciousness and developed an awareness of how labor mobilization could be used to achieve their own demands for better working conditions and equal pay (Bellin, 2002). Further, the partial integration of native Tunisians into trade union structures[2] endowed indigenous workers with an aptitude for organization, ultimately leading to the creation of all-Muslim docking, mining, and agricultural unions in the early 1920s (Ahmad, 1967, 57).

However, foreign influence did not prove to be an unequivocal benefit to the working class. For decades, persistent racial and national tensions undermined labor solidarity and delayed large-scale organization of indigenous workers. Discrimination in pay scales for

[1] Note that this number does not include agricultural workers (which numbered 319,000 persons, 99 percent of which were native Tunisians) or day workers (which totaled 121,000). According to Hermassi, overall 72 percent of Tunisian workers were employed in agriculture, 8 percent in industry, and 20 percent in services (Hermassi, 1966, 12–15).

[2] Although indigenous Tunisians were largely discriminated against within the CGT (Ahmad, 1967, 57; Bessis, 1974 cited in Ben Romdhane, 1981, 90), several Tunisians participated actively in the union and a few held positions of leadership. One prominent leader was Mokhtar Ayari, who was principal adjutant of Jouchim Durel and General Secretary of the Tramway Workers' Union.

Europeans galled Tunisians, leading to a general mistrust of foreign-dominated labor unions (Perkins, 2004, 85; United States Bureau of Labor Statistics, 1958, 11). Additionally, the denial of permanent job opportunities to Tunisian workers impeded the development of a robust proletariat that could lead the vanguard of the class struggle (Schaar and Ahmad, 1978, 260).

In 1946, the establishment of the Tunisian General Labor Union (*Union Générale Tunisienne du Travail*, UGTT) marked the inauguration of the first indigenous labor confederation that could credibly rival the influence of the CGT.[3] Founded by Farhat Hached in the coastal city of Sfax, the union quickly amassed a following among Tunisian workers in former CGT strongholds – gathering over 12,000 members in Tunisia's industrial regions of Bizerte, Tunis, and Gafsa. Despite intense competition from European federations, the UGTT expanded rapidly, establishing ten new regional unions in the Tunisian countryside and organizing workers in the most prolific sectors of economic activity: mines, ports, and transportation (Ahmad, 1967, 110–111). By 1956, the union increased its membership to 150,000 workers – roughly 4 percent of the population and 29 percent of employed persons[4] – over half of which were concentrated in the modern industrial and commercial services sector (ILO, 1960; Salah-Bey, 1965, 376; United States Bureau of Labor Statistics, 1958, 13).

During this period, the UGTT's expansion was bolstered by its progressive social vision and a concerted effort to recruit members from a broad cross-section of Tunisian society. Union organizing was not limited to blue-collar workers; instead, the UGTT worked to increase its ranks by incorporating unsalaried workers in agriculture, handicrafts, and the civil service. While several of these recruitment

[3] Prior to 1946, two additional autochthonous labor unions were founded in Tunisia. The first, founded by Mohammed Ali El Hammi in 1924, was dissolved in 1925 due to French repression. The second, founded by Belgacem Gnaoui in 1936, collapsed before the war due to internal struggles over the union's involvement in the anti-colonial struggle.

[4] Here, employed persons refers to wage earners and salaried employees, which totaled 509,000 in 1956. A separate figure, given by the US Bureau of Labor Statistics, which includes non-waged workers, increases the estimated labor force to 1,134,000 persons. Thus, at minimum, the UGTT comprised 13 percent of the total labor force, including waged and non-waged employees.

efforts were unsuccessful,[5] the UGTT managed to incorporate new federations of service employees, teachers, and bureaucrats, who comprised 25 percent of the union's base membership and its primary intellectual leaders.[6] More generally, the union established itself as a mass organization by providing direct assistance to members of the local community in the form of medical aid, literacy classes, and Quranic schools in several regions of Tunisia (Ahmad, 1967).

Most important, the UGTT's commitment to defending Tunisian workers' interests in the face of colonial objections cemented the union as one of the forefathers of the anti-colonial struggle. In the early years of its existence, the union struck an alliance with the pro-independence Neo-Destour Party and began orienting its mobilization efforts toward the nationalist cause, launching strikes in protest against the arrest of Neo-Destour leaders and organizing guerrilla activity in the nation's interior (Achour, 1989). Moreover in 1952, when colonial repression forced the withdrawal of the Neo-Destour from political life, Farhat Hached became the de facto leader of the nationalist movement, making the UGTT the foremost political actor in the independence movement. On the international stage, the UGTT used its public platform to press for Tunisian independence in forums with foreign partners such as the United Nations, the International Confederation of Free Trade Unions (ICFTU), and the American Federation of Labor

[5] Owing to the familial nature of the handicrafts industry, and lagging employment following the Second World War, the UGTT was unable to organize a significant portion of Tunisia's traditional craftsmen, which totaled roughly 70,000 employees. The union also struggled to organize agriculture workers (some 700,000 employees) due to the seasonal nature of their jobs (Ahmad, 1967, 116; United States Bureau of Labor Statistics, 1958, 9). However, it did succeed in organizing farm-workers on large estates, which represented about 10 percent of the agricultural working class (ibid). According to internal reports, in 1956, the UGTT's agricultural federation housed 50,000 members or roughly 1/3 of the union's total membership. This estimate is contradicted by external reports, which claim that agricultural wage earners compromised no more than 6 percent of the UGTT's total membership (Salah-Bey, 1965, 394).

[6] Following the election of Ahmed Ben Salah at the UGTT's Fifth Congress, the most prominent members of the union's national administration were middle-class intellectuals. However, at the sub-national level, union leadership remained overwhelmingly working class, with 80 percent of union officers in Sfax, 75 percent in Bizerte, 65 percent in Sousse, and 50 percent in Tunis being blue-collar workers with less than secondary education (Ahmad, 1967, 118, n29).

and Congress of Industrial Organizations (AFL-CIO) (Riddell, 1961, 12). In leading the vanguard of both the class and nationalist struggles, the UGTT was rapidly elevated into the ranks of a "kingmaker" in the Tunisian political landscape – a role that was cemented by France's invitation to the union to serve as official interlocutor during independence negotiations.

Morocco

Like the UGTT, the Moroccan labor movement does not owe its debt of origin to the Moroccan state. Prior to the arrival of the French, the traditional orientation of the Moroccan economy prevented the development of a unified working class; as Benomar notes, most of the precolonial population was dispersed across the countryside, working either as subsistence farmers or as self-employed artisans and merchants (Benomar, 1991, 54).

However, two features of the colonial government created auspicious conditions for the development of organized unions. First, the wealth of French investment into state infrastructure gave rise to a new industrial sector, generating the foundations for a native working class. As a result of foreign investment, Morocco's urban population ballooned from 245,000 citizens in 1900 to 865,000 in 1936, reflecting the vast numbers of Moroccans seeking employment in coastal cities where French enterprises were most prevalent (Ayache, 1956, 272). By 1929, the indigenous labor force had grown to 100,000 employees, the majority of whom worked in "modern" sectors of activity such as mining, docking, construction, and commercial agriculture (Menouni, 1979, 24).

Second, the influx of European migrants introduced trade unions to Morocco. Rooted in previous syndical experiences and desirous of the privileges they enjoyed back home, European workers led the vanguard of the movement for labor rights. In 1919, French employees of the colonial administration formed the first professional association, the General Association of Civil Servants of the Protectorate (*Association Générale des Fonctionnaires du Protectorat*, AG), and soon began unionizing workers in the postal service, education, and banking sectors. In 1930, under the guidance of the French left, these diverse associations consolidated to establish the first trade union on Moroccan soil, the Departmental Union of the General Confederation of Labor (*Union Departementale de la Confédération Générale du Travail*, UD-CGT).

Yet, if the protectorate regime created the conditions for organized labor in Morocco, it did not encourage its advancement. Due to legal restrictions that prohibited Moroccan citizens from engaging in union activities, it was not until 1936 that the seeds of an indigenous labor movement began to take root. That year, Moroccan workers participated in their first protest when they joined a strike led by European employees at the Casablanca sugar refinery, COSUMA. Although the strike call was issued by the European-dominated UD-CGT, Moroccan employees responded to the call in overwhelming numbers, spreading the strike from the COSUMA factory (June 11), to the central electricity works (June 12), to the phosphate mines in Khouribga (June 13). By June 19th, when the strike action had ended, over 2,118 employees (1,400 of whom were Moroccan citizens) had participated, making the 1936 strike wave the largest in Moroccan history to date (Ayache, 1982, 143). Significantly, Moroccan strikers came from sectors where European penetration was either weak or nonexistent suggesting that native workers had engaged in protest independent of foreign leadership (Benomar, 1991, 225; Menouni, 1979, 31). According to Miller, this marked a crucial turning point in Moroccan labor history – as the journal *Clarté* announced: "The Moroccan proletariat has finally shown that it has acquired a class consciousness and will stand without retreat alongside European workers to defend the right to work for its daily bread" (Clarté cited in Miller, 2013, 142).

Following World War II, the indigenous labor movement in Morocco experienced a virtual renaissance. In an attempt to recoup members lost during the war,[7] the UD-CGT intensified its efforts to recruit Moroccan workers, organizing new unions in native-heavy industries such as the ports, mines, dams, and large construction sites. As a result, the number of unionized workers grew rapidly in the postwar period – by 1944, 20,000 Moroccans were unionized, and by 1950, this figure had increased to 60,000 (Ayache, 1993, 87;

[7] During the German takeover of France, labor organizations in Morocco were brutally suppressed. Trade unionists, rumored to be allied with Communists, were sacked from their jobs, arrested, or deported to France, and the CGT was officially dissolved. The decision of the Labonne government to reverse its prohibition on Moroccan unionization alleviated this situation postwar.

Menouni, 1979, 54). With the massive influx of native workers into unions, the autochthonous labor movement officially cemented its presence in Moroccan society. In March 1955, Moroccan citizens held the founding congress of the first native union on Moroccan territory, the Moroccan Labor Union (*Union Marocaine du Travail*, UMT).

Like the UGTT, the UMT was founded as a mass organization with close ties to an influential nationalist party, the *Istiqlal*. Although created less than a year before Moroccan independence, it organized quickly, announcing twenty-two regional committees at its initial congress. By May 1956, the union had amassed over 400,000 members, representing a third of the Moroccan labor force and nearly 4 percent of total population. As in Tunisia, the UMT attracted members from a wide range of professional categories. According to estimates provided by Ashford (1960), the most prolific sectors of union activity were in heavy industries (e.g., mining, transport, and fisheries, <50 percent of sectoral membership), followed by the civil service (~33 percent) and traditional agriculture (~20 percent).

During its formative period, the UMT's participation in the independence movement enhanced its popular appeal, paving the way for organized labor to become a major player in national politics. Given its informal alliance with the *Istiqlal*, the union adopted an anti-colonial stance geared toward the full independence of Morocco. When the *Istiqlal* was forced underground, union leaders called upon their members to "fight for the repeal of the Protectorate … [and] demand that the Moroccan people take charge of themselves" (Benomar, 1991, 286). From 1955 until independence in March 1956, the UMT mobilized 76,486 workers in 1,987 protests, the majority of which had the explicit aim of expelling the protectorate regime (Moore, 1970, 193). As in Tunisia, these nationalist efforts granted the union a reserve of popular legitimacy that spread beyond its traditional working-class base – besides the *Istiqlal* and the King himself, no other organization could claim as great a sacrifice for Moroccan independence or as encompassing support from the country's politically active citizenry (Ashford, 1960, 312).

Summary

In sum, the developmental trajectory of organized labor in Tunisia and Morocco cannot be understood without an appreciation of its pre-independence origins. In both cases, unions' advocacy for indigenous workers garnered support from the working class and transformed labor unions from small, parochial institutions to one of the nation's chief mass organizations. At the same time, their substantial involvement in independence struggles endowed unions with political legitimacy that rivaled that of the modern state. While these factors would contribute significantly to the strength and prestige of organized labor in Tunisia and Morocco, they would also make unions a clear target for authoritarian control once independence was achieved, as discussed below.

Challenges of Postindependence Rule and Authoritarian Labor Control Strategies

The achievement of independence from France marked a critical turning point in North African politics and the development of state–labor relations. Although much of Tunisia and Morocco's institutional infrastructure would be inherited from the colonial period, the regimes that came to power under Habib Bourguiba and Mohammed V faced the dual challenges of neutralizing threats to their rule and consolidating control over their newly independent states. Initially, both leaders employed similar strategies to contain labor unrest, creating inclusive corporatist systems to pacify worker militancy through a combination of financial and legal inducements. When these tactics proved ineffective, both initiated political crackdowns, repressing trade union activity and political groups.

However, following increased turmoil in the late 1960s, labor policies in Tunisia and Morocco began to diverge. While Bourguiba continued to pursue an exclusive strategy that marginalized labor elites, Mohammed V's successor, Hassan II, reversed course, creating an inclusive, pluralist system that incorporated union leaders into key state and partisan institutions. These differing control strategies – exclusionary in Tunisia and inclusionary in Morocco – had profound effects on the political development of unions postindependence. Whereas the UGTT was able to maintain a unified, autonomous organization with strong links to its members and a diverse political community, Moroccan unions developed an ideologically and organizationally divided labor movement, fractured along party lines.

Tunisia

Early Labor Control in Tunisia: Between Alliance and Exclusion

With the achievement of independence underway, the Tunisian government found itself at a fork in the political road. While the triumph of the nationalist movement ended Tunisia's subjugation by France, it also exposed new challenges that the forthcoming regime would have to confront. On the one hand, the Neo-Destour faced a damaging internal split between factions concentrated around party leaders Habib Bourguiba and Salah Ben Youssef.[8] On the other, the regime would have to contend with a robust and independent labor movement, whose nationalist credentials and organizational strength rivaled that of the Neo-Destour.

In many ways, the solution to first of these problems provided a ready-made fix for the latter. At the 1955 Neo-Destour congress, Bourguiba deftly convinced the party's labor contingent to support him over in exchange for making the UGTT a "junior partner" in the new regime. Organizationally, he afforded the union monopoly representation and facilitated its solvency through the institution of an automatic check-off system for the collection of dues (Bellin, 2002, 96). He also encouraged the Neo-Destour to adopt the UGTT's comprehensive economic agenda and voiced his support for progressive labor legislation in the upcoming constitution (Moore, 1970, 177). On the political front, he reserved several spots for union representatives on the Neo-Destour's joint electoral list – garnering the UGTT nineteen Constituent Assembly seats – and awarded four key ministerial posts to labor leaders in the first postindependence cabinet (Boubaker, 1983, 230–255 cited in Bellin, 2002). Finally, he incorporated the union into a number of secondary executive institutions – the National Planning Commission, the Social and Economic Council, and the Neo-Destour politburo – granting UGTT leaders a measure of influence over policymaking and a hand in shaping the economic agenda for the future Tunisian state (Salah-Bey, 1965, 380).

Through granting these concessions, Bourguiba hoped to mollify the union and reduce its ambitions by (partially) incorporating it within the regime. Yet his hopes were quickly dashed; emboldened by the

[8] The disagreement between Bourguiba and Ben Youssef centered around Bourguiba's support for autonomy negotiations with France, which Ben Youssef openly deplored. After independence, Ben Youssef cultivated support amongst Tunisia's more radical rural areas and agriculturalists, while Bourguiba found support in the urban and industrial areas of the country.

regime's patronage, UGTT leaders pushed for deeper involvement with the party-state. During a contentious union congress in 1956, UGTT secretary-general Ahmed Ben Salah called for the "organic fusion" of the union and the Neo-Destour, with the hopes that the UGTT's socialist doctrine would become a guiding strategy for Tunisia's future (Ahmad, 1967, 181). Rather than pursue parochial class interests, he argued, the union should be actively engaged in political life and join forces with the ruling party to promote a "democratic social and economic program" that addressed the conditions of the country's economic backwardness (ibid).

Such a bold declaration proved too ambitious for Bourguiba's tastes, setting the union on a course of confrontation with the party-state. Fearing the subordination of the Neo-Destour to the UGTT, Bourguiba quickly moved to suppress the union and remove Ben Salah from political life. Playing upon existing tensions between Ben Salah and rival union leader, Habib Ben Achour, Bourguiba tacitly encouraged the creation of a splinter union,[9] which he then promptly endorsed. He also publicly supported the appointment of a new secretary-general, Ahmed Tlili, to head the UGTT and organize a unity congress to rejoin the factions at the behest of the regime. The conditions outlined for reunification – that Ben Salah retire from the union and that UGTT ministers relinquish their trade union functions – could not have made Bourguiba's motives more clear: he sought to neutralize the union and marginalize it within the political sphere. With Ben Salah's departure from the UGTT, the regime achieved its goal. For the next several years after reunification, the UGTT would remain subordinate to the party, choosing to confine itself to performing "exclusively economic and social tasks" (Ahmad, 1967, 190).

Labor Exclusion in Tunisia: The Suppression of the UGTT

The aftermath of the Ben Salah affair marked a turning point in the character of state-labor relations in Tunisia. As Alexander notes, in the immediate postindependence period, the government's labor policy sought to satisfy two distinct imperatives:

[9] This splinter federation, the Tunisian Union of Labor (*Union Tunisien du Travail*), was created by seven UGTT dissidents on October 18, 1956. As of December 24th, the union reportedly lay claim to 50,000 members, not including workers in the civil service (L'Action 12/24/1956).

"[The Tunisian government] has tried to maintain the support of a union whose cooperation has been vital to the country's economic development and the government's stability. At the same time, however, it has tried to keep the UGTT from threatening the party's political monopoly over the government's development strategy" (Alexander, 1996a, 181)

However, in the confrontation between Ben Salah and Bourguiba, the difficulty of maintaining this "checkered alliance" (Bellin, 2002) became clear. If incorporation could not curb the union's political ambition, more drastic measures would have to be taken. Thus, from the 1960s onward, the government implemented a repressive control strategy designed to undermine the influence of the UGTT and subordinate the union to the regime's political will.

During this period, labor repression was enacted at three main levels – that of formal legislation, that of the individual enterprise, and that of the union's internal bureaucracy. In the policy arena, Bourguiba betrayed his previous commitments to the UGTT by enacting labor laws that failed to cohere with the progressive social rights promised to workers at the 1955 Neo-Destour congress. Draft articles affirming the state's obligation to provide education, work, and medical care for citizens, for example, were absent from the final text of the 1959 constitution, as were provisions for collective bargaining and enterprise unions (Moore, 1965, 78; Ahmad, 1967, 245-248; Toumi, 1989, 33). Similarly, references to the right to strike, which had previously been described by Bourguiba as "sacred" a few years earlier, were omitted from the draft constitution and the 1966 labor code.[10] Most critically, legislation promulgated in January 1959 introduced limitations on union organizing by excluding non-Tunisian workers from holding leadership positions in the UGTT and proscribing their engagement in political affairs (Moore, 1965, 79). Although these measures were billed as supporting the government's policy of "Tunisification" – a reform initially supported by the UGTT – the policy's ultimate consequence was to expel militant leaders from the union and strip

[10] In addition to failing to guarantee the right to strike, business allies in the National Assembly also pressed for harsher punishments against strikers. According to a speech given by Bourguiba, strikes occurring before a proper appeal had been made to the government would be "regarded as a crime against the state ... The worker does not have the right to stop the country's economic machine, nor can he reject a verdict by a government because it does not please him" (Bourguiba 1957).

it of its best-trained and most educated cadres. In conjunction with institutional reforms that saw labor's power in the administration and Neo-Destour significantly reduced,[11] such measures had the combined effect of excluding the UGTT from the political arena. Under these legal provisions, intended to depoliticize labor and weaken linkages between political elites and the UGTT, the union would retain a significant measure of autonomy from the Neo-Destour and remain open to the influence of alternative political forces.

At the level of the enterprise, the government created barriers to plant-level organization and actively intervened to discourage unionization among the working class. Social legislation giving managers greater discretion over hiring and firing dissuaded workers from joining unions by permitting employee dismissals on the basis of vague justifications such as "professional inadequacy" and "evident bad will" (Moore, 1965, 172). Furthermore, the constitution's failure to explicitly endorse enterprise unions (*syndicats*) rendered base union leaders vulnerable to employer reprisals, as these individuals enjoyed no official status or protections under the law (Alexander, 1996a, 114). Consequently, conditions for workers inside enterprises were harsh, and attempts to combat exploitation through strikes were often met with fierce repression by employers or police (Appendix B: TU-4, 10/1/2013; TU-5, 10/3/2013). In several factories, these despotic shop-floor practices became the first source of workers' political consciousness, generating tensions between employees and the state, which failed to adequately protect them against employer abuse.

Perhaps the most damaging blow to plant-level organizing, however, came with the establishment of party-supervised "professional cells" within Tunisian enterprises. Originally created to coordinate resistance between the UGTT and the Neo-Destour at the height of the nationalist movement, professional cells were party-directed labor

11 Several changes introduced in the 1959 constitution significantly reduced the influence of Tunisia's legislative and executive institutions. The constitution produced a weak National Assembly that served to "rubberstamp" executive decisions rather than to independently make laws or act as a check upon presidential power (Moore, 1965, 77). Similarly, institutions such as the Social and Economic Council and National Planning Commission were routinely sidestepped and addressed only after consultation had occurred within executive commissions (ibid 79). Finally, reforms to the party in the late 1950s reduced the influence of the Politburo by increasing the number of members in the bureau and making all appointments subject to presidential approval.

organizations tasked with overseeing the "political organization and education of workers" (*La Presse*, March 17, 1963, cited in Ahmad, 1967). Following independence, however, these cells were used as a means to undercut the UGTT's organizational strength and preempt worker mobilization in its most militant branches. In 1962, when the party began reviving professional cells in earnest, they proliferated in traditional union strongholds – Sfax, Tunis, and Gafsa[12] – typically as a warning to the UGTT's more outspoken and popular leaders (Ahmad, 1967, 278).

Moreover, as these cells began to assume trade union functions, they undermined the efficacy of advocacy undertaken within the *syndicats*. In Tunis, a professional cell partially satisfied construction workers' demands for increased production bonuses after having obtained a sizable government loan for a workers' building cooperative (Moore, 1965, 169). Such actions drew the ire of UGTT leaders, who argued that the intervention of professional cells into trade union matters delegitimized local syndicates and frustrated union efforts to expand into weakly organized sectors (ibid; Achour, 1989, 73). In a 1962 meeting of the union's National Council, union leaders excoriated the cells for "creating confusion" among workers about the rightful channels through which to express their interests and "threatening the concept of a harmonious national front" (Ahmad, 1967, 278–279).

Finally, the most serious government assault on the union was undertaken at the level of the UGTT's bureaucracy and principal leadership. As would become characteristic of his political style, Bourguiba routinely interfered with the union's internal organization, using a combination of manipulation and direct intervention to restrain labor militancy. In 1963, he provoked a second change in the UGTT's leadership by having Ben Salah's replacement, Ahmed Tlili, removed from his post as secretary-general. Growing suspicious of the latter's advocacy for reforms to the Neo-Destour (Ahmad, 1967), Bourguiba quietly encouraged party militants to vote against Tlili's reelection at the union's ninth congress, and select his rival (and seemingly loyal Neo-Destourian), Habib Achour, to serve in his stead.

Ironically, two years later, a second confrontation between Bourguiba and the UGTT prompted the ouster of Achour. That year,

[12] In 1944, these were the first three regions organized by the UGTT and the main industrial centers of Tunisia (Ahmad, 1967).

conflict broke out over the union's demands for increased wages to offset the effects of the country's growing economic crisis. Infuriated by the decision to launch parochial demands during a moment of national crisis, Bourguiba immediately had Achour arrested and initiated a retaliatory campaign against the UGTT. Organizing a special congress in July, Bourguiba purged the union of its militant leadership: of the nine members on its Executive Bureau, only one member of the previous administration was re-elected, and more than half of its regional and federal leaders were replaced by party affiliates (Ahmad, 1967, 298). In addition, Achour was dismissed from his post and replaced as secretary-general with known party loyalist, Bechir Bellagha. Emasculated for a second time, the UGTT was successfully relegated to a subordinate position in the single-party regime; as Bellagha announced during a UGTT press conference; henceforth, the union would adopt an orientation that was "identical to that of the party" and pursue full collaboration with the Bourguiba regime (Ahmad, 1967, 299).

Ultimately, these oppressive practices – meant to subjugate the union to the will of the regime – created tensions between the UGTT and the government that would shape its future development as an opponent of Tunisia's authoritarian regime. Bourguiba's attempt to forestall the emergence of labor opposition and preempt linkages between workers and political groups produced two unintended consequences for the regime. First, the absence of effective workplace institutions radicalized union militants within the rank-and-file. Frustrated by the lack of representative channels through which workers could express their interests vis-a-vis employers and the state, rank-and-file workers became increasingly alienated from the government and motivated to use militant tactics, such as strikes and public demonstrations, to press for their demands. Moreover, because state officials frequently colluded with employers to condone despotic shop-floor practices, workers began to link their economic exploitation to their political oppression, forming a consciousness about their political environment that would lay the foundations for opposition during the neoliberal era.

Second, regime insistence on a functional separation between the Neo-Destour and the UGTT gave the latter a measure of autonomy vis-a-vis the state. Although the Neo-Destour remained a strong presence in the union, given its interlocking membership and shared leaders, close relations between the two at the national level masked more independent practices at the local level, where the regime failed to adequately capture rank-and-file support. Such autonomy was clearly reflected in the activities of the UGTT's regional branches, which often criticized the complicity of the national leadership with the Neo-Destour and actively resisted partisan attempts to control the union through its professional cells.[13] Moreover, the party's failure to establish organic linkages with the UGTT further enhanced the union's independence by enabling it to remain open to constituencies from varying political groupings and ideological trends. By the early 1970s, the UGTT was one of the most ideologically heterogeneous organizations operating within Tunisia, claiming members from groups as diverse as the Tunisian Communist Party, Islamist parties, and banned leftist movements such as the Movement of Popular Unity (*Mouvement de l'Unité Populaire*, MUP) and the Movement of Socialist Democrats (*Mouvement des Démocrates Socialistes*, MDS). As we shall see in the next chapter, this heterogeneity would prove critical to the politicization of the UGTT in the neoliberal period, paving the way for an alliance between organized labor and opposition elites when the closure of the political system made it impossible for political parties to operate freely within the regime.

Summary

In sum, the Bourguiba regime employed a strategy of repression and exclusion to control organized labor. Although Bourguiba initially incorporated union leaders into government positions, these appointments came with significant constraints on labor organizing, revealing the regime's aim to subordinate rather than include the union in its ruling coalition. Moreover, outside of these structures, labor freedoms were harshly suppressed and unionized workers were offered little protection on the shop floor. Combined with state intervention in

[13] In Gafsa, members of the local UGTT branch ran for seats in the party's professional cells and then, after winning a majority of these seats, voted to dissolve the cells (Ahmad, 1967, 273–274). Similarly, after a member of the Neo-Destour's coordinating commission placed himself as a candidate in the local *syndicat* elections in Metlaoui, the union's secretary-general and members of the outgoing bureau threatened to resign in protest of the party's infiltration (ibid). Other episodes of conflict between intermediate unions and the Neo-Destour/UGTT central are elaborated in (Moore, 1965, 170–172).

union affairs, this exclusion radicalized the labor movement and intensified workers' grievances against the state. Ultimately, such repression would draw labor into the opposition and encourage union militancy against the regime during the period of neoliberal reform. This pattern of state–labor relations differed dramatically in Morocco, where authoritarian leaders made more concerted efforts to formally incorporate unions into the regime.

Morocco

Early Labor Control in Morocco: An Iron Fist in a Velvet Glove

In Morocco, as in Tunisia, the achievement of independence marked a period of uncertainty for the nation's political elite. Although the state had been blessed with a centralized authority structure (makhzen) and a ready-made leader in the person of Sultan Mohammed Ben Youssef, on the eve of independence, the country's territorial integrity and the stability of its government were still very much contested. On the political front, the monarchy faced fierce competition from an organizationally robust nationalist party, the *Istiqlal*. On the social front, it needed to subdue a growing labor movement that had proven twice – once during the independence struggle and then again shortly thereafter – its capacity for political action.

Assuming this task with consummate political skill, Mohammed V spent most of the postindependence period neutralizing the *Istiqlal* and the UMT through a combination of tactical and political maneuvers. To curb the party's influence, he instituted multiparty elections and manipulated divisions within the *Istiqlal* to split the party between its left-wing and conservative factions.

Adopting a different tack with the UMT, he incorporated the union into the regime's ruling coalition by granting it a number of legal, institutional, and organizational privileges. In the legal arena, he granted the UMT a de facto monopoly over labor representation and enacted generous legislation which codified a minimum wage, instituted procedures for collective bargaining, and gave agency to worker's organizations in enforcing wage agreements (Ahmad, 1966, 174). Institutionally, the king ensured labor an official position in the state by affording it representation within a number of legislative and consultative bodies. In Morocco's first parliament, the UMT was given ten out of seventy-six seats, and its secretary-general, Mahjoub Ben Seddik, was appointed to serve as Vice-President of the assembly. Additionally, through its membership in the *Istiqlal*, the union acquired a direct voice in the Council of Government, where three labor-affiliated party members – Abdallah Ibrahim, Abderrahman Bouabid, and Maati Bouabid – could serve as spokespersons on its behalf. Finally, with its vast network of intra-elite relationships, the union gained limited influence within several decision-making bodies. Through its leaders' involvement in the Ministry of Interior, the Superior Council of the Plan, the Central Commission for Prices, and the committees of the Fund for Social Aid, the union could advise the regime on issues of policymaking and play a role in developing the country's economic plans.

Notably, in contrast to Tunisia, labor representation within these institutions was not merely perfunctory; rather, it provided the UMT with useful avenues for expressing its interests. Even in the context of a regime dominated by a powerful monarchy, the latitude given to the union to participate in decision-making during the early years of independence was "unquestionably great" (Moore, 1970, 181). According to Ashford, UMT leaders enjoyed regular access to the King, who often consulted with them on policy matters regarding social legislation (Ashford, 1960, 319). Additionally, through its participation in auxiliary institutions such as the Superior Council for the Plan and High Commission for Collective Conventions, the union had a direct role in guiding economic policy and could significantly influence legislation governing state–labor relations. Finally, within parliament, unionists could openly question ministerial decisions, serving as a litmus test and, at times, veto-player for key government initiatives. The extent of union's room for maneuver was clearly demonstrated in 1956, when UMT leaders blocked a controversial labor code that would have given the Minister of Interior the right to dissolve unions during threats to public order, despite alleged endorsement of the law by the King (Moore, 1970, 181).

Finally, from an organizational standpoint, the UMT benefited from numerous financial and material privileges afforded by the state. According to union sources, some 20 percent of the union's total budget was provided through subsidies by the state, amounting to 200,000 MDH of annual revenue (Moore, 1970, 186; Filali-Meknassi,

1989, 25). In efforts to help the UMT build its organizational base, the government provided syndical detachments for all union leaders in the public and private sector and gifted the union rent-free premises in Casablanca to serve as its national headquarters (Clement and Paul, 1984, 21). Substantial advantages were also afforded to the union in the management of public enterprises – in addition to high-ranking positions in state-owned firms, UMT leaders received prestigious posts in several mutual societies and were placed in charge of administering Morocco's Social Security Fund.

However, the brief honeymoon between the UMT and the monarchy would soon come to an end with the death of Mohammed V and the ascension of his successor, Hassan II. Unlike his father, Hassan II had little interest in appeasing a strong, directive labor movement – already, through his efforts to suppress the UMT's monopoly with the legalization of a rival federation, the General Union of Moroccan Workers (*Union Générale des Travailleurs du Maroc*, UGTM), the king demonstrated that he wanted the division of his opposition, not partnership with it. Thus, in the early years of his tenure, Hassan II responded to union activism with an impressive combination of co-optation and repression. While the 1962 constitution spelled out progressive labor legislation – including provisions for labor complaint courts, union representation in the workplace, and the right to organize and strike – actual labor demonstrations were met with harsh intervention; on several occasions, the military was called in to disrupt worker mobilization and union leaders were jailed for displaying any hint of opposition to the regime.[14] In 1963, several dozen union members were arrested during a strike for allegedly plotting against the king, leading to a definitive rupture in state–labor relations and the systematic erosion of benefits afforded to the UMT (Miller, 2013, 167). In an attempt to weaken the union, the government promoted the formation of two new labor confederations, abrogated cost-of-living indexing for wages, and froze pay rates in the civil service, the UMT's strongest sector (Clement and Paul, 1984, 22). When these measures failed to curb labor unrest, the regime cracked down hard, issuing a state of emergency and ushering in a decade-long period of

[14] Famously, in 1967, the king ordered the arrest of the UMT's secretary-general, Mahjoub Benseddik, for his criticism of the monarchy's close relationship with Israel after the Arab-Israeli War.

political repression known colloquially as "les années du plomb" (the years of lead).

Labor Inclusion in Morocco: "Representation Qua Control"

In many ways then, the early postindependence experience of trade unions in Morocco mirrored that of Tunisia: a brief period of alliance followed by an era of extreme repression and control. However, in the early 1970s, important changes in the country's political environment generated incentives for a reversal in the monarchy's draconian containment strategy. In May 1970, Morocco's rising unemployment touched off a series of domestic protests, culminating in a general strike in Rabat's public universities and neighboring schools (Lust-Okar, 2005, 56). Moreover, amid the wave of growing unrest, sectors of the military defected from the regime, launching two unsuccessful coups against Hassan II within a period of thirteen months.[15]

Spurred by these events, the monarchy sought to broaden its political base by re-integrating labor into its ruling coalition. In July 1970, Hassan II formally ended Morocco's state of emergency and began easing his repression of labor opposition.[16] Simultaneously, the regime redoubled its efforts to establish clientelistic relationships with unions, rewarding union cadres with policy concessions, political appointments,[17] and lucrative promotions within state-owned firms. This incorporative turn toward labor was solidified by the creation of a nominally inclusive parliament in 1970, which elevated trade unions' political influence at the expense of parties (Storm, 2007, 27). Following the adoption of constitutional reforms in 1972, union members were granted reserve seats in the country's new bicameral legislature and were invited to field candidates in the nation's forthcoming municipal elections.

[15] For more information on the 1971 coup, see Waterbury (1972), who provides a detailed discussion of these events.

[16] From 1972 to 1979, only four complaints were made by Moroccan unions to the ILO relating to the government's suppression of union organizing by force. As a point of comparison, twelve such complaints were made from 1961 to 1971.

[17] Maati Bouabid, who had affiliations to the *Istiqlal* (and later to the National Union of Popular Forces, UNFP) and UMT, was appointed to serve the Minister of Justice in 1977 and as Prime Minister in 1979.

Although the regime succeeded in placing such "representative" institutions under its tight control, the limited space offered in parliament became a place where issues with the monarchy could be presented and labor grievances could be expressed. If parliament was not a place for "producing policies" (i.e., enacting real political change), it was a space for "doing politics" (e.g., articulating interests and receiving benefits from the regime). In open sessions, legislators could check the behavior of the government by questioning ministers appointed by the King. Additionally, by submitting policy resolutions, legislative blocs could exert influence on decision-making at the margins. Most important, parliament served as a formal institution through which the monarchy could co-opt and pacify opposition elites. Consequently, the 1970s would be marked by a growing consensus between organized labor and the King, bolstered by a military campaign in the Western Sahara and new legislative elections which secured substantial representation for labor affiliates (Storm, 2007, 40).

Ultimately, the combination of inclusive labor control policies and a freer political system produced distinct legacies on the development of organized labor in Morocco. First, monarchical efforts to incorporate labor into formal institutions created linkages between unions and the government that would ultimately bind the fortunes of trade unions to those of the regime. By enacting friendly labor laws, granting union leaders prestigious positions in government, and providing direct subsidies to support union growth, regime elites transformed organized labor into a client of the authoritarian state. Although unions would benefit tremendously from these advantages, these benefits would serve as important levers of control through which the state could bring oppositional trade unions to heel in times of crisis.

Second, the integration of union elites into parliament created the conditions for the establishment of party-union linkages and – as noted in Chapter 2 – the fractionalization of the labor movement. Given that union seats in the parliament were fixed by quota,[18] parties saw allying with trade unions as an efficient way to acquire more power in the legislature by capturing unions' delegate seats (Appendix B:MA-19, 4/9/14). Similarly, the organizational strength of

[18] As of 1970, ten seats were specifically reserved for labor representatives in parliament, although members of labor unions could and did serve outside of these seats as representatives of individual parties.

labor made trade unions attractive partners for alliance – by winning the loyalty of a major confederation, party elites could ensure that union members would vote for their candidates in direct elections. For a trade union, alliance with a political party was useful because of the organizational and political benefits that parties could provide. In addition to acquiring high-level party positions[19] and forming networks with political elites, union leaders could have a direct influence on policy-making and receive organizational support from partisan partners when fielding their own candidates in elections (Appendix B: MA-19, 4/9/14, MA-20, 4/14/2014).

In the context of a pluralist party system, however, this desire for alliance meant that the labor movement was increasingly fragmented along party lines. As rival parties attempted to acquire their own labor constituencies, they frequently manipulated intra-union divisions – at times with the help of Hassan II himself – to encourage dissident unionists to form splinter unions. In the late 1950s, such partisan manipulation gave rise to the birth of a new trade union, the UGTM, with ties to the *Istiqlal*. Over the course of the 1960s and 1970s, union development would continue to track along the lines of party formation: as Figure 3.1 shows, the combination of labor incorporation and a plural party system engendered a dynamic whereby each new party was compelled to found its own labor union. As we shall see in the next chapter, this division fostered bitter rivalries within the labor movement that would impede effective collective action in the neoliberal period.

Finally, linkages between labor organizations and political elites had considerable effects on unions' internal bureaucracy. As labor leaders began to rely on political appointments to shore up their personal power, they became increasingly divorced from their constituents in the rank-and-file. Renewed militancy in the postal services sector (PTT) in 1963, for example, was immediately denounced by the UMT central administration after the monarchy threatened union leaders with the withdrawal of their rent-free premises and their paid government leave (Clement and Paul, 1984, 22). Additionally, party resources were frequently used to maintain the dominance of "cooperative"

[19] Traditionally, at least one member of a partner union is selected to sit on their party's Political Bureau, and other peak or intermediate leaders may be called to serve on the party's Executive or Central Committee.

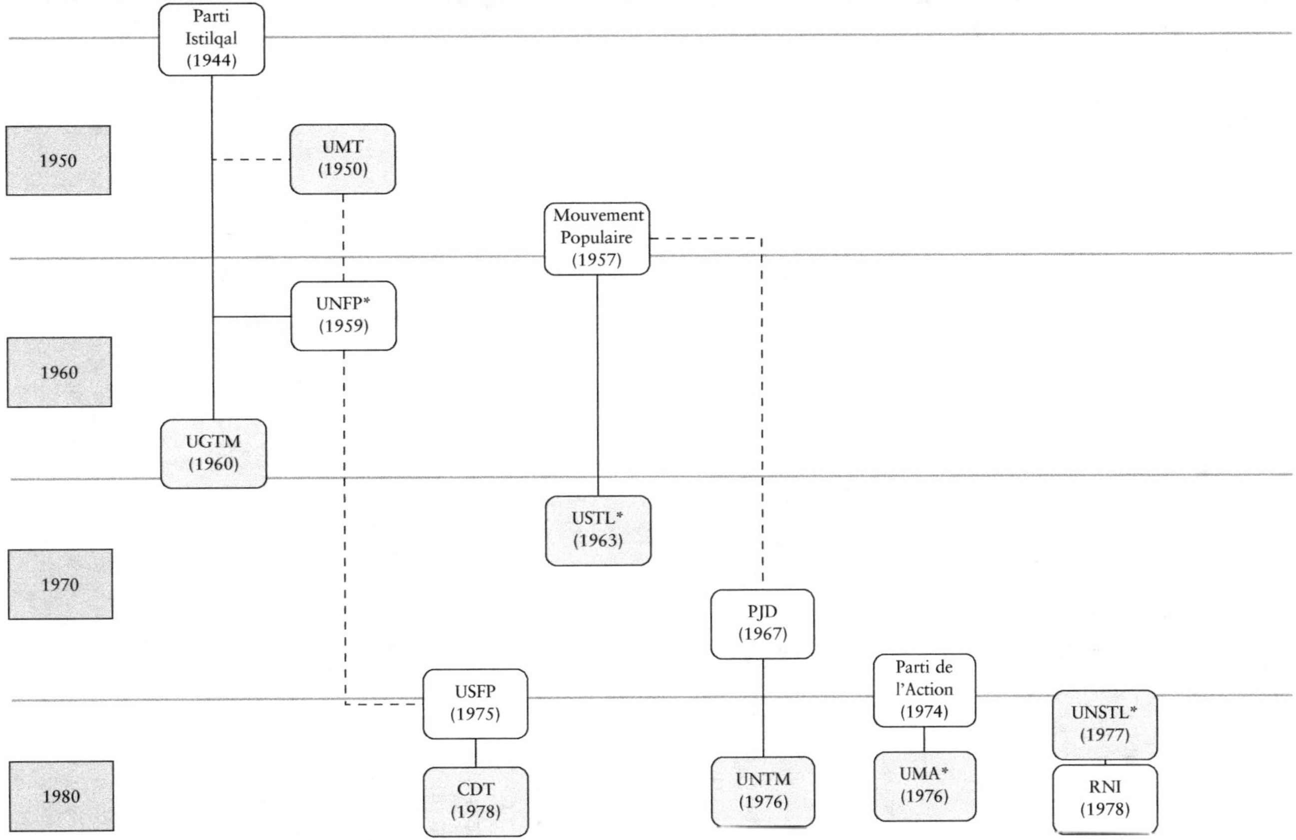

Figure 3.1 Party-union alliances in Morocco
Note: Founding year of party/union in parentheses. A solid line signifies alliance continuation, a dashed lined signifies a discontinued alliance or party split. An asterisk signifies a defunct organization.

labor elites over competitors and restrict the access of base unionists to positions of authority, as evidenced by controversial elections in the railways federation and the PTT.[20] At the national level, union congresses were regularly postponed or subject to direct manipulation by party or union leaders. Consequently, internal democracy within labor organizations fell into precipitous decline – from 1958 to 1975 only five out of twenty of the UMT's top leadership were removed from office, paralleling developments in the country writ large, where leaders were known to remain in their positions "*jusqu'à la mort* (until their death)" (Appendix B: MA-10, 3/19/2014; MS-16, 4/4/2014).

Summary

In short, state–labor relations in Morocco were based on a balance of representation and control, but there was more of the former than the latter. Although, in many ways, the strategies used to contain labor opposition in Morocco were similar to those implemented in Tunisia, the above discussion reveals that the extent of labor incorporation in Morocco was more systematic, thorough, and enduring. In contrast to the Bourguiba regime, which intensified its repression of the labor movement in the late 1960s, Hassan II's regime gradually reversed its authoritarian practices over the same period, signaling a meaningful change in its position vis-a-vis labor and political opposition as a whole. By enacting progressive labor reforms, granting concessions, and creating institutional avenues through which workers could express their interests before the state, the regime successfully co-opted labor into its ruling coalition, transforming it into an effective client of the autocratic regime. Additionally, by nurturing the relationship between parties and unions with the institution of a multiparty parliamentary system, the monarchy fragmented unions along ideological lines, generating tensions within the labor movement that it could manipulate to impede collective action in the future. Thus, in contrast to Tunisia, where the government's progressive exclusion of the labor

[20] In 1963, after the head of the postal federation decided to approve a strike against the Executive Bureau's wishes, members of the central administration had him forcibly removed from office and suspended the PTT federation. In 1973 similar tactics were used to curb the militancy of the rail workers federation, whose entire executive committee was dissolved by fiat (Clement and Paul, 1984).

movement lead to a contentious relationship between unions and the state, the Moroccan regime's efforts to incorporate organized labor into workplace and political institutions generated a new state–labor alliance built around the principle of "representation qua control" (Aidi, 2008, 79). As a consequence, when neoliberal reforms forced leaders to abandon their traditional clientelistic relationships with organized labor, unions in Morocco would remain politically captive and quiescent, while they served as a basis for militant opposition in Tunisia.

Conclusion

This chapter has reviewed the different incorporation policies employed by dictators in Tunisia and Morocco to contain labor and political opposition, highlighting their impact on unions' alliances and capacities as they entered the neoliberal period. In it, I examined how different strategies of political control – incorporation versus exclusion – affected labor's organization as well as its relationship with other political actors. Whereas Bourguiba's use of exclusionary corporatism fostered radicalism within the labor movement and granted a measure of autonomy to the UGTT, the incorporative and pluralist strategies adopted by Moroccan monarchs facilitated party-union linkages which moderated labor opposition. These differing political conditions underscore the importance of formal institutions in shaping the strategies and alliances of collective actors.

Nevertheless, scholars have suggested that factors outside of the incorporation period were instrumental in shaping patterns of labor mobilization in these two cases. Three additional variables – regime type, the structure of class alliances, and union's pre-authoritarian legacies – stand out as credible alternatives to the historical institutionalist argument advanced here. Each of these explanations points to fundamental differences between the Moroccan and Tunisian cases, which influenced leaders' institutional choices and shaped the variants of labor mobilization that unions would ultimately adopt. Below, I discuss each of these in turn, demonstrating why they fall short of explaining differences in Tunisia and Morocco and addressing concerns about the endogeneity of political institutions to antecedent conditions.

A first alternative suggests that the differing structures of Moroccan and Tunisian regimes in the postcolonial period account for variations in their institutional choices and trajectories of labor opposition. Specifically, Morocco's ability to retain its monarchy after the colonial period is said to have provided Mohammed V with greater flexibility to pursue incorporative policies and withstand political threats over the long term. According to this view, monarchies have unique capacities for policy innovation and institutional flexibility – unlike presidents, monarchs can position themselves "above the fray" of everyday politics, facilitating liberalizing reforms (Herb, 1999; Lucas, 2004). Additionally, in kingdoms like Morocco, where the ruling family lays claim to religious ancestry, the monarchy's traditional legitimacy can be leveraged during crises to prevent potential challenges to its rule (Frisch, 2011; Schlumberger, 2010).

However, while the differences between monarchies and presidential republics are significant, their impacts on long-term political developments and survival have often been exaggerated. A review of the historical record reveals that monarchies are not immune to collapse; since the 1950s, as many Middle Eastern monarchies have fallen as have managed to survive (Bank et al., 2014; Yom and Gause III, 2012). Moreover, although royalism may render certain institutional options less risky than they would be under republicanism, it doesn't make them impossible to select. As Gandhi and Przeworski (2007) note, since the beginning of the Third Wave, a number of presidential regimes have governed with legislatures or multiparty institutions to maintain their hold on power.

Specifically, in the cases of Tunisia and Morocco, differences in regime type neither predetermined leaders' institutional choices nor completely foreclosed alternative options. As noted above, both leaders initially pursued similar paths of incorporation and repression, only diverging after all alternatives had been exhausted. Additionally, although the Moroccan regime may have faced a lower threat of collapse due to Mohamed V's religious legitimacy, his position as Morocco's sole political leader was far from secure. Indeed, in the early years of independence, the monarchy faced serious political challenges from the *Istiqlal*, which aimed to transform Morocco into a constitutional monarchy with the king as a figurehead (Zartman and Duga, 1965). Moreover, Hassan II enjoyed less legitimacy than his father, who benefited dually from his position as "Commander of the Faithful" and his preeminent role in the independence struggle. The presidential regime in Tunisia also evolved qualities akin to a monarchy. After deposing the ruling bey, Bourguiba sought to endow himself with the traditional legitimacy of the palace, adopting a unique style of personalistic rule known as "presidential monarchy."[21]

Thus, in neither case did regime type preclude the selection of alternative political options. Both leaders faced significant threats to their rule that forced them to consolidate power in specific ways. Just as opposition parties in Morocco advocated for greater regime openness, liberal factions in Tunisia pressed for power sharing between Bourguiba and the country's political elite, though these efforts were ultimately futile (Moore, 1965). Additionally, while Hassan II's loss of military support following the 1971 and 1972 coups undoubtedly influenced his shift toward greater incorporation, similar coup attempts in Tunisia had the opposite effect,[22] prompting Bourguiba to concentrate power and demobilize his opposition to forestall future threats (Grewal, 2020; Nassif, 2015). While I am not suggesting that institutional differences should be attributed to the idiosyncratic characteristics of Bourguiba or Hassan II, one cannot cleanly link them to pre-existing differences in regime type. Instead, as my argument suggests, there is an increased role for contingency during periods of political upheaval: at moments of uncertainty, such as the founding of regimes, even the smallest decisions can have out-sized impacts over the progression of political life.

A second perspective emphasizes the role of class configurations in shaping institutional and political outcomes. Long-standing research suggests that class conflicts and the coalitions they engender are critical for understanding institutions' origins (Ruschemeyer et al., 1992; Thelen, 2004). In the context of labor, Collier and Collier's work in Latin America finds that incorporation policies were directly

[21] The term "presidential monarchy" was first used by Clement Henry Moore to describe the unique political style of the Bourguiba government. According to Moore, this term "conveys the dual nature of Bourguiba's style of leadership – reminiscent of that of the traditional autocrat [(i.e., monarch)] yet depending upon modern political structures" (1965, 71).

[22] In 1962, a coup attempt was made against Habib Bourguiba by members of Neo-Destour militia forces that supported Salah Ben Youssef for party president. For more details on the events surrounding the coup and the Bourguiba regime's response to it, see Borsali (2008).

influenced by class coalitions formed in the pre-incorporation period (1991, 103–106). Similar arguments have been made in the Middle East, focusing on the importance of rural/urban divides and populist alliances in driving institutional choices (Bellin, 2002; Buehler, 2015; Cammett, 2007; Clark, 2018). Thus, more inclusive incorporation efforts are expected when the state is supported by peasants and labor, while exclusionary policies are anticipated when the state aligns with landed elites (Collier and Collier, 1991).

However, in Tunisia and Morocco, the alliance of class coalitions during the post-independence period does not align with these expectations. While the Bourguiban and Mohammedian/Hassanian regimes relied on different bases of social support, their institutional choices contradicted those predicted by theory. In Tunisia, Bourguiba formed a classic populist alliance after dismantling the traditional precolonial elite, garnering support from the peasantry, labor, urban professionals, and the petite bourgeoisie (Cammett, 2007). In contrast, following early conflicts with the mostly urban *Istiqlal*, Mohammed V relied on the support of Morocco's traditional agrarian elite to sustain his rule (ibid). Per Collier and Collier's predictions, we should expect the Moroccan regime to initiate more limited labor reforms and for Tunisia to pursue more extensive worker incorporation. Yet as the previous discussion shows, this was not the case. Further, the different paths of economic development pursued by these regimes do not explain differences in their institutional structures. Indeed, Bourguiba's socialist development plan should have led to more efforts to incorporate workers into the state, while Morocco's relatively liberal development strategy should have fostered closer ties between the state and capital interests.

Finally, a third argument focuses on the pre-authoritarian period as a critical juncture, arguing that precolonial differences among labor unions account for their distinct protest patterns. In her 2020 article, Dina Bishara presents a comparative historical argument that stresses the role of historical political struggles and organizational development in influencing two of this study's main outcomes: the degree of union autonomy and the likelihood of labor opposition. She argues that the UGTT's prominent role in the anti-colonial struggle, in conjunction with the credibility and strength it amassed as a nationalist actor, "severely constrained the capacity of authoritarian rulers to completely subjugate the organization" (2020, 126). Consequently, when the union was confronted with the opportunity to participate in the 2011 pro-democratic uprising, it could draw upon this legacy to more effectively oppose the Ben Ali regime.

While I do not disagree with her analysis of the Tunisian case, I argue that tracing the UGTT's militant roots to the precolonial period – for the purposes of comparison with Morocco – points to the wrong critical juncture. As detailed above, the UMT had a similar level of nationalist legitimacy and organizational clout but was unable to resist the Moroccan regime's attempts at domination. What differed between the two unions was not their precolonial history but the ways in which they were co-opted after authoritarianism began. While the Bourguiba regime excluded the UGTT from important avenues of institutional power, Mohammed V and his successor, Hassan II, pursued a more inclusionary strategy meant to weaken unions through gradual co-option and efforts to divide and rule.

Ultimately, we cannot trace protest outcomes to pre-authoritarian antecedents, but to specific choices made by political leaders during the state-building period. As the following chapters will show, the legacy of these decisions significantly influenced how labor unions interpreted their political environments and, ultimately, the choices they made regarding their modes of mobilization in the neoliberal era.

4 *Workers in an Era of Change: Union Responses to Early Neoliberal Reforms*

The 1970s marked a period of profound change in the political economy of North Africa. In the early years after independence, favorable economic conditions facilitated state-labor bargains based on the principles of economic stability, interdependence, and mutual exchange. Rising global commodity prices and import-substituting industrialization led governments to embrace state-led development, which combined centrally planned economies with high levels of public investment. To support this strategy, authoritarian elites established corporatist systems that provided meaningful benefits to workers – higher wages, job security, and welfare benefits – in exchange for political loyalty and quiescence on the shop floor.

However, by the mid-1970s, the favorable conditions that undergirded state-labor bargains began to deteriorate. Having tried, and failed, to promote inward-looking development, North African states turned outward and introduced neoliberal reforms to reverse stagnating growth. In addition to opening up their economies, governments experimented with austerity measures designed to reduce public spending and pave the way for private sector investment. These changes, while sometimes accompanied by institutional innovations to secure unions' support called into question clientelistic bargains between workers and the.

In Tunisia and Morocco, labor unions responded to these reforms with an increase in militancy, organizing strikes and sit-ins to combat declining purchasing power, weak job prospects, and poor living conditions (Figure 4.1). Yet despite broad similarities in the frequency of opposition, the character and aims of labor protests differed dramatically. In Tunisia, labor mobilization united rank-and-file workers, union leaders, and radical leftists in a wave of unrest that was political as much as it was economic. By the late 1970s, the UGTT had transformed into one of the only opposition forces in Tunisia that could challenge the dominance of Habib Bourguiba's single-party

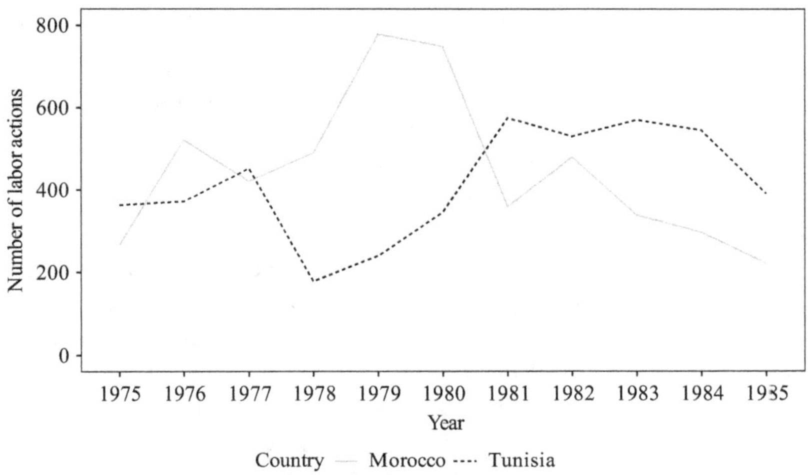

Source: ILO Database

Figure 4.1 Comparative labor protests in Tunisia and Morocco, ILO (1975–1985)

regime. Labor opposition went beyond material demands, critiquing the centralization of the regime, its growing authoritarianism, and the lack of union and political freedoms. In the 1970s and 1980s, this political transformation led workers into direct conflict with the Tunisian state, resulting in the near evisceration of the UGTT by 1985.

In contrast, labor mobilization in Morocco remained segmented and apolitical. While workers engaged in strike activity as a sign of opposition to reforms, they did not do so under a common banner, nor did unions emerge as an influential political force. Instead, competing unions adopted divergent methods of opposition, which often pitted workers against one another in the pursuit of limited, parochial goals. This fragmentation weakened the labor movement, preventing it from advancing a unified agenda for political change, as did the UGTT in Tunisia.

These divergent responses raise several questions that will be explored in the balance of this chapter. Why did unions in Tunisia and Morocco respond to economic reforms with increased militancy? Why, despite similar reforms, did the character of militancy in these cases differ? How did labor mobilization in Tunisia transcend traditional economic concerns and develop into a broad-based movement for political change? Why did the same fail to occur in Morocco?

I argue that the answer to these questions lies in an examination of the formal institutions that governed state-labor relations during the reform period. I move beyond an analysis of the economic costs of reforms to focus on how political institutions designed to contain labor militancy generated new dynamics between unions, opposition groups, and authoritarian elites. In Tunisia, exclusionary corporatist institutions alienated key segments of the labor and political elite, resulting in highly politicized labor protests. In contrast, inclusionary workplace and political institutions in Morocco strengthened mechanisms for workers to express their interests, solidifying linkages between unions, established parties, and the monarchical regime. These institutions exacerbated rivalries within the labor movement, resulting in surge of labor militancy. However, they also prevented organized labor from developing a broad-based coalition that could unite workers around a common agenda for political change.

The remainder of the chapter is organized as follows. The next section outlines the reform period in Tunisia and Morocco and details the effects that neoliberal reforms had on organized labor. I examine how liberalizing reforms disrupted preexisting state-labor bargains, creating new incentives for workers to strike. I then turn to unions' reactions to reforms, highlighting the differences between political militancy in Tunisia and apolitical protest in Morocco. Finally, I investigate the roots of divergent labor mobilization, emphasizing how formal institutions shaped unions' interests and capacities for protest. I detail how labor incorporation shaped unions' relationship with political elites and their own rank-and-file members, affecting their ability to mobilize and sustain political action.

The Evolution of State–Labor Bargains: "Etatist" Development and Neoliberal Reforms

Early State Sponsorship of the Working Class

In Tunisia and Morocco, the origins of state-labor bargains trace back to the rise of government intervention in the economy. Although leaders in each country initially pursued different methods of development, by the early 1970s, both converged on a "state-led" development model characterized by significant public investment, government ownership of key enterprises, and control over the means of production (e.g., capital, infrastructure, and waged labor). In Tunisia, state-led development mirrored Egyptian state socialism: inspired by Nasser, Bourguiba's economic plan called for the collectivization of agriculture, state-led industrialization, and substantial investment into public and private enterprise. In Morocco, a looser "state capitalist" model predominated in which the state controlled key resources (e.g., mines, railroads, sugar refineries) while supporting the formation of a domestic capitalist class.

In both countries, state intervention increased the government's influence over the economy, fostering organic linkages between incumbent regimes and organized labor. The advent of import-substituting industrialization in Tunisia led to the creation of 160 new state-owned enterprises by 1970, boosting employment in heavily unionized sectors such as textiles, phosphate mining, and manufacturing (Grissa, 1991, 111). Government-funded works programs absorbed a substantial share of unemployed workers into the formal economy, creating 250,000 temporary jobs by 1962 (Zaanouni, 1963). Additionally, substantial investments in human development (~ 90 million dinars per year) generated long-term benefits for the working class, significantly reducing poverty and increasing education (Institut Nationale de la Statistique, 2013).[1]

Similarly, in Morocco, state control of the economy forged new links between organized labor and authoritarian elites. Following a boom in global phosphate prices, the state tripled its investment in the public sector, increasing wages by over 26 percent in 1974 and establishing 215 new firms in agro-business, steel manufacturing, and petrochemicals (Findlay, 1984, 204; Saulniers, 1993a). The state also expanded its sponsorship of organized labor by augmenting consumer subsidies and increasing social spending. By 1975, state-financed welfare programs generated 41.5 million working days for Morocco's nonunionized workforce and contributed subsidies of up to 50 percent on the prices of basic goods and housing (Findlay, 1984).

[1] By 1969, the poverty rate had dropped by nearly 30 percent, and 40 percent of youths were enrolled in secondary school (DeGorge, 2002, 587).

These conditions laid the foundation for stable, clientelistic bargains between labor and the state based on the principle of mutual exchange. In return for interventionist policies that channeled benefits to the working class, union leaders were expected to suppress dissent among their members and support the regime's (often autocratic) political aims. However, the eventual failure of state-led development models cast doubt on these bargains and the economic policies that undergirded them. By the late 1960s, the étatist model was showing signs of collapse, raising concerns about the viability of continued state-sponsorship of the working class.

Bargains under Stress: Economic Opening and Initial Adjustments

In the 1970s, external price shocks and disappointing revenues forced governments to retreat from their traditional roles as guarantors of economic growth. Recognizing the difficulty of fueling development through government largesse, states withdrew from the public sector and experimented with limited economic reforms. Although the timing, pace, and content of these measures varied, they were all implemented around a set of common goals: cutting public expenditures, stimulating private enterprise, and removing government subsidies for welfare and consumer goods. In Tunisia and Morocco, such measures imposed painful sacrifices on workers, disrupting preexisting bargains between unions and autocratic regimes.

Tunisia: "Infitah" and Early Economic Reforms

In Tunisia, the transition to a market economy began in 1970 with the adoption of *infitah* ("economic opening"). As in many countries, the primary goal was to reduce Tunisia's debt by streamlining public investment while integrating the country more deeply into the global market. To this end, the government implemented a suite of liberalizing reforms: currency devaluation, the provision of export incentives, and favorable legislation to increase foreign investment. This shift marked a clear departure from the previous command economy to one in which market forces would play a greater role in driving economic growth.

A key aspect of Tunisia's new economic program was to reduce state expenditures by promoting private sector investment. To achieve this objective, the government created a new Industrial Promotion Agency (*Agence des Promotion des Investissements*) to support investors and enacted two new laws – Law 72-38 and Law 74-74 – which gave entrepreneurs special incentives to develop export industries. In addition, the government liberalized export trade and introduced various incentives to encourage domestic firms to compete on the open market. In 1969, Bourguiba signed an association agreement with the European Economic Community (EEC), followed by a cooperation agreement in 1975, ensuring free access to European markets.

Despite these liberalizing reforms, the government did not withdraw from the public sector entirely. During most of the *infitah* period, the Tunisian state continued to support industrial efforts that "exceed[ed] the capabilities of private initiative" (Tunisia Ministry of Plan, 1968, 141–142). Following an increase in revenue during the 1973 oil boom, the Tunisian state expanded its role in manufacturing, creating 140 new state-owned enterprises in construction, electrical, and chemical production (Pfeifer, 1996, 43). Additionally, the government boosted spending on public goods, devoting significant resources to consumer subsidies, welfare programs, and infrastructure projects. Consequently, government expenditures increased over the *infitah* period, doubling from 1972 to 1984 (Grissa, 1991, 112–113). While the share of private investment grew by 20 percent, the government maintained its influence in the economy, with its share of total capital investment remaining above 45 percent from 1960 to 1985 (Bellin, 2002, 27).

Initially, these policy measures had a positive impact on Tunisia's economy. Between 1970 and 1974, the value of Tunisia's exports quadrupled to 398 million Tunisian dinars (TD), placing Tunisia among the top ten countries in the world in terms of GDP growth per capita (Alexander, 2010, 77; Ben Romdhane, 1985, 277–279). By the mid-1970s, however, this prosperity waned. In 1977, EEC import restrictions led many European countries to close their borders to Tunisian exports, reducing export revenues to 29 percent of GDP (The World Bank, 2016). At the same time, a decline in agricultural production increased food imports by TD 735 million, straining Tunisia's current account. Combined with increased state spending to fund subsidies and float underperforming firms, these imbalances drove the Tunisian government into a spiral of increasing debt. By 1986, commercial borrowing had pushed Tunisia's external debt to roughly $5 billion, with debt service consuming nearly 26 percent of government receipts.

Effects on Labor

If liberalization failed to produce lasting benefits for the Tunisian economy, its effects on the labor market were mixed. On the one hand, state and private sector investment created thousands of jobs for the country's growing workforce. In addition to the 86,000 jobs created by the private sector, state-owned enterprises generated 242,500 new jobs by 1977 (Bank al-Markazī al-Tūnisī, 1978; Findlay, 1984). Since many of these positions required minimal skills, they were ideal for absorbing Tunisia's unemployed population, the majority of whom were young and lacked professional training.

Additionally, the state established new corporatist institutions to integrate unions more deeply into policymaking. In 1973, a new wage bargaining system, the *convention collective cadre* (CCC), formalized the relationship between organized labor, employers, and the state. Through the CCC, the UGTT, the employers' association (*Union Tunisienne de l'Industrie, du Commerce et de l'Artisanat*, UTICA), and government officials met on an annual basis to negotiate wage accords, set pay grids (including a minimum wage), and establish standards for working conditions and productivity standards. The government also strengthened the role of the Economic and Social Council and established new workplace institutions, joint consultative commissions (*commissions paritaires consultatives*, CPCs), to enforce wage accords.

With the help of the CCC, workers realized important gains in their wages and living conditions. Between 1970 and 1977, wage agreements increased the average annual income by 23–40 percent in real terms (Table 4.1). Minimum wages also increased by 35 percent due to successive wage increases in the private sector (Bellin, 2002, 103). Additionally, investments in welfare and education reduced poverty and significantly improved both the standard and quality of living for the working class (Murphy, 1999, 91–92).

However, these improvements failed to address deeper issues in income inequality and the cost of living. While the average real salary grew 18 percent from 1971 to 1975, employers' profits grew 68 percent, highlighting the vast disparities in the liberal economy (Ben Romdhane, 1981, 282). Furthermore, wage rates failed to keep

Table 4.1. ***Average annual salaries in Tunisia (in real terms), 1970–1977***

Year	Declarations to the Caisse Nationale de Sécurité Sociale	Census of industrial activities
1970	100	100
1971	100.2	105
1972	100.4	108.8
1973	103	106.5
1974	112.2	113.5
1975	127.1	119.4
1976	139	120.3
1977	146.6	123.6

Source: Ben Romdhane, 1981, 445 cited in Bellin (2002, 104.)
Notes: Relative values using 1970 as a base rate. Salary data excludes civil service workers.

pace with rising inflation, which averaged 5 percent per year. According to one union estimate, consumer prices rose 36 percent between 1970 and 1976 (UGTT, 1977, 12), meaning that wage increases were used to maintain rather than improve workers' lives. In the 1980s, workers' living conditions deteriorated further – following new austerity measures imposed by the International Monetary Fund (IMF), real salaries dropped by more than 5 percent, while the proportion of basic food subsidies was dramatically reduced (Nsouli et al., 1993).

On the employment front, job creation also masked larger issues. Population growth and increased feminization of the workforce meant that new job opportunities could not absorb all of Tunisia's unemployed. In the public sector, overemployment in state-owned firms gave way to mass layoffs as export revenues subsided. In the private sector, investment in capital-intensive industries reduced the ability of private firms to compensate for public sector losses. Consequently, the official unemployment rate remained above 10 percent throughout the 1970s, with higher levels among the youth and in major cities (Perkins, 2014, 163). Despite government efforts to expand job creation during the Sixth Economic Plan (1982–1986), by 1986 national unemployment had reached 15 percent, with even higher rates in southern and interior regions.

Morocco: Stabilization and Adjustment

As in Tunisia, the failure of state-led development in Morocco led to a reorientation of the national economy. Faced with a balance of payments crisis, the monarchy realized the need for stabilization measures to curb public sector growth and address macroeconomic imbalances. Thus, on two occasions – 1977–1978 and 1980–1982 – the government implemented fiscal reforms to avoid continued crisis. In 1977, it slashed public expenditures, adopted restrictive credit policies toward domestic enterprises, and reduced capital expenditures by more than 50 percent (Horton, 1990, 32–33). The following year, it complemented these measures with an increase in tax rates, salary freezes in the civil service, and a 36 percent reduction in public investment (Azam and Morrison, 1994, 90).

In the short run, these policies spawned a brief economic recovery, boosting GDP growth to 4.7 percent and reducing the current account deficit to less than 10 percent of GDP (The World Bank, 2016). However, the government quickly abandoned its stabilization program due to several external challenges. Costly food imports combined with escalating tensions in the Western Sahara increased budgetary demands for consumption subsidies and defense spending. Additionally, severe droughts and external price shocks negatively impacted fiscal revenues, exacerbating the budget deficit. By the 1980s, the government realized that short-term measures would not be enough to restore economic balance. What was needed was a longer-term approach, which combined both demand and supply-side restrictions.

Thus, in 1980, the government requested assistance from the IMF, implementing a second stabilization program through a three-year Extended Fund Facility (EFF). As with previous stabilization measures, the goal of the EFF was to eliminate Morocco's budget and current account deficits by curbing government expenditures and increasing domestic savings. To reduce spending, it called for a 10–50 percent increase in the price of subsidized goods, effectively returning consumption subsidies to their 1979 levels in real terms (Horton, 1990, 35). On the supply side, it demanded that capital formation be driven by the private sector, with state resources redirected from underperforming state-owned enterprises to export-oriented firms in agriculture, fisheries, and phosphates. In 1982, the policies initiated with the EFF were reinforced through an IMF-sponsored standby agreement. Per this agreement, the government further tightened its budget by freezing wages in the public sector and increasing the prices of public utilities.

Despite these ambitious goals, stabilization policies failed to achieve lasting success. In the wake of severe droughts, agricultural output fell by 23 percent in 1981, increasing the demand for imported goods (Azam and Morrison, 1994, 90). At the same time, an unexpected appreciation of the dollar raised import costs, placing negative pressure on Morocco's current account. Although the government attempted to offset these trends by lowering consumer subsidies, widespread rioting in June 1981 forced the monarchy to increase spending on public assistance. Since much of this spending was financed by foreign borrowing, this led to a surge in external debt, which reached an all-time high of $11.8 billion in 1983 (Denoeux and Maghraoui, 1998, 57). By March, Morocco's foreign exchange reserves were depleted, triggering a full-fledged economic crisis. In the years that followed, the government would embark on more stringent economic reforms that placed the monarchy in direct conflict with labor interests.

Effects on Labor

Similar to Tunisia, economic reforms imposed painful sacrifices on Moroccan workers, as reflected in unemployment and wage statistics. By 1982, the number of unemployed Moroccans had increased to 640,000, representing 13 percent of the working population (ILO, 1983). As fiscal austerity progressed, job prospects worsened: in 1983, budget revisions cut 19,000 planned public sector jobs and instituted a hiring freeze in the civil service (Azam and Morrison, 1994, 100). By 1983, the number of new public sector positions decreased to less than half of its 1982 level, leading to a spike in urban unemployment (Boudarbat, 2006, 166).

Workers' incomes also declined substantially during the reform period. In the public sector, wage freezes implemented from 1980 to 1983 reduced real incomes by 13 percent (Azam and Morrison, 1994, 92). While the government eventually raised wages in the mid-1980s, these increases failed to keep pace with high inflation, averaging 10 percent annually (The World Bank, 2016). In the private sector, nominal wages lagged behind price increases due to unfavorable conditions such as low productivity and rising unemployment.

Finally, workers suffered from sharp declines in social spending. Between 1978 and 1982, cuts in public expenditures led to a reduction in real government spending on public health and housing. Although investments in education increased, the growing number of university graduates strained the public sector, which struggled to absorb the demand for well-paying civil service jobs (Rhazaoui, 1987, 148). Restructuring Morocco's subsidy scheme to target the urban poor also negatively impacted workers in the long term. Price increases and revised tax policies disproportionately affected middle-class workers, resulting in a decrease in real average incomes by over 20 percent from 1981 to 1986 (Azam and Morrison, 1994, 92).

Labor's Response to Reform: Radical Political Unionism versus Apolitical Militancy

In sum, economic reforms initiated during the 1970s significantly altered the terms of existing state-labor bargains. However, unions in Tunisia and Morocco reacted very differently to these reforms. In Tunisia, the UGTT responded with increased militancy that challenged not only the government's neoliberal policies but the legitimacy of the regime itself. Conversely, in Morocco, labor militancy remained divided and apolitical. In what follows, I explore these differences in greater depth, focusing on the composition of labor protests, their strategies, and their divergent demands. This discussion lays the foundation for my analysis in the remainder of the chapter, which provides an institutional explanation for protest in these two cases.

Labor Opposition in Tunisia: The Birth of a Militant, Political Movement

As progressive liberalization threatened workers' traditional patron–client relationship with the state, organized labor in Tunisia experienced a resurgence of militancy not seen since the colonial period. As Table 4.2 shows, the number of strikes increased rapidly during *infitah*, with particularly intense years of protest – 1975–1977 and 1982–1984 – exceeding the intensity of the previous four years combined. This surge in labor opposition was driven by the rank-and-file, who initiated numerous wildcat strikes to protest their deteriorating wages and unjust treatment in the workplace. Faced with a resistant national leadership, strikes were also led by sectoral and local unions, with the highest concentration in newly industrialized sectors such as mining, transport, and manufacturing.

However, in the latter half of the decade, the composition of strike participants broadened to include a more diverse cross-section of the workforce. While industrial workers still played a critical role in organizing strikes, they were soon joined by public sector workers in the civil service. These included university professors, postal workers, and engineers, who were responsible for over 30 percent of protests from 1976 to 1985. In the private sector, strikes drew participation from poorly organized and previously quiescent workers, such as banking and textile employees. Most notably, in the middle of the reform period, strikes saw increased involvement from trade union leaders, with the UGTT's executive bureau approving an average of 41 percent of strikes from 1977 to 1985 (Table 4.2).

Yet, the most distinguishing feature of labor protest during the *infitah* period was not its increased militancy but rather its engagement with political concerns. Beginning in the late 1970s, the politicization

Table 4.2. ***Strike activity in Tunisia, 1975–1985***

Year	Strikes (ILO)	% Legal	Strikes (MENALC)	% Approved
1975	363	—	5	0
1976	372	—	16	0
1977	452	—	28	10
1978	178	—	7	14
1979	240	—	—	—
1980	346	5	13	20
1981	575	9	44	43
1982	530	11	30	57
1983	570	15	36	55
1984	545	26	42	45
1985	391	12	26	85

Source: Strike levels reported by the Ministry of Social Affairs reprinted in the ILO Yearbooks, 1971–1980 and data collected by this author, available in the MENALC Dataset; Percentage legal reported by the Ministry of Social Affairs, available through internal documents; Percentage approved recorded by this author, available in the MENALC Dataset

of labor protest in Tunisia marked the UGTT's transition into a broad-based opposition force. Implicitly, labor politicization was evident through the participation of various social actors in strikes, including students, the dispossessed, and opposition elites. For instance, transportation and postal strikes in April and May of 1976 garnered support from Tunisia's politically progressive students' union, *Union Générale des Étudiants Tunisiens*, which staged solidarity demonstrations for the protection of union rights (*Afrique-Asie*, 6/13/1976). Similarly, protests at the *Office de Terres Dominales* in October 1976 drew participation from university professors, local citizens, and members of the Tunisian Communist Party, transforming a simple labor dispute into a multiday episode of popular revolt (*Le Monde*, 12/1/1976, 5).

In one of the best examples of the UGTT's politicization, in 1977, unionists, opposition elites, and representatives of Tunisia's bidonvilles joined in a series of rolling strikes against government repression and economic reforms. These events culminated on January 26, 1978, when thousands of Tunisians gathered with the UGTT to hold the country's first general strike since independence. During the protests, citizens and workers attacked symbols of regime corruption, looting government enterprises and storming state buildings (Parti Socialiste Destourien, 1978). In a similar series of events in 1984, price increases led to massive riots, with students, unemployed youths, and seasonal workers targeting "the symbols of luxury, corruption, and foreign influence" that characterized the Bourguiba regime (Walton and Seddon, 1994).

Explicitly, the politicization of labor protest was demonstrated through the evolution of workers' demands, which shifted to include political as well as economic concerns. While the majority of strikes focused on industrial issues (wages, working conditions, personnel management, etc.), in the late 1970s, strike rhetoric adopted a more political tone, expressing grievances about repression and political corruption alongside traditional workplace demands (Figure 4.2). Exemplifying this shift, the 1978 general strike contained strong political overtones, with unions coupling demands for economic reforms with broader claims for political pluralism and democratic freedoms. This rhetoric was echoed in the union's official press outlet, *Echaab*, which criticized the regime for its "rapid and illicit enrichment" and "hardening of political, partisan and informational structures whose

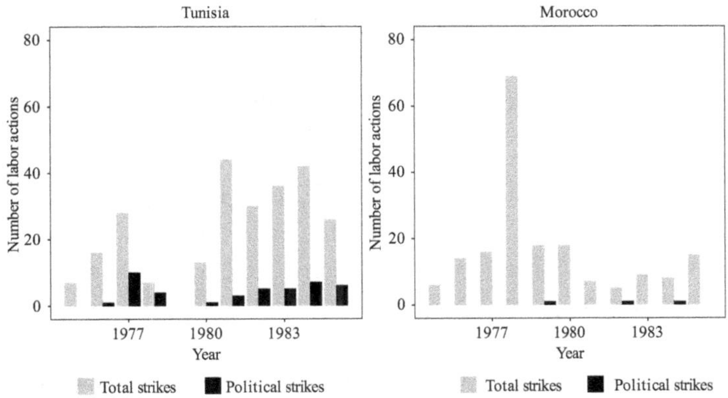

Source: MENALC Database
Note: Year 1979 missing due to press censorship

Source: MENALC Database
Note: Years 1982–1983 missing for Liberation due to press censorship

Figure 4.2 Comparative labor protests in Tunisia and Morocco, MENALC (1975–1985)

evolution has not accompanied that of the Tunisian people" (*Echaab*, 11/11/1977 cited in Karoui and Messaoudi, 1982).

Finally, as government repression intensified, members of the central union leadership became more willing to adopt militant positions against the regime. In a statement following the appointment Zine El Abidine Ben Ali to the Ministry of Interior, the UGTT's secretary-general indicated a new oppositional stance vis-à-vis the regime: "Unionists have begun to doubt the sincerity of the government toward us. Workers have demanded that we no longer speak of friendly collaboration with the regime" (Kraïem, 2011, 505). By the mid-1980s, political activity within the UGTT reached its peak. In 1985, over one-fifth of all strikes coded by this author promoted some form of political demand (Figure 4.2).

Labor Opposition in Morocco: Apolitical Militancy

In contrast, labor mobilization in Morocco evolved in a very different manner. As in Tunisia, unions reacted to reforms with increased militancy: according to official statistics, from 1977 to 1985, workers launched an average of 459 strikes per year, resulting in roughly three million working days lost. Additionally, strike intensity increased significantly in response to reforms. During the early years of stabilization (1977–1982), the number of workers involved in strikes averaged 61,983 annually. Data collected by this author confirms this pattern (Figure 4.2). Not only did strikes become more frequent, but they were also lengthier, lasting an average of nine days during the reform period.

However, labor militancy in Morocco developed in a qualitatively different fashion than it did in Tunisia. Unlike Tunisian protests, Moroccan strikes failed to mobilize broad cross-sections of the working class and suffered from a lack of internal cohesion. In large part, this was due to the concentration of strike activity within individual firms. In contrast to Tunisia, unions rarely coordinated strikes across regions or industries. Even within single factories, strikes were typically split among unions from different federations, particularly the UMT, UGTM, and the newly formed Democratic Confederation of Labor (*Confédération Démocratique du Travail*, CDT). Indeed, the relatively high volume of labor protests can be attributed to competition among these organizations rather than coordinated opposition to neoliberal reforms. As Figure 4.3 shows, sectors with the highest protest activity were those in which national unions had established rival branches, such as mining, transportation, and education.

At the national level, protest patterns also reflected the extent of competition among rival federations. An examination of unions' reactions to price increases in May 1981 reveals their lack of coordination in response to economic reforms. Despite workers' universal objection to subsidy removals – which would increase the cost of basic commodities by 14–77 percent – Moroccan unions failed to organize collective opposition. Instead, labor militancy reflected the conflicting and often contradictory aims of different labor unions. For example, CDT strike patterns highlighted the more militant response of leftist organizations, characterized by recurrent mobilization. In early June, the CDT began opposing austerity reforms by organizing local strikes to force the government to rescind price increases. When these actions failed to yield measurable results, the union escalated its militancy by calling for a nationwide general strike in coordination with the UGTM and UMT. Although both federations rejected the call, on June 20th, the CDT proceeded with a 24-hour general strike, which drew the participation of thousands of workers across Morocco's main commercial centers. Notably, as the strike spread to cities surrounding

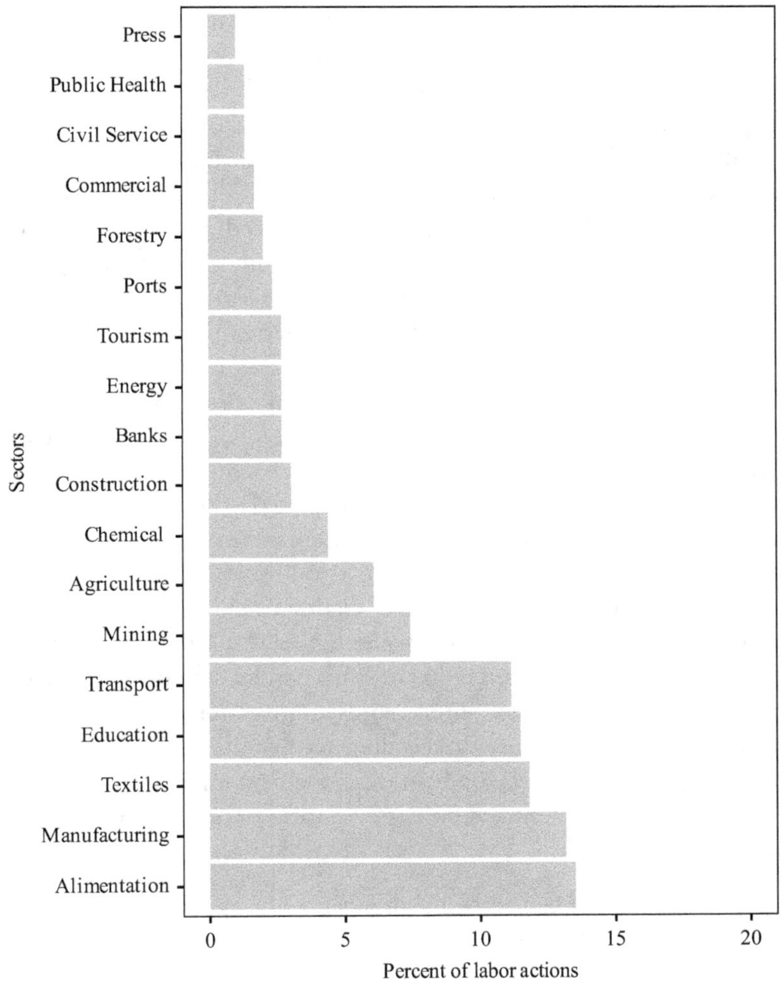

Source: MENALC Database

Figure 4.3 Strike activity by sector in Morocco (1977–1982)

the capital, it attracted the support of students and local citizens, triggering one of the largest and most intense episodes of political unrest in Morocco's post-independence history.

In contrast, opposition from the UMT and UGTM displayed a more moderate response to neoliberal reforms. Although the UMT organized its own general strike (1981) in response to the price increases, this effort was delayed and garnered only marginal participation from workers in Casablanca and neighboring areas. Moreover, the timing of the strike (June 18th) undermined planned strike action by the CDT, highlighting the antagonistic and incoherent nature of Moroccan labor mobilization. Finally, the UGTM adopted a conciliatory strategy that directly contradicted the efforts of both the UMT and CDT. Rather than participate in strikes, which it denounced as "opportunistic" (*L'Opinion*, 6/22/1981), the UGTM leadership conducted repeated negotiations with the government to revise the price increases, using as its main interlocutor the parliamentary bloc of the *Istiqlal*.

Lastly, labor mobilization did not acquire an explicitly political character as it did in Tunisia. Of the 79 strikes recorded from 1977 to 1985, only two included political demands, which focused on foreign issues, specifically opposition to Israeli aggression in Palestine. More commonly, strike demands emphasized traditional economic grievances such as wage increases, the application of collective agreements, or improvements in working conditions. Notably, even the larger strikes of the period were distinguished by their lack of political demands. For instance, while the CDT's 1981 general strike sparked local riots that included anti-monarchy slogans and attacks on symbols of the regime, union representatives remained noticeably distant from these actions. According to Benhilal (1984, 242), the union's absence during the opposition movement underscored the fundamentally apolitical and "*khubziste*" nature of Moroccan unionism during this era:

> The political scene occupied by the disinherited and the armed forces was deserted by the legitimate representatives of the aspirations of popular masses [parties and unions] ... no political or syndical movement intervened to channel the crowds or to offer them an instrument capable of transforming their diffuse energies into a vast current of reform

Explaining Labor Opposition: Existing Arguments

How can we account for the distinct patterns of labor protest witnessed in Tunisia and Morocco? One key explanation centers on the consequences of "corporatist collapse" and the effects of neoliberal reform on workers' well-being (Hartshorn, 2019). According to this theory, the decline of Tunisia's corporatist bargaining system alienated rank-and-file workers, reducing the regime's ability to co-opt labor interests or channel discontent away from the streets. In particular, the loss of expected privileges – stable wages, guaranteed employment, and welfare benefits – violated the "moral economy" that undergirded workers' harmonious relationship with the state, fostering resentment within the working class and triggering a new wave of labor unrest.

However, the case of the UGTT challenges this view. In addition to demands for higher salaries, Tunisian unionists advocated for sweeping political reforms, including greater press freedoms, human rights protections, and the establishment of representative democracy. From a moral economy perspective, labor demands should be limited to "bread and butter" issues, aimed at compensating workers for their losses rather than challenging the established political order. If violations of the moral economy drive labor protests, why did the UGTT transcend economic grievances to engage in political opposition against the Bourguiba regime? Moreover, why did Moroccan workers, who faced similar economic conditions, fail to do the same?

A second and related explanation focuses on workers' structural position in the economy. This theory posits that labor militancy coincides with periods of regime crisis and worsening economic conditions for workers relative to industrial elites. In some respects, this prediction holds true – the largest increases in Tunisian strike activity occurred when declines in workers' purchasing power were particularly severe (e.g., 1975 and 1984), despite rising prosperity for elites. However, in other ways, this structural perspective fails to explain certain qualitative aspects of labor opposition.

One such aspect is the timing of labor mobilization – why did strike activity in Tunisia surge between 1972 and 1978 and again from 1980 to 1984, rather than in some alternative period? While these years did correspond to significant economic downturns, workers had faced even worse conditions in previous decades. For example, during the socialist period, workers had to contend not only with declining living standards but also wage freezes that more severely impacted their purchasing power than the challenges posed by liberalization. If economic grievances were the sole catalyst for labor mobilization, why didn't Tunisia witness a similar surge of labor militancy in the 1960s?

Additionally, a structural perspective cannot account for the variation in protest behavior among unions in Morocco. Despite differences in sectoral membership composition (see Chapter 2), liberalizing reforms negatively affected all Moroccan unions uniformly. A focus on economic conditions, therefore, cannot explain why some unions why some unions, adopted more militant strategies than others. It also does not explain the high levels of militancy among relatively "privileged" public sector and civil service workers.

These limitations indicate the need to look beyond structural economic explanations to understand how specific patterns of labor protest emerge in response to reform. In the next section, I propose an alternative theory, focusing on how political institutions shape labor's interests and capacity for collective action.

Explaining Labor's Divergent Responses: An Institutional Approach

The divergent trajectories of labor opposition in Tunisia and Morocco provide a useful case study for the theory developed in Chapter 2; that is, that exclusionary labor control policies should incentivize union militancy, while inclusionary policies should pacify labor activism. As noted above, in Tunisia, the UGTT reacted to the state's liberal economic shift with a wave of demonstrations and strikes which evolved into political opposition. According to the theory, this reaction should be explained by the union's exclusion from economic and political institutions, which forced workers to adopt more militant behaviors to restructure their relationship with the state and regain their ability to act effectively in the labor market.

Tunisia

Labor Militancy in Tunisia: The Weakness of Collective Bargaining Institutions

At first glance, the coincidence of labor militancy with new collective bargaining institutions in Tunisia seems to challenge this prediction.

On paper, the convention collective cadre represented a new, inclusive means through which labor could engage with the state and participate in policy decisions that would directly affect their members. At the national level, annual wage bargaining between the state, UTICA, and sectoral labor leaders gave unions an opportunity to negotiate over measures that could improve workers' living conditions. Additionally, through the establishment of CPCs, the convention opened new avenues for workers within the enterprise to give voice to their concerns and address grievances jointly with management officials.

Yet, in reality, the system of labor representation created by the CCC functioned differently. At its core, the convention operated according to the same logic of previous policies enacted by the Bourguiba regime – to stifle labor opposition in service of maintaining the hegemony of the single-party government. By engaging in regular dialogue with labor officials, it could provide an outlet for social grievances without engaging in the type of political liberalization that produced social-democratic institutions in Europe. Moreover, by centralizing the bargaining process, it could reduce the costs of developing a robust national arbitration machinery, while simultaneously depriving militant rank-and-file workers of an organizational basis for opposition against the state's development policies.

Paradoxically, however, it was this very centralization that prevented the convention collective cadre from functioning as an effective check on labor militancy. In fact, the convention was so centralized that it failed to adequately incorporate labor representatives at lower levels of union organization, leading to a rash of wildcat strikes. At the plant level, enterprise commissions failed to provide workers with meaningful opportunities for representation due to several shortcomings in their design. Despite the important tasks assigned to these committees,[2] workers' role in CPCs was restricted to an advisory

[2] According to the convention collective cadre, the joint consultative commissions (CPC) were responsible for "overseeing the application of collective agreements" within individual firms. As part of this task, they were permitted to set enterprise scales for promotions and bonuses, oversee employee transfers within the firm, receive employee demands about wage and working conditions, establish disciplinary councils to adjudicate on labor disputes between workers and employers, and perform tasks of professional development within the firm (Article 42, Convention Collective Cadre, Journal Officiel du Republique de la Tunisie, 5/25/1973).

capacity, limiting the amount of influence they could have in changing workplace relations. According to Band, enterprise committees often failed to alter the balance of power between capital and labor at the shop floor, functioning mainly as one-way communication channel whereby managers could explain company policy to interested employees (Band, 1977, 25).

Moreover, the fact that such institutions were only mandated in firms with more than twenty employees meant that the majority of Tunisia's private enterprises – which housed on average one to ten employees – existed without any system for labor representation. Indeed, as a result of this organizational vacuum, trade unionists in the private sector reported wide variation in union's influence in different industries and firms, with many commenting that enterprise committees existed "on paper only" or were non-functional in the early 1980s (Appendix B: TU-3, 10/3/2013, TU-6, 10/3/2013). Research conducted in the public sector roughly supports this assessment of CCC-mandated workplace committees. According to Zghal, out of 18 industrial firms surveyed in Sfax in the 1970s, over half had no enterprise union or shop steward to represent workers' interests (Zghal, 1989, 89).

In part, this absence of representative institutions was facilitated by the lack of formal union rights at the enterprise level. Although the CCC implicitly recognized workers' right to organize, it failed to supplement this right with additional legislation that protected union members in individual plants. In line with the constitution and labor code, it left open to employers how and whether "legally constituted unions" would be recognized within CPCs, and further stipulated that in no case should the exercise of union rights "oppose the laws or internal regulations" governing an enterprise (Safi, 1989, 221). However, since the notion of labor representation was antithetical to the prerogatives of most employers, many managers did not approve of CPCs and took deliberate steps to impede their creation. In several firms, employers refused to grant workers' requests for enterprise commissions and, in extreme cases, shut down operations to avoid applying the recommendations of the convention collective cadre (Zghal, 1989, 89). In others, owners illegally hired relatives to avoid paying negotiated benefits and threatened union representatives with layoffs and various harassments (Alexander, 1996a, 174).

Notably, because the *infitah* period coincided with the government's shift toward a pro-capital orientation, state officials often colluded with employers to limit worker organization at the enterprise level. As Alexander(1996a) notes, owners routinely bribed regional labor inspectors not to report violations at their firms, enabling them virtually unchecked freedom to fire labor agitators or to refuse to enforce wage accords. Further, because new investment laws incentivized local leaders to attract foreign funding to their regions, governors within the ruling party – the Socialist Destourian Party (*Parti Socialiste Destourien*, PSD) – also turned a blind eye to employers' efforts to block CPCs (ibid). Even in the few state-owned firms where workplace committees did exist, the government allocated limited resources for the functioning of CPCs, preferring instead to establish their own "professional cells" to compete with unions for support and curtail labor activity. In certain industries, managers used special bonuses and promotions to buy off workers' representatives, thereby ensuring that they would not use enterprise commissions to levy worker demands. As a result, most CPCs in existence by 1977 were barely functional: out of the 188 enterprise commissions that had been established, only 38 were able to meet with any regularity (Zouari, 1989, 337).

Ultimately, this dysfunction of plant-level institutions created a crisis of representation for rank-and-file workers. Rather than stabilizing industrial relations, the workers' committees (or lack thereof) led to resentment and unrest on the shop floor. Subject to arbitrary harassment by employers and equipped with few avenues through which they could express their interests, strikes became workers' only method for voicing their grievances and achieving their demands. For many workers, strikes came to be seen as the sole means by which they could correct the power imbalances that privileged employers' (and by proxy, the state's) interests over their own. As one unionist in the banking sector commented about his colleagues' perceptions of strike action:

> We realized that [with the strike] we were stronger than we had been previously ... For us, the strike became a thing of joy; a joy of consciousness, a joy of strength in numbers, a joy of being able to weaken the employers. Now, it was us who had control, not them. (Appendix B: TU-28, 11/13/2013)

At the sectoral level, too, the laxity of representative institutions provided a strong incentive for labor militancy. Although on paper, the convention collective cadre permitted collective bargaining to occur within each sector – thereby allowing union leaders to set wage conditions within their individual industries – in practice, the negotiation process bypassed these channels in favor of direct dialogue with the UGTT's peak leaders. In many ways, such centralization benefited the regime by simplifying the negotiation process. Instead of establishing working conditions within each firm, which would require an extensive institutional apparatus and adequate worker representation at the enterprise level, peak-level bargaining could determine basic principles in a global collective convention that would serve as a basis for future sectoral agreements. However, by centralizing the bargaining process, the regime ultimately eroded its vertical integration within union structures and the regional and federal levels. In most cases, communication between government officials and sectoral union leaders was superficial, amounting to little more than periodic consultation with union representatives beyond the UGTT's central committee (Alexander, 1996a, 184).

Most important, marginal involvement of sectoral unions in the bargaining process undermined the government's efforts to encourage mid-level union officials to enforce labor restraint. For sectoral union leaders, such exclusion created serious uncertainties over whether their interests would be faithfully represented within the bargaining system – a fear that was realized when negotiations reduced wage increases for workers in a number of skilled sectors (Table 5.4). Whereas under state-led development, public sector unions could use their influence within the government to press for more favorable agreements on the basis of specific needs and demands, centralized bargaining yielded national-level policies with little differentiation among categories of workers. Without assurances that they could influence the bargaining process through their direct participation, sectoral leaders began organizing strike campaigns to force union executives and state officials to attend to their concerns.

In April 1976, a general assembly of railroad workers decided, against the wishes of the central leadership of the UGTT, to maintain the ultimatum addressed to the administration of the Tunisian National Railway Company (SNCFT) regarding the stalling of salary negotiations (*Afrique-Asie*, 6/13/1976). Similarly, strikes in the transportation, postal, and docking sectors held later that year, all advocated for salary increases to reverse deterioration in workers' purchasing power. In some cases, such as the high school teachers'

Table 4.3. ***Wage disparities between categories of workers (1975–1985)***

Professional category	1975	1977	1980	1985	%Δ 1975–1977	%Δ 1980–1985
Unskilled worker	100	100	100	100	–	–
Skilled worker	140	124	138	132	−11.4	−4.3
Supervisor	285	277	248	219	−2.8	−11.7
Engineer and manager	581	515	502	408	−11.4	−18.7

Sources: Data from the *Institut d'Economie Quantitative* cited in Zouari.

strike of 1981, workers used wage homogenization as the basis of their salary demands, claiming that workers with similar educational qualifications should receive similar pay. In particular, skilled white-collar workers felt alienated by their exclusion from the negotiation process. In 1982–1983, this category of employees created their own autonomous union at the national airline, Tunis Air, to lobby for pay increases similar to those received by minimum wage workers several months prior (Zouari, 1989, 345).

Interestingly, although centralized bargaining generated tensions among sectoral unions, it did not significantly strain industrial relations within the working class. Because public sector unions could no longer achieve gains through the lobbying tactics employed during state-led development, they had to compensate by mobilizing workers across the occupational spectrum in order to place maximum pressure on employers. In addition, when economic crises threatened wage decreases for all employees (1977–1979 and 1984–1986), union leaders were induced to set aside their individual interests and devote themselves to coordinated action to force the government to improve their working conditions. As a consequence, many of the high points of union-led collective action (1977 and 1984) coincided with the increased use of cross-sectional strike campaigns that united workers from both blue- and white-collar sectors.

Finally, at the national level, the timing of the collective bargaining process generated uncertainties over whether the CCC provided a credible mechanism for peak union leaders to influence labor policies. In its original formulation, the CCC specified that wage negotiations would take place once every three years, after which the social partners would reunite to adapt pay scales to current economic conditions. However, in 1980, this provision was amended to reduce the time between negotiations to no longer than a year. While this shift was credited with making the bargaining process more flexible to changes in inflation, ultimately this policy created perverse incentives for labor leaders to increase militancy on an annual basis in efforts to wrest as much as they could from employers. Furthermore, since the CCC did not explicitly tie wages to inflation, union leaders had no guarantees that they would continue to receive salary increases beyond the current year. By the early 1980s, peak leaders were skeptical of whether the government would continue to uphold its commitment to meaningful collective bargaining, a criticism that became stronger after the onset of economic crisis in 1984.

The negative impact of these policy changes was all the more serious because workers' economic situation did not improve significantly despite the expansion of economic growth in the early 1980s. While collective accords produced substantial wage increases from 1980 to 1982, these gains were largely consumed by increases in inflation – which had reached a reported 20 percent by 1984 – and failed to match gains in productivity and commercial profits achieved over the same period (UGTT, 1977, 1984). Moreover, negotiations had not weathered previous episodes of stress, which meant that labor leaders had little on which to base their expectations of government behavior except individual ties and personal loyalties. Ultimately, these factors created a situation in which high hopes quickly soured into disillusionment and feelings of mistrust when government ministries and employers refused to implement new wage accords.

Indeed, during protracted negotiations in 1983, union suspicions were piqued when government officials refused to hear union proposals containing a "material dimension," and stipulated that any further wage increases would be tied to production rather than continued bargaining (*Jeune Afrique*, 11/13/1985). Moreover, breakdown of social dialogue in April of the following year further increased peak leaders' diffidence about the credibility of the convention collective cadre. As one labor representative noted, wage accords under the revised CCC were no more than "scraps of paper" that failed to secure worker's interests over the long term (*Réalités*, 04/19/1985). In a press conference given on April 16, 1985, UGTT secretary-general Habib Achour confirmed this sense of general distrust between union officials and the government, stating that "the government has no faith the UGTT and we no longer have faith in them given that many of the agreements we have made with them have not amounted to anything" (ibid). In direct response to failed negotiations, the UGTT central committee organized a wave of rolling strikes within critical sectors throughout the summer of 1985, culminating in an October strike that shut down Tunisia's rail system for two days (*Jeune Afrique*, 11/13/1985).

Thus, the structure of collective bargaining institutions in Tunisia worked paradoxically to encourage unions to adopt more militant behaviors in response to economic reforms. Despite an outward appearance of inclusivity and representativeness, the corporatist institutions that underlay Bourguiba's "social partnership" offered labor representatives at all levels of union organization few means to express their interests or to credibly influence policy on their behalf. Faced with insufficient options for addressing their grievances, strikes became workers' and unions' only method of making themselves heard, particularly in the face of intransigent employers and government officials. In this way, the regime's corporatist institutions created the very problem they were intended to solve, generating incentives for strike activity that resonated across all sectors of the labor movement.

Politicization of Labor Protest in Tunisia: Corporatist Decline within the Single-party Regime

Yet if an examination of the institutions that governed state-labor relations helps to explain why workers and unions became more militant during the *infitah* period, two critical questions remain: why did labor mobilization acquire a political character, and how did it evolve into a broad-based opposition movement? Again, a focus on institutions is crucial for addressing these questions. Just as the exclusionary nature of the corporatist bargaining system sheds light on why workers and unions felt compelled to express their grievances through strikes, the decline of institutions that regulated political representation explains why these strikes became political. In particular, the progressive centralization and despotism of the single-party regime explains labor's transition to more radical demand-making in the late 1970s and 1980s. By limiting opportunities for both labor and political elites to represent their interests within the single-party system, the Bourguiba regime unintentionally drove these groups into alliance, creating the conditions for the UGTT to evolve into a broad-based force for political opposition.

Corporatist Collapse under the Bourguiba Regime

As noted in Chapter 4, by the early 1970s, the institutions that governed state-labor relations in Tunisia had already begun to show signs of hardening. Although Bourguiba initially tolerated the UGTT as a necessary ally of the regime, in the wake of renewed unrest in the mid-1960s, the government converted to repression, restricting the union's participation in representative institutions and demoting it from its subordinate position as a "junior partner" in the regime. In 1962, it reanimated efforts to replace enterprise unions with party-directed professional cells in order to discourage labor mobilization. Additionally, in 1965, it intervened in the UGTT's internal elections to install a more pliant leadership composed of PSD loyalists. Within the legislature, the party began purging militant unionists from the PSD's electoral lists, resulting in a 50 percent decrease in the number of labor representatives in the National Assembly. Finally, within the ruling party itself, Bourguiba progressively marginalized the UGTT from positions of influence, opting instead to extend greater privileges to representatives within the business community.

Collectively, these measures led to a crisis of representation in the labor movement, exposing serious deficiencies in the corporatist structure of the single-party regime. However, organized labor was not the only group affected by Bourguiba's repressive policies. Having established temporary control over the UGTT, Bourguiba soon moved to monopolize political power within the PSD and state bureaucracy. Shortly after independence, he deposed the ruling bey and assumed the latter's "full executive and legislative powers" (Moore, 1965). Similarly, in 1957, he adroitly eliminated all remaining opposition through the institution of two new legal provisions, which permitted the government to jail wealthy Tunisians for alleged collaboration with the protectorate regime (Perkins, 2004). A series of internal reforms to the PSD in 1958 further consolidated Bourguiba's control by increasing linkages between the party and state's bureaucratic apparatus. Reforms stipulating that the president of Tunisia must also be the president of the ruling party, for example, concentrated all executive authority within Bourguiba's hands, while measures to homogenize the organizational structure of the party-state gave the president greater control over the party itself (Moore, 1965). Heads of party federations, who had previously been elected by branch members, were replaced by regional officers appointed by the

Politburo of the PSD, itself appointed and controlled by Bourguiba. At the same time, key deliberative organs of the party, such as the National Council and annual Congress were suppressed,[3] and representative institutions within the Tunisian state – namely the National Assembly – were stripped of their decision-making abilities and subordinated to presidential control.

As economic reform deepened in the early 1970s, the regime's disregard for political opposition became more evident. In an effort to secure support for economic liberalization, Bourguiba rejected the types of political reforms that accompanied similar transitions in Western Europe. In his view, successful liberalization required the leadership of a strong state, backed by a dominant party that could project an image of political stability to foreign investors (Murphy, 1999, 60). Thus, Tunisia's economic liberalization was not accompanied by a political opening but rather by a tightening of control within the single-party regime.

Consequently, over the course of the 1970s, the Tunisian regime descended down a path of increasing authoritarianism and political decay.[4] Playing upon factional rivalries within the PSD, Bourguiba purged all liberal voices from the party and replaced them with loyal technocrats who were more sympathetic to his mission to liberalize the economy without pluralizing the political regime. Subsequently, he expelled all liberals and socialists from the National Assembly, using a controversial clause that prevented non-PSD members from serving in the legislature. During a 1974 party congress, the PSD rejected proposals to institute multi-partyism and allowed Bourguiba to appoint his own successor, Prime Minister Hédi Nouira. Finally, at his urging, remaining PSD members in the National Assembly voted unanimously to establish Bourguiba as "president [of the republic] for life," cementing his permanent monopoly over the Tunisian state.

3 In 1956, reforms to the PSD changed the schedule of party congresses from an annual timeline to every two years, and then to every three years in 1959. In practice, only one congress was held in the span of eight years (from 1956 to 1964). Additionally, the National Council suffered tremendous decline. Although National Council meetings were scheduled to be held every six months, from 1956 to 1962 it met only four times: twice in 1956, once in 1957, and once again in 1962 (Moore, 1965, 114).

4 The discussion in the following paragraph draws heavily on histories presented in Perkins, 2004, Alexander, 2010, and Murphy (1999).

Outsider Coalitions: The UGTT and the Radical Left

In the absence of meaningful political representation, the corporatist character of the regime fell into noticeable decline. Yet, paradoxically, it was this effort to forestall the emergence of opposition that contributed to the further politicization of the UGTT. With formal institutional avenues blocked, calls for political reform were pushed into non-corporatist organizations, such as radical social movements and clandestine political parties. Between 1970 and 1973, discontented militants from the PSD formed a range of unofficial organizations, including the Popular Unity Movement (led by Ahmed Ben Salah), Movement of Socialist Democrats (*Mouvement des Démocrates Socialistes*, MDS), and *Perspectives* (led by former members of the PSD Youth). Denied the opportunity to reform the system from within, these groups viewed protest as the only way to place pressure on the regime and force it to open the political system. However, given the myriad restrictions placed on associational freedom, adopting such a strategy would require that opposition leaders use preexisting organizations to mobilize opposition against the regime.

For a number of reasons, the UGTT provided the most conducive environment for pursuing this goal. As one of Tunisia's first mass organizations, the UGTT possessed numerous resources – an official press, independent financial holdings, and numerous local and regional offices – that were uncommon within the country's civil society landscape. Furthermore, as one of Tunisia's most ideologically diverse organizations,[5] the union provided a ready-made base of support for the left, particularly within its newer federations in the civil service and public sector. Indeed, due to demographic changes during the socialist era, these federations had gained younger, better-educated cadres emanating from Tunisia's progressive student union who were eager to promote a more radical vision for Tunisia's economic and political future (*Afrique-Asie*, 6/13/1976; Zeghidi, 1989, 285). Additionally, the broad scope of trade union issues and the extent of

[5] According to an article published by the Tunisian magazine *Le Maghreb*, the UGTT could count up to twelve different political trends, including leftists, Ba'athists and some Islamists (*Le Maghreb*, 4/25/1981). These statements were confirmed by a number of different interviewees (Appendix B: TU-4, 10/01/2013; TU-6,10/3/2013; TU-43, 12/13/13) and in scholarship published by Taieb Baccouche (1989) and Christopher Alexander (2000).

labor autonomy offered fertile ground for protest activism that could evolve into political opposition. By organizing strikes that defended workers' rights to organize and called for greater protection for union officials, opposition activists could subtly push for liberalization without incurring the wrath of antagonistic party officials (Appendix B: TU-31, 11/20/2013; TU-33, 11/21/2013).

Thus, in the early 1970s, political elites from a variety of leftist groups began to invest heavily in the UGTT as a base for opposition. Between 1970 and 1973, leftist activists entered the union en masse, establishing a notable presence within the UGTT's civil service unions, such as its education, postal, and banking federations. In 1975, these cadres began organizing wildcat strikes in many of Tunisia's major urban and industrial centers, including Sfax, Gafsa, and Tunis. Reflecting the critical influence of the left, these strikes articulated a more nuanced understanding of workers' grievances, which highlighted both the regime's economic liberalism and its increasing authoritarianism as reasons for the neglect of workers' interests.

Economic issues also encouraged tighter integration between organized labor and leftist groups. While a small minority in the UGTT had always been sympathetic to the left's progressive political agenda, transforming the union into an effective counterweight against the regime required leftist leaders to galvanize support among blue-collar workers in Tunisia's industrial working class. During the Ben Salah affair, these workers displayed the greatest opposition to calls for "organic fusion" between the UGTT and Neo-Destour, advocating for an apolitical brand of syndicalism that focused primarily on workers' economic interests(Ahmad, 1967). Moreover, given the numerous benefits afforded to unskilled workers as part of the CCC, it was this class of workers who were seen as the least likely to embrace a platform of political change that could threaten existing patronage from the Bourguiba government.

However, in the context of economic crisis in the late 1970s, changing social conditions strengthened affinities between the left and the industrial working class. In particular, mounting frustration over the unequal distribution of wealth provided fertile ground for wedding various left and labor issues. As blue-collar workers found themselves subject to deteriorating wage conditions amid increased corporate profits and rising GDP, they began to embrace a political message that tied their poor economic conditions to the regime's corruption and pro-capital stance. Additionally, the government's decision to suspend wage negotiations in October 1977 led workers to doubt the regime's promises to maintain social dialogue or compensate for their future losses. With institutional remedies within the labor market foreclosed, blue-collar unions began pursuing more radical forms of demand-making, often joining civil service unions in organizing wildcat actions to express their growing dissatisfaction with the Bourguiba regime. Most important, while these strikes maintained their focus on economic issues (i.e., wages, employment), they also touched on a range of political concerns – associational rights, government corruption, repression – that spoke to the necessity of liberalizing the institutional structure of the regime.

Government Repression and the Radicalization of Union Elites

Beyond solidifying connections between rank-and-file unionists and leftist elites, two additional factors help to explain the gradual politicization of the UGTT. First, the union's persecution at the hands of the state intensified conflict between labor officials and the regime, prompting the leadership to undergo its own process of political radicalization. As noted previously, the increase in wildcat strike activity during the 1970s precipitated severe repression against the UGTT's base – in the face of workers' rejection of its corporatist bargain, the regime proved more willing to use force to secure its desired "social peace." At the leadership level, this desire for social control also provoked a series of repressive actions from the regime.

Convinced that the outbreak of wildcat strikes indicated the peak's inability to control its base, the regime soon turned its antagonism toward prominent members of the UGTT's executive bureau. In June 1977, the government announced its intention to replace Habib Achour as the union's secretary-general, selecting instead his personal rival and loyal PSD militant, Ferhat Dachraoui (Kraïem, 2011, 412). When Achour refused to step down without a vote at the union's national congress, the regime initiated a large-scale offensive campaign against the UGTT. In November 1977, hardliners within the PSD devised a plot to assassinate Achour in order to forcibly remove him from union executive. Later that year, PSD militants created a splinter union to sow division within the labor movement and elect a new union leadership that was more willing to comply with the economic designs of the regime. In efforts to deprive the union of political allies, Bourguiba expelled six UGTT sympathizers from his ministerial cabinet and replaced them with party loyalists known for their willingness to use force to curb labor militancy. Finally, the government organized coordinated attacks against the union's regional offices, culminating in three days of successive violence against the UGTT's national headquarters in Tunis (*Echaab*, 11/11/1977a).

Ultimately, this rise in government hostility did much to politicize the UGTT's peak leadership. As government attacks against the UGTT mounted, the union's executive bureau became more willing to endorse rank-and-file strikes and even to support some of workers' more radical demands. In response to death threats against Habib Achour, for instance, the executive bureau approved a series of rolling strikes in the transportation, banking, and civil service sectors that critiqued "the hardening of a government which is visibly engaged in a battle against the labor movement" (*Echaab*, 11/11/1977b). As it had done to the left, the increasing despotism of the Bourguiba government convinced labor leaders that militant opposition was the only viable mechanism through which they could express their grievances. According to Achour, in the face of such naked repression, "the natural choice of the [UGTT leadership] was none other than to strike" (Achour, 1989, 199).

Moreover, the UGTT leadership, like the rank-and-file, gradually came to view their grievances not solely in economic terms but as a consequence of deficiencies within Tunisia's broader political environment. While the executive bureau was initially reluctant to fuse labor issues with critiques of the regime, denouncing political slogans as the "work of foreign elements" who wished to "use ... [the UGTT] for non-union ends" (La Presse, 5/5/1973 cited in Alexander, 1996a), as repression intensified, union officials began to discuss workers' grievances in explicitly political terms. In comments made following attacks on local UGTT offices, the secretary-general of the Sfax regional union blamed workers' poor economic conditions on "a military occupation with a relationship with a minority that holds power ... [which] controls the country and keeps it in a state of increasing dependency" (Ghorbal quoted in Parti Socialiste Destourien, 1978, 79). Similarly, several issues of the union press outlet, *Echaab*, published pointed critiques of the government's liberal economic program, denouncing it for its unjustified bias toward the "interests of certain social categories to the exclusion of others" and highlighting the issues of mismanagement, corruption, and "suspicious and fraudulent enrichment" at the heart of the regime (*Echaab*, 11/25/1977, see also Karoui and Messaoudi, 1982; Sadiki and Saleh, 2024). In one of the last issues of *Echaab* published before the January 26th general strike, the intimate connection between workers' economic and political conditions was made clear. In a fierce critique of the regime's "savage capitalism" the union blamed strikes on the:

> increasingly clear contradiction between the aspirations of the Tunisian people and the government's policy ... the contradiction between the great progress realized in the field of liberty and democracy ... and the hardening of the political and party structures. (*Echaab* cited in Dhiaf, 1977)

The Genesis of Union Democracy

Finally, the UGTT's politicization also emerged as a consequence of its own internal bureaucracy. Unlike many of its North African counterparts, the UGTT enjoyed a surprising amount of autonomy from the regime, particularly in the management of its local and regional affairs. While administration at the top of the union often reflected the designs of the Bourguiba regime, bureaucracy and elections at the lower levels were free from government control, providing a space of internal debate and democracy that was unprecedented in Tunisian society (Appendix B: TU-6, 10/3/2013; TU-43, 12/13/13; Ahmad, 1967, 295). Moreover, despite periodic attempts to influence the union's executive, the leadership was never completely divorced from its accountability to the rank-and-file. Instead, due to the routinely conflictual relationship between the union and the regime, the peak leadership existed in a "precarious equilibrium between autonomy and dependence vis-á-vis the government as well as the union base" (Yousfi, 2015, 34).

For the leftist opposition, these features provided a unique opportunity to advance its political program beyond the rank-and-file. By infiltrating the UGTT and winning elections at the local level, opposition elites could gain a measure of influence over union administration, which could then be used to pressure peak leaders to orient labor agendas toward more political ends. As previously mentioned, this strategy largely succeeded in producing the left's desired results – by 1975, leftist activists had won prominent positions in the higher education and banking federations, and by 1977 had achieved enough standing to contest for elections in the union's executive bureau. To influence policy at the national level, however, opposition elites would have to successfully force union officials to shift their allegiances away from the Bourguiba regime.

Indeed, since Bourguiba's purge of the UGTT's peak leadership in 1965, elections at the national congress had been subject to heavy intervention by the government. Although union delegates were still permitted to vote for their preferred representatives, state officials – in collaboration with union elites – manipulated the nomination process to keep unfavorable candidates off of election lists. In extreme cases, government officials serving as "election monitors" bribed susceptible delegates to sway voting decisions or directly intervened to falsify election results (Ahmad, 1967, 292). As a result from 1965 to 1976, the composition of the executive bureau witnessed very few changes, with only six incumbents failing to secure re-election.

Fortunately for the opposition, the progressive exclusion of union elites from the regime's ruling coalition helped to shift the leadership's loyalty squarely in their favor. Realizing that the threat of his replacement meant that he could no longer rely on the support of the regime, Achour began improving his position among his remaining base of support – the rank-and-file. To do this, he expanded opportunities for workers to participate in union politics and permitted popular base union leaders the chance to secure positions of power. In addition to more frequently convening National Council meetings, where executive, sectoral, and regional union leaders could debate and decide upon union policies, Achour oversaw the first UGTT national congress in twenty years that was relatively free from government intervention (Kraïem, 2011, 411). Consequently, leftist leaders were elected by substantial majorities into the UGTT executive bureau and were later appointed to important posts in the union newspaper, *Echaab*, and the Office of Studies and Research.

The ascendance of leftist militants into positions of power within the union executive marked a milestone in the politicization of the UGTT. With opposition elites securely at the head of the organization, the left was able to construct a cross-sectional alliance that could act collectively to achieve political goals. Using their authority over its press and research wings, leftist elites began infusing the union's rhetoric with more explicitly political content (Karoui and Messaoudi,

1982). Moreover, under the influence of leftist members inside the UGTT's executive bureau, the peak leadership became more willing to support radical protests from the rank-and-file, accounting for the rise in political strike activity after 1977.

Most importantly, the growing influence of the base within the UGTT's decision-making bodies triggered a shift in the union's relationship with the state. As they gained positions of power, base militants became more willing to distance the union from Bourguiba's government and challenge some of the collaborationist policies of the peak leadership. During the 1977 Congress, for example, 600 unionists signed a petition rejecting the executive bureau's decision to formalize a "Social Pact" with the regime because the peak had not consulted with the base before agreeing to it (Disney, 1978). Additionally, during a National Council meeting, opposition to the practice of dual leadership[6] compelled Habib Achour and two others to resign from the PSD Politburo, signaling a definitive rupture between the union and the regime.

Following this, the UGTT was propelled into a state of open opposition. After a series of government attacks on union premises, the executive bureau announced its decision to hold a general strike – the country's first since independence – on January 26th. In a manner reflecting the political evolution of the UGTT, this strike contained strong political overtones that challenged the legitimacy of the Bourguiban party-state (Disney, 1978; Sadiki and Saleh, 2024). In addition to calling out the government for its economic excesses, the union also condemned "enmity of the party leadership" to the existence of independent civil society and the agenda of political pluralism that was gaining traction in Tunisia at that time (Parti Socialiste Destourien, 1978). The resulting conflict was brutal – after 24 hours of protests and violent repression, some 1600 workers were arrested, several hundred were injured or dead, and all but two of the UGTT's executive bureau (including Achour) were charged with insurrection by the state.

[6] Prior to 1978, union members could hold leadership positions in the UGTT and PSD simultaneously.

The Resurgence of Union Militancy in the 1980s

Similar factors explain the resurgence of political militancy in the 1980s. Initially, the regime's efforts at political liberalization, led by Prime Mohammed Mzali, signaled the possibility of labor peace. In 1981, the government pardoned and reinstated the UGTT's former leaders, inviting them to form a common front with the PSD in forthcoming legislative elections. That same year, it announced an end to Tunisia's one-party system, promising legal recognition to any group that received at least 5 percent of the vote.

These inclusionary gestures aimed to co-opt the union leadership and fracture the informal alliance between the UGTT and the left. However, labor militancy persisted for two key reasons. First, the regime failed to incorporate the union's most radical elements. When allowing union members to run for parliament, Bourguiba excluded some of the UGTT's most militant leaders, whose detention after the 1978 strike barred them from holding public office (Murphy, 1999). Additionally, legislative elections insufficiently co-opted leaders from the political left. Despite presenting multiple candidacies, opposition parties failed to secure enough votes for legalization, prompting leftist elites to continue mobilizing within the UGTT.

Throughout the 1980s, pressure from these groups drove the UGTT back into political conflict with the regime. Opposition movements organized strikes in the education, banking, post, and communications sectors, citing the decline in workers' purchasing power and poor economic conditions as a pretext for their militancy. Although these strikes frustrated the leadership's attempts at compromise, the UGTT central frequently supported them, attesting to rank-and-file's increasing influence on the peak's radicalization. Additionally, leftist elites sought to distance the UGTT from the party-state. In 1982, the UGTT's National Council refused to participate in government talks over the Sixth Plan, arguing that it had not been contacted early enough for its recommendations to be taken into consideration. Similarly, in 1983, the UGTT boycotted the Economic and Social Council, protesting its lack of autonomy over membership selection (Bellin, 2002). Finally, the UGTT's Administrative Commission voted to exclude seven members of the executive bureau for their collaboration with the regime by joining the PSD-led "National Front."

These moves paved the way for the left to strengthen its position within the UGTT and instrumentalize its activities for political purposes. Through repeated public sector strikes, the left discredited the government's economic policies, widening the rift between the union's leadership and the Bourguiba regime. Furthermore, perceiving its increased militancy as a threat, Bourguiba intensified repressive tactics against the UGTT, pushing its leaders further into opposition. In response, the UGTT resumed its role as a key opponent of the autocratic party-state. Following mass arrests of striking unionists in 1985, the UGTT executive prepared for a second general strike to protest the regime's "politics of intransigence and authoritarianism," which threatened "an explosive situation similar to the bread riots of 1984" (*Echaab* 6/7/1985 cited in Bras, 1987).

Ultimately, the UGTT's militancy solidified its politicization but weakened the labor movement overall. Efforts to protect union autonomy led to internal divisions, culminating in the creation of a rival union, the National Union of Tunisian Workers, by PSD-affiliated unionists in 1984. This split allowed the government to use divide-and-rule tactics to curb labor opposition, undermining the UGTT. Additionally, labor politicization sparked a new, more virulent round of government repression. In 1984, the government banned trade union meetings, arrested workers for "syndical activities," ended the automatic check-off for dues, and seized union assets in Amilcar Hotel and Ettihad Insurance (Bras, 1986, 713; Bras, 1987, 991). In 1985, it took direct action against the UGTT by invading local offices, imprisoning trade union officials, and replacing elected leaders with "provisional syndical committees" composed of party loyalists ("*chourafa*"). Thus, by 1986 organized labor had lost its capacity to act as a force of opposition. Besieged by internal and external pressures, the UGTT was reduced to a "transmission belt" for the policies of the Bourguiba regime (Hibou, 2011, 124).

Summary

The above discussion highlights that trade unions' responses to economic reforms are more complex and varied than current analyses present. In contrast to the viewpoint advanced by traditional theories, the UGTT's political behavior suggests that unions are not so bound by material demands that they are unwilling to adopt new strategies to address the challenges they face in new political and economic circumstances. If unions are unable to influence labor market conditions from the inside because institutional channels are closed off, they will pursue extra-institutional strategies that seek to reshape the structure of the political environment in which workers live. In Tunisia, the absence of institutions for labor representation played a critical role in generating labor militancy because crucial constituencies in the UGTT were alienated from the policymaking process, increasing uncertainties for both rank-and-file militants and union elites. Although the state expanded opportunities for interest articulation through the creation of the collective contention cadre, the dysfunction of plant-level institutions embedded in this social pact created a crisis of representation among the rank-and-file, who saw militant protest as the only way to force employers to attend to their concerns. Similarly, the high degree of centralization in the bargaining process disabled federal union leaders from expressing their interests, generating additional incentives for labor opposition. Annual wage negotiations also created uncertainties about whether the convention collective cadre was a reliable mechanism for influencing labor policy. Particularly as worsening economic conditions triggered a withdrawal of the state from collective bargaining, this short time-horizon increased mistrust among peak union leaders and government officials, encouraging the former to organize strike activity to express their discontent with the state and press for their demands.

At the same time, deficiencies in the corporatist system of political representation played a role in politicizing the UGTT and transforming the labor movement into a force for opposition. As the single-party state became more exclusive and authoritarian, opposition elites were driven outside of the PSD to enact liberalizing reforms to the regime. The integration of these elites into trade unions helped to bring a new, more radical vision of labor politics into the UGTT – one that connected workers' grievances to the pro-capital orientation, corruption, and democratic deficiencies of the regime. By facilitating an alliance between opposition groups and workers, political institutions converted the UGTT into a locus of resistance against the autocratic state. As prominent leftist and UGTT secretary-general, Taieb Baccouche, observed, "The development of the union movement and its opening to new educated, politicized constituencies, destabilized the former relations [between the Bourguiba regime and the UGTT] which had become progressively anachronistic and stifling" (Baccouche, 1989, 167).

Finally, the UGTT's internal bureaucracy helped to create a cross-sectional alliance that could support the opposition's efforts to mobilize collective action against the regime. Within the union's base, democratic organization of local branches allowed leftist militants to influence union agendas and imbue strike activity with political aims. Within the leadership, horizontal relations between the UGTT elite and the rank-and-file in the context of increased antagonism between the union and the state compelled labor leaders to support rank-and-file militancy and promote opposition elites into prominent leadership positions. Consequently, leftist elites were able to form a broad coalition of interests across the union hierarchy that could organize opposition to the regime. This cohesion and politicization of labor protest in Tunisia would contrast sharply with the pattern of labor militancy witnessed in Morocco, as I discuss below.

Morocco

At first glance, labor relations in Morocco during the 1970s bear a striking resemblance to those in Tunisia. Leaders in both countries implemented economic reforms that reduced the state's presence in the economy, and altered the terms of previously clientelistic relationships between organized labor and the state. Although Morocco never adopted the sort of "socialist" development model implemented by Bourguiba, the government's decision to scale back public investment following the 1976 oil crisis subjected workers to lower wages and poorer living conditions than ever before. In response, unions mobilized on an unprecedented scale, launching hundreds of strikes, sit-ins, and public demonstrations to protest losses in their purchasing power and jobs.

However, in one critical way, labor opposition in Morocco differed from that witnessed in Tunisia. While the level of labor militancy was comparable in both countries, labor unions in Morocco never developed an organized strike campaign as a part of a broader political movement. Instead, strikes remained confined to individual workplaces and industries, and focused on parochial concerns or economic grievances. In stark contrast to the UGTT, the Moroccan labor movement never coalesced into a political force capable of uniting broad cross-section of workers in opposition to the authoritarian regime.

To explain this difference, I argue that a focus on political institutions is necessary. In contrast to Tunisia, where leaders developed exclusionary corporatist institutions that united workers and social movements in opposition to the regime, Moroccan leaders modified existing institutional structures to more tightly incorporate labor and political parties into the monarchy's ruling coalition. In both the workplace and the polity, the government strengthened channels for labor representation and provided opportunities for unions to access influential political networks. In so doing, the regime exacerbated competition among rival unions and institutionalized demand-making within the confines of the monarchical regime. Ultimately, this approach prevented unions from building a broad coalition of interests that could unite workers around a common political agenda.

Labor Militancy in Morocco: Personnel Delegate Elections and the Battle for "Most Representative Union"

As noted in Chapter 4, the early 1970s marked a significant shift in Morocco's labor containment strategy. Although the government continued to exercise tight control over labor unions, political developments at the beginning of the decade pushed the monarchy to expand its coalitional base and pursue closer collaboration with organized labor. Between 1970 and 1972, Morocco witnessed two unsuccessful military coups and a surge of wildcat strikes, involving over 200,000 workers and occasionally deteriorating into violence. This wave of unrest highlighted a dangerous loss of public confidence in the regime. Without more inclusive policies and institutions, the monarchy could struggle to manage the social discontent triggered by economic reforms.

Thus, in the early 1970s, the government moved to establish a more inclusive system of labor control. As in Tunisia, its goal was to create institutions in the workplace and polity that could pacify resistance to neoliberal reforms and enforce wage restraint. Already, the personnel delegate system provided a de facto method of labor representation at the plant level. Although Moroccan law did not explicitly establish union rights in the enterprise, it did allow workers to represent themselves by electing worker delegates in firms with ten or more employees. Through these delegates, workers could bring individual and collective complaints to company management, which could then be resolved through negotiation or arbitration by regional officials (Filali-Meknassi, 1989, 44–45).

However, following the surge of labor protests in the early 1970s, the government sought to enhance the personnel delegate system by introducing two key innovations. First, it institutionalized employee–employer relations by introducing the designation of "most representative union" (MRU), which granted unions with the largest share of elected delegates in a given sector special privileges in wage setting and negotiation. At the firm level, MRU delegates would be tasked with defending workers' interests and advising managers on salaries, promotions, and employment decisions (United States Bureau of Labor Statistics, 1966, 4). At the national level, these delegates played a direct role in economic policymaking through their participation in key institutions like the Central Commission on Prices and Wages, the Office for Vocational Training and Promotion of Work, and the National Social Security Fund.

From the point of view of its architects, Morocco's revitalized personnel delegate system was meant to neutralize labor opposition by strengthening worker representation and dialogue. Unlike their Tunisian counterparts, Moroccan workers enjoyed more opportunities to express their interests and influence decision-making. In the workplace, personnel delegates could settle labor disputes, weigh in on salary decisions, and win better working conditions and indemnities for their constituents. In state institutions, union-affiliated delegates could advocate for their policy preferences and gain political support to advance labor agendas. Importantly, because personnel delegates enjoyed lengthy tenures and legal protections, workers could credibly rely on this system to promote their interests over the long term.

Yet, contrary to expectations, the personnel delegate system often incentivized labor militancy. Unlike Tunisia's highly centralized bargaining system, which generated wildcat strikes by concentrating bargaining power at the peak, Morocco's decentralized system turned individual enterprises into battlegrounds. Because unions had ambiguous standing at the plant level, personnel delegate elections became the principal means for them to gain recognition within firms and access the benefits of representation. However, the need to rally workers' support for these elections created perverse incentives for rival unions to engage in competitive striking behavior. For newly formed unions like the Democratic Labor Confederation (*Confédération Démocratique du Travail*, CDT), strikes served as a means to build legitimacy and draw workers away from established federations (Menouni, 1979).

For established unions, increased militancy was necessary to defend their membership and maintain their credibility as representatives of the working class.

This competition created the conditions for the surge in labor activity witnessed in Morocco from 1977 to 1982. The years with the highest strike counts – 1979 and 1980 – coincided with the establishment of the CDT as a national confederation, reflecting its efforts to build constituencies in sectors already dominated by the UMT and UGTM. The rise in strike activity in the transportation sector provides a case in point. In January 1979, a rail-workers union affiliated to the CDT, *Syndicat National des Cheminots* (SNC), began organizing strikes to protest workers' low wages. In a communiqué accompanying the strike, the SNC criticized the complacency of existing unions in refusing to attend to workers' demands, calling out the UMT's *Fédération Nationale du Transport Routier* (FNTR) for its "doctrine of ignorance and hostility toward the interests of the working class" (*Libération*, 01/26/1978a). In response, the FNTR and SNC organized a series of rolling strikes, culminating in a sixteen-day-long strike in the national railways and the complete closure of bus services in Casablanca. Although the strikes primarily focused on material demands, including a 30 percent pay increase, most labor observers saw the movement as "a consequence of rivalries between unions," rather than a sincere effort to address rail workers' needs (Appendix B: MA-4 2/19/2014). The resolution of the strike wave confirms this view: after two weeks of negotiations, rail workers received only a 60- dirham salary increase (roughly 7.5 percent). That same year, the SNC triumphed over the FNTR in one of the most contentious personnel delegate elections in the railway's history.

In one key way, however, the structure of the personnel delegate system allowed company managers to curtail labor militancy and prevent it from coalescing into a unified opposition force. While state regulations stipulated that only workers could vote in personnel delegate elections, labor laws gave employers significant discretion over the distribution of worker members among unions and the number of seats allocated to each. This enabled managers to manipulate the electoral process to divide and weaken labor unions. On the one hand, ambiguity in the criteria for determining union representativeness enabled managers to selectively deny representation to more militant unions while inducing their competitors to cooperate in exchange for more delegate seats. According to labor representatives from the CDT, employers used various manipulations to enhance union competition and suppress potential dissenters – including excluding militant unionists from candidate lists and offering bonuses or time off to elected representatives (Appendix B: MA-3, 2/19/2014). On the other hand, because the legal statute governing personnel delegates did not require them to be affiliated to a union, plant directors could fill delegate positions with less militant, nonunionized workers if union representatives became too recalcitrant. In many enterprises this led to an increase in personnel delegates designated as unaffiliated to any union (*sans appartenance syndical*), exacerbating tensions between unionized and the nonunionized working class.

Additionally, because designation as the "most representative union" at the national level was tied to a union's ability to win the majority of seats in worker delegate elections, state bureaucrats often used their discretion over the seat allocation process to empower cooperative unions over their less cooperative counterparts. As mentioned previously, representative unions enjoyed direct participation in a number of influential labor boards responsible for setting pay scales and distributing social benefits to Moroccan workers. However, because the Minister of Labor Affairs designated which worker representatives would sit on these boards, unions often found themselves at the mercy of governing officials in exercising these privileges. In many cases, such as the aforementioned rail workers' strike, union leaders struck deals with ministers that traded quiescence for pay increases, promotions, and extra indemnities for their members (*Libération*, 01/26/1978b). In cases where such inducements failed to compel a union to be cooperative, ministers relied on subjective criteria such as "lack of patriotic spirit" or "non-independence" to deny militant unions their rights (Bouharrou, 1993). In extreme circumstances, bureaucrats collaborated with employers to fire workers not yet designated as personnel delegates, thereby eliminating the support base of unions that stepped out of line (Appendix B: MA-3, 2/19/2014, MA-25, 5/5/2014).

In this way, the personnel delegate system kept union militancy in a delicate balance. While delegate elections incentivized unions to strike to secure a support base, they also checked this behavior by allowing the state to deny critical resources to militant unions. Most important, by allowing employers and government officials to utilize divide-and-rule tactics to manage labor opposition, the delegate system further institutionalized competition among rival federations, limiting workers' ability to act collectively toward common goals.

Apoliticism of Labor Protest in Morocco: The Moderating Effects of Legislative Institutions

If a focus on institutions helps to explain why labor mobilization in Morocco remained militant yet divided, it also helps us understand why the labor movement was unable to evolve into an effective political force, as it did in Tunisia. In the political arena, unions' strategies and modes of opposition were directly influenced by their level of incorporation into the regime and their ability to rely on partisan allies to mediate their concerns. Although all unions had grievances that could have been channeled into political militancy, those with institutional ties to the state and alternative channels for expressing their demands moderated their behavior, opting to work within the state's existing institutional framework. Even for unions existing on the margins of the regime's ruling coalition, the fractionalization of the labor movement and the new "consensus politics" promoted by the King prevented the formation of anti-government opposition and hindered political militancy.

Co-opting Labor through Consensus Politics

As noted in the previous chapter, political developments in 1970s Morocco were characterized by the relative liberalization of the political arena. At the beginning of the decade, King Hassan II officially ended the 1965 state of emergency, reinstated Parliament, and promulgated a new constitution that increased the power of civil society groups. When these efforts failed to co-opt key interests,[7] the monarchy initiated a second round of reforms aimed at incorporating opposition elites into its ruling coalition and pacifying the political sphere through the creation of a "government of national consensus." In August 1971, the King invited representatives from the *Istiqlal* and the leftist National Union of Popular Forces (*Union Nationale*

[7] Claiming that the 1970 Constitution maintained an unequal division of power between the opposition and the regime, the UNFP and *Istiqlal* called for a boycott of the constitutional referendum (Pennell, 2000, 330).

des Forces Populaires, UNFP)[8] to discuss the creation of a new constitution and a multiparty government. In 1972, the government held a referendum on the draft constitution which, while boycotted by several parties, made significant concessions to key opposition demands.

Notably, new provisions specifying that two-thirds of Parliament would be elected by direct universal suffrage appeased demands for better representation, making it more difficult for the King to manipulate its composition through indirect appointments. Additionally, a reduction in the timing of legislative elections from six to four years slightly improved citizens' chances of selecting a Parliament less beholden to the King. Most important, the 1972 constitution restricted some of the King's prerogatives to unilaterally enact laws by decree, instead requiring two-thirds approval from the parliament for new legislation. Revisions to article 98 concerning the King's right to revise the constitution also marginally increased parliament's power vis-à-vis the monarch by stipulating that this right was to be shared between the two.

Through these measures, King Hassan II hoped to secure the monarchy's political survival by co-opting opposition elites into the regime and building national consensus around the legitimacy of his rule. However, this goal would not be fully realized until the mid-1970s when two unforeseen political developments – one foreign and one domestic – helped to restore broad support for the monarchy. First, the Spanish withdrawal from the Western Sahara sparked a national military campaign that served to restrain some of the regime's most critical opponents (Pennell, 2000, 339). Under the banner of "national unity," most opposition parties fell into line behind the monarchy, softening their criticism and endorsing the King's political program (Storm, 2007). Second, a new round of competitive[9] municipal and

[8] The UNFP was formed in 1959 as part of a splinter between a leftist and more conservative element of the *Istiqlal*. While the leftist faction, led by Mehdi Ben Barka, broke away to form the UNFP, the conservative element remained under the banner of the original, right-wing *Istiqlal*.

[9] The competitive nature of elections was primarily due to the influx of new parties on the Moroccan political scene in the late 1970s. Along with the Socialist Union of Popular Forces (USFP, to be discussed in more detail below), two other new opposition parties participated in elections the Party of Progress and Socialism (Parti du Progrés et Socialisme, PPS) and the Action Party (Parti de l'Action, PA). Additionally, at the request of the opposition, new election

legislative elections (1976–1977) reanimated participation within the regime, bringing labor unions and opposition elites back into the political fold. As a result of their electoral successes, members of the UMT and UGTM gained significant positions in local and national government,[10] while the UGTM's partisan affiliate, *Istiqlal*, returned to power for the first time since 1963.

Ultimately, the liberalization of Morocco's political system did much to depoliticize organized labor's response to economic reforms. By incorporating unions and their partisan partners into formal politics, the monarchy created incentives for these groups to avoid open confrontation with the regime and to refrain from organizing protests that excluded opponents could exploit. It is important to emphasize that unions' failure to engage in political militancy does not imply that they lacked substantive grievances or did not oppose government policies. Rather, the specific ways in which this opposition was expressed were shaped by their institutional environment and the availability of alternative channels for voicing their concerns.

Union Reactions to Economic Liberalization: Variations on a Common Theme

A comparison of unions' reactions to IMF-sponsored price increases in 1981 underscores the significance of political institutions in moderating labor opposition. The UGTM's decision to adopt a conciliatory response to reforms, for example, was a direct consequence of its renewed integration into the regime's ruling coalition. Initially, the UGTM viewed price hikes as a threat to their members' interests and vehemently opposed the reforms; Just three days after the price

identity cards were issued to voters and electoral districts were redrawn. However, the redrawing of electoral districts ultimately served to undermine the competitiveness of elections by unduly favoring pro-monarchist parties such as the MP (Storm, 2007, 40; Clark, 2018, 122).

10 As a result of the parliamentary elections, the *Istiqlal* gained the second highest number of seats (50 in direct elections, 1 in indirect elections), while the UMT gained seven seats (all in indirect elections). Subsequently, the *Istiqlal* was incorporated into the government through the Ministry of Foreign Affairs (M'Hammed Boucetta) while the UMT was incorporated through the Ministry of Justice (Mâati Bouabid). On a subnational level the UMT was afforded positions in several public agencies and enterprises connected to the monarchy, specifically through the directorate of the *Caisse Nationale de Sécurité Sociale* (CNSS) (Vermeren, 2002, 79–80).

increases were announced, the UGTM National Council released a critical communiqué denouncing the government's decision and threatening to use "all methods of struggle to repair the damage caused to poor sectors of society and workers" (*L'Opinion*, 6/19/1981a). Additionally, in open sessions of parliament, UGTM and *Istiqlal* representatives sharply questioned Prime Minister Maati Bouabid about the decision to raise prices without proper consultation or parliamentary approval (Azam and Morrison, 1994). On June 5, the *Istiqlal*-UGTM parliamentary bloc rejected government's decision to maintain the price increases and joined forces with the Party of Progress and Socialism in demanding the immediate annulment of all new prices.

However, despite this vocal opposition, UGTM leaders never threatened to withdraw from the government and opposed calls for a general strike. In a statement released in the *Istiqlal's* press outlet, *L'Opinion*, the UGTM emphasized the importance of dialogue with the regime as an alternative to militant opposition:

> In reiterating our refusal of any increase in the prices of basic goods, we note that the *Istiqlal* and the UGTM have always displayed their opposition to such increases via democratic methods in the Chamber of Representatives ... it is one thing to fight against this process and another to select a general strike date that coincides with a period when the country needs unity and cohesion. (*L'Opinion*, 6/22/1981)

Rather than resorting to protest, UGTM representatives chose to express their grievances within the existing institutional system using a strategy that Burgess describes as "norm-based voice" (Burgess, 2004, 9). UGTM leaders had three key reasons for limiting their opposition to "within-system" strategies. First, union leaders were encouraged to moderate their behavior due to the government's willingness to compromise on critical issues. Shortly after the price increases were announced, the King convened a special council to discuss potential revisions, inviting delegations from *Istiqlal*, PPS, UGTM, and UMT to participate in the talks (Azam and Morrison, 1994). Additionally, the Prime Minister privately met with the *Istiqlal* parliamentary bloc to discuss their proposed amendments to the price reforms. Following a June 6th meeting, union leaders praised the government for its "willingness to open a dialogue on fundamental questions whenever necessary" and its recognition of the "opinions of the Chamber of Representatives in their evaluation of ... previous price increases" (*L'Opinion*, 6/19/1981b). The next day, the government announced a 50 percent reduction in the price increases on subsidized goods and an 8 percent wage hike to offset additional costs, conforming to many of the UGTM and *Istiqlal's* recommendations.

Second, given their integration into the political system, the UGTM's leaders found it less costly to work within the government to seek a compromise than trying to force a solution from the outside. Among the unions opposing price reforms, the UGTM arguably had the most power to affect policy change – of the 263 seats in parliament, the UGTM and *Istiqlal* held nearly one-fifth,[11] making them the largest non-loyalist parliamentary bloc (Europa Publications, 1977; García, 2000). The UGTM also enjoyed moderate influence in the ministerial council, where *Istiqlal* representatives held key positions in several secondary ministries (e.g., the Ministries of Handicrafts and Social Affairs, Justice, Education, and Foreign Affairs). Combined with the union's commanding performance in the previous year's local elections, this gave UGTM leaders significant leverage over municipal and national governments, enabling them to pressure regime elites to reconsider the price increases without resorting to militant tactics. As a result, most UGTM leaders opted to replace traditional methods of protest with a formalized – and privileged – form of intra-elite bargaining, which they strictly preferred over external pressure (Appendix B: MA-12, 3/25/2014; MA-25, 5/5/2014).

Even more important, the UGTM's close relationship with the Istiqlal made it an indispensable partner in the government's ruling coalition, thereby limiting the union's ability to oppose price reforms. As part of one of the largest partisan groups in government, the UGTM was heavily reliant on economic privileges from the state, including union secondments and salary bonuses for parliamentary representatives (Clement and Paul, 1984). Additionally, organic ties between the *Istiqlal* and the UGTM increased the union's dependency on political elites, making its leaders more accountable to partisan

11 Although Garcia and Europa have the *Istiqlal* recorded as winning fifty seats in the 1977 parliament, Santucci (1979, 233) records slightly different statistics, claiming that the *Istiqlal* captured fifty-one seats (including the one seat won by the UGTM in indirect elections).

interests than to the workers they represented. At the union's national congresses, the party hierarchy guided labor delegates on which candidates to support and whom to exclude from election lists, giving labor leaders significant autonomy from the rank-and-file (Appendix B: MA-20, 4/14/2014; MA-25, 5/5/2014). The party also controlled the UGTM's access to candidate slates for legislative and municipal elections, allowing party leaders to exert pressure on the union leadership. When the *Istiqlal* was in the opposition, these factors worked to increase militancy within the UGTM as a way of boosting the party's profile among its more restive constituents. However, with the party firmly embedded in the regime's ruling coalition, these dynamics incentivized labor leaders to restrict opposition and support government reforms, even when they conflicted with workers' interests.

Finally, the attractiveness of working within the system was compounded by the UGTM's weak presence within the labor force. By the late 1970s, the UGTM had failed to expand its influence beyond 10 percent of the working class (Clement and Paul, 1984, 24). In delegate elections it lost to the UMT by significant margins in sectors such as metallurgy, textiles, tourism, and transportation (Morocco Ministry of Labor, internal document). Reflecting its weak position among worker representatives, the UGTM secured only one of the ten seats reserved for unions in parliament, compared to the UMT's seven.

This organizational weakness was critical in deterring the UGTM from pursuing radical protest. Faced with the likelihood that strikes would not garner sufficient support, UGTM leaders opted for a negotiated strategy that was less likely to result in failure (Appendix B: MA-12, 3/25/2014). By adopting a conciliatory approach, the union aimed to secure concessions that would bolster its legitimacy among workers without sacrificing its privileged position within the regime. Union leaders also hoped to avoid the harsh repression typically directed at more militant unions (ibid).

The UMT's response to price increases further demonstrates the moderating effect of institutional incorporation on union behavior. Although UMT leaders openly criticized the government's economic policies – organizing meetings to demand the cancellation of price increases and launching a regional strike in Casablanca – their actions adhered to a logic of "within-system" opposition rather than radical militancy. Amid its anti-reform efforts, the UMT invested in its alliance with the regime, balancing the threat of militancy with a constant emphasis on dialogue. In the lead-up to its June 18th strike, the UMT participated in several rounds of government-initiated talks about revisions to the price reforms. Moreover, in planning its protest campaign, UMT leaders took pains to secure government approval and to highlight the "peaceful" nature of its general strike (Al-Bayane 6/17/1981). Most important, the union made a deliberate effort to limit its opposition to a single strike action focused exclusively on price reforms. Despite sharing common cause with more radical unions that pledged to continue strikes until all price increases were rescinded, UMT leaders refused to join a general strike organized by the CDT on June 20th, for fear that "[the CDT's] motivations were driven by subversive, partisan concerns" (Appendix B: MA-28, 5/7/2014).

Like the UGTM, the UMT's strategy of apolitical militancy reflected its precarious position within industrial and political institutions. On one hand, its disappointing performance in personnel delegate elections drove union leaders to call for a regional strike. During the late 1970s, the UMT lost key constituencies in the mining sector to the UGTM and suffered divisions in the civil service, leading to the formation of the CDT. Worse still, just two years after its creation, the CDT captured former UMT strongholds in education, the postal sector, and transportation, winning 95, 78, and 47 percent of delegate seats, respectively. Although the UMT retained its status as the most representative union, these results shattered its expectation that the CDT was a fringe group, supported only by its political partner, the Socialist Union of Popular Forces (*Union Socialiste des Forces Populaires*, USFP).[12] To defend its legitimacy and counter the CDT's critique of its "reprehensible collaboration with employers and the government" (Benhilal, 1984, 237), the UMT had to mobilize protest actions to demonstrate its commitment to protecting workers' interests.

On the other hand, the UMT's reluctance to engage in political militancy was driven by its desire to protect its privileged position within government institutions. In addition to occupying the majority

12 The USFP was created in 1975 as a result of a division between the Rabat branch of the UNFP, comprised of party leaders, intellectuals and the party youth, and the Casablanca branch, mainly composed of trade unionists and labor-sympathizers.

of seats reserved for unions in parliament, the UMT also held prestigious appointments in the government's central administration and maintained loose alliances with key regime elites, including Prime Minister Maati Bouabid. As Morocco's "most representative union" the UMT benefited from representation in the social security administration, mutual societies, and international labor boards, as well as a wide range of economic subsidies from the state. These latter benefits were especially significant, as the state financed nearly all of the UMT's local and regional offices as well as its wage and utility bills (Clement and Paul, 1984).

Opposing the state directly could have jeopardized these privileges and risked potential exclusion from the regime. Furthermore, as UMT leaders wisely anticipated, forming an alliance with the CDT could provoke massive state repression, potentially crippling the union's organizational base. Thus, while the union had reason to oppose the government's economic agenda, it could not do so in a way that would directly threaten the regime. As a result, UMT leaders opted for a mobilization strategy that allowed workers to express their dissatisfaction with austerity policies while staying within the bounds of government-sanctioned opposition (Appendix B: MA-4, 2/19/2014).

Finally, the CDT's militant response to the price increases stemmed from its marginal position within formal institutions and its lack of influence in the political system. Of the trade unions discussed in this chapter, the CDT was the least well-integrated into formal politics. Although it had a partisan partner in the USFP, the party held no ministerial positions and only fifteen parliamentary seats (5.7 percent of the total), limiting its ability to influence government decision-making. Nevertheless, the CDT initially attempted to engage in "within-system" opposition to persuade the government to soften price reforms.

Shortly after the price increases were announced, the CDT Executive Bureau sent a letter to the ministerial council, demanding the cancellation of price reforms and the "opening of a dialogue about the [union's] urgent demands: a 50 percent increase in salaries, an increase of the minimum wage by 1200 DH, etc." (Jibril, 1981, 28). Similarly, on May 31st, the union requested a meeting with Prime Minister Bouabid to discuss a reduction in prices, though this request was ultimately rebuffed. For the CDT, this rejection suggested that the socio-economic crisis had reached unprecedented levels, making it clear that working within the system would not be effective in achieving reforms (Appendix B: MA-5, 2/19/2014; MA-23, 4/25/2014). Consequently, in early June, the CDT organized a "plan of union action," orchestrating strikes across various industries and regions to pressure the government. When the government refused to reduce price increases beyond 50 percent, secretary-general Noubir Amaoui called for a nationwide general strike on June 20th to "compel the government to account for the price increases and press for the satisfaction of workers' demands" (Benhilal, 1984, 239).

It is important to note that, unlike the UMT's regional strike in Casablanca, the CDT's strike activity clearly traversed the bounds of "within-system" opposition. On the day of the general strike – which had not been previously approved by the authorities – labor demonstrations disrupted economic activity in many of the country's largest industrial centers. Further, like the 1978 general strike in Tunisia, these protests devolved into widespread violence in Casablanca's *bidonvilles*. According to the Ministry of Interior, sixty-six people were killed, 110 were injured, and numerous buildings were ransacked, vandalized, or set ablaze during the unrest. Reflecting the regime's antagonism toward the CDT's strike activity, nearly sixty CDT members were arrested before the protests began, and an additional hundred militants from the CDT and USFP (including their secretary-general and members of the executive committee) were detained after the riots.

Despite this, it would be incorrect to view the CDT's militancy as a direct political challenge to the regime. Although government statements emphasized the seditious nature of the strike and accused union militants of "mobilizing agents provocateurs ... giving marching orders, and issuing threats" (*Maroc Soir* 6/23/1981), CDT leaders – both before and after the strike – sought to distance themselves from any association with violence or revolutionary demands. In a statement given to *Le Continent*, the CDT's adjoint Secretary-General denied any political motivation for the strike, insisting that the labor action arose solely from "the government's refusal to cancel the price increases or engage in dialogue with the CDT" (*Le Continent* 6/25/1981). Additionally, in an interview with *Jeune Afrique* following the strike, partisan representatives of the union expressed a willingness to work with the monarchy to resolve the country's political issues, emphasizing that the USFP-CDT bloc was prepared to participate in government if granted "certain guarantees" (*Jeune Afrique* 7/8/1981).

Ultimately, the CDT's decision to limit its opposition to apolitical militancy was driven by two tactical considerations by its leadership. The first was a concern over the success of potential political opposition: acting alone, the union was unlikely to garner enough support to pose a credible challenge to the regime, leaving it vulnerable to government repression (Appendix B: MA-5, 2/19/2014). Second, union leaders were constrained by the climate of "national consensus" that had emerged in the aftermath of the Saharan War. Much like their partisan partners in the USFP, CDT leaders realized that opposing the monarchy while the country was at war would be tantamount to an act of treason (Appendix B: MA-19, 4/9/14). Thus, although the union's dissatisfaction with price reforms led it to violate the terms of the state-labor alliance, the CDT could not push for an all-out scission with the regime. As a result, labor opposition in Morocco remained both apolitical and fragmented. With unions institutionally bound to the government and pursuing different strategies to advance their demands, organized labor failed to develop into a cohesive force capable of uniting workers behind a common agenda of opposition to the regime.

Conclusion

In this chapter, I have argued that divergence in unions' responses to economic liberalization in Tunisia and Morocco is best explained with a focus on formal institutions. When confronted with the deterioration of their clientelistic bargains with the state, unions' reactions were conditioned by their ability to advance their interests within the regime's key economic and political institutions. Where labor was excluded from formal politics, as in Tunisia, workers had fewer opportunities to address their grievances and adopted more militant tactics, both in their methods of interest articulation and in the substance of their demands. Additionally, where exclusionary policies forced unions to operate as political outsiders, authoritarian suppression not only radicalized rank-and-file workers but brought them into alliance with marginalized opposition groups and disenfranchised political elites. Consequently, organized labor came to project a more radical vision of labor politics, centered on active resistance to economic reforms and political opposition to the Bourguiba regime.

By contrast, in Morocco, selective incorporation of unions and their partisan partners into the regime's institutional framework contained labor activism within formal politics. Although institutions governing labor representation at the shop floor encouraged militancy by fostering competition among rival unions, they also limited labor opposition by enabling employers to exploit these divisions. Simultaneously, political incorporation of labor unions into parliament channeled workers' grievances into formal politics and increased government leverage over labor leaders. By enabling regime elites to use divide-and-rule strategies to co-opt moderate unionists while punishing militants, incorporative labor policies fractured the labor movement, ensuring that labor militancy could not be translated into an effective challenge against the regime. Thus, organized labor in Morocco was unable to form the broad coalition of interests necessary to become a force for political opposition, as it did in Tunisia.

One alternative explanation of these trends worth mentioning before concluding centers on the role of union leaders in driving labor activism (Ahlquist and Levi, 2013; Darlington, 2009; Ganz et al., 2001; Kelly, 1998; McAlevey, 2015). In the social movements literature, leadership is seen as critical in activating collective identities and fostering the group cohesion necessary to sustain collective action (Ganz, 2010, 2011; Polletta and Jasper, 2001; Taylor et al., 1989). Leaders can persuade members of the validity of strikes by securing material benefits for workers or convincing them that militancy can succeed (Ahlquist and Levi, 2013; Murphy, 2016). In countries where union leaders are drawn from leftist traditions (i.e., Communism, Trotskyism, socialism), workers are expected to be more willing to protest and advance progressive social and political demands.

Applied to the cases of Tunisia and Morocco, this theory suggests that union leaders in Tunisia were more ideologically left-leaning than their Moroccan counterparts, and therefore, more predisposed to initiate militant action against the regime. While it is true that several UGTT leaders had connections to the political left, it is also the case that Moroccan union leaders had similar ties. In fact, leaders of both organizations were formerly members of the Communist-oriented CGT before distancing themselves from the Communist party and forming independent labor unions aligned with prominent nationalist parties (Ahmad, 1967; Benomar, 1991). After independence, leftist influences persisted in both unions – while prominent UGTT leaders were members of the Tunisian Communist party and the MDS,[13] UMT leaders came from the leftist UNFP and the Communist-influenced Party for Progress and Socialism.[14]

Moreover, UGTT leaders were no less vulnerable to co-optation than their Moroccan counterparts. For example, prior to 1975, Habib Achour was considered an "unquestionably loyal Destourian" and was handpicked by Bourguiba to serve UGTT secretary-general in an effort to quiet labor unrest (Ahmad, 1967, 158; Bellin, 2002, 100, fn. 12). Unlike former UGTT leaders like Ahmed Ben Salah or Ahmed Tlili, Achour "believed in the apolitical nature of trade unionism" (Ahmad, 1967, 159) and upheld this principle throughout much of his early career.[15] In this respect, he was similar to Mahjoub Ben Seddik, the head of the UMT, who was also known for his commitment to a separation between trade unionism and politics (Forst, 1976).

Thus, while union leaders were undoubtedly influential in shaping labor politics in Tunisia and Morocco, it is not the case that leaders in either country were inherently more likely to lead their organizations down a militant path. Instead, as I have argued, UGTT leaders were alienated by state repression and were forced to align with union militants as a way of reclaiming their power. This reinforces the need to investigate political institutions in order to understand the specific patterns of labor mobilization that emerge. To explain why unions engage in militancy and moderation, we must understand how the institutions that govern labor representation shape leaders' perceptions of their interests and influence the coalitions that they form to advance these interests vis-a-vis the regime. In the next chapter, I demonstrate how changes in political institutions and the coalitions they create can shift labor strategies, even after a stable pattern of state–labor relations has been formed.

[13] For example, Taïeb Baccouche was affiliated with the Tunisian Communist Party and Mustapha Ben Jaafar was a founder of the MDS.

[14] For example, Omar Benjelloun was a prominent member of the UNFP (and later founder of the USFP).

[15] Indeed, part of the reason that Achour was chosen by Bourguiba to lead the UGTT in 1962 and 1970.

5 Workers in an Age of Adjustment: Union Reactions to Structural Adjustment Programs

On the morning of December 14, 1990, thousands of workers flooded the narrow streets of the old city (*medina*) in Fez. Frustrated by rising inequality and recent hikes in the prices of consumer goods, they demanded a comprehensive suite of reforms, including a $130 increase in the minimum wage, expanded social benefits, and basic protections for workers' rights. More troubling for the authorities, workers' grievances were not limited to economic concerns – in addition to material concessions, they called for a "democratic framework," issuing a direct challenge to the monarchical regime. As the protests escalated and spread to major northern cities, labor unrest descended into violence against the Moroccan state. By the end of the demonstrations on December 16th, some 200 protesters were either injured or killed, and the state had incurred over 15 million dollars in damage to government properties.

These events marked a significant shift in labor politics in Morocco witnessed during the late 1980s. Once passive allies of the Moroccan monarchy, trade unions began to adopt a more critical and confrontational stance toward the regime. Between 1989 and 1997, Moroccan unions organized 2,822 protests, including two general strikes that brought hundreds of thousands of workers into the streets (Figure 5.1). Many of these protests were held in coordination with opposition parties, signaling the growing politicization of Moroccan labor unions during the period.

In contrast, in Tunisia, labor mobilization became much more quiescent. While workers continued to strike, most actions were limited to individual factories and focused on traditional bread-and-butter issues like wages, unemployment, and working conditions. Despite important changes in the government's economic and political program – including the growing authoritarianism of the Ben Ali regime – union leaders did not mount serious efforts to resist government reforms. Instead, the UGTT underwent its "own [process

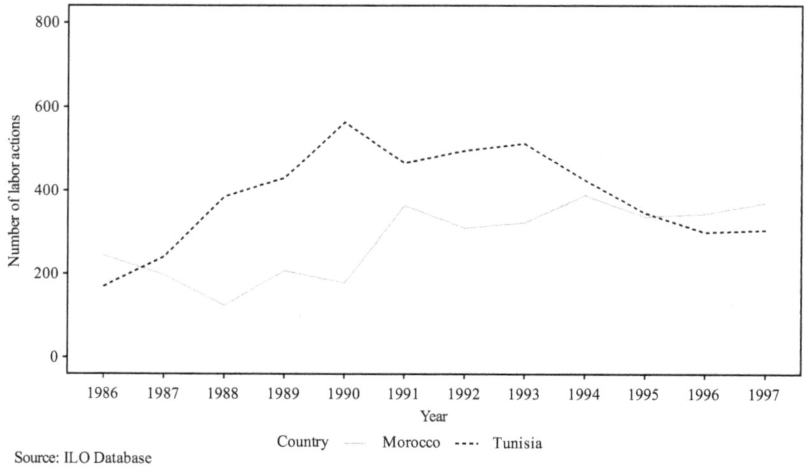

Figure 5.1 Comparative labor protests in Tunisia and Morocco, ILO (1986–1997)

of] structural adjustment," wherein union leaders suppressed protest activity and depoliticized demands in order to maintain a tacit alliance with the authoritarian regime.

How do we explain this surprising reversal of fortunes? In both countries, leaders implemented austerity programs that shattered the terms of existing state–labor bargains. Nevertheless, unions' responses to economic reforms in these countries differed sharply. While the UGTT retreated from its position at the vanguard of opposition to the regime, Moroccan unions coordinated numerous strike campaigns against the monarchy's economic policies and its exclusionary political reforms.

These contrasting developments are puzzling for two key reasons. First, despite broad similarities in economic policies in both countries, organized labor reacted differently. According to traditional theories of labor behavior, neoliberal reforms should produce *similar* reactions from unions experiencing shared grievances. If this is the case, why was labor opposition in Morocco more militant and cohesive than that witnessed in Tunisia?

Second, from a historical institutionalist perspective, the divergence in protest patterns is equally surprising. Given the trajectories outlined in the previous chapter, one might have expected the opposite pattern of behavior to emerge – that is, continued militancy in Tunisia and quiescence in Morocco. However, during the structural adjustment period, this pattern suddenly reversed. What changed to make Moroccan unions more willing to oppose the government and Tunisian unions more accepting of reforms?

In what follows, I link this unexpected divergence in protest behavior to changes in the institutions that governed labor and political representation in Tunisia and Morocco during the structural adjustment period. In Tunisia, changes to the corporatist bargaining system provided new channels for labor leaders to express their interests, which muted opposition to the regime's economic policies. At the same time, limited political liberalization under President Zine Ben Ali integrated opposition elites into the political system, upending the alliance between leftist groups and organized labor. In contrast, in Morocco, existing institutions for labor representation combined with worsening economic conditions to produce new uncertainties for workers and union leaders. Alongside the closure of political avenues for interest articulation, this generated new incentives for unions and their partisan affiliates to work together to oppose the exclusionary practices of the monarchical regime.

This chapter thus explores the dynamics of *institutional change* and their impact on labor behavior. I highlight two mechanisms of change – innovation and drift – and examine how each influenced unions' interests and capacity for collective action in response to economic reforms. I pay special attention to how institutional reforms reconfigured political coalitions in support of labor militancy, disrupting previous patterns of labor mobilization and generating unexpected responses to economic change. In so doing, I challenge path-dependent explanations that predict "institutional lock-in" following critical junctures. By focusing on the coalitional foundations of political institutions, I emphasize the contested nature of institutional equilibria and uncover some of the mechanisms that drive processes of institutional change.

The remainder of the chapter is organized as follows. First, I outline the specific policies that comprised reform programs in Tunisia and Morocco, highlighting their negative effects on organized labor. Next, I analyze unions' responses to these reforms, drawing on a combination of publicly available and original quantitative data. In the third section, I provide an institutional explanation for unions' divergent responses, focusing on how changes in political and economic institutions shifted unions' incentives and affect their ability to contest neoliberal economic reforms. Finally, I conclude by evaluating my argument against theoretical alternatives and discussing its implications for path-dependent explanations of political behavior.

Labor in the Age of Structural Adjustment: The Shattering of the Nasserist Social Bargain

The beginning of structural adjustment marked a period of radical transformation for North African economies. After decades of unsuccessful state-led growth, governments across the region turned to neoliberal reforms meant to reduce the state's role in the economy, and make domestic businesses more competitive and efficient. In many cases, these reforms were adopted out of necessity; without some form of economic restructuring and international aid, North African regimes would have collapsed under the dual burdens of economic crisis and external debt. However, structural adjustment also jeopardized key sources of domestic support. If the adoption of reforms in the 1970s called into question the Nasserist social contract, structural adjustment shattered the preexisting patron–client relationship between labor unions and authoritarian regimes. As governments cut state expenditures and withdrew from the public sector, workers could no longer rely on the "*état providence*" to ensure their collective welfare. Instead, they would have to adapt to a new state–labor bargain that undermined long-standing worker interests.

Structural Adjustment in Tunisia: Continued Crisis and the New Liberal Economy

As we saw in Chapter 4, by 1986, Tunisia's rising debt and inefficient public investments had plunged the country into a full-blown economic crisis. At its worst point, the Central Bank only had enough foreign exchange to cover two weeks of imports (Alexander, 2010, 79), prompting a dramatic shift in economic policy. To stave off further financial collapse, the government initiated an economic structural adjustment program (SAP) with assistance from the World Bank and IMF. Like many others, this SAP called for sweeping changes to the

Tunisian economy: market liberalization, fiscal austerity, privatization, and labor market deregulation.

The cornerstone of Tunisia's SAP was reducing government spending. By 1985, Tunisia's public sector investments totaled TD 1.26 billion, roughly 5 percent of GDP (Bank al-Markazī al-Tūnisī, 1985, 133). To alleviate this burden, the state implemented a two-fold austerity program aimed at reducing consumer subsidies and divesting from public enterprises. The first step in this initiative was lifting price controls on several manufactured goods and increasing the price of staple grains by 10–15 percent (Nsouli et al., 1993). In subsequent years (1987–1992), these increases were accompanied by the gradual elimination of consumer subsidies, which were replaced by targeted assistance for the urban poor. Additionally, general welfare programs, including housing benefits, food assistance, and health insurance, were restructured and replaced by need-based programs and direct income support for those most affected by the reforms.

Perhaps the most extensive budget-reduction measures, however, came with the privatization of the public sector. By the mid-1980s, public expenditure on state-owned enterprises (SOEs) accounted for 37 percent of investment, and SOEs represented a quarter of total employment and GDP (Alexander, 2002b; Ferchiou, 1991). Consequently, the government implemented a gradual divestiture policy focused on the restructuring of unprofitable firms *(mise á niveau)* and later transferring them into the private sector. In 1989, the government established the National Commission on the Restructuring of Public Enterprises (CAREPP) to oversee the sale of SOEs and began the first phase of privatization with the transfer of small-to-medium enterprises in textiles, tourism, and construction. Although the pace of privatization began slowly, by the mid-1990s, the government expanded its efforts to include larger firms in strategic sectors, such as transportation, banking, and telecommunications. By 1999, a total of 89 firms had been partially or fully privatized, generating approximately $461.5 million for the Ben Ali regime (The World Bank, 2008).

Finally, in efforts to open up the Tunisian economy and increase the country's competitiveness abroad, trade was targeted for significant reform. Soon after signing the SAP, the government launched an import liberalization program to reduce quantitative restrictions and streamline import duties. Between 1986 and 1988, the Ben Ali regime lowered the maximum tariff rate by 41 percent and decontrolled

70 percent of manufactured goods (Bassani, 1993, 147). Further liberalization followed Tunisia's accession to the General Agreement on Tariffs and Trade in 1992, with 85 percent of imports freed from quantitative restrictions and the average tariff rate reduced to 43 percent (Dillman, 1998, 9). In a major step toward global integration, Tunisia signed an association agreement with the EU in 1995, creating a free-trade zone that opened domestic markets to 500 million new consumers (White, 2001, 164).

Effects on Labor

By the mid-1990s, these initiatives – boosted by favorable harvests and tourism receipts – began to yield positive results for the Tunisian economy. Heralded as one of the textbook cases of successful reform, Tunisia was able to halve its external debt ratio, manage inflation, and sustain average GDP growth of 4 percent throughout much of the adjustment period (1985–1995) (Alexander, 2010; Pfeifer, 1996; Richards and Waterbury, 1990).

However, for organized labor, the outcomes of structural adjustment were far less favorable. Unemployment remained a persistent problem during the reform period, partly due to redundancies caused by privatization. According to one CAREPP study, in 1990, 6,500 workers were affected by industrial restructuring, with 41 percent either forced into early retirement or dismissed (Saghir, 1993, 19). Additionally, between 1996 and 1998, privatization was responsible for approximately 2,000 annual layoffs in the public sector (Layachi, 1999, 4). In total, approximately 6 percent of the pre-privatization workforce lost their jobs due to structural reforms (Posusney, 2003, 279).

Trade liberalization further exacerbated unemployment. As Ghali and Mohnen (2004, 17) note, market integration benefited large export-oriented firms at the expense of small and medium enterprises, which were considered the "most dynamic in terms of job creation." Although losses were concentrated in tradable sectors, nearly 1,000 small enterprises struggled to adjust to competitive pressures, putting an estimated 25,000 jobs at risk (ibid). As a result, industrial nonmanufacturing employment decreased as a proportion of total employment, while agricultural employment – most negatively impacted by European trade – fell to less than 22 percent (Charmes, 2001).

Coincident with job losses, employment in all economic sectors became more precarious. In response to World Bank recommendations for labor market deregulation, the 1996 labor code increased hiring flexibility for private firms, enabling managers to use fixed-term and part-time contracts to recruit employees (Alexander, 2001; Ennaceur, 2000). Although employers still faced penalties for dismissals, the net effect of these reforms was to encourage owners to hire workers on an increasingly short-term basis – for periods less than four years – limiting stable employment opportunities for new labor force entrants.

Moreover, available jobs were concentrated in low-skill sectors despite an increasingly skilled workforce, leading to rising inequality and underemployment. In response, many workers transitioned to the informal sector, where employment was more readily available but wages were lower, and protections were minimal (Pfeifer, 1996, 47). As a consequence, Tunisia maintained one of the highest unemployment rates in the world during the reform period, averaging 15 percent, with even higher rates in rural areas and among educated youth (Rama, 1998, 59).

Additionally, labor market reforms severely undermined the social safety net that had long underpinned the government's corporatist relationship with labor. Not only did workers lack a robust scheme for unemployment insurance, but under the new labor code provisions, wage increases and job security were directly tied to plant-level productivity (Ennaceur, 2000). Furthermore, the government reduced employer contributions to the National Social Security Fund from 17.5 percent to 15.5 percent (Alexander, 2001), meaning that workers had to contribute more to the system while receiving fewer and lower-quality benefits.

Finally, economic reforms and austerity measures predictably worsened workers' living conditions. During the early years of stabilization (1986–1990), real average annual wages fell by 2.3 percent, due partly to wage freezes in the public sector in effect since 1983 (Nsouli et al., 1993). While these decreases were later compensated by salary raises of 8–9 percent for public and private sector workers and 5–6 percent for minimum-wage earners, these raises failed to keep pace with declines in purchasing power caused by inflation and subsidy cuts (ibid). Moreover, as targeted assistance programs replaced general social spending, unionized workers lost access to many social welfare benefits, which were increasingly directed toward the rural and urban poor.[1]

[1] Since many of these recipients were employed in the informal sector, they were unlikely to be union members.

Structural Adjustment in Morocco: Economic Collapse and the Return to Liberalism

In Morocco, small cracks in the government's development policy that emerged in the late 1970s had evolved into deep fissures by the early 1980s. Given the failure of domestic efforts to resolve the country's debt crisis, in 1983, King Hassan II turned to the IMF to prepare a SAP in exchange for SDR 300 million in debt relief and financial support (Horton, 1990). In line with standard IMF recommendations, the program called for a range of reforms, including cuts to public spending, privatization of SOEs, reductions in trade and investment barriers, and revisions to labor laws. To jumpstart these changes, the government announced an initial raft of reforms that liberalized exchange rates, rationalized Morocco's tax system, and reduced capital expenditures to their 1982 levels.

As in Tunisia, the main objective of Morocco's SAP was to reduce public spending. Despite previous efforts to stabilize government budgets, public expenditures still accounted for 35 percent of GDP, a level that became unsustainable after phosphate revenues declined in 1979 (Nsouli et al., 1995). To improve its fiscal position, the state needed to drastically reduce its economic intervention, beginning with its spending on the wage bill. Thus, in 1981, the government implemented a four-year wage freeze in the public sector, which was later reinstated from 1992 to 1995 (ibid; Seddon, 1989). To support wage controls, it slowed the expansion of civil service employment and introduced reforms tying future wage increases and promotions to productivity (El-Said and Harrigan, 2014). At the same time, it implemented a broad initiative to streamline subsidy expenditures and target welfare assistance more effectively toward the poor (Seddon, 1989).

Parallel to these efforts, the government embarked on an ambitious effort to restructure public enterprises. In 1989, it passed its first privatization law, which established guidelines for restructuring SOEs and identified 112 businesses for transfer to the private sector (Saulniers, 1993b). Unlike Tunisia, Morocco's privatization program was far-reaching, targeting both strategic and non-strategic firms. Between 1992 and 1996, the government sold twenty-five public enterprises and seven hotels, generating $1.3 billion in revenue (Khosrowshahi, 1997, 243). In subsequent years, the program expanded to the critical energy, infrastructure, and banking sectors, liquidating larger, more profitable firms such as the *Société Anonyme Marocaine de l'Industrie de Raffinage* (1997), the *Banque Marocaine de Commerces* (1997), the public water-works (1997), and *National Gaz* (1998).

Finally, in tandem with austerity measures, the Moroccan government introduced significant reforms to liberalize the trade regime. Within two years of adopting the SAP, King Hassan II reduced price controls, deregulated foreign investment, freed interest rates, and depreciated the dirham by 30 percent (Nsouli et al., 1995, 39). In 1985, the government reduced the number of goods subject to quantitative restrictions from 61 percent to 13 percent and lowered the maximum average tariff from 400 percent to 45 percent (Bassani, 1993; Cherkaoui et al., 2011). Additionally, in 1987, it reaffirmed its commitment to free trade by joining the General Agreement on Tariffs and Trade and signing a free-trade agreement with the EEC in 1995. As in Tunisia, these measures were complemented by institutional reforms, including a domestic industrial upgrading program, rationalizing investment codes, and moving toward full convertibility of the dirham by 1996 (Cammett, 2007).

Curiously, despite pressure, the Moroccan government resisted significant reforms in labor legislation. Fearing the social costs of layoffs, it reinforced strict labor protections to limit labor flexibility and retain employment. In the private sector, the government maintained regulations that restricted employers' ability to dismiss workers and increased the compensation due to workers found to have been unjustly dismissed (El-Mikawy and Posusney, 2002, 66). Additionally, to mitigate job losses from financial restructuring, the state implemented an informal freeze on layoffs within privatized enterprises and stipulated that firms that expanded after downsizing rehire previously laid-off workers (ibid).

Effects on Labor

Taken together, these measures did much to improve the Moroccan economy. By 1996, Morocco was seen as one of the few success stories of structural adjustment, having achieved an average annual growth rate of 4.7 percent from 1986 to 1991 (Nsouli et al., 1995).

The effects of structural reforms on workers, however, were much more mixed. On the one hand, the government made concerted efforts to protect social welfare and improve living conditions as part of its economic restructuring plan. Between 1983 and 1996, GDP per capita rose to $1,365, effectively doubling from its pre-adjustment level, while the number of people living below the poverty line was halved to 3.3 million by 1991 (Pennell, 2000, 377; Nsouli et al., 1995). Social indicators in health and education also saw considerable improvement, with reductions witnessed in the number of pupils per teacher, inhabitants per physician, and the infant mortality rate from 1984 to 1995 (The World Bank, 2016).

Despite these improvements, however, poor and low-income earners did not necessarily *feel* any richer during the structural adjustment period, nor did they experience significant gains in the short term. Although inflation rates declined, they still hovered at an average of 6 percent, peaking at 12.4 percent in 1984 (ibid). Moreover, food prices rose even more quickly, with a 5.7 percent increase in August 1985 alone (Seddon, 1989, 255). Because food purchases made up the largest share of expenditures in poor households, these price hikes disproportionately impacted the poor, leading to a rise in the number of people living below the food poverty line (El-Said and Harrigan, 2014).

Similarly, for much of the working class, the government's SAP did little to protect living standards or employment. Due to wage restraint in the public sector, real average wages for civil servants fell by 20 percent from 1981 to 1985, a loss from which they did not recover until the early 1990s (Horton, 1990; Nsouli et al., 1995). Manufacturing workers also saw significant declines in wages, particularly as currency appreciation made Moroccan exports more expensive abroad (Lane et al., 1999). In the private sector, the impact of liberalization was even more striking – in addition to lower wages, a 10 percent reduction in tariffs led to an estimated 1.65 percent decline in firm-level employment (Currie and Harrison, 1997).

On the employment front, structural adjustment had more limited effects, though specific sectors faced serious dislocations. Early privatizations had little impact on overall employment, as the firms listed for privatization represented less than 1 percent of the labor force. However, in firms privatized after 1996, layoffs were more substantial, since they were concentrated in more inefficient, overstaffed firms. According to reports cited in *L'Économiste*, factory closures in the late 1990s were the second-largest contributor to unemployment, pushing the national unemployment rate above 16 percent (*L'Économiste*, 12/11/1998). Unemployment was particularly concentrated in urban areas, where rates reached as high as 25 percent by 1995 (Pfeifer, 1999). As in Tunisia, unemployment disproportionately affected the young and educated, who found it increasingly difficult to secure public sector jobs due to government cuts (El Aoufi, 2000). As a result, organized labor lost the opportunity to recruit a new wave of workers, as many young job seekers were forced into the informal economy, where workers were often unprotected and unorganized (Aita, 2008, 76).

Summary

In sum, in both Tunisia and Morocco, structural adjustment had negative effects on organized labor. Privatization and liberalization cut jobs, while stabilization measures increased prices and reduced purchasing power for most of the working class. Labor code reforms also diminished social benefits and made employment opportunities more precarious. These developments thus gave unions in both countries strong incentives to oppose government policies. However, as I discuss in greater detail below, Tunisian and Moroccan unions responded to structural reforms in markedly different ways.

Labor's Response to Reform: Tacit Acceptance versus Political Militancy

Labor Opposition in Tunisia: Depoliticized Protest and the UGTT's "Own Structural Adjustment"

Despite harming organized labor, structural adjustment did not elicit a militant reaction from the UGTT. While peak union leaders occasionally criticized aspects of the government's reform program, they did not undertake systematic efforts to challenge these reforms or to mobilize against them. In sharp contrast to previous periods, union leaders facilitated reform efforts by organizing fewer labor protests and moderating wage and policy demands. In a 1993 interview, a member of the UGTT's executive bureau revealed the leadership's new conciliatory approach to reform:

> [The UGTT] must revise its conceptions to adapt to the new economic situation that it is confronting ... Old union organizations have gradually

abandoned their commitment to "class struggle" in order to adapt to a situation marked by unemployment, reductions in work, and ... the reduction of union activism (*Réalités*, 4/22/1993)

Nonetheless, acceptance of structural reforms by UGTT leaders did not reduce strike activity among the rank-and-file. According to official statistics, from 1986 to 1997 workers launched a total of 4,639 strikes, representing a 10.5 percent increase over the previous decade. This trend is corroborated by the data collected by this author – despite an official policy of moderation, the early years of structural adjustment saw some of the highest rates of strike activity in Tunisia's history (Figure 5.2).

However, labor militancy during structural adjustment differed from that of previous periods in three key ways. First, in contrast to the 1970s, strike activity was confined to individual plants, mainly involving blue-collar workers in recently privatized firms. Sectors with the highest levels of strike activity were those that faced the greatest threat from structural reform: textiles, apparel, public works,

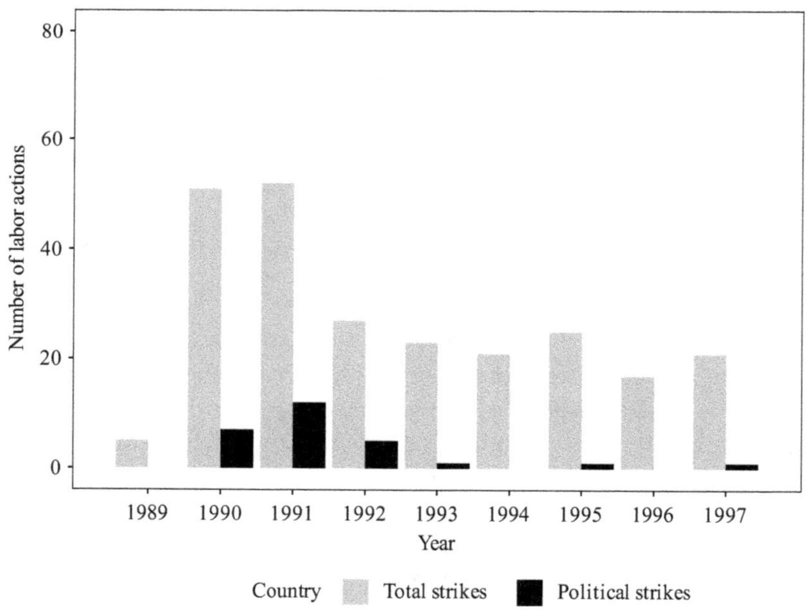

Source: MENALC Database

Figure 5.2 Labor protests in Tunisia, 1989–1997

and export-oriented manufacturing. Moreover, in contrast to the *infitah* period, this mobilization was not frequently accompanied by militancy from "intellectual" segments of the working class. Despite an increase in the number of solidarity strikes held during the period, labor mobilization failed to attract engagement from civil service employees or high-skilled workers. Out of the 238 strikes recorded, only 16 percent were held by workers in the public administration, reflecting the dissolution of the cross-sectoral coalition that fueled labor opposition during the *infitah* years.

Second, labor demonstrations were shorter than they had been in the previous period. Although some strikes went to for weeks, on average they lasted no more than three or four days before being called off by union officials. Moreover, reflecting the leadership's push for moderation, strikes were frequently organized by rank-and-file workers without approval from the central bureaucracy. At the national level, union executives refused to mobilize general strikes and forbade sectoral and regional strikes during economically sensitive periods (Appendix B: TU-39, 12/2/13). Most important, UGTT leaders discouraged cooperation between sub-national unions and social movement campaigns by enforcing "political neutrality" upon union members and leaders.

Finally, labor militancy during structural adjustment was distinguished by its lack of political engagement. Although workers organized a few political strikes, these mainly focused on foreign policy issues (i.e., the Gulf War, the Palestinian Intifada) and received explicit endorsement from the Ben Ali regime. As (Figure 5.3) shows, the majority of strikes held between 1987 and 1997 were centered on traditional economic or organizational issues. Three key issues gained prominence or were newly introduced to labor's agenda during the 1990s: organizational rights, employment issues, and opposition to economic reforms. These shifts reflect the transition from a command to a market-oriented economy and indicate extent of the UGTT's "own structural adjustment." By the mid-1990s, the political militancy that once defined the Tunisian labor movement had become a thing of the past. In addition to moderating their protest activity union leaders also gave tacit support to the Ben Ali regime's more authoritarian practices, such as curbing political opposition and suppressing the Movement of Islamic Tendency (*Mouvement Tendance Islamique*, MTI).

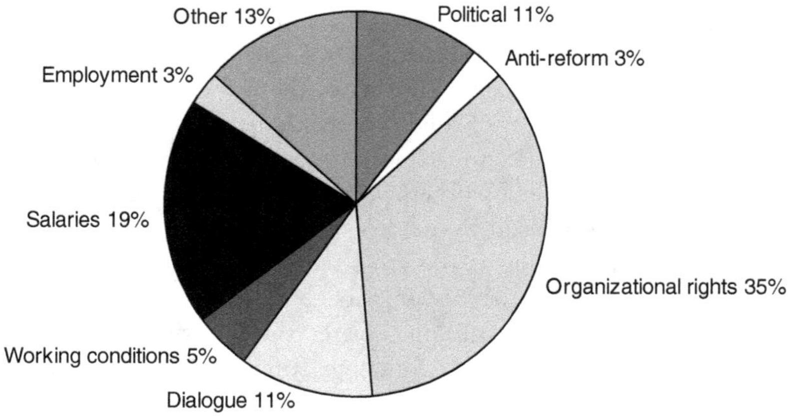

Source: MENALC Database

Figure 5.3 Labor protests in Tunisia by demand type, 1989–1997

Labor Opposition in Morocco: The Rise of Political Opposition

In contrast, in Morocco, organized labor exhibited stronger opposition to economic reforms. Labor mobilization unfolded in two distinct phases, reflecting the changing relationship between unions and the state and workers' growing dissatisfaction with neoliberal policies. In the first phase, lasting from 1983 to 1989, union mobilization was marked by "norm-based voice," where unions openly criticized reform measures but made little effort to actively mobilize against them. According to official statistics, strike activity declined significantly – between 1983 and 1989, workers participated in 1,632 strikes, a nearly 50 percent decrease compared to the previous five years (1977–1982). While this lull in labor militancy was occasionally punctuated by major unrest, such as the 1984 bread riots in Al Hoceima and Marrakesh, official unions remained largely uninvolved and confined their resistance to verbal critiques of government policy.

However, this period of relative labor quiescence did not last long. After several years of achieving small gains without overturning the regime's socioeconomic program, unions reversed their approach, significantly increasing the number of protests and strikes held through 1997 (Figure 5.4).

Alongside this increase in protest activity, labor militancy also underwent important qualitative changes. First, in contrast to the

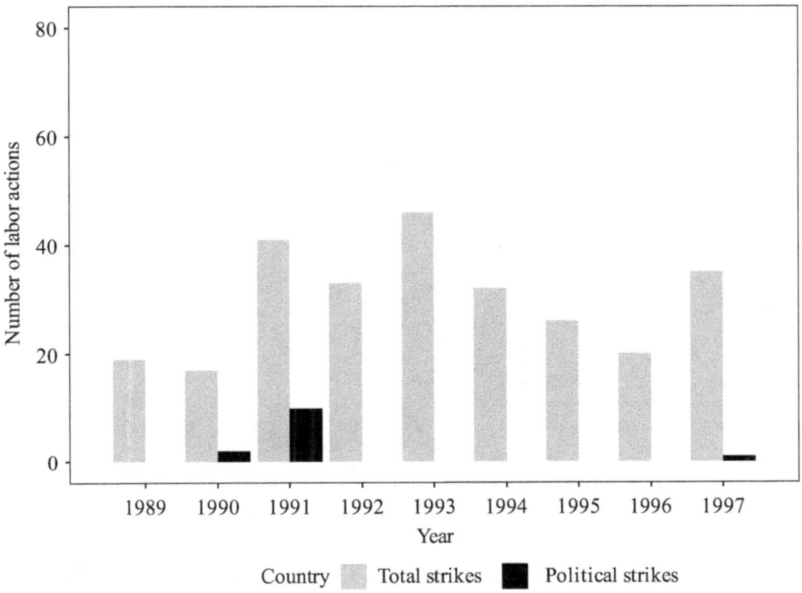

Source: MENALC Database

Figure 5.4 Labor protests in Morocco, 1989–1997

previous period, strikes became more dispersed across different sectors of the labor movement. While traditionally militant unions like the CDT continued their high levels of strike activity, more moderate unions, such as the UGTM and UMT, also displayed increased militancy (Figure 5.5). Moreover, strikes in the later years of reform exhibited an unprecedented degree of coordination across union federations. Notably, the UGTM and CDT regularly organized joint actions, and coordinated strike campaigns in key sectors such as education, transportation, and public health. In December 1990 and June 1996, this coordination culminated in two general strikes in which 60 percent of workers participated.

Finally, labor militancy during the structural adjustment period took on a more overtly political character. Although most labor demands remained focused on economic and organizational issues, such as salary increases and calls for tripartite negotiations, strikes by the CDT and UGTM were frequently supported by political parties and carried implicit political overtones. For example, a series of rolling strikes coordinated by the UGTM and CDT in 1993 criticized the government

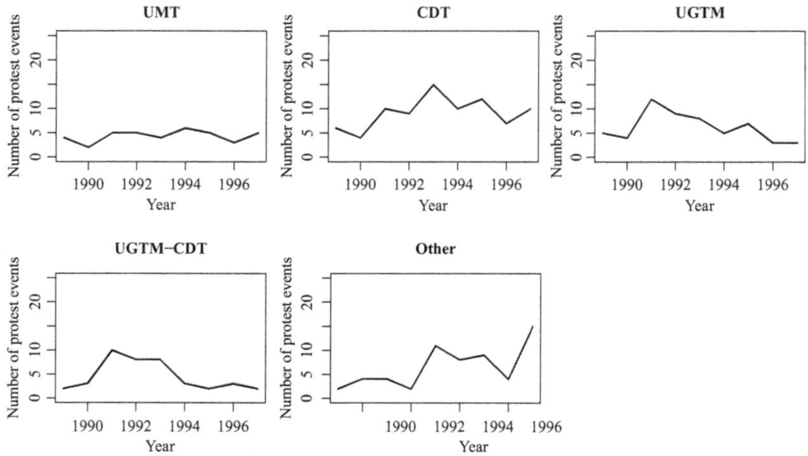

Figure 5.5 Labor protests in Morocco by federation, 1989–1997

for its "utter intransigence toward workers" and its willingness to "falsify popular will, violate public and individual liberties, and perpetuate poverty" (*Libération*, 02/11/1993). The timing of these strikes, just months before parliamentary elections, and the explicit support they received from the *Istiqlal* and USFP underscore the increasing politicization of the labor movement.

Explaining Labor's Divergent Responses: Existing Explanations

An analysis of labor's reaction to structural adjustment in Tunisia and Morocco presents a number of empirical puzzles that will be addressed in the remainder of this chapter. Why, in the face of economic policies that negatively impacted their constituents, did labor unions pursue different mobilization strategies compared to previous periods? What explains the increased willingness of union leaders in Tunisia to cooperate with the government's reforms while rank-and-file workers were less willing to follow suit? And, what accounts for the surge in labor militancy in Morocco during the 1990s, particularly the newfound cooperation between sectors of the labor movement?

For many observers of North African politics, the answers to these questions lie in labor's organizational conditions during structural adjustment. Several analyses suggest that labor was among the primary losers of market-oriented reforms (Forteza and Rama, 2006; Rudra, 2005). While privatization and budget cuts reduced union membership in the public sector, increased employment flexibility threatened labor interests more broadly (Djankov and Ramalho, 2009; Posusney and Cook, 2002). Therefore, neoliberal development policies are said to have undermined unions' traditional sources of power, effectively disabling them from launching concerted opposition to economic reforms.

In both Tunisia and Morocco, structural adjustment policies weakened labor's organizational capacity and, by extension, its ability to mobilize. In Tunisia, the emphasis on private sector growth fragmented labor solidarity by dispersing workers across small, spatially scattered firms and concentrating economic activity in sectors where the UGTT was traditionally weak (Alexander, 2002a). At the same time, budget cuts in the public sector targeted industries where labor had historically found its strongest base, while layoffs and rising unemployment further reduced the union's potential membership. Consequently, the UGTT saw its membership decline sharply from a high of 500,000 in 1977 to just 300,000 by 1993 (Upham, 1993; Waltz, 1984).

Similarly, in Morocco, neoliberal reforms weakened unions' organizational power by decreasing job security and discouraging workers from engaging in strikes. In the public and semi-public sectors, where the UGTM and CDT were concentrated, highly publicized layoffs underscored the precarious nature of employment, while hiring freezes decreased the possibility of re-entry into new jobs. Faced with high unemployment and shrinking membership, organized labor was structurally ill-positioned to mount effective opposition. According to membership figures reported in Trade Unions of the World, by 1989, Moroccan unions represented no more than 18 percent of Morocco's working-age population – and even this number is likely inflated (Upham, 1993; Appendix B: MA-22, 4/21/2014). As Alexander (1996b, 188) notes, for many union leaders, the realistic question was not "whether or not" to oppose reforms but how to modify them to suit labor's needs given its weakened organizational position.

Yet, while organizational conditions help to explain some elements of labor behavior, they cannot account for the full trajectory of labor protest witnessed in these two cases.Specifically, an emphasis on how neoliberal reforms eroded labor's structural power fails to explain the timing and location of labor opposition. If unions' weak structural position hindered their ability to strike, why did protests in Morocco increase in the early 1990s, when organized labor was at its weakest and unemployment was at an all-time high? Similarly, if sectors most threatened by structural adjustment are the least able to mobilize, why were blue-collar workers in Tunisia more likely to engage in militant protest to oppose neoliberal reforms?

Additional questions concern the characteristics of labor militancy itself. From a historical institutionalist perspective, Moroccan unions should have been less willing to mobilize against structural adjustment than their Tunisian counterparts, not more. If critical junctures "lock-in" patterns of behavior, Moroccan unions should have continued on their path of strategic moderation. Yet the opposite occurred – Moroccan unions expanded their protest agendas to include political demands and confrontational tactics, while Tunisian unions retreated from their previous political activism. What explains this surprising reversal of strategies?

Explaining Labor's Divergent Responses: The Consequences of Institutional Change

I argue that the answer to these questions lies in an assessment of the political institutions that governed labor and political representation during the structural adjustment period, and how these interacted with the state's development policies. In particular, I argue that two contrasting processes of institutional change – innovation and drift – generated novel incentives among union leaders for anti-regime contention, shifting their modes of mobilization in unexpected ways. In Tunisia, updates to existing institutions decentralized collective bargaining and introduced liberal political reforms meant to induce labor cooperation with the regime. These changes rehabilitated the UGTT, moderated wage negotiations, and incorporated labor and opposition elites more fully into the government's ruling coalition. By contrast in Morocco, shifts in the economic system that gave employers more control over labor institutions alienated unions from formal politics and produced shared grievances among previously divided members of the working class. In line with the theory presented in Chapter 2, these changes are expected to moderate labor opposition in Tunisia and produce greater cooperation between unions and the state, while radicalizing protest in Morocco.

Tunisia

Labor Quiescence in Tunisia: Co-optation and Innovation in Collective Bargaining

Although structural adjustment was initiated during the tenure of Habib Bourguiba, it wasn't until his successor, Zine El Abidine Ben Ali, took office that this economic transition was accompanied by significant institutional reforms. Much like Bourguiba, Ben Ali devoted the early years of his presidency to consolidating power and solidifying his regime. Coming to power on the heels of a "bloodless coup," Ben Ali quickly distinguished himself from his predecessor's exclusionary authoritarianism by promoting a new model of state–society relations grounded in consensus and dialogue. Central to this model was the creation of the 1988 Tunisian National Pact.

At its core, the National Pact aimed to solidify the regime's authority by uniting Tunisian society under a new inclusionary social contract. In its main sections, the document outlined several broad principles to guide the new Tunisia, including competitive elections, freedom of association, and the right to freely express one's opinions. Importantly, for the UGTT, the section on development laid the groundwork for a new corporatist bargain between labor and the state, which promised "broad participation of the masses in identifying the objectives and instruments of development" (Tunisian External Communication Agency, 1994, 14). As compensation for their contributions to development, workers would receive greater freedom to express their interests and a "fair distribution of the fruits of production" (ibid).

However, the National Pact was not the only element of Ben Ali's new state–labor bargain. To further demonstrate his commitment to incorporating organized labor, Ben Ali took direct steps to restore the UGTT to its former capacity as a dynamic national organization. As noted in Chapter 4, the union had been severely weakened as a result of government repression following the 1984 bread riots, which saw hundreds of militants arrested and the dismantling of the UGTT's leadership structures. Yet, in the early years of Ben Ali's rule, the UGTT experienced an unexpected revival due to several incorporative gestures initiated by the regime.

In 1988, Ben Ali signaled the beginning of harmony between the union and the regime by ordering the release of former trade union leader Habib Achour and pardoning hundreds of union activists imprisoned during the 1985 crackdown on the UGTT (Bellin, 2002, 116). Later that year, he announced the reinstatement of public sector workers dismissed for union activities and encouraged similar actions in the private sector (*Réalités*, 9/2/1998). Additionally, Ben Ali helped rescue the union from financial collapse by forgiving nearly TD 5 million in UGTT debts and returning control of two of its commercial properties, the Amilcar Hotel and Ettihad Insurance, to the UGTT's executive management (United States Department of Labor, 1989, 4). Politically, the regime expanded the union's role in the reinstated Economic and Social Council, which advised the government on the country's Seventh and Eighth development plans (United States Department of Labor, 1991, 4). Most significantly, under the guidance of a "reconciled" National Labor Commission, Ben Ali facilitated new union elections at the local, regional, federal, and national levels, restoring many former trade union leaders to their previous positions.

As Bellin (2002, 120) argues, it was this state-led restoration of the union that helped "prevent the UGTT from being the focal point of contestation [against the regime], as it had been in the 1970s." With the union's survival and vitality dependent on the regime's goodwill, labor leaders were far less inclined to challenge Ben Ali's economic agenda.

The Revitalized Collective Convention Cadre and the Pacification of Labor Militancy

However, beyond its organizational rehabilitation, another factor explains the UGTT's reluctance to challenge government reforms during this period. In an effort to restore the "social partnership" between capital, labor, and the state, the government introduced significant changes to the collective bargaining system, which made labor more willing to adopt a conciliatory stance despite the harsh effects of structural reforms on Tunisian workers.

In large part, these institutional changes resembled innovations from the 1973 *cadre convention collective* (CCC). Like the CCC, the new wage bargaining system provided a regularized means for labor representatives to engage in dialogue with employers and to influence policies affecting their constituents. By granting formal provisions for union representation at the plant level, the bargaining system reinforced the cadre's commitment to workers' rights within individual enterprises (Journal Officiel du Republique de la Tunisie, 1/20/1995).

However, in three critical ways, the new collective bargaining system improved upon the CCC, reducing leaders' incentives for labor militancy. First, the new system decentralized wage bargaining by involving labor representatives from the national and sectoral levels. As discussed in Chapter 4, a major drawback of the CCC was its extreme centralization, which limited the bargaining process to a few peak union leaders and increased uncertainty among sector representatives, who feared that the UGTT executive could not adequately advance their demands. During the 1970s and 1980s, this uncertainty drove federation leaders to organize sector-specific strikes to force union executives and employers to address their concerns.

To alleviate this pressure, the new collective bargaining framework granted sectoral representatives greater influence in tripartite negotiations. During the first round of negotiations in 1990, the government stipulated that all bargaining would occur between two four-person teams – one from the UGTT and one from UTICA – composed of representatives from relevant sectors. Although peak leaders retained control over setting general wage margins, federation leaders were responsible for all other aspects of collective agreements, such as determining pay scales, bonuses, and working conditions (Alexander, 1996a, 282). Should negotiations stall, a separate arbitration committee – comprising the secretaries-general of UTICA, the UGTT, and the Minister of Social Affairs – would be convened to resolve lingering issues. In this way, the system balanced the imperatives of both the union's intermediate and peak leadership, while ensuring the peak could still exert meaningful control over the bargaining process.

During the latter half of the structural adjustment period (1990–1996), this decentralized format was credited with liberalizing the social sphere and creating new opportunities for cooperation. In 1990, over 1,000 union cadres participated in wage talks – significantly more than the estimated three or four reported in 1983 (*Réalités*, 05/13/1993). Decentralization also allowed wages to better reflect differences in individual markets and sectoral bargaining power, decreasing incentives among stronger federations to use militancy to gain support (Alexander, 1996a; Appendix B: TU-35, 11/27/2013). Furthermore, centralized arbitration allowed weaker federations to rely on UGTT central leadership to lobby for wage increases in case of failed negotiations. For example, in 1993, textile and construction workers secured salary increases of roughly 10 percent thanks to the intervention of the UGTT central committee and government officials (*Réalités*, 04/29/1993).

In addition to reducing militancy within individual sectors, the government's revised bargaining system disincentivized confrontational behavior within the union's peak leadership. The establishment of accords-cadre between UGTT and UTICA leadership helped prevent gridlock by identifying and barring contentious issues from sectoral wage talks. For instance, in 1993, the accords-cadre helped resolve tensions between labor and business over salary increases and labor flexibility. While employers argued that wage hikes would cripple firms already struggling due to liberalization, labor representatives railed against employer initiatives to cut labor costs by increasing flexibility (*Réalités*, 02/11/1993).

In an effort to reach a compromise, the Ministry of Social Affairs allowed the UGTT to include controversial proposals – such as plant-level union rights, promotion protocols, and standards for workplace discipline – on the bargaining agenda, provided that the union "not demand a cent more" from struggling firms (Ismail Sahbani quoted in *Réalités*, 03/25/1993). While this agreement represented a "second-best" solution, the accords-cadre was credited with creating an important "convergence of interests" between the UGTT and UTICA and ensuring that sectoral negotiations proceeded on time (*Réalités*, 04/30/1993; Alexander, 1996a, 192).

Finally, the government extended the timeline of wage negotiations from one year to three years, addressing the problem of uncertainty created by the previous CCC system. Under the 1973 framework, annual wage bargaining exacerbated tensions between labor and business because employers could refuse to bargain during economic downturns, as occurred in 1978 and 1985. However, the new three-year timeline reassured both parties that their interests would be protected. While the timeline represented a compromise for both workers and employers,[2] three-year wage accords served the critical function of making wage accords more credible by extending both

[2] While UTICA complained that the timeline limited their flexibility, unions worried about its effect on purchasing power during inflationary periods (Appendix B: TU-44, 1/8/2014).

parties' time horizons. Additionally, the lengthier timeline gave unions meaningful assurances that their constituents' interests would be protected, even in the case of unexpected crises (Appendix B: TU-44, 1/8/2014).

This newfound stability was further reinforced by the government's and UTICA's commitment to honor the new negotiation timelines. In 1990, the decision to renegotiate all collective agreements merely after they were concluded, at the UGTT's request, demonstrated employers' willingness to make concessions in the name of promoting "social peace." Similarly, the government's decision to continue negotiations in 1993, despite financial upheavals from the Gulf War and slowing GDP growth, convinced union leaders that it was serious about its commitment to social dialogue and that it would uphold the corporatist bargain outlined in the National Pact (Appendix B: TU-5, 10/3/2013). Indeed, the state acted as a neutral arbiter during contract negotiations in 1993, at times intervening to secure better benefits for workers than they had received in the past[3] (Alexander, 1996a, 202). Thus, despite the weakening of unions' structural power during structural adjustment, the institutionalization of labor participation in wage bargaining reduced labor militancy by providing greater assurances that workers' interests would be protected. As a result, union leaders praised these new institutions in the press, crediting them with improving state–labor relations (UGTT, 1995).

Taken together, institutional innovations in Tunisia's collective bargaining system, coupled with the government's willingness to ensure their proper functioning, played a crucial role in incentivizing moderation among national and sectoral union officials during structural reform. Extended accord timelines diffused conflicts over the state's and employers' credibility, while expanded participation in wage talks addressed wage disparities and reduced the need for sectoral strikes. Although base-level strikes continued, they were largely aimed at strengthening unions' bargaining position rather than organizing coordinated campaigns, as had been done in the 1970s and 80s. For many leaders, such militancy was unnecessary, given Tunisia's more inclusive bargaining environment. As one union executive remarked,

[3] According to Alexander (1996a), following the refusal of the Finance Minister to negotiate wage accords in the banking and finance sector, Ben Ali personally intervened to win members of the General Union of Banking and Finance a better wage deal than it had been able to negotiate in 1990.

> The sincerity and engagement on the part of militants has not changed. On the contrary, it is the social and political situation that has changed ... With different social partners, dialogue is fruitful, that is what explains the numerous accords signed and the better working conditions that have existed since 1989 until today. It is also what explains the revisions of collective conventions and salary increases that have been obtained over the past six years ... the union movement is conscious of the challenges that face our country and that require increased cohesion and national solidarity. (Mohamed Trabelsi quoted in *Réalités*, 04/13/1995)

Depoliticization of Labor Protest in Tunisia: The Specter of Incorporation

In addition to adopting more moderate tactics than they had in previous periods, union leaders also displayed less militant attitudes toward the state and the Ben Ali regime. In contrast to labor activism in the 1970s and 1980s, which linked economic grievances to broader political struggles, union opposition to structural reforms was largely devoid of political concerns. While issues like arbitrary layoffs and associational rights remained key priorities, union leaders framed these concerns in purely economic terms, without linking them to systemic political issues. In part, this reflected the changes in the relationship between organized labor and the state following the new framework for social dialogue. Yet, in larger part, this shift was influenced by broader institutional changes that reshaped the union's relationship with political organizations and its own internal dynamics.

Political Liberalization and the Collapse of the UGTT-Leftist Alliance

Upon his assumption of the presidency, Ben Ali worked to recast Tunisia's political landscape in a more inclusive and participatory mold. Recognizing that the strength of the Bourguiba regime lay in its corporatist character, Ben Ali aimed to restore linkages between the state and national organizations while incorporating new political interests into the regime. Unlike his predecessor, Ben Ali saw political liberalization as key to the success of modern corporatism and, coincidentally, an externally oriented development strategy. Thus, in the National Pact, the government positioned Tunisia as "a state of law and institutions" built upon the principles of democracy, pluralism, and "the legitimate right to difference which signifies neither sedition nor division" (Tunisian External Communication Agency, 1994, 14). To demonstrate his commitment to these ideals, Ben Ali initiated his tenure by instituting a number of political reforms, including the release of prominent opposition figures, easing press restrictions, and revoking provisions that established the "presidency-for-life."

The government's new liberal orientation was further evident in two key areas of institutional reform: restructuring the ruling party and reforming the electoral system. Early in his presidency, Ben Ali reorganized the PSD to attract a wider range of political perspectives. In February 1988, he renamed the party to the Democratic Constitutional Rally (*Rassemblement Constitutionnel Démocratique*, RCD), signaling his personal commitment to democratic reforms. An extraordinary party congress held later that year brought opposition elites and party members together to discuss the revision of party statutes and broader political transformations promised by the government. In preparation for this event, RCD elites launched a massive recruitment drive aimed at younger members to rejuvenate the party and reform its ideology. According to official sources, this effort was largely successful: by the end of Ben Ali's first year, the proportion of new members in RCD cells had risen by 60 percent, and the average age of party delegates had dropped to the mid-thirties (Anderson, 1991, 251). Additionally, Ben Ali expanded the RCD's central committee from 90 to 200 members, replacing much of the PSD's conservative old guard with younger members from Tunisia's emerging business elite (Murphy, 1999, 210). These changes helped convince the secular opposition of the regime's credible commitment to liberalization, bringing some of the more liberal PSD-defectors, like Hamouda Ben Slama (MDS) and Habib Boulares (Independent), back into the party's ranks.

In addition to restructuring the RCD, the regime also reformed the electoral system to allow for more political competition. In November 1988, the government moved up presidential and legislative elections to April 1989 and amended the electoral law to grant legal recognition to most opposition parties. Along with increasing the number of seats in the National Assembly from 125 to 141, this improved the opposition's chances for political representation. To further ease barriers to competition, the government permitted opposition parties to distribute voting cards and approved the legalization of several opposition-run media outlets.[4]

It is important to note that by implementing these reforms, Ben Ali was not building a truly competitive democracy. Instead, much like the National Pact, his vision of democracy emphasized liberalism and political expression while limiting their exercise in the service of consensus. Notably, the regime did not concede to the opposition's principal demand: changing the majoritarian electoral system. Instead, to assuage fears that his reforms would not be enough to help them secure political office, Ben Ali created an independent commission to oversee the elections and offered opposition parties the chance to field candidates on a coalition list with the RCD.

Nonetheless, Ben Ali's liberal reforms, cast as they were in the language of democracy and inclusion, significantly undermined the political alliance between the leftist opposition and the UGTT. For leftist elites who rejoined the RCD, the restoration of participatory mechanisms within the party provided a new space to discuss their political perspectives and advocate for future reforms (Appendix B: TU-31, 11/20/2013). For others, legal recognition of their parties made the strategy of working within the UGTT to advance their political demands obsolete. As a former syndicalist and member of the Socialist Rally for Progress (now Republican Party) explained, "In the generation [of liberal democracy] everyone could have their own mission – political parties could focus on political issues, unions on labor issues, human rights groups on human rights … there was no need for confusion between politics and syndicalism" (Appendix B: TU-33, 11/21/2013).

As a consequence, the UGTT's political activism quickly deteriorated. With leftist elites no longer using the union as a platform for political expression, most rank-and-file workers shifted their focus to

[4] As part of his "Historic Change," Ben Ali relaxed bans on the sale of opposition journals Al-Moustaqbal (MDS), Tarik el-Jedid (Communist Party), and Sawt-Echaab (Tunisian Worker's Communist Party, PCOT) (Report, January-February 1988, 8). In 1990, a second set of opposition papers – Al-Badil (PCOT) and Al-Watan (Democratic Unionist Union) – began publication (Chouikha and Labidi, 1992, 101–103). However, the regime also repressed critical press outlets, withdrawing copies of Al-Mawqif and Realités (independent) when they critiqued the government too harshly (Alexander, 2010, 55).

economic concerns, neglecting to link these issues to broader deficiencies within the regime. Moreover, since most of the union's peak and intermediate leadership was co-opted, no figure emerged who was willing to advocate for political reforms. Indeed, the combination of state repression and co-optation eliminated most of the radical left from positions of power – at the 1993 UGTT national congress leftist unionists comprised only 10 percent of the total number of delegates, compared to 25 percent at the national congress just four years before (*La Presse*, 12/15/1993).

Elite Incorporation and the Retreat from Union Democracy

Finally, internal changes within the UGTT's bureaucracy further contributed to its depoliticization. In order to protect its corporatist bargain with the regime, the union's leadership distanced itself from its grassroots base. In the lead-up to the UGTT's 1989 national congress, the National Labor Commission approved fewer than 50 percent of base union elections, leaving federations from traditionally militant regions underrepresented among congressional delegates (Table 5.1). At the national level, "*chourafa*" unionists collaborated with the regime to remove radical members from electoral ballots by claiming that these members had not submitted their candidacy by the appropriate deadline. Even for those militants who did make it onto electoral lists, the union leadership – in collaboration with the RCD – deliberately undermined their success by making them the subject of smear campaigns in the national press[5] and preventing their supporters from reaching the voting floor (*La Presse*, 04/15/1989; *Le Temps*, 04/22/1989). As a result, union elections that reinstated "legitimate" labor activists to the UGTT's leadership actually solidified the union's subordination to the regime, as many leaders owed their positions to government intervention.

Under the leadership of Ismail Sahbani (1989–1999), the union further weakened its ties to the rank-and-file by centralizing authority around the executive bureau. To begin, the executive bureau

[5] For example, the candidate list led by Ali Romdhane was decried as an Islamist list despite including only one candidate – Mokhtar Belhaj Khelifa – with alleged ties to the Movement of Islamic Tendency. Similarly, three independent candidates (Mustapha Kenzari, Habib Ben Achour, and Sadok Allouche) withdrew their candidacy due to the "personal and egoistic" attacks launched against their running mates (*La Presse*, 04/15/1989; *Le Temps*, 04/22/1989).

Table 5.1. ***Delegates to the 1989 UGTT Congress***

Governorate	No. of mandated delegates	No. of delegates present
Tunis*	204	140
Zaghouan	8	4
Bizerte	30	26
Beja	13	13
Jendouba	16	14
Kef	13	13
Siliana	7	7
Gafsa	45	45
Kasserine	12	12
Sidi Bouzid	7	7
Gabès	17	13
Tozeur	6	6
Medenine	20	19
Sfax*	45	12
Monastir	21	17
Mahdia	5	5
Kairouan*	11	7
Sousse*	36	29
Nabeul	28	28
Total	**544**	**417**

Sources: Le Temps 5/1/1989
Note: Militant unions indicated with an asterisk

expanded the powers of the Office of Interior Regulation and Disciplinary Committee to dismiss militant unionists for "indiscipline" and "bad behavior," a tactic that was used to purge the UGTT of its Islamist membership in 1989 (Appendix B: TU-43, 12/13/2013). During the 1990s, these provisions were used to curb the militancy of traditionally political federations and to eliminate left-leaning unionists from their positions at the regional and sectoral levels.[6] Occasionally, such measures were directed against prominent members

[6] Three leaders of the Nabeul regional union were expelled from their positions for having voted out their secretary-general, who was a protégé of Ismail Sahbani. In a similar fashion, a prominent leader in the Post, Telegraph and

of the UGTT's central administration who sympathized with militant factions or otherwise challenged the secretary-general's hold on power.[7]

Additionally, the central leadership modified bureaucratic statutes to weaken base-level unions and reduce rank-and-file workers' capacity to strike. In 1989, the executive bureau upheld a regulatory provision requiring that central administration approve strikes in order for them to be considered legitimate. That same year, amendments to union dues collection procedures centralized financial control by requiring dues, previously collected by base unions, to be transferred to the UGTT headquarters in Tunis. Funds would be allocated to regional unions based on need, following formal requests (Appendix B: TU-11, 10/17/2013). According to regional leaders, the procedures for requesting such monies were cumbersome, and allocations to militant unions were frequently denied by union executive (ibid; Appendix B: TU-42, 12/11/2013). Consequently, labor activism in militant regions languished, with some unions lacking sufficient funds to hold regular meetings or to mobilize their members.

Most notably, in contrast to previous periods, members of the union executive actively intervened in regional and local elections, undermining democratic procedures during the UGTT's National Congress. In collaboration with the RCD, UGTT officials created disciplinary committees that vetted candidates, expelled critics, and limited local constituencies' ability to elect or sanction their own executive bureaus. In one of the more dramatic examples of the union's authoritarian turn, votes for the executive leadership during the 1993 Congress were tallied by a show of hands, a practice which had previously been used to confirm "*chourafa*" candidates when the PSD manipulated union elections. As a result, from 1989 to 1997, only five of the unions' top sixty leaders were voted out of office.[8] Under the domination of a co-opted and autocratic leadership, oppositional voices within the union were effectively silenced. Henceforth, the UGTT executive committed itself to a policy of "social stability" by supporting the government's

Telecommunications Federation was transferred out of Tunis because his federation had organized a strike (Hamzaoui, 1999, 375).

7 For example, Abdelmajid Sahraoui, Abdennouar Maddahi, and Ahmed Ben Remila were all removed from the Executive Bureau for their disagreements with the Secretary-General (Hamzaoui, 1999, 375).

8 Author's calculation based on Database of Tunisian Union Leaders.

initiatives to maintain its privileged position within the Ben Ali regime.

Summary

This shift in the UGTT's mobilization strategy – from radical political militancy to tacit cooperation – poses a number of challenges for existing theories of labor politics. Contrary to standard economic accounts, the UGTT did not mobilize significant opposition when threatened by neoliberal reforms, nor were the most vulnerable workers (i.e., the rank-and-file) completely passive in the face of austerity measures. In addition, the shift from militancy to moderation confounds comparative historical accounts that stress the enduring effects of political institutions on labor behavior. If early institutional choices "lock in" stable patterns of labor politics, why did the UGTT's response to neoliberal reforms suddenly change?

In the preceding discussion, I have argued that a thorough explanation of the shift in labor militancy requires a focus on unions' political relationship with the state and the consequences of institutional change. After coming to power in 1987, Ben Ali introduced innovations to the collective bargaining and political system in Tunisia, moderating union's response to reforms. On the industrial side, the government revised the CCC to include previously marginalized sectors of the union hierarchy, and lengthened the time horizon of wage accords to provide better assurances to workers and labor elites. On the political front, the inclusionary character of the Ben Ali regime permitted partisan elites to maneuver within the political system, upending the previous alliance between the UGTT and Tunisia's leftist elite.

The Tunisian case thus confirms the inverse relationship proposed in Chapter 2 between labor militancy and institutional incorporation. Since the UGTT's executive bureau was co-opted by the state, and opposition parties were incorporated into the government, the union retreated from its former militancy, opting instead to work within the institutional structures of the state. At the same time, institutional incorporation of labor elites spurred organizational changes that distanced rank-and-file workers from union leaders and subverted traditional mechanisms of mobilization (i.e., regional autonomy and union democracy). The evolution of state–labor relations in Tunisia would differ dramatically from that witnessed in Morocco, as I discuss in greater detail below.

Morocco

Labor Militancy in Morocco: Institutional Drift and the Challenges with Decentralization

In contrast to Tunisia, Morocco's implementation of structural adjustment was not accompanied by significant institutional reforms. Because government officials believed that decentralized negotiations were still the most efficient means to address workers' concerns, they introduced no new mechanisms for collective bargaining and kept the personnel delegate system in tact. As discussed in Chapter 4, during the initial phase of economic reform, the personnel delegate system kept union militancy locked in a delicate balance – while delegate elections incentivized competitive striking among rival unions, they also checked this militancy by allowing employers to use their discretion over worker delegate seats to reward moderate unions and punish militant ones. On the national front, the spirit of consensus fostered by Hassan II in the wake of the Saharan War helped to rally social forces around the regime, limiting the potential for militant labor mobilization.

During the early years of structural adjustment, these factors – combined with deliberate inducements from the state – continued to suppress labor opposition to economic reforms. Personnel delegate elections held in 1983 reinforced existing rivalries among unions, facilitating the government's use of divide-and-rule strategies to weaken labor protests. Unlike the 1977 elections, in which the UMT won a majority of worker delegate seats, the 1983 elections saw significant gains made by the UGTM and CDT, who won majorities in key public enterprises and gained two and three seats in the Moroccan parliament, respectively. In the short term, the weakening of the UMT's dominance hindered labor mobilization by elevating tensions between the UMT and CDT, whose leaders the UMT accused of breaking away to undermine its representative hegemony (Appendix B: MA-33, 5/15/2014).

Additionally, the government's reluctance to implement economic reforms helped to temporarily stave off labor opposition. Despite early recommendations by the IMF to implement privatization to reduce redundancies in the public sector, the government delayed such measures until 1989, with the first privatizations beginning in earnest in 1993. Similarly, labor code reforms were postponed to avoid antagonizing unions that openly opposed the IMF's calls for increased flexibility. Finally, favorable harvests allowed the government to provide fresh inducements for organized labor in the form of salary increases in the civil service and the minimum wage. As a result, for much of the early structural adjustment period, state–labor relations remained in a stable equilibrium. While unions criticized aspects of the government's economic program, they limited their resistance to norm-based voice and confined their demands to the institutional structures of the state.

State Retrenchment and Institutional Drift

By the late 1980s, however, continued economic deterioration and new structural reforms disrupted this balance in two key ways. First, additional budget cuts curtailed the government's ability to provide labor unions with sufficient benefits to maintain their quiescence. In 1986, restrictions on government spending under the SAP prevented the creation of 22,000 new jobs, while subsidy removals disproportionately impacted the poorest workers (Moutadayene, 2001; Seddon, 1987). Moreover, effective wage freezes eroded workers' purchasing power in the civil sector. According to a USAID report, per capita incomes in Morocco dropped by 19 percent from 1981 to 1988, while public sector salaries decreased by some 200 percent relative to the minimum wage (ibid).

Second, the state's gradual retrenchment from the public sector reduced its control over industrial relations. In the 1970s, the government played a critical role in mediating labor disputes, with provincial governors overseeing conciliation commissions and labor inspectors ensuring compliance with national labor regulations. However, in the context of declining government spending, such robust intervention became untenable. By 1993, Morocco had fewer than 200 labor inspectors, rendering the Ministry of Labor incapable of monitoring workers' conditions outside of a small number of public firms (Appendix B: MA-2, 2/17/2014). Additionally, employers began demanding more control over the management of employee relations within their enterprises. To adapt to changing economic conditions, they argued, managers needed greater flexibility to initiate layoffs, replace permanent workers with temporary ones, and determine their own pay and promotion criteria. Although the government avoided agreeing to these demands in order to prevent labor opposition, it informally struck a deal with employers to reduce its oversight of personnel decisions within certain firms.

Consequently, in the later years of structural adjustment, mechanisms for labor representation and negotiation fell into decline. To a greater extent than in previous periods, employers used their expanded authority to dismiss workers for engaging in union activity under the pretext of "financial difficulties" or "enterprise restructuring" (Douieb, 1987, 1). In multiple firms, managers violated workers' rights by failing to implement collective agreements or refusing to meet with workers' designated representatives. In an emblematic case of labor suppression, managers at state-run sugar refineries unilaterally implemented wage provisions from a previous 1975 agreement without consulting personnel delegates (ICFTU, 1991). At the same time, the failure to convene labor tribunals left workers with few avenues to address grievances outside of the shop floor. In the latter half of the structural adjustment period, labor inspectors rarely intervened to enforce consultation among workers and employers, and court cases to challenge arbitrary firings were often lengthy and prohibitively expensive (United States Department of State, 1994, 1).

The Coalescing of Labor Opposition

This subversion of labor institutions had profound effects on the labor movement, from the shop floor to the union central. For workers, employer abuses and the erosion of dialogue exacerbated their grievances and increased uncertainty. The withdrawal of the state from industrial relations empowered employers to use collective dismissals to evade mechanisms for labor representation. Additionally, the failure to accompany employer autonomy with new tripartite bargaining institutions left workers without assurances that their interests would be protected in the long term. Employers routinely skirted labor regulations, and increasingly relied on temporary employees to cut costs, undermining the credibility of previous labor agreements (Harrison and Islam, 1993; *L'Opinion*, 4/29/1990). One private sector worker captured the growing frustration with the absence of dialogue:

> The private sector has initiated a systematic anti-union policy that tries to annihilate all union organizations by firing and persecuting all who wish to create a force to defend workers ... it is to counteract the offensive

of the employers which is facilitated by the unpopular choices of the government that the working class mobilizes. (*Al-Bayane* 1/20/1987)

It is important to note that, in contrast to the previous period, opposition to employer abuses was not limited to the CDT. In their efforts to curtail labor activism, employers targeted union members across the labor spectrum, including traditionally moderate unions like the UGTM and UMT. In 1990, 190 members of the UGTM's tourism federation were dismissed from Sahara Tours after management refused to negotiate wage revisions (*L'Opinion*, 3/9/1991). Similarly, in 1994, the UMT reported the dismissal of 20 union officials in Casablanca following trade union elections (ICFTU, 1995). From 1990 to 1996, unions other than the CDT lodged thirty-five complaints with the ILO about employer violations, ranging from refusal to honor collective agreements and harassment of unionized employees.[9]

Consequently, in the new era of structural adjustment, even unions that had previously benefited from the personnel delegate system had reasons to oppose it. Trapped in enterprises where managers could bypass workers' assemblies and neglect their demands, formerly quiescent unions had sufficient cause to challenge existing labor arrangements and upend the status quo. As a result, strike activity quickly spread across multiple sectors, including traditionally moderate unions in white-collar professions and the civil service. Furthermore, by closing off opportunities for unionists of all types, employers weakened their ability to use divide-and-rule strategies to preempt labor solidarity, laying the groundwork for collective action among once-rival trade unions.

Additionally, for peak labor leaders, the intensification of structural adjustment tested the depth of their loyalty to the regime. As patronage resources dwindled due to declining budgets, union leaders lost the ability to control their constituents, while the monarchy had fewer levers to co-opt labor elites. The frequent harassment of union officials at local and federal levels also alienated intermediate labor leaders and spurred an increase in regional- and sector-wide strikes. Most important, the failure of the monarchy's decentralized bargaining

[9] Author's calculation based on ICFTU (1990–1996).

system highlighted the need for more formal, centralized mechanisms for negotiation. To recoup their losses at the firm level, union representatives in parliament demanded a greater role in designing institutional safeguards that could minimize the costs of reform borne by workers. Specifically, union leaders wanted to help the government develop a Tunisian-style bargaining system that would preserve union rights at the plant level while establishing new institutions for collective bargaining and conflict resolution at the shop floor, federation, and peak.

Union leaders' frustration with the state of labor affairs was evident in their pointed critiques of the regime. At its 1986 national congress, the CDT denounced the government's economic plan, claiming that its reliance on the IMF was "mortgaging the country's future" at the expense of political and trade union rights (Santucci, 1988). In a 1989 press release, the executive bureau of the UGTM condemned the Laraki government for deepening the social crisis, accusing the monarchy of having "lost its credibility" by siding with capitalists over workers (*L'Opinion*, 2/23/1989). Even the UMT, while more restrained in its critique, called out the monarchy for having adopted an economic program without engaging in sufficient dialogue with unions beforehand to reduce its social costs. Speaking before the Regional African Association, UMT secretary-general Mahjoub Benseddik stressed the need for labor participation in policymaking, demanding that unions "be present in all national policy discussions, including those with the World Bank and IMF" to develop policies that more directly "conform to the aspirations of the working class" (*L'Économiste*, 10/13/1994).

As relations with the government deteriorated, union leaders increasingly saw strikes as the only viable means to voice labor demands. The government's reluctance to establish national bargaining institutions, coupled with the economic hardships of structural adjustment, reinforced the perception that confrontational tactics were necessary to force the government to address labor concerns. The UGTM emphasized this rationale in a 1990 press release, citing the government's lack of cooperation as a key driver of labor militancy:

> We are in an institutional state: [the] government, which does not cooperate with other institutions, cannot, in public opinion, manage its affairs correctly. These are thus the two reasons which motivate the militant in favor of the call to strike. (*Al-Alam* 11/29/1990)

Similarly, the CDT cited the absence of social dialogue as the primary justification for its 1994 general strike:[10]

> When the paths for social dialogue have been blocked off by the will of the executive, when arbitrary dismissals have sharply risen, when the social partners are the last concern for those directing public policies ... there is only one choice left: militancy. (*Libération*, 02/18/1994)

Labor Politicization in Morocco: Government Exclusion and the Rise of the "Kutla"

The uncertainties generated by employer abuses within Morocco's personnel delegate system shed light on the growth in strike activity over the course of structural adjustment. They also help to explain why previously divided segments of the labor movement began to display greater cohesion in their platforms and agendas. However, they do not account for the politicization of labor protests or the increased collaboration between the UGTM and CDT. What changed to make these unions more willing to engage in political militancy in the early 1990s?

To answer this question, I argue that we must turn our attention to broader political changes that took place in Morocco after 1989. As noted in the previous chapter, a key mechanism that the monarchy used to contain political opposition was the selective incorporation of union leaders into formal institutions. By giving unions and their partisan partners seats in the legislature, the monarchy effectively channeled labor opposition into formal politics, as unions found it more efficient to express their demands through inter-elite bargaining than in the streets.

In the early years of structural adjustment, the monarchy once again employed incorporative tactics to stave off social and political challenges. To co-opt the USFP-CDT bloc, Hassan II appointed USFP leader Abderrahim Bouabid as minister of state in 1983. Additionally, to maintain the loyalty of parties already incorporated into the regime, he expanded ministerial portfolios for *Istiqlal* and re-integrated party leaders with ties to the UMT into his executive council.

[10] In February 1994, the CDT called for a general strike in response to the government's delay in beginning social dialogue negotiations that it had promised in 1992. However, after the government declared the intended strike illegal, and King Hassan II responded publicly to the unions' demands, the strike was postponed to a later date.

Initially, these appointments kept unions from mobilizing against the government's economic reforms. Though most unions opposed price hikes and public sector cuts, they were reluctant to organize protests for fear of inviting repression and losing their remaining opportunities for institutional voice within the regime (Appendix B: MA-25, 5/5/2014). This was especially true for the CDT, which had suffered the most from state repression following its 1981 general strike. Labor-affiliated parties also cautioned against labor militancy, hoping to increase their chances of success in the 1984 parliamentary elections (Appendix B: MA-19, 4/9/2014). Thus, in the early years of structural adjustment, unions adopted a nuanced approach to neoliberal reforms. While they publicly condemned the regime's structural adjustment policies, they refrained from challenging the SAP with a general strike, agreeing to accept austerity measures on the condition that workers would not be unduly burdened.

Elections and Exclusion

Yet if labor and opposition elites believed that cooperation with the government's agenda would help them to expand their political presence in the regime, they were quickly disappointed. In 1983, long-awaited municipal elections were marred by discrimination and fraud, benefiting regime-backed parties at the expense of the USFP and *Istiqlal*. New electoral rules that redrew several districts limited the influence of urban-based parties by increasing the number of voters necessary to obtain a council seat (García, 2000, 86). As a result, urban constituencies accounted for only 11.6 percent of seats on the municipal councils, while rural districts, where loyalist parties dominated, retained significant weight.[11] Additionally, opposition candidates faced routine harassment and complained of irregularities at the ballot box. According to allegations by the *Istiqlal*, government officials tampered with results before making them public, undermining the legitimacy of the municipal councils – and the one-third of parliamentary members they would elect (*Le Monde*, 6/24/1983; *L'Opinion*, 06/23/1983).

[11] 83.3 percent of seats were filled in rural areas even though only 68.6 percent of registered voters resided in these constituencies. Ultimately, this disproportionality benefited rural-based parties such as the National Rally of Independents and the Popular Movement.

The 1984 parliamentary elections yielded similar results. Despite marginally increasing their seat share from 1977, the USFP and *Istiqlal* still lagged behind pro-monarchy parties, ranking fourth and fifth, respectively, in seats gained in the House of Representatives.[12] Accusations of vote manipulation, including allegations that the government bought unused ballots and inserted its preferred candidates, marred the election's credibility (Santucci, 1986, 908). In one district, elections observers recorded 500 votes for loyalist parties, even though only 115 votes had actually been cast (García, 2000, 149). As a consequence, unions' influence in the government was significantly weakened. In addition to diminishing the size and strength of their parliamentary blocs, elections also resulted in a cabinet that was composed almost entirely of pro-regime candidates.

This marginalization gave unions and opposition elites clear incentives to mobilize protests as a means of making their voices heard (Appendix B: MA-4, 2/19/2014; MA-19, 4/9/2014). However, three factors hindered mobilization in the short term. First, the ongoing conflict in Western Sahara continued to preoccupy the country, limiting the opposition's capacity for protest. Framing the conflict as a national security issue, the monarchy positioned dissent during wartime as a treasonous act, discouraging opposition parties and unions from taking militant action (ibid).

Second, domestic unrest triggered by structural adjustment also hindered mobilization. In January 1984, a series of violent riots broke out in the northern and southern regions of Morocco in response to proposed austerity measures in the 1984 budget. Unlike the 1981 protests, these demonstrations were not led by institutionalized social actors; instead, unorganized social movements and radical Islamist groups capitalized on public discontent to stoke opposition against the regime (Seddon, 1986). The unrest that followed – which included weeks of rioting and up to 200 deaths – showed both the monarchy and the legal opposition that radical forces could channel popular grievances in ways that neither could control (Lust-Okar, 2004). Thus, despite experiencing some repression, the opposition rallied behind the regime, hoping to contain the spread of Islamist influence (Appendix B: MA-19, 4/9/2014, Appendix B: MA-20, 4/14/2014).

12 In indirect elections, however, the *Istiqlal* managed to surpass the total seat share of the USFP, winning seventeen indirect seats to the USFP's one (García, 2000).

Finally, parties and unions suffered from internal divisions that weakened their ability to oppose the regime. Debates about the benefits of collaborating with the monarchy created rifts between parties that hampered unified action (Bras, 1991, 611–616). Particularly within the USFP/CDT bloc, public conflicts threatened to split the group into separate factions. While soft-line USFP parliamentarians, led by Abderrahim Bouabid, believed collaboration was the best path forward, CDT militants favored opposition, leading to heated debates between Bouabid and CDT secretary-general Noubir Amaoui (Appendix B: MA-4, 2/19/2014).

Nevertheless, by the late 1980s, opposition and labor elites recognized the need to put pressure on the regime, lest they remain in an unacceptably stifling position (Appendix B: MA-4, 2/19/2014; MA-19, 4/9/2014; MA-34, 5/14/2014). Two changes in the political environment paved the way for a shift in unions' strategies. In 1987, cuts in government spending reduced military funding for the Western Sahara, prompting the regime to seek a more peaceful resolution to the conflict. Additionally, successful repression of radical activists after the 1984 riots reduced public fears of the Islamist opposition, while exacerbating tensions between the monarchy and opposition parties that suffered from intense human rights violations and arrests (Appendix B: MA-19, 4/9/2014).

More important, the government's own actions solidified the opposition's belief that militant action was necessary. In 1988, a parliamentary by-election resulted in an overwhelming victory for the Constitutional Union,[13] prompting renewed accusations of government manipulation and fraud. The same year, the opposition accused the monarchy of undermining parliament by removing controversial bills from public debate and excluding foreign policy issues from the legislative agenda. In 1989, fears about exclusion deepened when the King requested parliament to approve the postponement of legislative elections, citing the need to allow the situation in the Western Sahara to improve. While opposition parties agreed to this demand, USFP members were angered by what they perceived to be an attempt to prolong the pro-monarchy parliamentary majority and preclude their access to power (Lust-Okar, 2004). Finally, the regime's unilateral

[13] The Constitutional Union is a pro-monarchy party founded by Maati Bouabid in 1983. It is alleged to have been created with the support of King Hassan II (Cavatorta et al., 2020).

ratification of the 1989 Privatization Law and 1990 Finance Law highlighted its willingness to circumvent institutionalized channels for dialogue (*L'Opinion*, 12/7/1989).

For the opposition, these events demonstrated that the government was no longer committed to incorporating them into its ruling coalition, nor to creating a political system in which their voices could be heard. Fearing continued marginalization, opposition elites began to collaborate in order to present a united front against the regime. Initially, such alliance-building was loosely organized and occurred exclusively among party elites. At a party congress in July 1987, PPS secretary-general Ali Yata called for pro-democratic forces to unite under a common program for "national salvation," mirroring the *Kutla-al-Wataniya*[14] of the 1970s. In response, the USFP and *Istiqlal* issued joint declarations supporting the idea of shared proposals for constitutional reform and encouraging social mobilization for political change. In the following years, coordination between these groups produced sporadic cooperation on a series of draft laws. However, the degree of cohesion within the alliance remained low due to disputes over political ambitions[15] and the prospect of participation from the Organization of Popular Democratic Action (*Organisation de l'Action Démocratique Populaire*, OADP) and the UMT.

The Consolidation of the Kutla and the Politicization of Moroccan Labor

The turning point in opposition mobilization occurred in May 1990, when the government convened an extraordinary parliamentary session to ratify the 1990 Finance Law. Aimed at addressing Morocco's ongoing debt crisis, the law proposed more stringent austerity measures, including a 15 percent reduction in state spending, devaluation of the dirham, and a transfer of social sector expenses to the municipal level. The opposition, led by the USFP and *Istiqlal*, vehemently opposed these reforms, criticizing the government's "confused financial and economic policy," which maintained spending limits despite

[14] The Kutla-al-Wataniya (National Bloc) was a parliamentary group formed by the *Istiqlal* and UNFP to oppose the monarchy's domination of the political system in the early 1970s.

[15] According to Santucci (1988, 682–684), the USFP and the PPS accused the *Istiqlal* of being more interested in regaining government power than reviving the Kutla alliance.

two years of economic growth (*L'Opinion*, 5/5/1990). Moreover, arguing that the government's insistence on passing the law without parliamentary debate was unconstitutional, the opposition joined to launch a motion of censure against the government – the second in the nation's parliamentary history (ibid). Though the motion was ultimately unsuccessful, such coordination marked a new era of opposition unity, distinguished by its use of confrontational tactics. After years of infighting the opposition coalesced under a single political banner, the *Kutla al-Dimuqratiyya*, supported by the *Istiqlal*, USFP, UNFP, PPS, OADP, CDT, and UGTM.

The formation of the *Kutla* helps explain the intensification of labor militancy during the later years of structural adjustment. As a means of pressuring the regime to enact liberal political reforms, opposition parties encouraged their union affiliates to launch strikes beginning in mid-1990. For the opposition, labor activism was a tool to strengthen their position vis-à-vis the regime – by highlighting the negative effects of the government's economic program, they could solidify their credibility with the public and convince the regime to include them in governance. Moreover, given their limited influence within an increasingly sidelined parliament, strikes and demonstrations provided an alternative way for partisan elites to force the regime to attend to their concerns.[16] For trade unions, strikes became essential for compelling the regime to take their demands seriously in a closed political system. As unions found themselves increasingly excluded from institutional politics, they became "constrained to strike" to make their voices heard (*Libération*, 11/12/1990).

The development of the Kutla alliance also fostered unprecedented cooperation between the UGTM and CDT. With their political partners united, the two unions gained incentives to coordinate their efforts to achieve workers' goals. In November 1990, union leaders Abderzzak Afilal (UGTM) and Noubir Amaoui (CDT) formed a "commando of joint action" to organize protests in key industries, such as mining, transportation, and education. By leveraging their strength in civil service and SOE, they aimed to force the regime

16 As with strike wave in the early seventies, which led Hassan II to end the Morocco's state of emergency, party leaders hoped to spark a crisis of confidence within the monarchy that would force the King to engage in meaningful political reform (Denoeux, 2001).

into a national-level social dialogue, giving unions a voice in shaping wage and economic policy. After weeks of rolling strikes failed to elicit a response, the UGTM and CDT issued a joint declaration, calling for tripartite negotiations and threatening a nationwide strike on December 14 if the government refused to engage in serious talks. At the center of the statement was a list of economic and political grievances, including an increase in the minimum wage, prohibition of arbitrary dismissals, protection of the right to strike, and the "unfreezing of parliamentary debates," regarding economic policies related to the SAP (*Libération*, 11/30/1990).

The 1990 general strike marked the high point of union cooperation between the UGTM and CDT. As the fifth general strike in Morocco's history – and the first that the UGTM and CDT organized together – this demonstration clearly broke with the "politics of national consensus" and the competitive unionism that had characterized industrial relations in the past. The strike reflected a new understanding among union leaders that cooperation was beneficial in a closed political environment. Operating as political outsiders, unions saw joint action as an essential way to push for institutional reforms that would restore their influence on issues of mutual concern, like workplace rights, enterprise reform, and job protections. Furthermore, joint strikes often resulted in concessions from the government, reinforcing the view among union leaders that alliance-building was necessary to achieve their goals (Appendix B: MA-4, 2/19/2014; MA-12, 3/25/14). Cooperative striking also offered a layer of protection to unions – by coordinating, union leaders and workers had greater assurances that their strikes would not be easily manipulated or broken by the regime (Appendix B: MA-25, 4/25/2014). The Kutla alliance thus coincided with a wave of union cooperation, evidenced by three consecutive joint May Day celebrations between the CDT and UGTM and a series of coordinated public sector strikes from 1992 to 1993.

Finally, the Kutla's formation contributed to the growing politicization of labor protests. In large part, this politicization stemmed from the influence that the USFP and *Istiqlal* exerted over their union partners. As part of their campaign for increased political power, opposition parties pressured union leaders to infuse their strike agendas with political demands. Although labor officials insisted that protest agendas were determined internally, evidence suggests that opposition parties played a significant role in orchestrating some strikes. For instance, the 1990 general strike was heavily promoted by the *Istiqlal* and USFP, and included numerous political demands alongside unions' economic grievances. As Moutadayene (2001, 78) observed, opposition parties "profited from [the strike] to reinforce their credibility," emphasizing the need for democratic and inclusive governance as a foundation for economic reform. Similarly, a symbolic strike in 1991 called to express solidarity with Iraqi citizens during the Gulf War was used by Kutla-affiliated parties to pressure the monarchy to condemn the U.S.-led offensive and withdraw Moroccan troops from Saudi Arabia. The spike in public sector strikes from February to May 1993 is also thought to have been politically motivated. Hoping to boost their political profile in advance of parliamentary elections in June, opposition elites called on workers to "unify their efforts in mobilizing for demands relating to a dignified life and true democracy," framing the elections as essential to achieving these political goals (*Libération*, 05/01/1993).

Summary

The rise in militant labor opposition in Morocco illustrates the consequences of political exclusion amid institutional drift. In contrast to Tunisia, Moroccan leaders did not adopt institutional reforms to accompany economic liberalization; instead, they continued to rely on the decentralized bargaining system that had previously maintained labor peace. However, in the context of structural adjustment, this approach had the opposite effect. Rather than fostering labor quiescence, it created new uncertainties for union leaders and workers who saw their influence in the bargaining system gradually diminish. Furthermore, indiscriminate labor repression incentivized unions of all types to strike, leading to a new wave of labor militancy and inter-union cooperation.

Simultaneous exclusion in the legislative arena also pushed union opposition in a more political direction. During the 1980s, the gradual exclusion of unions and their partisan partners from positions of influence in government forced labor unions to protest as a means of advocating for political reforms. Fearing their complete exclusion from politics, union leaders forged a historic alliance with opposition parties to resist the closure of the political system and demand political liberalization. Consistent with the theory presented in Chapter 2, exclusionary policies drove labor unions toward more confrontational tactics – absent "official" channels to express their interests, unions were forced to reshape the political environment in which their demands could be pursued.

Conclusion

The reversal in labor protest patterns – from militancy to moderation in Tunisia, and the inverse in Morocco – poses a challenge for existing theories of labor politics. In both countries, authoritarian leaders implemented neoliberal reforms that threatened workers' interests and undermined unions' structural power. By some accounts, these actions should have made unions less willing to mobilize against economic reforms; with their structural position weakened, unions should have been less capable of organizing resistance to austerity measures. Other perspectives, such as moral economy theories, argue that economic reforms should increase unions' willingness to mobilize in an effort to reclaim their foregone privileges.

In either case, both theories would predict a similar pattern of labor protest in Tunisia and Morocco. Since unions in both countries faced similar reforms and suffered similar consequences, their responses should have been congruent. However, as this chapter demonstrates, this was not the case: Moroccan unions adopted a far more militant stance against austerity reforms than their Tunisian counterparts. Additionally, these patterns of labor opposition defy the expectations of historical institutionalism. Path-dependent theories would predict the continuation of prior protest patterns – strategic moderation in Morocco and political militancy in Tunisia. However, the opposite occurred. Moroccan unions expanded their protest agendas to include confrontational tactics and political demands, while Tunisian unions retreated from their previous political stance. If critical junctures "lock-in" patterns of behavioral regularity, what explains this surprising reversal?

In the sections above, I argue that existing theories fail to explain these changes in protest behavior because they overlook the role of political institutions and processes of *institutional change*. In both countries, economic conditions interacted with existing institutional structures, leading to new patterns of labor opposition. In Tunisia, deliberate updates to the collective bargaining system decentralized wage negotiations and brought union leaders back into the regime's political coalition. Moreover, liberalizing reforms in the political system weakened the alliance between labor unions and opposition groups, diminishing a key source of labor opposition to the authoritarian regime.

In Morocco, neoliberal reforms disrupted the functioning of previous bargaining institutions, creating new uncertainties for workers and union leaders. In the context of economic austerity and state retrenchment, government officials were less willing to curb employer abuses of union rights, leaving workers more vulnerable to economic reforms. At the same time, the closure of Morocco's political system marginalized union leaders and their partisan allies from key centers of power within the government, cutting off their primary avenue for making peaceful demands. As a result, labor opposition shifted to the streets, where unions adopted increasingly radical positions against both the regime's economic policies and its exclusionary political practices.

This analysis thus nuances historical institutionalist theories, which view labor protest patterns as the inevitable consequence of a previous "critical juncture." While critical junctures create institutions that shape labor behavior, these patterns persist only as long as the mechanisms supporting them remain intact. In the cases of Tunisia and Morocco, one key mechanism is the coalition between union leaders, opposition parties, and regime elites. If institutions foster cooperation and "buy-in" from these groups, labor mobilization is likely to moderate, and unions will continue to operate within institutional channels to make their demands. However, if institutions push these groups into conflict – even through unintentional processes like institutional drift – defection and labor militancy are likely to result. Another mechanism, as explored in Chapter 6, is the relationship between union leaders and rank-and-file members. When internal governance structures compel union leaders to accommodate the radical demands of their members, labor opposition can evolve from narrow economic militancy into a broad-based movement for political reform.

6 Workers in the Shadow of Reform: Labor Protest in the Autumn of Autocracy

For many observers, the end of structural adjustment augured a period of economic and political stability for North Africa's autocratic regimes. The successful implementation of neoliberal reforms generated impressive levels of growth, which scholars and citizens alike expected to yield positive externalities over the long term. Improvements in human development eased social tensions that had previously threatened incumbent regimes, fostering a robust middle class seen as critical for supporting authoritarian stability. Consequently, countries as diverse as Tunisia, Morocco, and Egypt were hailed as success stories of neoliberal reform, generating hopes for sustained progress into the new millennium.

By the late 2000s, however, it was clear that much of this optimism had been misplaced. While many countries continued to enjoy economic growth, macroeconomic indicators masked systemic issues that became apparent in the wake of structural adjustment. Economies, while growing, were unable to keep pace with rising populations and employment demands from upwardly mobile, educated youth. In addition, the benefits of prosperity did not accrue evenly to all sectors of the population, leading to a growing divide between "privileged" and "disinherited" social groups.

As a result, the mid-to-late 2000s was characterized by rising levels of social unrest across diverse segments of the population. By 2011, the political order undergirding authoritarianism was seriously threatened as citizens protested against uneven economic development and corrupt, repressive regimes. However, organized labor's reactions to these developments varied markedly – while some unions tracked the course of social protests and experienced a resurgence of political militancy, others remained firmly aligned with authoritarian rulers. Labor mobilization in Tunisia and Morocco reflects these divergent trajectories; while UGTT in Tunisia resumed its militant opposition

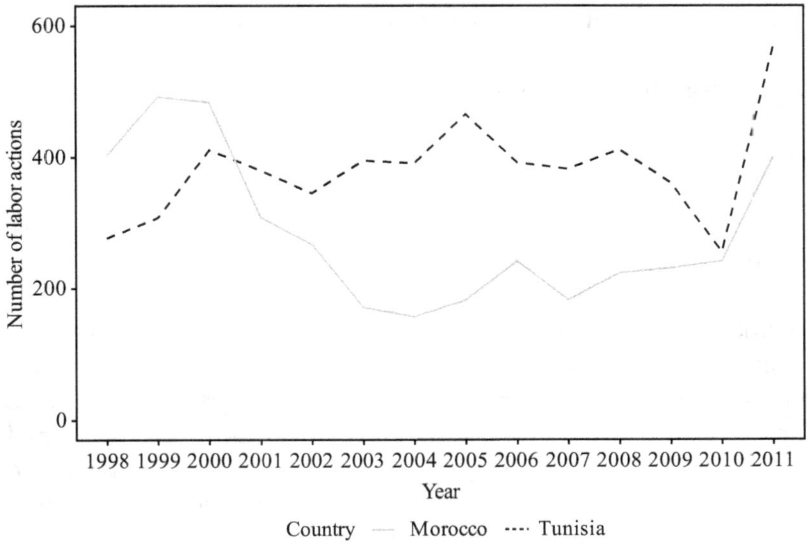

Source: ILO

Figure 6.1 Comparative labor protests in Tunisia and Morocco, ILO (1998–2011)

to the regime, Moroccan unions opted for more moderate protests focused exclusively on economic concerns (Figure 6.1).

The central goal of this chapter is to explain this divergence. I argue that differences in the institutional structures governing state–labor relations provide the most compelling explanation. In Tunisia, the closure of channels for collective bargaining and interest articulation reanimated an alliance between union leaders, workers, and opposition elites, propelling organized labor into direct confrontation with the regime. By contrast, in Morocco, the development of new representative institutions helped to quell labor and political opposition, stabilizing the foundations of authoritarian rule.

However, understanding divergent patterns of labor militancy also requires investigating unions' internal organization. While external factors, such as the nature of state–labor relations, set the stage for opposition, unions' internal dynamics determine the course of action taken and the success or failure of these tactics. In Tunisia, the persistence of democratic institutions within the UGTT enabled organized labor to pursue militant protests in the late 2000s and adopt an openly political role during the 2011 Arab Spring. Institutions linking union leaders to regional branches and rank-and-file militants incentivized the UGTT to directly oppose the Ben Ali regime, while increased antagonism between government officials and labor elites facilitated an alliance with Tunisia's pro-democracy movement. Ultimately, these developments proved crucial to the country's political future. In the final days of the revolution, UGTT-sponsored protests forced the ouster of the Ben Ali regime and paved the way for labor to influence the democratic transition that followed.

In contrast, in Morocco, a lack of internal democracy impeded political opposition despite rising protests. In the initial months of contention, unions' responses were primarily shaped by their partisan alliances and relationship with the state. Politically incorporated unions criticized the pro-democracy February 20th Movement and collaborated with the regime on reforms, while more marginalized unions supported the movement and promoted anti-government opposition. However, when the monarchy announced a plan for constitutional reform – which guaranteed union participation in parliament – a lack of internal democracy inhibited labor opposition within even the most independent of unions. Particularly within the UMT, hierarchical governance helped to silence rank-and-file dissents and expel union leaders who supported political militancy. This, in turn, fragmented organized labor and further weakened the pro-democracy coalition.

This chapter thus offers a rare examination of the internal politics of labor unions. I focus on three features of union bureaucracy that contribute to labour opposition: 1) the inclusion of rank-and-file members in decision-making, 2) the dispersion of resources and authority among lower levels of the organization, and 3) the existence of governance structures, such as regular elections, which link union elites to their members. I link the development of these structures to the institutional relationship that unions have with the state – only unions excluded from the formal political system are expected to establish and maintain democratic organizations. Thus, a counterintuitive finding of the chapter is that labor unions may be better equipped to challenge authoritarian rule when they are repressed and excluded from the formal political process.

The remainder of the chapter is organized as follows. First, I review the socio-economic conditions faced by unions at the end of structural adjustment before turning to an analysis of their varied responses. Next, I discuss existing explanations for this variation, and, finding these wanting, provide an institutional account of labor protest. I detail how shifts in formal institutions governing state–labor relations motivated different paths of militancy in Tunisia and Morocco, especially with respect to political demands. I also highlight the role of internal governance in helping unions to sustain political mobilization in the face of internal and external threats to their success. The chapter concludes by discussing the impact of labor mobilization on regime survival, paying special attention to how unions' specific mode of protest impacted the success of pro-democracy movements. I draw insights from the Tunisia-Morocco comparison for studies of labor mobilization in authoritarian regimes and offer preliminary conclusions.

Labor in the Shadow of Reform: Corporatist Collapse in the New Millennium

In North Africa, as in much of the developing world, governments entered the new millennium in a complex economic position. On the one hand, structural adjustment generated macroeconomic benefits that fueled prosperity and social progress. Between 2000 and 2010, regional GDP grew at a rate of more than 3 percent per capita, reducing public debt and spawning significant improvements in human development (Cammett et al., 2015; The World Bank, 2016). Additionally, privatization and freer trade led to an increase in foreign direct investment and created thousands of jobs in the private sector.

Despite these successes, the post-structural adjustment period also produced numerous distortions that undermined regional stability over the long term. In Tunisia and Morocco, structural reforms created dualistic economies characterized by high unemployment, rising corruption, and growing economic inequality. These issues negatively impacted workers and led to a fundamental shift in state-labor relations. In the latter half of the 2000s, grievances emerging from these trends contributed to new patterns of labor militancy and incentivized unions to challenge their preexisting bargains with authoritarian regimes.

Economic Challenges in the Post-structural Adjustment Period

Two core problems arising from structural adjustment were the rise in unemployment and the growth of the informal sector. As noted in Chapter 5, job creation failed to keep pace with the region's changing demographics, producing national unemployment rates of 15–18 percent. In the early 2000s, this problem worsened; continued public sector retrenchment fueled job insecurity, while first-time entrants to the labor market were increasingly funneled toward risky, low-paying work. In Tunisia, this produced unemployment rates above 14 percent from 2000 to 2005. In Morocco, unemployment was lower (~10–13 percent), but considerably elevated among the young and well-educated (ILO, 2016; Badimon, 2007, 3; Badimon, 2013, 195).

Pro-market policies also failed to turn North African states into competitive, market-driven economies. Persistent government regulation enabled elites to direct markets in ways detrimental to economic growth. For example, in Tunisia, provisions in the investment code requiring executive approval for large contracts created opportunities for rent-seeking within Ben Ali's ruling coalition. According to Rijkers et al. (2014), these measures concentrated investment in the hands of a few wealthy, well-connected families at the expense of smaller, more dynamic, labor-intensive firms.

Additionally, privatization sales were marred by allegations of corruption and nepotism. While there is no systematic data on the extent of bias in these sales, anecdotal evidence suggests that private transfers directly benefited members of Ben Ali's extended family and network of friends. For instance, in 2009, the Mabrouk Groupe, then headed by the president's son-in-law, Marwan Ben Mabrouk, won an offer on telecommunications firm Orange Tunisie (Tesquet, 2011). Similarly, after receiving favorable terms from the state-controlled Banque Nationale Agricole, Ben Ali's other son-in-law, Sakher El Materi, acquired a 41 percent share in Nestle (Duparc, 2011).

In Morocco, market intervention by government elites undermined the dynamism of the private sector, crippling economic growth. Regional observers allege that privatization sales were made to close friends and relatives of the monarchy, who used their political power to stifle domestic competition and gain preferential access to investment funds (Benchenna et al., 2017; Guazzone and Pioppi, 2007; Oubenal and Zeroual, 2017). Market concentration among

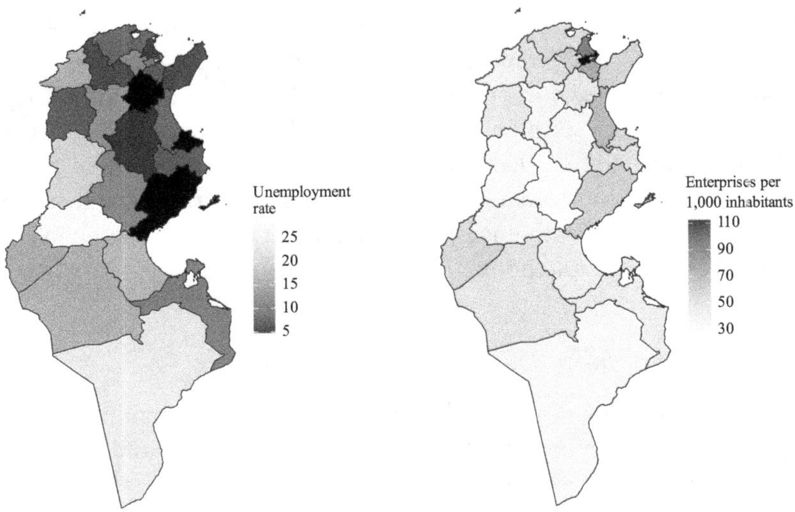

Figure 6.2 Regional disparities in Tunisia, by governorate

makhzen-connected firms facilitated cronyism, contributing to widespread perceptions of corruption in the country's business environment. Consequently, Morocco was ranked as one of the most corrupt countries in the Middle East and North Africa, with an average corruption index of 3.3 from 2001 to 2010 (Transparency International, 2010).

Finally, the distribution of economic growth was less inclusive than it had been in the past, creating new divisions between "central" and "peripheral" regions. Because private investment was concentrated among government elites, development projects were disproportionately located in regime-favored areas along the coast (Figure 6.2). Employment opportunities in cities like Sousse expanded rapidly at the expense of traditional industrial centers like Gafsa and Sfax (Bashir, 2018, 88; UGTT, 2010). Moreover, because investments in infrastructure typically accompanied firm creation, uneven development gave rise to significant disparities between coastal cities and the interior/southwest in public goods provision and social welfare.

In Morocco, economic growth exacerbated inequality between rural and urban areas, leading to a growing divide between coastal and peripheral regions. Government-sponsored programs to reduce urban poverty, for example, exaggerated the problem of uneven growth by transferring funding from rural municipalities to coastal cities like Tangier, Rabat, and Casablanca (Zemni and Bogaert, 2011). According to a 2007 report, 70 percent of Morocco's multidimensionally poor were concentrated in rural villages, resulting in poverty rates nearly twice as high in rural areas than those in urban ones (Abdeljaouad, 2022). Unsurprisingly, in the late 2000s, these areas became focal points for anti-regime opposition, as citizens gathered to express frustration with lingering social inequities and declining living standards for the rural poor.

Effects on Labor

Structural adjustment also had pernicious effects on organized labor. Workers bore the brunt of economic liberalization and suffered greatly in the wake of structural reforms. For example, flexibilization and underemployment weakened unions' organizational power and increased workers' vulnerability to employer abuse. In Tunisia, some 36,000 jobs in the textile sector were retrenched between 2000 and 2005, undercutting the UGTT's fledgling private sector base (Embassy of Tunisia, 9/24/2007). Similarly, the privatization of large state-owned firms in Morocco, such as *Maroc Telecom* and *Régie des Tabacs*, led to significant job losses in the public sector. This created labor surpluses in both countries, which increased vulnerability for unionized workers. With a significant "reserve army" of unemployed persons, business owners exploited their employees and threatened to replace them should they make excessive or costly demands (Appendix B: TU-36, 12/10/13).

Corruption and inequality also had negative effects on organized labor. Corrupt business practices employed by the Ben Ali government exacerbated unemployment and decreased wages for many private sector employees. A survey of "politically connected" firms in Tunisia showed that enterprises owned by the Ben Ali family employed only 1 percent of the labor force, though they accounted for nearly 21 percent of all private sector profits in 2010 (Rijkers et al., 2014). Additionally, new businesses created through foreign direct investment – an area highly regulated by the regime – employed fewer than five persons per year and provided low-technology, low-skilled, and low-paying jobs (Achy, 2011, 10–11).

In Morocco, government corruption impacted organized labor in a more indirect manner. The concentration of wealth allowed large businesses to gain control over the economy, leading to a lack of medium-sized firms. However, because such firms were traditionally the leaders in productivity and job creation, this contributed to rising unemployment and growth in informal work (Cammett et al., 2015; Cammett and Diwan, 2016; Rijkers et al., 2014). By 2008, over 80 percent of the Moroccan labor force was employed in the informal sector, perpetuating a cycle of poverty that disproportionately affected rural citizens and educated youths (Angel-Urdinola and Tanabe, 2012; Charmes, 2010, 9).

Finally, uneven development harmed workers in peripheral regions and worsened living conditions for unionized workers in interior cities. As investment and infrastructure moved to the coast, workers in peripheral areas found it increasingly difficult to find or maintain decent employment. In addition to high rates of regional joblessness – nearly double the national average in regions like Sidi Bouzid (Tunisia) and the Rif (Morocco) – workers had to cope with the effects of downsizing due to the displacement or closure of their firms.[1] Middle-class workers frequently complained that reduced purchasing power brought their status closer to that of the poor, while the number of vulnerable workers in interior regions increased (Appendix B: TU-40, 12/3/2013, TU-41, 12/10/2013, TU-42, 12/11/13).[2] Ultimately, the depth of socio-economic deprivation in the periphery strained the government's relationship with organized labor. As one unionist in Tozeur province put it, "People believe that the region is being left behind … The government is not trying to create jobs for people … this is a cause of frustration for most workers, they get angry and then they revolt" (Appendix B: TU-42, 12/11/13).

Summary

Thus, challenges from the structural adjustment period continued to harm organized labor and jeopardize workers' relationship with the

[1] One notable example of such downsizing took place within the Gafsa Phosphate Company (Compagnie Phosphates du Gafsa, CPG), which saw its workforce reduced from 15,000 to 5,000 workers from 1985 to 2006 (Appendix B: TU-36, 12/10/13).

[2] Such complaints were particularly prevalent among workers in rural areas, where it was estimated that over 80 percent of families lived on an income of less than MAD 5,163 ($668) per month (*La Vie Éco*, 07/06/2009).

state. In both Tunisia and Morocco, the end of structural adjustment coincided with job losses, economic marginalization, and increasing frustration from unionized workers. While these issues catalyzed labor protests in both countries in the late 2000s, the way that such opposition developed varied. In the following sections, I detail these differences, focusing on Tunisian unions' return to political militancy and Moroccan unions' emphasis on apolitical protests.

Labor's Response to Reform: Political Opposition versus Depoliticized Acquiescence

Labor Opposition in Tunisia: The Resurgence of Political Militancy

In Tunisia, economic imbalances in the post-structural adjustment period sparked a resurgence of broad-based worker militancy (Figure 6.3). While the overall frequency of strikes remained consistent with previous periods, the character and intensity of labor militancy shifted considerably in the late 2000s. Strike intensity – as measured

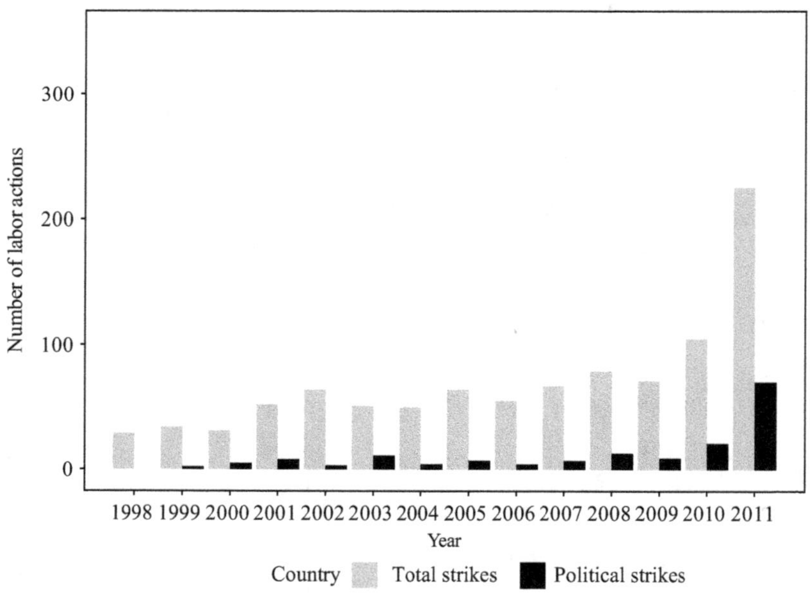

Source: MENALC Database

Figure 6.3 Labor protests in Tunisia, 1998–2011

by the number of workers participating in strikes – increased by an average of 23 percent from 1998 to 2011. Similarly, the duration of labor protests increased to an average of 7.2 days, with some strikes, such as the 2008 miners' demonstrations in Gafsa, lasting for over five months.

During this period, labor opposition was marked by enhanced solidarity among workers and an increasingly militant leadership willing to support workers' demands. Data from the Ministry of Social Affairs reveals that the number of solidarity strikes increased in the latter half of the 2000s, peaking at 23 percent in 2008 (Tunisian Ministry of Social Affairs, 2012). In contrast to previous periods, strike activity was more frequently organized at the sectoral level, involving a broad cross-section of workers from both private and public firms. Crucially, the UGTT leadership became more willing to endorse militant protest actions; by the end of the decade, roughly 31 percent of strikes were officially approved by the UGTT executive bureau (Figure 6.4).

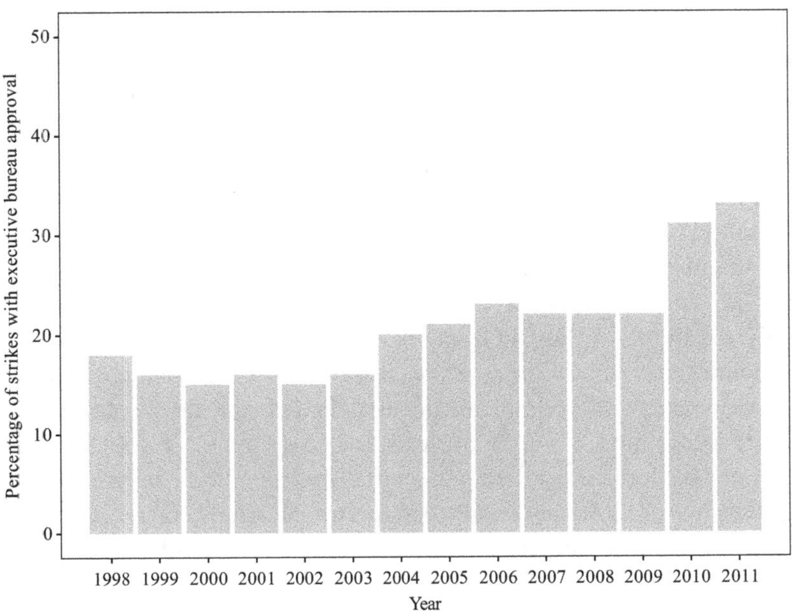

Source: Ministry of Social Affairs, Tunisia

Figure 6.4 Approved labor protests in Tunisia, 1998-2011

Additionally, during the late 2000s, labor protests in Tunisia became much more political. Three episodes of contention illustrate this evolution within the UGTT. First, in March 2005, sporadic demonstrations broke out in response to President Ben Ali's invitation to Israeli Prime Minister Ariel Sharon for the World Summit on the Information Society in Tunis. Although the UGTT leadership limited its opposition to official statements, regional offices organized spontaneous protests critiquing the regime's "Zionist collaboration" (Appendix B: TU-14, 10/23/2013). On March 4th, labor conflict reached a peak when several union federations, in coordination with human rights and opposition groups, organized an anti-Zionist rally in the heart of Tunis. Although the UGTT leadership distanced itself from these actions, the movement is celebrated as one of the earliest instances of political opposition to the Ben Ali regime.

Second, from January to June 2008, unionized workers participated in a months-long rebellion against government corruption in Gafsa. That year, labor unrest erupted when the state-owned mining company, the Gafsa Phosphate Company (*Compagnie des phosphates de Gafsa*, CPG), announced the results of a recruiting competition that locals alleged privileged the relatives of wealthy elites and politically connected members of the UGTT. In the conflict's initial weeks, a popular committee composed of local unionists, workers, and unemployed graduates sought to defuse the crisis through negotiations with CPG management. However, when negotiations foundered, local unions continued to protest, utilizing a wide array of tactics – hunger strikes, work stoppages, barricades, and roadblocks – to force the regime to attend to their concerns (Appendix B: TU-41, 12/10/2013). As the movement developed, worker demands broadened to include not only a critique of the CPG's nepotistic hiring practices but a general denouncement of the regime's security apparatus, unequal regional development, and widespread poverty. Evidencing the "political and contestatory nature" of the protests, the government's response to the Gafsa rebellion was violent and swift – by June 2008, security forces arrested over 200 demonstrators, many of whom faced sanctions for their syndical activities (Chouikha and Gobe, 2009; Appendix B: TU-41, 12/10/2013).

Finally, the UGTT played a leading role in organizing protests that led to the ouster of Ben Ali during the 2011 Jasmine Revolution. Following the self-immolation of Mohammed Bouazizi on December

17, 2010, union activists in Sidi Bouzid coordinated with local citizens to mobilize daily strikes protesting the regime's indifference to the region and complicity in his suicide (Appendix B: TU-38, 12/2/2013). When labor protests were met with violent repression, local UGTT branches intensified their opposition, calling for an end to the government's brutality and launching subversive slogans against the regime.[3] By January 4th, protests had expanded throughout Tunisia, prompting the UGTT's executive bureau to release a statement expressing "complete solidarity with the grievances of protesters in Sidi Bouzid" (*Echaab*, 01/08/2011).

The turning point of labor opposition, however, came on January 11th, when the UGTT Administrative Commission issued a decision allowing regional unions to organize general strikes against the Ben Ali government. Like the rolling strikes held by the union in 1977, these demonstrations highlighted the revolutionary nature of union militancy by advancing explicitly political demands. In advocating for the fall of the regime, the protests marked a decisive shift in the UGTT's relationship with the state and the end of its "tacit acceptance" of authoritarian rule. After a decade of gradual politicization, the union officially resumed its opposition to Tunisia's autocracy, organizing nationwide general strike that demanded an end to the Ben Ali regime and paved the way for an (eventual) transition to democracy.

Labor Opposition in Morocco: Depoliticized Acquiescence

By contrast, in Morocco, labor opposition during the early 2000s was much more restrained. Despite facing similar constraints on purchasing power and working conditions, unions did not engage in political militancy against the regime. Instead, they mediated workers' demands through moderate channels like intra-elite negotiation and compromise. As Figure 6.5 shows, in contrast to the structural adjustment period, strike levels *decreased* from 1998 to 2007, reaching a low of 154 strikes in 2004.[4] Consequently, labor mobilization transitioned from its previous intensity to a "dead age" of Moroccan unionism in

3 One such slogan was "A job is a right you pack of thieves" (Appendix B: TU-40, 12/3/2013; Beinin, 2015).

4 These trends are slightly different in the data collected by this author, available in Figure 6.6.

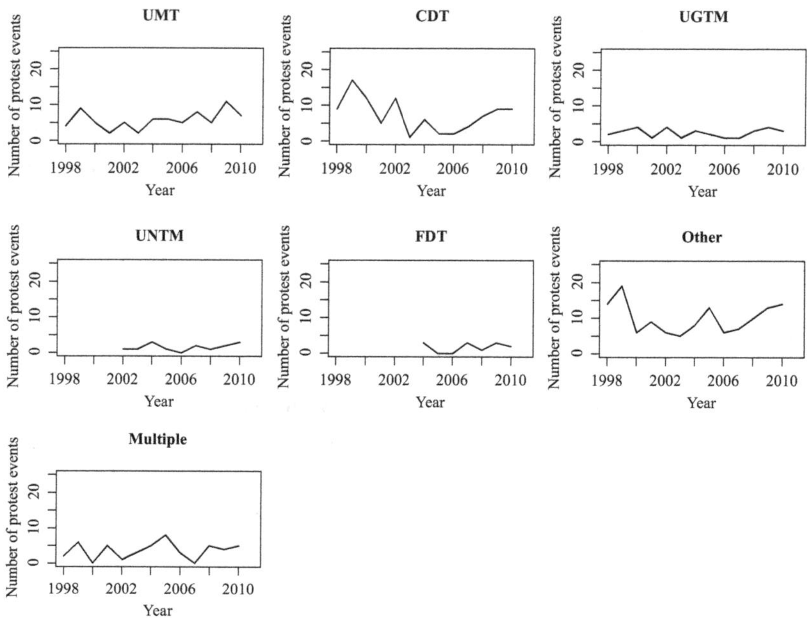

Figure 6.5 Labor protests in Morocco by federation, 1998–2011

which "unions [were hamstrung] in a logic of partnership with the government and business" (*L'Économiste*, 11/12/2007).

Beneath this general trend of quiescence, however, lay considerable variation in protest patterns over time and among different federations (Figure 6.5). While traditionally militant unions, such as the CDT, continued to mobilize strikes, formerly activist unions like the UGTM remained quiescent for much of the period. Of Morocco's three main unions, the UGTM displayed the lowest levels of strike activity, a trend that became more pronounced after 2007. Additionally, the entry of two new unions into the labor movement – the Democratic Federation of Labor (*Fédération Démocratique du Travail*, FDT) and the National Union of Labor in Morocco (*Union Nationale du Travail au Maroc*, UNTM)[5] – contributed to a noticeable increase in strike activity from 2006 to 2011.

[5] The FDT was created in April 2003, following a split between the CDT and its partisan ally, the USFP. Since that date it has become the new union wing of the USFP while the secretary-general of the CDT formed his own political party, the Congrès National Ittihadi (National Unionist Congress, CNI). The UNTM which resurfaced in 2004, is the union affiliate of the Justice and Development Party (Parti du Justice et du Développment, PJD).

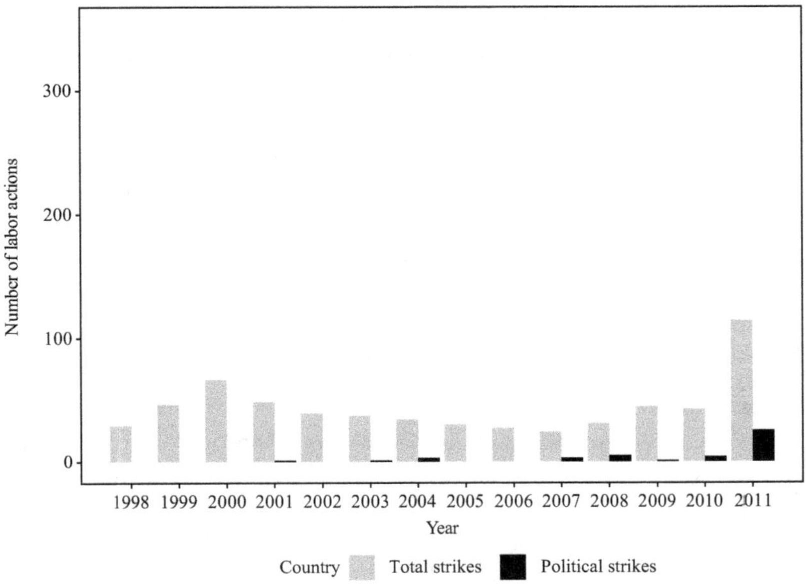

Source: MENALC Database

Figure 6.6 Labor protests in Morocco, 1998–2011

As in previous periods, strike activity was characterized by competitive militancy and inter-union rivalries. Reflecting the large number of workers who chose to disaffiliate from traditional unions, the majority of strikes were held by employees with no clear syndical affiliation. Moreover, the rise in strike activity after 2005 was largely due to rival strikes held by the CDT and its parent/splinter unions, the UMT and FDT. In a striking example of competitive labor militancy, in 2008, the CDT and a coalition of unions led by the UMT organized separate general strikes in Morocco's public administration a mere eight days apart (*L'Économiste*, 05/12/2008).

Finally, in contrast to labor mobilization in Tunisia, Moroccan labor protests were largely apolitical (Figure 6.6). The behavior of unions during the 2011 Arab Spring clearly illustrates their political passivity. That year, the pro-reform February 20th Movement (F20M) emerged to contest Morocco's poor economic conditions and demand democratizing changes to the regime. Thousands of Moroccan citizens protested, calling for administrative resignations and the promulgation of a new, more liberal constitution. However, in the face of public protests, Moroccan unions demonstrated a lackluster response. While a few unions supported demonstrations and offered logistical support, most distanced themselves from F20M and openly criticized its revolutionary demands. Notably, after the monarchy announced constitutional reforms, even unions that initially endorsed the movement disassociated themselves, opting instead to negotiate with the regime. Henceforth, unions limited their protest campaigns to economic issues and supported the monarchy's proposals for superficial reform.

Explaining Labor's Divergent Responses: Existing Explanations

Given the protest patterns witnessed in the previous decade, the divergence in labor militancy in Tunisia and Morocco from 1997 to 2011 is surprising. In a manner recalling its activism in the 1970s, the UGTT resumed its political militancy, culminating in a wave of anti-regime strikes during the 2011 Arab Spring. This shift is counterintuitive, given the UGTT's close collaboration with the Ben Ali regime in the 1990s. What changed to spark a revival of political mobilization and opposition to autocratic rule?

Equally surprising is the behavior of labor unions in Morocco during this period. After a decade of fierce opposition, Moroccan unions suddenly became more willing to cooperate with the monarchical regime. The fact that such pacification occurred despite growing labor grievances confounds the expectations of existing theories of labor politics. If labor protest is rooted in economic deprivation, how do we explain the shift from militancy to moderation in light of broader developments in the Moroccan economy?

To a greater extent than in previous periods, existing explanations help us to address these questions. For example, Feltrin (2019) convincingly argues that Tunisian unions had more working-class power than their Moroccan counterparts, helping to explain the difference in their protest trajectories. While Moroccan unions suffered from internal division, Tunisian unions benefited from cohesive organization (i.e., monopoly representation of the labor force) and better structural conditions for workers; formal employment, job security, and social welfare spending were all higher in Tunisia than in Morocco. Thus, unionized workers in Tunisia could better leverage their structural power against the regime and organize opposition when workers' gains were threatened.

A second argument highlights the role of moral economic concerns in driving labor opposition. Rising unemployment and corruption in Tunisia harmed key labor interests, providing clear incentives for renewed militancy and opposition to the Ben Ali regime. As workers saw their job prospects and well-being decline while the Tunisian economy grew, resentment toward the authoritarian government intensified. Particularly in underdeveloped interior regions, moral economic concerns about "fairness" and "equality" spurred conflict between organized labor and the regime. As one labor militant in Sidi Bouzid noted, "The political and social situation in Sidi Bouzid was not stable because the regime no longer invested in the region, despite the fact that the Democratic Constitutional Rally (RCD) was quite strong" (Appendix B: TU-40, 12/3/2013).

However, if existing explanations clarify important aspects of labor protests, they also leave several questions unanswered. A focus on structural economic conditions, for instance, explains why Tunisian unions had greater capacity to mobilize than their Moroccan counterparts, but not why they were more *willing* to do so. The privileged position of unionized workers in Tunisia arguably could have made the UGTT *less* likely to challenge the regime (Bellin, 2002). Furthermore, given that many protests originated outside the formal labor movement – for example, the 2011 strike wave began because an informal worker had his vending cart confiscated by the police – it is puzzling why union members would join protests that did not directly affect them and could jeopardize their privileged position in the regime.

Moral economic arguments also fail to explain key characteristics of labor militancy. If violated expectations and material grievances drive labor opposition, we should expect only the most aggrieved workers to engage in protest. However, in neither Tunisia nor Morocco was this the case. Although strikes frequently started among disadvantaged workers, they quickly drew participation from industrial workers in "privileged" urban centers. Additionally, labor militancy was most frequent among civil servants, who had traditional ties to the regime and were considered to be members of the labor elite (Bellin, 2002; Naccache, 2009).

Finally, moral economic explanations have trouble accounting for the timing and character of labor militancy. As we saw in the previous chapter, Tunisian workers had expressed grievances regarding unemployment, arbitrary dismissals, and violated wage agreements since the mid-1990s. Yet during this period, workers' grievances did not translate into substantive demands for political change. Why did unions in Tunisia actively oppose the regime in the late 2000s? And why did Moroccan unions, who faced similar threats, limit their demands to purely economic reforms?

Explaining Labor's Divergent Responses: The Dynamics of Union Democracy

To understand these behaviors, I argue that we must examine how workers' interests and capacities for militancy are formed in interaction with their broader institutional environment. In line with the theory developed in Chapter 2, I attribute political militancy in Tunisia to the existence of *exclusionary* relations between unions and the Ben Ali regime and *democratic* organization within the UGTT. Persistent antagonism between the government and the UGTT fostered militancy among rank-and-file workers and labor elites. Additionally, the union's democratic governance, a legacy of historical conflicts with the regime, enabled UGTT members to sustain their militancy, even in the face of regime co-option. Armed with a cohesive organization and autonomy from ruling elites, rank-and-file unionists were able to compel their leaders to support their political aims and launch a revolutionary campaign against Ben Ali's authoritarian regime.

In contrast, *inclusive* relations between autocrats and union leaders in Morocco undermined union democracy and weakened militant mobilization. Renewed alliances between unions and regime elites reduced union leaders' incentives to challenge autocratic rule. Moreover, because decision-making among labor elites was highly centralized, when faced with the opportunity for militancy, unions lacked adequate grassroots support to sustain radical protests. Thus, a key takeaway of the argument is that political incorporation can weaken unions' internal organization, leaving them less capable of effectively mounting challenges to authoritarian regimes. By contrast, exclusion from political institutions pushes unions to focus on grassroots organization and mobilization, enabling them to successfully oppose authoritarian rule.

Tunisia

The Resurgence of Labor Militancy in Tunisia: Deficiencies in the State's Corporatist Bargain

Institutional Stasis and the Renewal of Labor Uncertainty

In contrast to previous periods, formal institutions for collective bargaining in Tunisia in the early 2000s were not marked by significant change. As mentioned in the previous chapter, by the mid-1990s, the government's triennial wage negotiations had largely prevented the UGTT from launching coordinated opposition to market reforms. Consequently, the government sought to maintain the collective bargaining system in tact, introducing no major modifications. Over the course of the 1990s, this produced two successful rounds of negotiations (1996 and 1999), both marked by the enthusiastic participation of national and sectoral union elites.

However, while Tunisia's collective bargaining system succeeded in institutionalizing state–labor relations, it also generated new tensions in the labor movement that fueled workplace militancy in the late 2000s. In particular, the *convention collective cadre* failed to adequately protect union members at the plant-level, leading to a resurgence of rank-and-file protest. Of all of the reforms included in the CCC, plant level union rights were the most late-in-coming and the least well-enforced. Although the UGTT made enterprise unionism one of its key platforms as early as 1989, the government did not legally recognize workplace unions until 1995 (Journal Officiel du Republique de la Tunisie, 1/20/1995). Moreover, given that the majority of private enterprises in Tunisia were small and thus exempt from creating workplace institutions, most unionized workers did not enjoy adequate protections under the law (Agence de Promotion de l'Industrie, 1992)

This institutional deficiency created a serious crisis of representation within the UGTT. One unionist described the poor state of labor relations in Tunisian firms thusly, "an unfortunately large number of employers … do not accept the presence of unionists in their enterprises. There is no lack of examples in which managers have proceeded to fire union representatives before their election" (*Réalités*, 4/13/1995, 13). As a result, shop-floor harassment against unionized workers became increasingly common. Recalling the behavior of firm owners in the 1970s, employers used mass layoffs to abusively fire union workers, hired subcontracted employees to avoid labor regulations, and intimidated striking workers through lock-outs and sporadic acts of violence (*Réalités*, 4/9/2008, 14; *Réalités*, 5/12/2008, 10–11; ICFTU, 2005, 70–71). At the same time, the introduction of new labor code provisions reducing courts' latitude to fine employers for abusive behavior left workers with fewer mechanisms to oppose employers' tyranny outside of the shop floor (Alexander, 2001, 119; *Réalités*, 3/11/1996).

In the absence of institutional avenues for labor representation, rank-and-file workers turned to militant protest to force employers to attend to their concerns. According to a 2010 report, the chief motivation behind solidarity strikes was the absence of adequate protections for unionized workers and the lack of effective dialogue at the firm level (Tunisian Ministry of Social Affairs, 2010). In the private sector, strikes were seen as a way of forcing recalcitrant employers to comply with collective agreements established in tripartite negotiations. As one unionist in the textile industry noted: "You cannot get managers to cooperate without [the strike]. Employers do not respect workers and they do not respect the negotiations, they only care about profits and [their personal] wealth ... They only respond to the possibility of loss. This is what motivates workers to strike" (Appendix B: TU-34, 11/22/13).

Struggles over shop-floor representation also created new divisions between business owners, government officials, and labor elites. The growth of wildcat strikes among rank-and-file workers alarmed members of the regime, leading them to question the UGTT's effectiveness in enforcing labor discipline and maintaining its credibility as a "responsible" social partner. Additionally, plant-level organization became increasingly important to labor elites in the wake of privatization. With their strength in the public sector severely diminished, UGTT leaders required a stronger institutional presence in the private sector to maintain their bargaining power. They also needed to consolidate intra-union loyalty by convincing existing members that their representatives were working hard to achieve their demands.

Thus, in the early 2000s, assaults on plant-level union rights became a major point of contention for labor elites. In 2002, the UGTT executive bureau made labor protections – specifically the ratification of ILO Conventions 98 and 135 – their chief issue in collective bargaining, causing a months-long delay in concluding the 2002 accords cadre.

Later that year, UGTT leaders in Monastir supported striking workers who were abusively dismissed in the textile sector, securing generous financial compensation despite resistance from factory owners and the regional labor inspectorate (*Agence France Presse*, 12/12/2002). In 2004, the UGTT officially increased its support for rank-and-file militancy concerning labor code violations and protection of union rights. According to a 2005 report, roughly half of the 400 approved strikes that year were driven by grievances related to the right to organize or failures to engage in social dialogue with employees (ICFTU, 2005).

Another flashpoint for UGTT leadership came during deliberations over the structure of wage negotiations in 2002. Representatives from UTICA proposed a return to annual wage talks, arguing that a three-year timeline unfairly burdened firm owners in the event of unexpected crises. The UGTT, for its part, vigorously opposed this change, fearing that it would allow incompetent business owners to shift the burden of "economic hardship" onto workers and disadvantage union representatives in negotiations (Appendix B: TU-5, 10/3/2013). Although changes to the bargaining system were never adopted, the public debate over reforms – and the government's alleged willingness to consider UTICA's proposal – raised suspicions about the regime's commitment to labor interests (ibid). Already, under the triennial structure of wage accords, workers purchasing power had been severely diminished; according to a 2001 report, despite "salary increases since 1990 [that] offset the reduction of purchasing power," workers still made less in 2000 than they did in 1984, the year of the UGTT's most virulent opposition to economic reforms (Union Générale Tunisien du Travail, 2001). Compounding this mistrust was the general perception among labor elites that Ben Ali could no longer serve as an impartial arbiter in business-labor disputes. Among many union members, highly publicized marriage of UTICA president Hédi Jilani's daughters to members of the Ben Ali family, was seen as clear evidence that the president's ability to act as a "good faith mediator" in private sector talks had been compromised (Appendix B: TU-5, 10/3/2013, Cable "05TUNIS768.", 3/25/2005).

Finally, the regime's own hostility toward labor unions in the public sector exacerbated union leaders' concerns about the efficiency of existing bargaining institutions. In one notable example, negotiations between members of the UGTT's higher education federation

(*Syndicat général de l'enseignement supérieur et de la recherche scientifique*, SGERS) and the education minister were blocked for nearly two years due to the minister's refusal to accept the federation's militant executive bureau as legitimate bargaining partners (Appendix B: TU-44, 1/8/2014). Without legal recognition, members of the education sector gained serious incentives to strike in order to wrest whatever they could from the government. In response to the continued blockage of negotiations in 2005, leaders in the SGERS launched the country's first administrative strike, which resulted in the closure of Tunisia's public schools for nearly five weeks (Tounsi, 2007).

Thus, persistent deficiencies in Tunisia's bargaining system explain many of the changes in labor militancy witnessed during the post-structural adjustment period. As the institutions regulating state–labor relations became more exclusive of key constituencies within the UGTT, economic concertation became a less viable method for addressing labor concerns. Rank-and-file workers adopted militant strategies to ensure their continued influence in the workplace, while weaknesses in the bargaining system incentivized labor leaders to adopt a more antagonistic view toward the state. Ultimately, this created the conditions for broad-based labor militancy and paved the way for a new elite-membership alliance that fueled anti-regime protests in the latter half of the 2000s.

Labor Politicization in Tunisia: Repression and Renewed Exclusion under Ben Ali

Labor Marginalization and the "Redressement" of Union Governance

Indeed, the deterioration of state–labor relations at the bargaining table catalyzed changes between the UGTT leadership and the rank-and-file, predisposing the union to future political militancy. By the early 2000s, the UGTT executive bureau faced a troubling dilemma. The breakdown in social negotiations necessitated a mobilization strategy that would demonstrate the union's strength and allow its leaders to place pressure on the regime for future economic concessions. However, the dual effects of structural adjustment and government co-option alienated several rank-and-file members, undercutting the UGTT's main source of associational power.

The need for organizational solidarity became all the more pressing due to the progressive closure of alternative sources of influence within the political system. By the mid-1990s, the façade of "changement" in Ben Ali's Tunisia had worn off, as the state initiated a policy of suppressing the UGTT and eliminating union leaders from the regime's ruling coalition. In 1994, Ben Ali denied the union an opportunity to form joint electoral lists with the RCD, using its doctrine of "political neutrality" to disqualify labor-affiliated candidates from running for office. Similarly, within the RCD, the president eliminated UGTT leaders from the party's central committee and replaced them with loyal technocrats and prominent members of the business elite.[6]

For labor leaders, these actions highlighted the extent of the regime's hostility and underscored the need to promote union interests through grassroots organizing. In 1999, an article printed in *Echaab* lamented the UGTT's weak presence in parliament, going so far as to suggest that the union form its own labor party to compete against the RCD. According to the article's author, the dearth of labor representation in the National Assembly required that the UGTT seek creative solutions to "defend its positions on economic, political and social issues" (*Echaab* cited in *Réalités* 1/13/1999). Thus, in the early 2000s, the UGTT sought to restore its hegemony by instituting a series of organizational reforms.

In 2001, the UGTT's Administrative Commission announced a new platform of "*redressement*" – correction – built around three key pillars of reform: democratization, transparency, and decentralization. To enhance internal democracy, the commission amended regulatory statutes to limit representatives to a maximum of two terms and disabled retired workers from running for executive office. Additionally, a specialized commission was appointed to review the results of previous elections and identify/address instances of fraud. In 2002, the UGTT Executive Bureau organized an extraordinary congress in Djerba, which rejuvenated the union's central administration by electing a new, more militant leadership. Transparency in union administration was

[6] In 1994, Ben Ali initiated a revitalization of the RCD by expanding its central committee and infusing the body with a new cohort of younger members. Of these, at least fourteen were members of the business elite. Moreover, six of these hailed from UTICA directly: Ali Slama, Habib Nciri, Mohamed Ben Abdallah, Romdhane Rahli, Béchir Ben Amor, and UTICA president Hédi Jilani.

ensured through the creation of a National Commission of Financial Control, requiring that all union expenses be subject to external audit. Finally, the union decentralized its internal bureaucracy by allowing regional branches more autonomy in managing their affairs, including decisions about strike authorization and the training of labor negotiating teams. To prepare future leaders for this role, UGTT officials encouraged active member participation in union meetings and established national training programs to educate workers about labor affairs.

These changes to the UGTT's internal bureaucracy had three complementary effects that strengthened labor mobilization. First, involvement of rank-and-file workers in decision-making enhanced union solidarity and politically socialized workers within the UGTT's base. Site visits to local union meetings revealed the extent of membership engagement in union affairs – workers regularly met with union officials to discuss shop-floor grievances, structure agendas, and coordinate plans for general strikes. Interviews affirmed the importance of such involvement for workers' political consciousness; although discussions typically centered around economic topics, union meetings frequently served as the only space in Tunisia where workers could engage in open political discussion and debate (Appendix B: TU-20, 10/29/2013; TU-44, 1/8/2014). This fostered a quasi-syndicalist collective identity within the UGTT. As one unionist noted:

> For me, Mohammed Ali Hammi [the union training program] was critical ... there I learned about the UGTT's historical past, the need for its autonomy ... It was there that I understood the role of the worker and his position in society ... I learned what it meant to be an activist and the necessity for workers to contribute to the social and political development of the state. (Appendix B: TU-24, 11/4/2013)

Second, the restoration of democratic practices within the union paved the way for further radicalization of labor protest by drawing leftist groups back into the UGTT. While the regime's limited political opening co-opted most of the political left, those parties that rejected co-optation faced harsh repression at the hands of the Tunisian state.[7]

[7] Interviews with opposition elites revealed numerous harassments – regime surveillance, media suppression, mass arrests – that made operating as an independent organization difficult or impossible.

For much of the opposition, this suppression created serious incentives for reintegration within the UGTT (Appendix B: TU-29, 11/17/2013, TU-33, 11/21/2013). In the early 2000s, members from a variety of political trends – Communists, Arab Nationalists, social democrats, and independent leftists – reactivated within the union, establishing a significant presence in its post, education, public health, and banking sectors. Moreover, at the Djerba congress in 2002, freer elections permitted many of these militants to gain leadership positions at both the national and regional levels.

Subsequently, opposition elites began using their influence to steer the UGTT's agenda in a more radical direction. By 2004, leftist groups had gained enough power within the union to force a real debate over whether the UGTT would endorse Ben Ali's fourth presidential term (Appendix B: TU-20, 10/29/2013; Beinin, 2015). In 2005, these same groups were the driving force behind the union's decision to renounce its seats in the newly created second chamber of parliament. According to unionists involved in the decision, the regime's offer was rejected because its rules for selecting candidates violated the UGTT's commitment to internal democracy (Appendix B: TU-7, 10/06/2013).

Finally, devolution of administrative authority to regional unions strengthened linkages between peak leaders and the rank-and-file, allowing base-level militants more freedom to orient labor agendas in a political direction. Throughout the UGTT's history, regional unions fulfilled an important task: responding directly to the needs of their local constituents (Appendix B: TU-5, 10/3/2013; TU-11, 10/17/2013). Unlike the executive bureau, which was physically distant from the grassroots, regional branches could more ably address workers' problems at their point of origin. Frequently, this involved addressing not only workplace grievances but also community issues such as access to government services, public goods provision, and poverty relief (Appendix B: TU-42, 12/11/2013).

Under the restrictive leadership of Ismail Sahbani, however, regional unions' ability to act as a voice for community interests was severely curtailed.[8] After *redressement*, changes to the union's internal

[8] Frequently, under Sahbani's rule, requests for regional strikes were denied by the executive bureau in order to preserve the image of "labor peace" so critical to maintaining the regime's co-optive state-labor bargain (Appendix B: TU-25, 11/5/2013).

bureaucracy counteracted this dynamic, giving regional leaders greater latitude to mobilize. New regulations requiring strike authorization from a majority decision at the regional level, for example, increased union leaders' capacity to organize strikes and respond to rank-and-file members' demands. For leaders known for their history of militancy, the decentralization of decision-making authority freed them to organize strikes without fear of reprisal from the central administration (Appendix B: TU-11, 10/17/2013). For moderate leaders, increased membership scrutiny over union affairs compelled them to adopt more confrontational strategies, lest they be accused of neglecting workers' interests (Appendix B: TU-38, 12/2/2013)

In almost all unions, the new regulations fostered greater accountability between regional leaders and the rank-and-file. According to a 2005 survey, nearly 94 percent of union members agreed that regional officials implemented their members' proposals either in whole or in part (UGTT, 2006).

Changes to the union's internal bureaucracy also strengthened regional leaders' control over union agendas, creating tighter links between the UGTT's administration and its base. Organizational reforms designed to decentralize authority increased the de facto power of the UGTT's Administrative Commission (AC), which included leaders from regional unions, sectoral federations, and national labor elites. Though the executive bureau still served as the union's official mouthpiece, it was expected to take strategic directives from the AC, making the commission the most important decision-making body in the UGTT. Moreover, proportional voting within the AC gave regional leaders more control over labor agendas, enabling them to elevate their constituents' interests over those of national elites.

Taken together, these organizational changes had a tremendous impact on the UGTT's political development. Driven by internal pressure from its members, the once-co-opted union was forced to take on a more oppositional stance vis-à-vis the Ben Ali regime. This shift occurred gradually and developed over the course of numerous conflicts between rank-and-file members and the UGTT elite. One such conflict, which proved critical to the union's political militancy during the Arab Spring, was the 2008 Gafsa mining rebellion.

The Trials of Union Democracy: The 2008 Gafsa Mining Rebellion

Analysis of the 2008 Gafsa mining rebellion demonstrates the radicalizing effects of intra-union politics on labor mobilization. Examining the sequence of events reveals how workers used their political leverage to impel the union's leadership toward a more confrontational stance after the UGTT's bureaucratic reforms. Although, initially, political mobilization was limited to marginalized segments of the union's base, as the movement grew, popular unrest – and the regime's harsh reaction to it – compelled the executive bureau to shift its position from conciliation to critique. This set the stage for additional reforms in the late 2000s that would prepare the UGTT for overt political opposition during the 2011 Arab Spring uprisings.

At the heart of the Gafsa rebellion was a conflict between the marginalized working-class and a "labor aristocracy tied to the status quo" (*Attariq al Jadid*, 7/8/2008 cited in Chouikha and Gobe, 2009). Protests began on January 5th, when the state-owned Gafsa Phosphate Company (CPG) announced a list of new hires drawn from families connected to the regime, rather than local residents and children of miners injured in the line of work. Despite previous agreements that stipulated 20 percent of the company's new hires should be allocated to such persons "on the basis of social considerations" (Chouikha and Gobe, 2009, 4), workers critiqued the recruitment process for being biased in favor of wealthy members of the RCD. Additionally, protesters alleged that the UGTT's regional secretary-general, Amara Abbassi (himself a member of the ruling party), had colluded with CPG management to favor employees from his subcontracting company, using his parliamentary position to influence hiring results.

Almost immediately, local unionists mobilized to support the protests, putting their organizational resources at the disposal of local activists. In the early days of the rebellion, members of the Redeyef primary education federation worked to connect protesters and government officials, using their privileged positions as intermediaries to win important concessions (Appendix B: TU-41, 12/10/2013). As demonstrations continued, militants deployed parts of the UGTT's organizational structure to support collective action: local leaders allowed meetings to be held in union assembly halls, financed protest materials, and facilitated connections with other activists, such as the Tunisian League of Human Rights (LTDH) (Appendix B: TU-41, 12/10/2013). In the most chaotic moments of the rebellion, regional union offices in Ben Arous and Kairouan set up protest committees to shelter Gafsa demonstrators fleeing from government repression and mobilized solidarity protests to raise public awareness about the revolt (Appendix B: TU-37, 12/1/2013).

Most important, local unionists helped to frame the protest events in Gafsa, giving the movement broader resonance and an explicitly political character. As members of the clandestine opposition and one of the most politically active federations in the UGTT, militants from Redeyef's education unions lent a radical interpretation to workers' demands. On February 9th, Adnane Hajji, a secondary school teacher, gave an impassioned speech denouncing

> "the [regime's] denial of unemployed and precarious workers' dignity; a lack of work; the pollution affecting the Gafsa region; the nepotism and corruption that plagued the distribution of jobs; and efforts of the Gafsa union bureaucracy and local RCD leaders ... to divide the protest movement" (*Al-Badil 'Ajil*, 2/14/2008).

Interviews further confirmed that leftist activists, such as Hajji, Bechir Laabidi, and Taeïb Ben Othmane provided the "intellectual leadership" of the protest movement (Appendix B: TU-38, 12/2/2013; TU-39, 12/2/2013; TU-41, 12/10/2013).

In addition to serving as interlocutors between protesters, the government, and the press, these militants facilitated contact between different groups active in the rebellion and unified their disparate goals through a single ideological framework. This framing, which drew upon Marxist rhetoric, moved beyond issues with the hiring contest to address the elitism and corruption that plagued all those left behind by the government's neoliberal development plan. As such, issues like social justice, human rights, and community empowerment were at the forefront of the Gafsa protest platform. This was clearly reflected in the movement's slogans: "Everyone has a right to a job," "No to corruption and opportunism" and "Work, Freedom, National Dignity" (Appendix B: TU-38, 12/2/2013; Chouikha and Gobe, 2009, 7; Sadiki and Saleh, 2024, 206).

However, if the actions of local unionists highlighted the extent of the UGTT's politicization, the responses of regional and national leaders illustrated how far it had left to go. In an effort to undermine the protest movement, the Gafsa regional union suspended Adnane Hajji's membership and accused local activists of using their union credentials to incite rebellion against the RCD. On March 31, the union's secretary-general further weakened the movement by organizing a counter-protest in Redeyef, during which beneficiaries of the CPG's recruitment contest demanded an accelerated hiring process for winners (*Akbar Al-Badil*, 4/2/2008). These actions were tacitly supported by the UGTT's central administration – in May 2008, the executive bureau endorsed the Gafsa office's decision to expel Hajji and remained silent about the events in the mining basin in the union's official press outlet *Echaab*.

Indeed, it was only after mounting pressure from the rank-and-file that the UGTT leadership changed its stance. Following mass arrests in Redeyef in June, base union leaders called on the executive bureau to take a stronger stand against government repression and work to free detained unionists (Appendix B: TU-44, 1/8/2014). Subsequently, the executive bureau issued a communique denouncing the arrests and hired lawyers to secure the release of Hajji, Ben Othmane, and others (Appendix B: TU-5, 10/3/2013). In October 2008, local unionists stepped up their pressure campaign by organizing a solidarity protest for the Gafsa miners outside of the UGTT's central headquarters in Tunis. During this event, demonstrators criticized the executive bureau's lackluster response and called for more vigorous support for the families of arrested workers (Appendix B: TU-44, 1/8/2014). Though reactions among the leadership were mixed, the executive bureau ultimately capitulated, sending material support to local families affected by the protests. A second grassroots campaign in 2009 further pressured the leadership to advocate for the release of Redeyef protesters by calling on the UGTT's secretary-general, Abdesslam Jrad, to lobby Ben Ali directly. In November 2010, this internal pressure paid off, as all union members arrested in the Gafsa rebellion were pardoned, and Adnane Hajji's membership was officially reinstated.

Ultimately, the union leadership's about-face underscores the importance of internal democracy in motivating political activism. The autonomy enjoyed by base union leaders enabled local unionists to engage directly in the protest movement and use their organization's infrastructure to sustain mobilization. Additionally, the UGTT's decentralized structure allowed local demands to be scaled up through the union hierarchy, despite close relations between certain regional leaders and the regime. This sensitivity to grassroots demands was driven by both external political conditions and internal dynamics within the UGTT. As an organizationally weakened union with limited political influence, the UGTT could not afford to challenge the regime directly, but neither could it remain neutral and risk losing its remaining support base. Thus, the central leadership was forced to channel rank-and-file demands, even if it meant confronting government elites. After 2009, this grassroots pressure compelled the UGTT toward a more equivocal relationship with the Ben Ali regime. In contrast to previous periods, the executive bureau adopted a dual strategy of negotiating with the government while actively encouraging protest among its membership base (Appendix B: TU-20, 10/29/2013). This also paved the way for more direct confrontation between the union and the regime during the 2011 "Arab Spring."

The Test of Union Democracy: The 2011 Jasmine Revolution

The 2008 protests in Gafsa were a critical precursor to the popular uprisings that began during the 2011 Arab Spring. Although the initial protests originated outside the labor movement, union members quickly took up the mantle of organizing demonstrations and spreading them beyond Tunisia's interior regions. Drawing from their experiences in Gafsa, these activists adapted preexisting mobilization strategies to "frame" the crisis and employed unique methods to transform local grievances into a national political movement. Additionally, local and intermediate union leaders leveraged their influence within the union bureaucracy to pressure the national administration to abandon its mediating role and support protesters' demands. Consequently, when protests broke out in Sidi Bouzid in December 2010, the union was able to quickly mount a direct challenge to the Ben Ali regime. By January 11, the administrative commission had approved a series of anti-government rolling strikes, culminating in a general strike on January 14, which prompted Ben Ali's departure.

From the earliest days of the revolution, local and federal union leaders played a pivotal role in mobilizing protests. On the day of Bouazizi's self-immolation, teachers from the local secondary education syndicate transported him to the hospital and accompanied his family to the prefectural office to express their anger over his treatment by government officials and the police. The following day, the regional executive bureau in Sidi Bouzid formed a "Committee for Supporting the Activities of the People" to coordinate protests and formally present citizens' demands to regional authorities. According to activists, this committee streamlined mobilization efforts among different participants and devised strategies to help demonstrators avoid government pursuit (Appendix B: TU-38, 12/2/2013). One such strategy, borrowed from the Gafsa repertoire of contention, was to split protests between day and nighttime demonstrations. Unionists led daytime marches, which drew more attention from the press, while youths and unemployed graduates carried out nighttime revolts to disrupt local infrastructure and "tire out the police" (Appendix B: TU-38, 12/2/2013).

Union offices also served as meeting locations and refuges for demonstrators fleeing police intimidation. Given the UGTT's historical legitimacy, union offices shielded citizens from government repression, because police were less likely to breach UGTT headquarters to engage in mass arrests (Appendix B: TU-37, 12/1/2013). Thus, local unions "incubated" the protest movement, allowing it to withstand repeated efforts at suppression by the regime.

In addition to mobilizing protests, local unionists also played a crucial role in framing contentious activities and expanding demonstrations to neighboring cities. Union officials in Sidi Bouzid described their coordination efforts with nearby offices in Regueb, Meknassi, and Menzel Bouzaiane: "On the 26th, after the death of our comrade in Menzel Bouzaiane we organized a committee that was called the 'Committee of Popular Resistance' to mobilize unionists, members of human rights organizations, parties … together we tried to spread the movement and organize popular insurrection in the street" (Appendix B: TU-40, 12/3/2013). Similarly, in Kasserine, civil service unions leveraged their historic ties with lawyers and professional syndicates to stage broadly populated joint demonstrations.

The spread of protests was further facilitated by unique framing strategies adopted by labor activists to garner widespread support. Unlike in Gafsa, union militants initially advocated for a set of apolitical, non-parochial slogans that would appeal to diverse publics. While reanimating popular protest slogans like, "Work is a right, you pack of thieves," union leaders made sure to frame these demands in terms of global issues such as regional development and corruption, rather than as local grievances about hiring and unemployment. According to some unionists, this allowed protests to gain broad salience early on:

> each city was able to identify with the slogans that were launched. When you talk about regional development, Kasserine is for regional development, Gafsa is for regional development, Siliana demands regional development, same with Jendouba, these cities did not just support Sidi Bouzid but they also adopted its demands which ultimately became the demands of all of the regions of the country. (Hafedh quoted in Yousfi, 2015, 66)

However, as the movement gained ground, union militants took more deliberate steps to politicize the movement by advocating oppositional slogans against the Ben Ali regime. Drawing upon existing grievances, these slogans linked socio-economic issues to critiques of Ben Ali and his family – i.e., "No, no to the Trabelsi's who robbed the budget." As in Gafsa, this effort was spearheaded by unions affiliated with the political left, who called on citizens to consider Bouazizi's death as closely connected to the regime: "[leftist unions] had a critical role in developing the movement … We wanted them to know that he did not commit suicide, he was a political martyr" (Appendix B: TU-44, 1/8/2014). In other instances, the politicization of popular protests was more spontaneous: "Sometimes we organized our own events and sometimes we would just join existing protests and politicize them, providing slogans that posed questions about the regime and not just about socio-economic issues" (International Crisis Group, 2011, 4).

Ultimately, this shift in unionists' messaging provoked a critical split between the UGTT's national leadership and the regime. Despite early misgivings about the radical nature of the protests, members of the union's executive bureau faced intense pressure to engage more deeply with the uprisings and endorse workers' political demands. In part, this pressure was driven by internal fears that continued moderation would cost the leadership dearly in terms of rank-and-file support. Heated debates within the administrative commission revealed that the executive bureau's success in forthcoming elections depended on the support they were willing to give to local unions that organized protests and suffered from government repression as a result (Appendix B: TU-7, 10/6/2013; TU-41, 12/11/2013; TU-44, 1/8/2014). Paradoxically, uncertainty about the success of revolutionary protests also drove deeper engagement with the protest movement. Given the rapid spread of demonstrations – many of which took place without the knowledge or endorsement of the executive bureau – several leaders reported feeling "overwhelmed" by the momentum of events, and obliged to "encapsulate the movement" to save face (Appendix B: TU-5, 10/3/2013, TU-14, 10/23/2013). In the event that protests were unsuccessful, this would allow the national leadership to claim control over its members in future talks with the regime. If the protests succeeded, it would enable union elites to maintain their legitimacy as genuine representatives of the working class.

Thus, in early January, the central leadership committed itself to more systematic engagement with mobilization efforts and protesters' demands. On January 4, the executive bureau issued a communique expressing "complete solidarity with the inhabitants of Sidi Bouzid" and calling for extensive reforms to "find an appropriate solution to the crisis" (*Le Temps*, 01/06/2011). As regime violence against labor activists escalated, the UGTT stepped up its critique, condemning the government's use of live rounds against demonstrators and supporting protesters' demands for "the promotion of democracy and strengthening of freedoms." On January 11, the union's administrative commission took its most dramatic step in opposing the regime by officially recognizing the "right of regional trade union structures to observe [anti-government] protests" in coordination with the national executive bureau (*Le Temps*, 01/12/2011). This marked a decisive shift in the momentum of the protest movement and the UGTT's politicization – after a string of successful regional strikes calling for the ouster of Ben Ali, the union executive was forced to accept the regime's eventual demise and position itself at the forefront of the pro-democracy movement by organizing its January 14th general strike.

Labor Opposition and Authoritarian Breakdown

If the UGTT's resurgence of political militancy was surprising to many,[9] it should not be considered counterintuitive. As I have argued in the preceding discussion, the UGTT's politicization was the natural consequence of nearly a decade of institutional changes both within the union itself and in its relationship with the regime. As avenues for interest articulation in the bargaining system broke down, rank-and-file workers became more militant, organizing coordinated protests against their poor economic conditions and the government's unwillingness to attend to their demands. At the same time, growing

[9] Several scholars and interlocutors argued that the UGTT's central leadership was too co-opted to launch a meaningful challenge against the state (Bellin, 2002; Hibou, 2011; Appendix B: TU-6, 10/3/2013, TU-23, 11/4/2013). While some scholars noted that the UGTT represented a "weak link" in Ben Ali's neo-corporatist regime (i.e., Hibou, 2011, 124), ultimately, she concludes that the federation was "an essential transmission belt for political authorities … the function that the UGTT is now expected to fill is that of relaying the wishes of the Palace of Carthage."

alienation of labor representatives from the political system led to internal reforms, enabling this militancy to become explicitly political. State repression not only reignited the potential for a union-opposition alliance but also highlighted the need to restore labor autonomy through democratic reforms. These reforms expanded member participation in decision-making and decentralized authority from the union central to local and regional branches, reducing the concentration of power. Over time, the institution of more democratic practices helped the UGTT to politicize its base and increase accountability between national leaders and the rank-and-file. During the events of the 2011 Jasmine Revolution, these features helped to propel the UGTT into a directly oppositional role, forcing union officials to take a clear stance against the Ben Ali regime.

While numerous factors contributed to the success of anti-regime protests, the critical role of labor militancy in the regime's ouster cannot be overstated. Symbolically, labor's participation fueled a sense among the population that the country was undergoing a historic moment of change and that protests might actually succeed. Practically, the UGTT's actions – first by its local branches and then by its national leadership – were crucial in mobilizing protests and expanding opposition to a point that the regime could no longer control. The union's regional strike in Sfax, for instance, marked a turning point in the protest movement and was instrumental in forcing Ben Ali to depart. When asked about the most important forces in the Tunisian revolution, several respondents emphasized the UGTT's critical role:

> In the end the role of the [union] was considerable ... at first it was the base unions who protested with the people, helped to organize ... these unionists wanted to change the regime, and wanted to reform the Tunisian state .... The union base imposed its decision upon the leaders, so in the final days of the revolution it played a considerable role. (Appendix B: TU-38, 12/2/2013)

Thus, while the revolutionary movement in Tunisia began with informal workers' economic grievances, its trajectory cannot be fully understood without acknowledging the UGTT. In a closed political system, the union became the natural focal point for anti-regime mobilization, and its involvement in political protests was crucial in precipitating Ben Ali's downfall. Most importantly, the UGTT's democratic structure enabled the protests to overcome several challenges to their success: sustaining frequent mobilization to pressure authorities, protecting movement leaders from repression and co-optation, and fostering internal solidarity to prevent divisions among movement actors. This dynamic contrasts sharply with labor mobilization in more inclusive environments, as I explore in the following discussion of labor protests in Morocco.

Morocco

Explaining Labor Quiescence in Morocco: The Pacifying Effects of "Social Dialogue"

Labor Inclusion as a Force for Change

The end of structural adjustment marked a turning point in Moroccan labor history. With the monarchy's powers of resource allocation severely diminished and labor unrest a persistent feature of social life, King Hassan II realized that top-down reforms without the support of popular constituencies – particularly organized labor – could no longer be sustained. A month-long strike at the national railways in May 1995 demonstrated how quickly wildcat demonstrations could spiral out of control without proper mechanisms for dispute resolution (Lust-Okar, 2005). Similarly, a general strike in 1996 suggested that if the monarchy continued its current approach, more workers might be tempted to defect. To address this situation, the regime needed to alter its methods of labor containment. Thus, in 1996 Hassan II inaugurated a new process of "social dialogue" meant to incorporate unions and their members more fully into the regime.

The development of social dialogue marked an effort to institutionalize the relationship between the state, employers, and organized labor. In August 1996, the first phase of this process was crowned by the adoption of a Joint Declaration, which systematized dialogue by setting regular intervals[10] for meetings, and establishing mechanisms for consultation at the sectoral level. As in Tunisia, the agreement outlined key issues to be addressed by the three parties, including wages, social protection, housing, and career advancement for civil

[10] According to the provisions of the Joint Declaration, negotiations were to be held in April and September of each year.

servants. Subsequent rounds of dialogue in 2000 and 2003 introduced collective bargaining procedures and led to the adoption of a more worker-friendly labor code, which codified union representation at the enterprise level and established new institutions for resolving labor disputes.

The institutionalization of social dialogue did much to dampen labor militancy in the early 2000s. To begin, the introduction of tripartite negotiation satisfied a key demand of union leaders and affirmed the role of labor representatives as legitimate social and economic actors (Appendix B: MB-3, 2/17/14; MU-32, 1/16/2015)). As mentioned in the previous chapter, one of the main drivers of unrest in the early 1990s was the lack of adequate mechanisms for labor representation at the national and enterprise levels. Because employers colluded with the state to bypass mechanisms for labor to express its interests, unions accumulated grievances that were frequently manifest through strikes. Under the new scheme of social dialogue, national labor leaders gained access to institutionalized channels for interest articulation, reducing the need to organize large-scale strikes. Additionally, the new labor code provided stronger protections for union representatives. For instance, new legislation prohibited employers from disciplining or firing workers for union membership, participating in union activities, serving as worker delegates, or filing complaints against employers (Essaidi, 2007, 141). In cases where employers violated these provisions, courts had the authority to reinstate unfairly dismissed workers and could compel employers to pay damages and back pay (ibid).

For many labor representatives, these protections signaled a shift in the relationship between unions, the state, and employers – from one based on conflict to one rooted in mutual understanding and compromise. As CDT secretary-general Noubir Amaoui noted in a speech celebrating the start of tripartite negotiations,

> Once our struggles ended in tragedy—deaths, injuries, lawsuits, and layoffs. Today, this struggle concludes in a civilized way through a historic agreement. This agreement is one of the most important achievements of the labor movement and of the CDT. (Noubir Amaoui, quoted in Benhilal, 1997)

Social dialogue further pacified labor opposition by providing unionized workers with an institutional mechanism to secure concessions from employers and the regime. In commemoration of the inauguration of the first round of accords, the government satisfied a long-held demand to reinstate dismissed civil service employees, providing the additional benefit of funding these workers' wage arrears (Conseil Economique, Social et Environnmental, 2015). In successive negotiations in 2000 and 2004 social dialogue accords produced wage increases of nearly 21 percent for the lowest-paid category of employees, with additional benefits for higher-scale workers (Royaume du Maroc, 2006).

Most importantly, by systematizing collective bargaining at the national level, social dialogue strengthened the ability of peak union leaders to control their members by delivering exclusive benefits. In exchange for obtaining material concessions from the state, labor leaders were tasked with moderating the demands of the rank-and-file. This had the effect of reducing labor militancy, as leaders could use economic privileges to exercise "social control" over their constituents. According to one labor activist:

> The possibility of resolving problems through dialogue gave union leaders a culture of negotiation more than of activism. Before there were always strikes, strikes for this or that union talking about the need for social dialogue, and today some unionists still strike … but now leaders understand that unionism needs to be professional and propositional … to give recommendations, to conduct studies … there is no longer a "combative unionism." (Appendix B: MA-9, 3/19/2014)

The Weakness of Social Dialogue and the Resurgence of Union Protest

However, if the success of social dialogue explains the relative passivity of organized labor in the early 2000s, its dysfunction accounts for the resurgence of labor militancy after 2008. Indeed, by 2009, most observers agreed that tripartite negotiation had "broken down" due to various issues in its implementation (Appendix B: MA-3, 2/19/2014; MA-24, 4/29/2014; *L'Économiste*, 04/22/2008). At the enterprise, provisions of the labor code were inconsistently applied: labor representatives were often excluded from consultations with employers, and collective bargaining occurred in only 15 percent of private sector businesses (Conseil Economique, Social et Environnmental, 2015; *L'Économiste*, 12/20/2006). At the national level, unions struggled to negotiate with the newly appointed prime minister, Abbas El-Fassi, who proved reluctant to accede to workers' demands.

In part, the government's inability to appease organized labor was due to its worsening financial position in the late 2000s. Entering office at the beginning of a global economic crisis, El-Fassi argued that the union's traditional demands for wage increases, promotions, and higher pensions could no longer be accommodated. The government had already spent 67 billion dirhams (10.2 percent of the budget) on public sector wages and had increased subsidies by 85 percent to offset living costs (*La Vie Éco*, 11/02/2007). Thus, El-Fassi offered a compromise solution: a progressive increase in the income tax exemption and a phased 8 percent raise in the minimum wage (*L'Économiste*, 04/04/2008).

Although relatively generous, this proposal fell short of unions' expectations and was promptly rejected by a majority of labor elites.[11] Further attempts to negotiate in 2009 failed to result in an acceptable compromise. In July, after a third round of talks, Moroccan unions collectively decided to withdraw from social dialogue, criticizing the government for its "lack of seriousness" in addressing their topline concerns. In response, the government hardened its stance: it refused to discuss further wage increases until 2011 and announced a draft law on trade unions that would give the state greater oversight of its internal operations, financial management, and bureaucratic affairs.

Ultimately, these developments reignited unions' and workers' incentives to strike. Public sector workers, in particular, leveraged their roles in essential services to extract substantive concessions from the regime.[12] By disrupting critical services like trash collection and education, they aimed to stoke the government's fears of social unrest (Buehler, 2015). From 2008 to 2010, workers struck in 139 government offices, resulting in 765,701 working days lost (ibid, ILO, 2016). In some instances, a generalized malaise among

[11] The only union that did not criticize the government's proposal was the UGTM, a union with historical ties to the *Istiqlal* and El-Fassi. Remarking on the government's plan, the union's then secretary-general stated "the government's proposal within the framework of social dialogue is reasonable ... 17 billion dinars have been granted by the government to improve the purchasing power of workers" (*L'Économiste*, 05/13/2008).

[12] For example, unions had routinely lobbied the government for public sector wage increases that would bring the minimum wage up to MAD 3500. However in successive government proposals, the minimum wage had only been raised to MD 2109.12 by 2008 (Appendix B: MA-1, 2/7/2014, L'Opinion 2/18/2011).

workers fostered rare cooperation between members of different union federations. For example, in November 2010, a nationwide strike by public sector employees from the Democratic Labor Organization (*Organisation Démocratique du Travail*, ODT), UMT, FDT, UNTM, and UGTM shut down municipal and government services for two days (*Libération*, 11/03/2010).

The intensity of labor unrest was especially noticeable during the events of the 2011 Arab Spring. As a social movement emerged that challenged the regime over its democratic deficiency and widespread corruption, workers launched an unprecedented number of strikes from January to June of that year (Figure 6.1). Like strikes in previous years, labor militancy was spearheaded by public sector workers, who shut down schools, municipal services, hospitals, and courts. However, while these strikes coincided with broader calls for political reform, the demands of striking workers were primarily material. Indeed, the vast majority of strikes were driven not by a desire for political rights or democracy, but by frustration with the government's refusal to negotiate and address workers' basic economic demands. Union leaders consistently emphasized the economic motivations behind their actions when explaining the rationale for the strikes. Commenting on the wave of public sector strikes, UNTM leader Mohammed Yatim held the government fully responsible for labor unrest, noting "a disengagement on the part of the government to meet the demands of the working class, hence our decision to undertake the fight" (*Aujourd'hui le Maroc*, 10/12/2010). Similar sentiments were echoed by national leaders of the CDT:

> For two years now, we have been asking for respect for the dialectic of consultations. Today, the government has accustomed us to opening debates, setting up committees that concern us and then decisions are taken unilaterally. Why meet if in the end we are not heard? … This is why we have chosen to withdraw and continue our activism outside of this approach in which social dialogue is held. (*Les Éco*, 4/11/2011)

Explaining Labor's Apoliticism: Moroccan Unions between Incorporation, Cooperation, and Conflict

Thus, changes in Morocco's system of labor representation help explain trends in union mobilization witnessed during the early 2000s. However, while a focus on social institutions sheds light on why labor militancy remained relatively moderate, it does not explain why it was explicitly apolitical. By 2008, unions had abandoned the logic of compromise and had begun adopting more militant tactics in response to the government's economic proposals. In the face of growing social and political unrest, why did this militancy fail to develop into a broad-based movement for political change?

To answer this question, I argue that a focus on political institutions is necessary. Alongside its efforts to incorporate labor into a new collective bargaining system, the Moroccan monarchy also developed new political institutions that provided avenues for organized labor and opposition parties to voice their concerns before government. These institutions tempered labor militancy by strengthening clientelistic linkages between regime-aligned parties, unions, and the state. They also altered the internal dynamics between union leaders and their rank-and-file, preventing militant unionists from effectively pursuing revolutionary goals.

Mechanisms of Political Incorporation: The House of Councillors and *Alternance*

Indeed, at the same time that the Moroccan monarchy introduced changes to the country's collective bargaining system, it also sought to reform the broader political regime. In the wake of structural reforms, a period of pessimism set in as parties lost faith in the government's economic program and its half-hearted attempts at political liberalization (Martin-Muñoz, 2000, 98). Following a sharp economic downturn in 1995, a scathing World Bank report emphasized the connection between Morocco's economic and political futures. If the monarchy "failed to invest in human capital … and to address the bureaucratic and legal archaisms of its excessively centralized administration," it would be "unable to adapt to economic growth," increasing the potential for social and economic unrest (*Al-Maghreb* 10/17/1995 cited in Martin-Muñoz, 2000).

Hoping to avert continued crisis and reduce the risk of a political challenge to the regime, Hassan II attempted to redefine the Moroccan monarchy through institutional reforms. On August 20, 1996 – just months after the initiation of social dialogue – he announced constitutional amendments that would pave the way for competitive parliamentary elections the following year. As a further sign of change, he promised that future governments would be formed based on direct elections to the House of Representatives, giving opposition parties a greater chance to assume executive office. Additionally, to ensure proper representation of civil society organizations, the constitution would establish a second chamber – the House of Councillors – where partisan representatives would share seats with appointed members of professional councils, employers' associations, and trade unions for renewable mandates of nine-year terms.

In creating this institution, Hassan II hoped to pluralize the political system without transferring any real power away from the authoritarian regime. Although both legislative bodies gained new prerogatives to initiate laws and censure the government, the monarchy retained its authority to appoint and dismiss the Prime Minister, dissolve parliament, and modify the ministerial council (Storm, 2007, 74). Despite this, most parties and professional organizations welcomed the second chamber and supported the monarchy's proposals for reform. In 1997, legislative elections led to a recomposition of the parliament in which opposition parties (and their affiliated unions) won a substantial portion of parliamentary seats (Table 6.3). Subsequently, elites from these groups were incorporated into the new government under the banner of "*alternance.*"

Throughout the late 1990s and 2000s, these institutional reforms restructured the relationship between opposition parties, unions, and the government, fundamentally reshaping protest mobilization against the regime. First, the inclusion of parties and unions into state institutions provided these groups with an alternative means of articulating their demands, reducing the need to rely on militant strategies to express their interests. Labor parliamentarians described the second chamber as a valuable space for receiving concessions and engaging in dialogue and debate (Appendix B: MA-14, 3/31/2014; MA-25, 5/5/2014; MA-33, 5/15/2014). While their individual powers to legislate or amend proposals without monarchical approval were limited, many believed that, in coalition with partisan allies, they could influence legislation on the margins and lobby jointly for reforms (Appendix B: MA-14, 3/31/2014; MA-25, 5/5/2014).

Second, the incorporation of opposition parties into the government neutralized criticisms against the regime, transforming former political rivals into a "quasi-loyalist" opposition. In particular, the appointment of Abderrahman Youssoufi (USFP) as head of the new *alternance* government signaled the domestication of the political left and its

Table 6.1. *Parliamentary elections in Morocco, 1997*

Party	Seats	Indirect	Total
USFP	57	16	73
UC	50	28	78
RNI	46	42	88
MP	40	27	67
MDS	32	33	65
Istiqlal	32	21	53
MNP	19	15	34
PND	10	21	31
MPDC	9	0	9
FFD	9	12	21
PPS	9	7	16
PSD	5	4	9
OADP	4	0	4
PA	2	13	15
PDI	1	4	5
MD	0	0	0
UMT	—	8	8
UGTM	—	3	3
CDT	—	11	11
Other trade unions	—	5	5
Total	325	270	595

Source: Moroccan Ministry of Communication (1997)

acceptance of a new "politics of consensus" (Storm, 2007, 199–210). Although this shift periodically caused friction between militant and moderate factions within opposition groups,[13] it generally reduced resistance to the regime when labor-allied parties were in power.[14] As one observer noted:

[13] In interviews with members of the CDT, the passivity of the USFP following its inclusion into the government, as well as its failure to implement progressive social reforms, was highlighted as the chief reason provoking the USFP-CDT split (Appendix B: MU-3, 2/19/2014; MU-23, 4/25/2014).

[14] For example, during the early years of the Jettou government, UGTM executives purposefully held back from organizing strikes as a show of solidarity with the *Istiqlal* (Appendix B: MU-25, 5/5/2014).

> The depoliticization of Morocco began with the government of *alternance*. Everyone wanted 'social peace', wanted this process of transition ... but this led to stagnation, where there was no longer a living rhythm ... it created a clientelistic relationship between parties, the state, and the unions. (Appendix B: MA-9, 3/19/2014)

Moroccan Unions and the February 20th Movement: Labor at the Crossroads of Opposition and Compromise

The effects of political institutions in neutralizing labor opposition to the regime are evident in the responses of Moroccan unions to anti-regime protests in February 2011. In contrast to Tunisia, where organized labor actively championed pro-democracy protests, Moroccan unions shied away from political confrontation and used protest mobilization instrumentally to advance their goals. By leveraging their connections with partisan elites and activists from F20M, unions combined public demonstrations and institutional lobbying to pressure the government to address their concerns. While this approach allowed labor elites to win significant economic concessions, it also hindered broader political transformations that could have secured workers' interests over the long term.

Indeed, a key factor shaping unions' responses to anti-regime protests during the Arab uprisings was their relationship with regime-affiliated parties. The two unions most reluctant to support F20M – the UGTM and UNTM – were linked to parties that were closely incorporated into the regime, retaining the highest share of seats in the legislature and key positions in the El-Fassi government. As a longtime ally of the ruling party, the UGTM distanced itself from revolutionary protests, denouncing them as "anti-Moroccan," and actively discouraging its members from participating in the demonstrations (*L'Opinion*, 02/18/2011). The UNTM, for its part, expressed interest in the movement's goals early on but reversed its position just days before the protests, ultimately withdrawing from the movement entirely (Appendix B: MA-24, 4/29/2014).

Even as pro-democracy protesters became actively involved in labor demonstrations, regime-friendly unions drew a clear distinction between the "political" protests of the F20M and the "apolitical" protests focused on unions' socio-economic demands. As one February 20th activist noted, "[The conservative unions] wanted nothing to do with us. The other unions at least provided symbolic support. They released communiqués, provided shelters, and some even marched with us" (Appendix B: MA-32, 05/09/2014).

Undoubtedly, ties between loyalist parties and unions constrained union militancy, disincentivizing solidarity with F20M and limiting their capacity for radical action. According to one *Istiqlal* official, overlapping leadership roles and hierarchical relations (Arabic: *tabaʿīa*) between parties and unions allowed the *Istiqlal's* secretary-general[15] to influence the UGTM decisions, pushing the union to scale back its protests and focus on submitting demands directly to the government (Appendix B: MA-20, 4/14/2014). Similarly, the UNTM's decision to withdraw from the February 20th protests was likely driven by directives from its political partner, the Justice and Development Party (PJD). Despite initially showing sympathy for the movement, UNTM leaders withdrew their support after PJD leader Abdelilah Benkirane announced the party's boycott of anti-government demonstrations on February 17th (*Ya-biladi*, 12/18/2011).

In some cases, labor's close partnerships with regime-aligned parties enabled unions to act as a counter-revolutionary force, weakening the influence of pro-democracy protests by promoting the monarchy's reform agenda. In Fez, for example, the intersection of state, party, and union leadership in the city's mayoralty allowed Hamid Chabat – a longtime government employee and secretary-general of the *Istiqlal* and UGTM – to openly campaign for a "yes" vote in the 2011 constitutional referendum, mobilizing hundreds of union members for a pro-regime demonstration.[16]

The Reanimation of Social Dialogue

Unions' willingness to engage in anti-regime protests was also constrained by the monarchy's effort to co-opt organized labor through the revitalization of social dialogue. The day after the February 20th demonstrations, Mohammed VI announced the government's return

[15] As noted below, the secretary-general of the *Istiqlal* in 2011 was Hamid Chabat, who simultaneously served as the secretary-general of the UGTM as well as the mayor of Fez.

[16] For example, UGTM banners in Fez displayed slogans with the following text, "We are mobilizing together for the success of the council chaired by the King to reform the constitution."

to the bargaining table and convened the long-anticipated Economic and Social Council, signaling the regime's commitment to fruitful talks. On April 4, 2011, Prime Minister El-Fassi met with four of the country's five major unions – the UGTM, UNTM, FDT, and the UMT – to address labor demands and propose a new package of reforms. While the first round of negotiations was unsuccessful, the government pledged to continue talks throughout April and refine its proposals until a satisfactory compromise was achieved (*Les Éco*, 04/30/2011).

Seizing on the government's willingness to negotiate, trade unions adopted a two-pronged strategy to extract concessions. Using the spread of social protest as a bargaining chip, unions ratcheted up their mobilization efforts and organized a series of joint public sector strikes in education, health, and transportation (Buehler, 2015). Leftist unions leveraged their connections with civil society groups like the National Association of Unemployed Graduates (*Association nationale des diplômés chômeurs du Maroc*, ANDCM) and the Moroccan Association for Human Rights (*Association marocaine des droits humains*, AMDH)[17] to threaten deeper engagement with pro-democratic protests if the government failed to satisfy labor demands (Appendix B: MA-31, 5/8/2014; MA-36, 1/13/2015). Simultaneously, union leaders continued to participate in social dialogue negotiations, quietly lobbying the government for their preferred reforms (Appendix B: MA-33, 5/15/2014).

Ultimately, these tactical maneuvers paid off. On April 26, 2011, the government agreed to a compromise that included wage increases, promotions, and pension reforms, meeting most of the unions' core demands. But, if institutional engagement helped organized labor to achieve its economic goals, these gains came at the expense of deeper political reforms. Following the April 26 agreement, labor support for the February 20th movement once again splintered, as the FDT and its partisan affiliate, the USFP, withdrew from the movement in favor of deeper cooperation with the regime. Although precise figures on FDT/USFP participation are unavailable, a temporal analysis of media coverage shows a sharp decline in FDT involvement after the start of social dialogue and the king's pivotal March 9th speech. While

[17] Both of these organizations were vigorous supporters of the February 20th Movement (Badran, 2022).

the FDT was initially mentioned as a key supporter of the February 20th protests, its participation was barely registered at the movement's March 20th and May 1st demonstrations. Moreover, by June 16th, both the FDT and its partisan partner had officially withdrawn from F20M and endorsed the monarchy's plan for constitutional reform (Appendix B: MA-19, 4/9/14; MA-26, 5/6/14).

"La Deuxième Chambre"

Another barrier to unions' participation in anti-government protests was their incorporation into formal institutions, as reflected in the debate surrounding Morocco's second parliamentary chamber, the House of Councillors (HoC). A key point of contention among February 20th protesters was whether the HoC should be dissolved. While opponents criticized the HoC as "useless window dressing," funded at the taxpayers' expense (Appendix B: MA-16 4/4/2014; *La Vie Éco*, 12/30/2005), supporters argued that it strengthened democratic representation by ensuring a diversity of voices in government (Appendix B: MA-33, 5/15/2014). For trade unions, the existence of the second chamber was significant due to the political and financial benefits it offered their leadership.

As previously noted, union representatives saw the HoC as a key platform for exercising political influence. In the HoC, labor representatives could propose legislation, challenge controversial laws, and exert direct, albeit limited, influence over policymaking. Labor parliamentarians reported leveraging the political connections they developed in the chamber to secure exclusive benefits such as investment funds for their constituents and appointments to influential positions in state-owned enterprises and pension boards (Appendix B: MA-14, 3/31/2014; MA-33, 5/15/2014). Most important, deputies in parliament received substantial compensation – around 36,000 Moroccan dirhams – a portion of which was routinely "kicked back" to unions' operating budgets as a form of patronage (Appendix B: MA-9, 3/19/2014; MA-11, 3/24/2014; MA-20, 4/14/2014; *Telquel*, 5/15/2012).

Given these benefits, it is unsurprising that the debate over the second chamber became a dividing line for unions in their support for pro-democratic protests. While members of F20M and unions excluded from parliament called for the dissolution of the HoC, unions integrated into it actively fought for its preservation, creating tension between pro-democracy activists and organized labor. Debates over the HoC's existence also highlighted divisions between militant and moderate factions within politically independent unions, such as the UMT. While local branches of the union provided support to anti-regime protests, the national leadership participated in the regime's constitutional reform process, using protests strategically to lobby for greater representation in the HoC.

Indeed, despite its historical ties to the left, the UMT failed to consistently support F20M. Initially, the UMT endorsed protesters' demands, but as the debate over constitutional reform intensified, its participation in the movement splintered. The main division occurred between its intermediate branches and national administration. As in Tunisia, regional and sectoral unions – historically the most militant and politically conscious[18] – drove much of the unions' initial political activism. In regions where militant unionists held executive office, union resources were made available to support the February 20th protests and unionists participated in F20M demonstrations. In Rabat, for instance, the UMT local served as a meeting space and safe house for demonstrators fleeing government repression during street marches (Appendix B: MA-021, 04/21/2014).

In contrast, the UMT's national administration took a more cautious approach to pro-democracy protests. While it initially voiced support for F20M, its practical involvement was limited to public statements and half-hearted participation in early demonstrations. Moreover, UMT's national leadership regularly engaged in negotiations with the government, undermining F20M's efforts to pressure the monarchy by boycotting regime-initiated talks. As negotiations progressed, national leaders distanced themselves from the movement, pressuring members to reduce participation and disciplining regional leaders who continued to host F20M protests. As one union leader in Rabat noted, "There was a section within the UMT that was very supportive of the February 20th movement, but the national

[18] For example, several members of the UMT regional branch in Rabat were members of Annahj Addimocrati and the Unified Socialist Party (Parti Socialiste Unifié, PSU). These unions also sought to revitalize the UMT's bureaucratic structure through internal reforms, such as holding regular elections, increasing financial transparency, and recruiting members from marginalized professions.

leadership was against it. There was a lack of institutional support" (Appendix B: MA-31, 5/8/2014).

The definitive rupture between the UMT's militant and moderate wings came in response to the regime's decision about the House of Councillors. Following the King's announcement of constitutional reforms, including the preservation of the HoC, the UMT's Administrative Commission endorsed an unprecedented "yes" vote, abandoning the more radical demands of F20M. This decision reflected the leadership's concern with preserving its institutional influence, illustrating the constraints that political incorporation can place on union behavior. As one member of the executive bureau explained,

> We opted for the 'yes' because the text of the Basic Law was largely in line with the proposal made by the UMT in its memorandum ... in addition to wage increases in the public sector and the signature of agreements in certain enterprises, the decision to protect Morocco as an *institutional state* militated in favor of the 'yes' for the project of the Constitution (Appendix B: MA-14, 3/31/2014, emphasis added).

Union Hierarchy as an Obstacle: The UMT between Militancy and Moderation

At the same time, this decision also reflected the undemocratic nature of the UMT's internal bureaucracy and the lack of accountability between its leadership and rank-and-file members. A distinguishing characteristic of Moroccan labor unions is the hierarchical nature of their internal governance. Most unions are led exclusively by their national executives, or, in cases where they are affiliated with political parties, in collaboration with their partisan partners (Appendix B: MA-20, 4/14/2014). While local and shop-floor unions exist, they are often weakly institutionalized compared to the central administration or sectoral unions in urban centers.

Moreover, leadership turnover is rare, and national congresses to elect new executives are infrequently held.[19] Access to leadership positions is tightly controlled by the executive bureau, with labor and party elites often intervening in elections to ensure that their political clients advance (Appendix B: MA-11, 3/24/2014; MA-36, 1/13/2015).

[19] For example, the first secretary-general of the UMT was in power from 1955 to 2010. Additionally, the former leader of the CDT served from 1978 until 2018.

Labor militants in the UMT described various harassments used to discourage rank-and-file members from seeking office, including denial of financial resources, displacement of militant leaders through workplace transfers, or freezing workers' membership to curb their political ambitions (Appendix B: MA-31, 5/8/2014; MA-36, 1/13/2015). In extreme cases, dissenting unions were completely dissolved, and their leaders subjected to violent repression from union militias and state police (ibid; see also Monjib, 1992).

During the Arab uprisings, this gross centralization eroded accountability between union elites and rank-and-file workers, weakening the capacity of militant unionists to mobilize. For example, at the UMT office in Rabat, union leaders Abdelhamid Amine, Khadijah Ryadi, and Abdellah Lefnatsa were censured by the executive bureau and repressed by government-sponsored thugs (*baltagiyya*) in an effort to stifle support for F20M (Appendix B: MA-31, 5/8/2014; MA-36, 1/13/2015). Similarly, in Errachida, the local secretary-general Mohamed Oualout, was stripped of his union secondment for leaving the choice to militants to vote according to their convictions on the constitution (Rassouni, 2012).

The central administration's dominance over regional branches also played a crucial role in securing a favorable vote for the monarchy's constitutional reform. Union leaders involved in the UMT's referendum vote described the draconian methods by which the Administrative Commission arrived at a "yes" decision:

> There was no internal democracy when decisions about how to engage with the February 20th movement were made ... Most of the decision-making occurred in the commission. The [leadership] refused to discuss the matter with anyone and dismissed people who supported the [February 20th movement] in its boycott. (Appendix B: MA-31, 5/8/2014)

Other unionists accused the executive bureau of "selling out" its members to curry favor with the regime:

> With the unions, the regime began negotiations with the unions and increased the salaries of public servants by 6,000 dh. Additionally, it made promises to satisfy demands that had not yet been fulfilled, under the condition that the unions vote "yes" during the constitutional referendum. *For the 1st time, the UMT voted "yes."* The regime expected the unions to not support the February 20th movement and close the doors of the regional bureaus to the activists. Finally, the regime requested

that unions expel the radical militants from the union because of their militancy ... The constitution passed, elections were organized, and in 2012, there was increased repression against militants. (Appendix B: MA-36, 1/13/2015)

Labor Passivity and Authoritarian Resilience

Ultimately, this internal split once again fractured labor's support for F20M, delivering a significant blow to pro-democracy activists and their platform for revolutionary change. With the UMT firmly backing the monarchy's constitutional reforms, only the CDT – unsurprisingly the sole union without meaningful partisan alliances or parliamentary representation – chose to boycott the referendum and align with F20M members in opposing authoritarian rule (Badran, 2022; Bennani-Chraïbi, 2021).

Absent effective political pressure from organized labor, Morocco's authoritarian regime was able to avoid the kind of substantive reforms that led to a democratic transition in Tunisia. For many, the regime's dexterity in co-opting union elites was critical to this outcome. As one political observer remarked, "the most decisive moment of the Moroccan Arab Spring was when the UMT chose to stay with the reformist, negotiated option and withdrew from the sit-ins and street demonstrations" (Appendix B: MA-9, 3/19/2014). While this assessment is likely overstated, it is evident that labor passivity played a significant role in shaping the trajectory of political opposition in Morocco and in sustaining authoritarian rule. With renewed legitimacy following a successful constitutional referendum, Mohammed VI was able to reconsolidate his authority over the Moroccan state and steer the course of political change. At the same time, the regime was able to roll back many of the concessions granted to workers in 2011, as I discuss in Chapter 7.

Conclusion

Analyses of the recent wave of labor mobilization in North Africa offer several explanations for the differences in these movements' evolution and success. While many focus on material grievances and corporatist policies as drivers of labor unrest, this chapter presents an alternative theory centered on the role of political institutions in shaping labor conflict. I argue that the tactics and trajectories of labor protest are fundamentally shaped by the political context in which labor movements operate, as well as its impact on unions' internal governance. While the emergence of protest may be driven by workers' discontent, the survival and effectiveness of labor militancy depends on the types of organizations unions construct and how these interact with the broader political environment.

Drawing on a comparison of labor protests in Tunisia and Morocco, I find that unions with democratic organizations are more effective in engaging in political militancy than those without. Union democracy fosters political opposition by enhancing intra-union solidarity, increasing accountability between leaders and the rank-and-file, and allowing local demands for political action to "scale up" through the union hierarchy. It also helps unions withstand typical threats to social movements under authoritarian rule, such as elite co-optation, loss of grassroots support, and deliberate efforts by regime elites to sow division. Where unions establish and institutionalize democratic practices, they can more capably sustain radical protests and pressure authoritarian elites to make meaningful concessions to citizens' political demands. Where they do not, labor movements tend to be fragmented and weak, leading unions to pursue institutional remedies and make limited demands for reform.

This chapter thus underscores the importance of internal organization in shaping patterns of labor mobilization. It highlights the symbiosis between unions' external and internal political environments. I find that more repressive authoritarian contexts may foster and even facilitate the creation of democratic labor unions. For instance, when union leaders are excluded from formal politics, they may be incentivized to invest in deeper connections with their constituents to increase their capacity to influence policy through strikes. Moreover, authoritarianism itself may serve as a negative referent, prompting union leaders to seek forms of organization that directly counter the tyrannical practices they endure.

This challenges conventional wisdom about the ideal modes of labor organization and helps explain why successful social movements can emerge in contexts with weak union rights and civil liberties. Although influential bodies like the International Confederation of Free Trade Unions (ICFTU) and the International Labour Organization (ILO) have pushed for more liberal labor practices, such as union pluralism and decentralized collective bargaining, I demonstrate how these can disempower unions and make them more susceptible to control by authoritarian elites. As I explore further in the book's conclusion, this dynamic also explains why many labor unions in newly democratized contexts struggle to mobilize effectively. Once the negative referent of autocracy is removed, the *raison d'être* for militant labor unions may disappear, leading to a weakening of internal solidarity.

Finally, this chapter nuances discussions of labor's contribution to the Arab Spring by examining the different ways labor opposition can influence political change. While much attention has been given to cases where labor mobilization helped usher in new democracies, such as in Tunisia and Egypt, less focus has been placed on instances where labor movements advanced democratic aims but fell short of achieving regime change. These cases highlight the diversity of labor protests and challenge us to critically examine why ambitious social movements sometimes fail. Unlike other scholars who attribute the failure of pro-democracy protests in Morocco to their limited goals or the monarchy's entrenched legitimacy, I argue that the weakness of political reform stems from unions' inability to sustain radical protest campaigns. In contrast to the UGTT, Moroccan unions were too fragmented to coordinate mass protests and too hierarchical to embrace the political demands of their members. Additionally, they operated in a more inclusive political environment, where regime elites could use multiple institutional levers – partisan connections, social dialogue, and parliamentary inclusion – to reduce union leaders' incentives to mobilize.

Still, it would be misleading to suggest that labor opposition is ineffective unless it leads to full democratization. Under authoritarian rule, social movements can contribute to political liberalization in more subtle ways, such as placing issues on the policy agenda, raising political awareness, or shifting citizens' expectations about the possibilities for change. This highlights the importance of looking beyond successful democratic transitions to fully understand the impact of labor mobilization. By appreciating the various forms of labor protest, we can better understand unions' roles as political actors and their potential to spur reform in politically closed environments.

7 *Workers after the "Spring": Labor Mobilization in an Era of Uncertainty*

This chapter concludes the book's empirical investigation by focusing on the fates of labor unions after the Arab Spring. The revolutionary uprisings that swept across North Africa in the spring of 2011 marked a critical transition in the region's labor politics. While 2011 is widely recognized as the peak of labor power in the Middle East (Beinin, 2015; Bishara, 2018; Feltrin, 2019; Hartshorn, 2019; Kerrissey and Schofer, 2018; Langohr, 2014), subsequent years saw workers face even greater challenges within newly pluralized political environments. In the wake of regime transition and constitutional reform, unions in Tunisia and Morocco encountered new opportunities for activism, testing their ability to effectively advocate for workers' rights amidst changing political conditions.

In Tunisia, the Tunisian General Labor Union (UGTT) navigated a fraught democratic transition in which its role as a political actor and representative of the working class was hotly contested. In Morocco, labor unions grappled with task of negotiating their influence amid a mix of co-optation and limited political reforms.

Within these transitions, the dynamics of labor mobilization and political liberalization diverged sharply. In Tunisia, the UGTT utilized the democratic opening to flex its organizational muscle and win significant concessions for workers. Although repeated strikes demonstrated UGTT's ability to exploit the political transition, they also raised important questions about the union's proper role in a democratic government. Ultimately, the resolution of these debates led the UGTT to assume a king-maker role in Tunisia's democratic transition, culminating in its participation in the 2014 National Dialogue.

In contrast in Morocco, a reconstituted alliance between labor and the state after constitutional reforms led to more limited political change. While liberalization opened up new opportunities for unions' participation in government, it did not significantly increase their policy influence or their ability to win economic concessions for workers. Instead, the government's strategic decision to ally with union leaders reinforced divisions within the labor movement and restricted union's capacity to press for additional gains. The fact that many of the elements of previous state–labor relations remained in tact limited workers' capacity to redress their needs or to secure concessions won in the process of reform.

This chapter presents a comparative analysis of these developments, focusing on three issues that constituted the most important labor concerns in the post-uprising environment: unions' organizational status, their role in the political system, and workers' socioeconomic gains. I argue that institutional legacies inherited from authoritarian rule created different starting points for Tunisian and Moroccan unions, shaping their trajectories during the post-uprising period. In Tunisia, militant unions drew upon vast organizational resources – internal democracy, autonomy, and cohesion – to shape political transitions and achieve meaningful policy reforms. In Morocco, labor unions faced a less protracted liberalization process but obtained fewer material and political gains through moderate tactics like negotiation and lobbying.

This chapter thus confirms the argument that labor unions are most likely to effect significant socioeconomic and political change when they remain outside of formal politics. Contra the conventional wisdom, political exclusion affords unions with unique resources – namely, autonomy and close connections to the grassroots – that they can use during political transitions to strengthen their power and influence the process of policy/political reform. Conversely, unions that retain close connections with political parties and elites face a unique dilemma: while they can leverage these ties to promote their interests, political alliances may also persuade them to prioritize the incumbent regime's electoral and governing goals, which require strategic moderation, over workers' redistributive demands. In this case, political incorporation is likely to inhibit the achievement of meaningful reforms since it suppresses workers' radical demands and makes division within the labor movement more likely.

The remainder of the chapter is organized as follows. The next section examines the conventional wisdom on labor mobilization during political transitions, outlining the various challenges that labor unions face and the ways that they are expected to respond based on existing theories. I then compare the divergent reactions of Tunisian and Moroccan unions, focusing on the UGTT's continued militancy and achievement of meaningful reforms and Moroccan unions' moderation and more limited policy gains. I attribute these outcomes to institutional legacies inherited from authoritarian rule and show how varying modes of labor incorporation shaped unions' relationships with the state and the organizational assets available to workers for advancing political reforms. Finally, I conclude the chapter by considering how institutional legacies might shift to enhance labor unions' political influence in the future.

Unions in Transition: Labor Mobilization during Political Liberalization

Scholars of labor politics generally acknowledge that political transitions present unique windows of opportunity for organized labor. Political liberalization expands the space for worker mobilization – as associational space is deregulated and the costs of repression increase, workers become more emboldened to press for their demands through collective action (Bermeo, 1999; O'Donnell and Schmitter, 1986; Przeworski, 1991; Sandoval, 1995). Political openings may also create a more favorable environment for adopting labor-friendly legislation, as newly established regimes seek to build broad-based coalitions to legitimize their rule (Collier and Collier, 1991). Particularly in contexts where trade unions have been suppressed, political transitions can catalyze labor revitalization. Amid the "resurgence of civil society" that often accompanies democratization, trade unions are well positioned to leverage the more permissive political environment to reassert their presence and attract new members (O'Donnell and Schmitter, 1986). In some cases, unions can use their influence to play a pivotal role in shaping the new political order, advocating for workers' rights and social justice as central components of the emerging democratic framework (Collier and Mahoney, 1997; LeBas, 2011; Lee, 2011).

However, political transitions also expose unions to new uncertainties that may diminish their influence in newly liberalized societies. The expansion of associational space can act as a double-edged sword: while it provides new opportunities for union organizing, it also introduces competition from rival unions that can weaken the labor movement and dilute workers' collective voice (Caraway et al., 2015). Additionally, the shift to market-oriented policies that frequently accompanies democratization can undermine unions' bargaining power by promoting labor flexibilization, weakening job security, and undercutting unions' organizational base (Burgess, 2004; Murillo, 2001). Increased mobilization can also strain the economy or provoke resistance from states and employers, leading to a protracted political crisis. For instance, efforts to implement labor-friendly reforms may encounter opposition from employers, causing them to reconsider their commitment to democratic change. Similarly, conservative and moderate politicians may be overwhelmed by the popular support for organized labor, viewing the growth of trade unions as a threat to their political authority (O'Donnell and Schmitter, 1986; Ruschemeyer et al., 1992; Valenzuela, 1989). In such cases, the revitalization of organized labor can provide a pretext for hardliners to initiate a counter-revolution and regain state power. Thus, the influence of unions during political transitions may be significantly curtailed, limiting their ability to shape policy and protect labor interests in the long term.

Given these opportunities and challenges, extant literature offers varying expectations of union behavior during political transitions. Some scholars argue that workers will seize the moment to aggressively push for labor demands, using the political opening to secure material gains and "expand the limits of mere liberalization and partial democratization" (O'Donnell and Schmitter, 1986, 53–54). Others suggest that labor unions will adopt a more cautious approach, noting that "complete docility and patience" are required from labor during democratic transitions to prevent destabilizing backlash (Przeworski, 1986, 63). Still others offer more complex predictions. For instance, Valenzuela (1989) expects an initial burst of union activity followed by moderation once the prospects for democratic consolidation seem more likely. The specific timing of such militancy and moderation is said to be contingent on several factors, including the strength of the labor movement, its treatment under the previous regime, the speed and nature of the political transition itself, and the broader socioeconomic context (ibid).

Common to all of these studies, however, is the expectation that institutional legacies, particularly those inherited from the previous authoritarian regime, condition the trajectory of labor mobilization. Important in this regard is the extent of labor incorporation and unions' relationship with partisan elites. Unions with experience in formal politics and strong partisan alliances are expected to moderate their behavior, strategically positioning themselves to gain the most in terms of political concessions and labor reforms (Lee, 2011; Murillo, 2001; Robertson, 2004). These unions mediate their demands through the political system, leveraging their partisan connections to secure substantial gains while maintaining political and economic stability. In contrast, unions that were excluded from the political process and failed to establish systematic linkages with political parties are expected to adopt more militant tactics (Caraway et al., 2015; Caraway and Ford, 2020; Lee, 2011; Valenzuela, 1989). Importantly, these unions are also expected to achieve fewer concessions, as they lack the political leverage necessary to influence the process of reform (Lee, 2011).

Viewed from this theoretical framework, Tunisian unions, which have a legacy of political exclusion, are expected to display greater militancy than their Moroccan counterparts. Additionally, Moroccan unions are expected to secure larger gains for workers in the post-uprising period due to their strategic positioning within the political system and their access to influential partisan elites.

Labor Mobilization and Reform Trajectories in Tunisia and Morocco

However, the reality of labor protest and reform in Tunisia and Morocco only partially fulfills these expectations. In Tunisia, unions were indeed more militant and confrontational, but this did not hinder their ability to win political concessions or to secure material gains for the working class. According to data from the Ministry of Social Affairs, in the post-uprising period (2012–2014), Tunisian workers held an average of 451 strikes per year – a slight decrease from their peak of 567 in 2011, but consistently higher than the pre-uprising average of 360 strikes per annum (Figure 7.1). These actions ranged from regularized, nonviolent demonstrations to more disruptive protests such as blockades, sit-ins, and hunger strikes, which became more prevalent after 2013. Additionally, although the majority of strikes were legally sanctioned and organized by unions, in 2014, the protest landscape became more fragmented, with the share of wildcat strikes increasing to 30.4 percent. Finally, strikes increased significantly in duration. In 2014, working days lost increased from 241,658 to 361,464, which had deleterious effects on economic

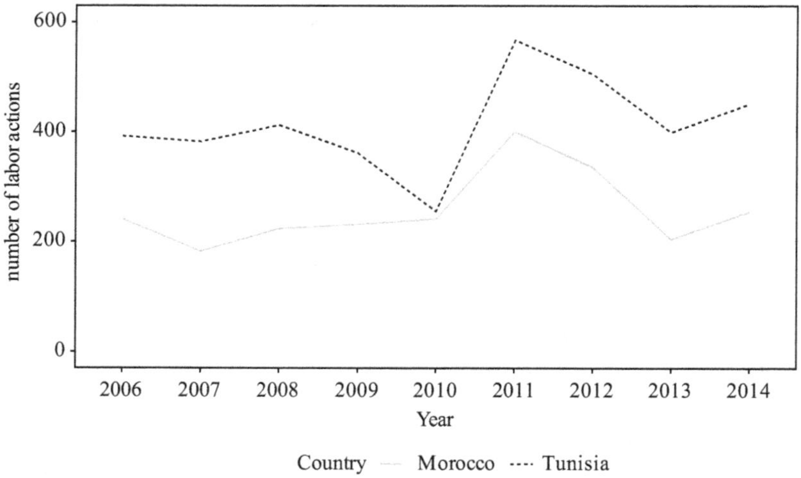

Source: Tunisian Ministry of Social Affairs, Moroccan Ministry of Labor

Figure 7.1 Comparative labor protests in Tunisia and Morocco, ILO, 2006–2014

stability, particularly in large industrial firms like the Gafsa Phosphate Company (CPG).[1]

Strikes during this period were also marked by their political orientation. Although the majority of strikes recorded by this author were socioeconomic in nature – focusing on working conditions, wages, and professional issues – a number of prominent strikes had explicitly political goals. For example, the Kasbah protests in January and February 2011 advocated for the removal of prominent Democratic Constitutional Rally (RCD) elites from Tunisia's government, demanding the creation of a protective body for the revolution to pilot the transition toward the democratic election of the National Constituent Assembly. Additionally, two of the three general strikes organized by the UGTT were held in response to political events: the first following the assassination of leftist leader Chokri Belaid and the second after the murder of MP Mohamed Brahmi. In both of these protests, unionists called for an end to political violence and the

[1] According to reports, UGTT planned strikes in the CPG led a 40 percent reduction in production, costing the company nearly $2 billion in revenues from 2010 to 2014 (Dahmani, May 7, 2015; Gall, May 13, 2014).

start of negotiations to solidify the country's democratic transition. Beyond protests, the UGTT also led efforts to establish the National Council for the Protection of the Revolution (*Conseil de Sauvegarde de la Révolution*, CSR) and the 2014 National Dialogue, enabling it to take decisive action to influence the direction of Tunisia's political transition.

Importantly, in contrast to expectations, labor protests in Tunisia were effective at winning concessions for workers and shaping the process of political reform. Although both the government and union officials expressed concerns about the potential economic damage caused by strikes, the UGTT achieved significant gains for workers, including increases in the minimum wage, public sector wages, and civil service jobs. Through its political activism, the UGTT played a critical role in steering the course of democratic transition. Following the Kasbah protests, the RCD-influenced government of Mohammed Ghannouchi was replaced by a more technocratic alternative, which was perceived as more responsive to the public's demands(Hartshorn, 2019). Additionally, the 2013 general strikes paved the way for a national reconciliation process that resulted in the creation of a new constitution, marking a pivotal moment in Tunisia's democratic transition.

In contrast in Morocco, labor militancy was much less prevalent. Although strike levels from 2012 to 2014 increased from the pre-uprising period (2006–2010), the increase was marginal, and by 2014, strike numbers had largely returned to their previous levels (Figure 7.1). Moreover, the number of strikes that occurred paled in comparison to those avoided through negotiation, which rose from a low of 930 in 2011 to a high 1,462 in 2014. This trend reflects the hesitancy of unions to organize militant protests following the 2011 uprisings, and their renewed preference for a "wait and see" approach to confrontation with the state. As the secretary-general of the Moroccan Workers' Union (UMT), Miloudi Moukharik, remarked, "We are now in the logic of negotiation before moving on to protest." (*L'observateur du Maroc*, 02/17/2014)

Indeed, majority of protests recorded during the period were organized by workers without union affiliation, accounting for roughly 60 percent of strikes overall. However, in the later part of the period, this dynamic shifted, with a larger share of strikes being organized by official labor federations. Especially active in this regard were the Democratic Confederation of Labor (CDT), the Moroccan Workers'

Union (UMT), and the Democratic Federation of Labor (FDT), which formed a historic alliance in 2014 to unify militant actions against the government. This marked a significant shift in the Moroccan protest landscape, signaling its movement toward more coordinated and unified collective actions.

In line with existing theories, protests in Morocco remained socio-economic throughout the post-uprising period. Of the strikes recorded by this author between 2012 and 2014, none were motivated by political concerns. Instead, demands were focused on parochial workplace issues such as unpaid wages, which accounted for approximately 35 percent of strikes, arbitrary dismissals, representing 25 percent, and the refusal to grant social benefits, making up another 25 percent of strikes. This focus on immediate, localized labor issues rather than broader political objectives reflects the unions' strategic orientation toward economic concessions and addressing specific workplace grievances.

However, despite their moderation, Moroccan labor protests achieved fewer gains than their Tunisian counterparts. Although strikes in 2011 brought promises of important concessions, by 2014, very few of these promises had been fulfilled. Six hundred-dirham wage increases in the public sector, for instance, were quickly undermined by wage freezes implemented as part of the 2013 Finance Law. Additionally, changes to Morocco's promotion system agreed upon in the 2011 round of social dialogue remained unenforced as of 2014. According to Moukharik, the lowest category of workers still awaited promotion, leading to extreme insecurity for low-income workers (*Finances News*, 04/09/2014). The government also moved to reduce pensions and increase the retirement age, further exacerbating the challenges faced by the working class (ibid).

Finally, after the Arab uprisings, the regime implemented new strictures on union organizing, which reduced unions' strength and ability to mobilize. Employers in the private sector instituted a de-facto reduction of salaries for striking workers and utilized penal codes (Article 288) to punish workers accused of militant activity. The government also proposed a restrictive union organizing law that increased government oversight of union budgets and made government funding contingent on their holding congresses every four years(La Vie Éco, 12/09/2014). These measures significantly curtailed the influence of Moroccan unions, leaving them in a weaker position than before.

Explaining Divergent Trajectories: The Influence of Institutional Legacies

What explains these divergent developments? A prominent body of scholarship stresses the macrostructural determinants of labor opposition and policy reform. According to this view, mobilization is more likely to occur in permissive political environments where constraints on organized labor are lax or where economic distress amplifies workers' demands. Particularly, where economic hardship accompanies the breakdown of authoritarian regimes, social movement claims can become more resonant, increasing the likelihood of movement success.

While it is true that Tunisia experienced a more severe economic downturn and a clearer break with its authoritarian past – marked by the ouster of Ben Ali and a subsequent power vacuum – these factors only partially account for the patterns of mobilization witnessed in Tunisia and Morocco. Indeed, while Tunisian workers faced harsher economic conditions, some business cycle theories would predict that this should have led to more restraint in labor mobilization to preserve macroeconomic stability. The worsening economic environment might have dissuaded workers from striking, out of fear that prolonged instability might exacerbate their already precarious situation. Moreover, although Tunisia's clean break from its previous regime arguably facilitated greater protest activity, it also introduced new challenges that potentially undermined the mobilizational capacity of the UGTT. For example, increased pluralism meant that the UGTT, once Tunisia's sole labor organization, faced competition from rival unions, potentially diluting its capacity to organize. Furthermore, the weakened state and economy following Ben Ali's departure should have reduced the government's ability to enact significant reforms, making the UGTT's achievements in obtaining concessions even more remarkable.

Conversely, Moroccan unions were arguably better positioned to secure concessions from the government due to their closer ties with the regime. According to prominent theories, their ability to maintain a degree of economic stability and their access to political allies should have enabled them to secure labor-friendly reforms. However, as noted earlier, this did not occur. Instead of leveraging their political connections to demand more substantial changes, union leaders often prioritized preserving their political relationships over pursuing radical reforms.

This discussion underscores the need to go beyond structural factors in explaining patterns of labor opposition and political reform. While macrostructural conditions may create a more conducive environment for labor protests, it is crucial to understand how unions operate within this environment and how they manage to capitalize on political opportunities to secure meaningful reforms. This requires an examination of their internal politics, as well as their positioning within the broader political landscape. In the sections that follow, I explore how institutional legacies, inherited from the authoritarian period, shaped unions' capacity to mobilize after the Arab uprisings and their ability to steer the course of political and economic change.

Tunisia

Labor Mobilization in Tunisia: The UGTT as an Architect of Tunisia's Democratic Transition

The ouster of Ben Ali in 2011 provided a window of opportunity – and several unanticipated challenges – for organized labor in Tunisia. The fall of the former regime sparked a turbulent political transition, which generated an explosion of mobilization and popular demands. Amid this unrest, the UGTT navigated an uncertain political environment in which its role as a social and political actor was actively questioned. Despite these challenges, the UGTT was able to leverage resources derived from its authoritarian past to win substantial concessions for workers and exert influence over the process of reform.

The legacy of exclusionary corporatism under Ben Ali endowed the UGTT with two critical resources – autonomy and organizational cohesion – that placed labor in an advantageous position once political liberalization began. Armed with these tools, the UGTT emerged as a central actor in the transition process, using its organizational clout to guide the democratic transition and act as a mediating voice in the contest for power that followed. At the same time, it secured impressive gains for workers, including labor-friendly policies, permanent contracts for public sector workers, and wage increases in the private and public sectors. Consequently, Tunisia was able to emerge as one of the few success stories of the Arab Spring, consolidating its fragile democratic transition and avoiding the counterrevolutionary pressures that plagued other North African regimes.

Legacies of Organizational Strength: Consolidating Autonomy and Solidarity

In many ways, Tunisia's successful transition to democracy, when compared to other North African countries, is surprising. Like its regional counterparts, Tunisia endured decades of authoritarian rule under leaders who tightly controlled political life and suppressed opposition. However, unlike in countries such as Egypt and Morocco, the extent of this repression was so severe that it eliminated virtually all political competition. The country's political landscape was shaped by a policy of exclusionary corporatism, where state institutions limited pluralism to maintain the hegemony of the ruling elite.

Given this, Tunisia entered the postrevolutionary period without a clear political agent to guide its transition. Existing parties had been co-opted by the former regime while newer parties had to establish national organizations and win constituents, leaving them ill-equipped to direct the process of political reform. Similarly, civil society organizations – save the UGTT – were organizationally weak. After decades of state co-optation or repression, most civil society groups lacked the organizational capacity and political expertise to advocate for broad-based democratic reforms.

Ironically, this legacy of organizational weakness helped the UGTT to steer Tunisia's political transition by maintaining its organizational autonomy from political elites. In previous periods, political autonomy was forced upon the union through government sanctions on union activities: authoritarian leaders deliberately avoided coalition-building with organized labor and prohibited unions from participating in political life(Alexander, 1996a). These efforts, meant to demobilize workers and isolate them from the political sphere, left the UGTT without a strong partisan ally to represent its interests in the post-uprising landscape. Although opposition parties were involved in the UGTT and sympathetic to labor concerns, they never developed an institutionalized relationship with the union that could be relied upon to advance labor demands. Moreover, in the fractured political landscape that predominated after the end of the Ben Ali regime, no party with programmatic commitments to labor emerged that was strong enough to unilaterally influence policy in the UGTT's favor.

Consequently, in the political contest that followed Ben Ali's ouster, the UGTT remained outside of formal politics. Although three union leaders initially accepted portfolios in the interim government led by Mohammed Ghannouchi,[2] protests from UGTT members outside of the ministerial headquarters [Kasbah] forced these leaders to resign the following day. The UGTT's continued detachment from institutional politics was, in large part, the result of legacies formed during the Ben Ali era. Due to their historical experience with government repression, many in the labor movement were suspicious of direct political participation and eschewed alliances with regime elites. For union militants, developing linkages with political parties was a violation of the UGTT's historical mission and risked exposing it to co-optive pressures that could undermine the union's independence. Activists stressed the need to protect the union against "infiltration" by the transition government, arguing that political neutrality was necessary to safeguard both the union and the popular revolution from nondemocratic forces (Appendix B: TU-12, 10/18/2013). While liberalization opened up the possibility for the UGTT to create its own labor party, union leaders worried that doing so would sow ideological divisions among workers and undermine unions' strength (Appendix B: TU-5, 10/3/13; TU-44, 1/8/14, see also Bishara and Grewal, 2022). Workers were also concerned that direct involvement in politics might compromise the UGTT's ability to negotiate effectively during tripartite discussions. As one unionist put it, "[The UGTT] cannot be both judge and jury ... its role is to defend the people and not the government" (Cherif quoted in Yousfi, 2015, 109).

Additionally, the union's history of grassroots organizing led it to favor a bottom-up approach to activism over reliance on institutional politics or partisan elites. As Tunisia's sole labor union, with over 500,000 members and an office in every district, the UGTT was technically well-equipped to deploy its organizational muscle to advance labor demands. However, consolidating support for militant mobilization was a more complex task. In the aftermath of the 2011 uprising, the UGTT faced two organizational challenges that compromised its internal unity and mobilizing strength.

First, while the union received widespread acclaim for its role in supporting revolutionary protests, it simultaneously faced intense criticism from its members. Younger, more militant, and geographically

[2] Mohammed Ghannouchi served as prime minister under Ben Ali from 1999 to 2011, and was a prominent member of the RCD.

isolated factions within the UGTT denounced the leadership for its delayed response to anti-government protests and its alleged collaboration with the Ben Ali regime (Yousfi, 2015). This discontent was exacerbated by the freeing of associational space during the transition period, which introduced competition from two new unions: the General Confederation of Tunisian Labor (*Confédération Générale Tunisienne du Travail*, CGTT) and the Union of Tunisian Workers (*Union des Travailleurs Tunisiens*, UTT). While the CGTT criticized the UGTT its perceived lack of internal democracy, the UTT offered a platform more focused on workers' socio-economic demands, sharply contrasting with the UGTT's increasing politicization.

To address these challenges, the UGTT embarked on a comprehensive process of internal reform. From December 25 to 28, 2011, it held its 22nd congress with the goal of uniting the union's membership and restoring its legitimacy in the post-revolution environment. Union leaders apologized for their complicity with the former regime and committed to a series of bureaucratic reforms aimed at ensuring greater transparency and accountability (*Tunis Afrique Presse*, 12/28/2011). In addition to upholding the union's commitment to term limits introduced in 2002, the congress also discussed several institutional changes that would strengthen union members' voice vis-à-vis labor elites: lowering the requirements for base union leadership, decentralizing union finances, and formally ending the ten-day strike authorization process (Appendix B: TU-44, 1/8/2014).

The congress also adopted a progressive social program that catered to the economically disenfranchised and more radical members of the union base. In a bold move, delegates rejected the government's request for a six-month moratorium on strikes and adopted resolutions condemning privatization, international loans, and government corruption (Hartshorn, 2019). The new executive elected to execute this agenda represented a victory for "left-wing" militants in the UGTT – heading the union was Houcine Abbasi, known for his activism against the RCD in Kasserine. Additionally, a diverse coalition of leaders from different regions, sectors, and ideological trends comprised the remaining members of the executive bureau.[3]

[3] For example, Samir Cheffi, Hfaiedh Hfaiedh, and Sami Tahri, all prominent members of leftist organizations were elected to the executive bureau. Despite this the bureau contained no female leadership.

Union pluralism presented another challenge that the UGTT had to address. To maintain cohesion and discourage potential defections, UGTT leaders framed union pluralism in terms of solidarity and betrayal, with continual references to the union's persecution under the Ben Ali regime. When discussing the rise of new unions, they emphasized the UGTT's legacy as the historical representative of the working class and blamed leadership defections on "counter-revolutionary forces," who hoped to divide the UGTT and dilute its organizational influence (Yousfi, 2015, 162). This antagonistic framing raised the costs of defection considerably; by portraying new unions as politically motivated spoilers, it equated defection with a betrayal of the working class at best and active collaboration with the previous regime at worst.

Although, in interviews, unionists recognized the need for pluralism in a democratic Tunisia, many viewed it as an attempt to undermine workers' unity during an already tenuous political transition. Loyalty to the UGTT also persisted because workers understood the importance of intra-union solidarity to preserve their rights in the enterprise. According to one unionist:

> It is true that now we are afraid [of trade union pluralism] ... The problem with the new trade unions is that instead of penetrating the vast terrain where the UGTT does not exist, they come in the same areas, in the same workplaces and amass two or three people, and say that they are forming a union. Sometimes they are manipulated by political parties that want to weaken the UGTT, and sometimes it's just a rivalry between two people ... Now, many employers will refuse to negotiate, they'll say 'you [two unions] are in conflict, so try to solve your problems and after that we'll negotiate.' Pluralism permits the employer to not negotiate, not to give rights to workers. (Appendix B: TU-20, 10/29/13).

Two additional institutional legacies reinforced organizational cohesion within the UGTT. First, the union's decentralized bureaucracy alleviated concerns from reform-minded unionists about their ability to organize within the union's existing structure. Although some of these militants defected to the CGTT, the experience of the 2011 uprising demonstrated that local and regional branches could exercise their functions without obstruction from the confederation leadership. Moreover, in the context of a pluralized union environment, confederation and regional leaders hesitated to regain control over local offices, fearing that such pressure could lead to further defections (Appendix B: TU-17, 10/23/2013; TU-44, 1/8/2014).

Second, affiliation with the UGTT still offered significant benefits due to the persistence of Ben Ali-era labor laws. Despite the rise of union pluralism, Tunisia's labor market continued to be governed by corporatist institutions developed under authoritarian rule. For example, as the country's "most representative union," the UGTT retained exclusive rights to collective bargaining and enjoyed numerous institutional advantages, such as union secondments and automatic dues checkoff. The interim government also erected barriers to new union's success to maintain the UGTT's organizational dominance. For instance, in 2012, the government denied the CGTT access to its membership dues and publicly questioned the union's legitimacy by disputing the accuracy of its enrollment numbers (Appendix B: TU-32, 11/21/2013). Strikes held by new unions often went unrecognized by the Ministry of Social Affairs and were brutally repressed by employers without consequence. As a result, new unions struggled to attract members in the post-uprising period – by 2014, the CGTT reported approximately 50,000 members, while the UTT claimed around 150,000 (Appendix B: TU-32, 11/21/2013; *La Presse*, 02/16/2014).

These developments profoundly shaped the UGTT's organizational trajectory during the early transition years. The hollowing out of civil society, combined with the persistence of corporatist institutions, allowed the union to maintain its organizational strength and attract a significant influx of new members.[4] Additionally, the UGTT's historical exclusion from formal politics and its commitment to grassroots organizing enabled it to preserve its autonomy from political elites, despite co-optive pressures. These dynamics were rooted in legacies inherited from the authoritarian period. Because exclusionary corporatism had emptied Tunisia's political environment, the UGTT entered into the transition period with few political allies and continued to operate outside formal institutional structures. During the transition, this reliance on extra-institutional politics would allow the union to assert itself as a significant social actor and exert considerable pressure on the government to achieve its demands. It would also empower

[4] According to Hartshorn (2019), the UGTT's membership increased to 800,000 members by the end of 2011.

the union to direct the process of political reform, as I discuss in the following section.

The UGTT as a Power-broker: Steering the Democratic Transition

The fall of the Ben Ali government in January 2011 marked a period of profound uncertainty for Tunisia's political future. In the aftermath of the regime's collapse, intense debates arose over the direction that the country's political transition should take. During these discussions, the UGTT emerged as a leading force in shaping Tunisia's democratic transition. In three key phases of the transition process – the establishment of the National Constituent Assembly (NCA), the crafting of the constitution, and the conclusion of the National Dialogue – the UGTT's influence was instrumental in guiding the country toward a negotiated settlement and advancing workers' democratic aims.

Creating a Constituent Assembly

At the heart of the initial debates about Tunisia's political future was the question of how its democratic transition should proceed. While many in the government, particularly those with ties to the RCD, favored a simple handover of power as stipulated by the 1959 constitution, the UGTT and opposition groups insisted on the creation of a new constitution by an NCA. For members of this latter group, a genuine democratic transition necessitated a decisive break with the former regime, which could only be achieved through the creation of a democratically elected, representative body. Thus, in the early months of the transition, the UGTT took a leading role in advancing the demand for an NCA and a new constitutional process.

To counteract the government's proposal, UGTT leaders spearheaded a pressure campaign to build momentum for the convening of the NCA. In February 2011, the UGTT formed a coalition with twenty-eight other civil society groups to found the National Council for the Protection of the Revolution (CSR), a civil society organization created to monitor the government's activities and facilitate negotiations with the opposition about the transition process. The CSR positioned itself as the "pilot" of Tunisia's democratic transition; by organizing joint meetings with the country's major stakeholders about the proposal for an NCA, the group aimed to chart a vision for Tunisia's future grounded in broad-based participation (International Crisis Group, 2011; Zemni, 2015). Additionally, by mobilizing public opinion it hoped to place the demand for the NCA at the forefront of the agenda, effectively challenging the government's preferred course of action.

In March 2011, this public pressure finally paid off when the government announced its decision to suspend the 1959 constitution and elect a popular assembly to draft a new one. The CSR's success in achieving its demands was bolstered by two key factors. First, the organization's diverse composition and political independence from former regime lent its proposals greater legitimacy than those offered by the government. For many Tunisians, the CSR possessed unique moral authority to guide Tunisia's democratic transition because its founders had resisted the Ben Ali regime and played an essential role in organizing opposition during the 2011 Jasmine Revolution (Appendix B: TU-24, 11/04/2013; TU-27, 11/08/2013). Despite internal disagreements about the Council's political aims,[5] the coalition was generally seen as the genuine representative of popular sovereignty in Tunisia. Indeed, its influence during the transitional period was so great that the interim government ultimately absorbed the CSR into its own advisory body, the High Commission for the Protection of the Revolution (ISROR), tasked with steering the country's ongoing political reforms and ensuring that the people's objectives were reflected in the new political order.

Second, the UGTT effectively utilized its organizational capacity to pressure the government into meeting the CSR's demands. In addition to hosting workshops and public meetings to promote the Council's plans for an NCA, the UGTT coordinated demonstrations, strikes, and sit-ins to ensure that the transition process adhered to citizens' revolutionary goals. For instance, when concerns arose that ISROR lacked sufficient representation from youth groups and interior regions – key actors in the anti-regime protests – the UGTT threatened to

[5] Although they were initially part of the CSR the Tunisian National Freedom Council, the Tunisian Association of Democratic Women, and the National Union of Tunisian Journalists later withdrew from the organization because they believed that the Council did not have adequate legitimacy to speak in the name of the Tunisian people (Zemni, 2015).

withdraw its representatives from the commission unless these groups were granted greater participation (*Echaab*, 03/19/2011). Similarly, when the government attempted to install a new slate of governors, including nineteen former members of the RCD, the UGTT activated its regional branches to lead protests, denouncing the appointments as a betrayal of the revolution's aims (*Echaab*, 02/12/2011). Despite officially dissolving the RCD on February 21st, unionists maintained pressure on the government, leading to its eventual decision to resign and suspend the 1959 constitution. This development paved the way for the creation of a National Constituent Assembly to guide Tunisia's political transition, setting the stage for a more liberal and inclusive transition process.

Drafting a New Constitution

With the framework for the NCA securely in place, the next step in Tunisia's political transition was to draft a new constitution. Early on, the UGTT showed a keen interest in influencing the constitution-making process. In mid-2011, the union began drafting its own constitutional proposal that included several key provisions aimed at advancing workers' rights. Its ultimate goal was to have a direct hand in shaping the constitution's content by winning seats in the NCA and using this institutional leverage to secure labor-friendly legislation, which politically minded unionists saw as essential to consolidating a successful democratic transition (Appendix B: TU-43, 12/13/2013).

Despite this ambition, the UGTT was unable to secure representation in the NCA. The assembly was dominated by a coalition of conservative and left-leaning parties, with Ennahda winning the plurality of seats and two other center-left parties, Ettakatol and the Congress for the Republic, helping to form the government. The UGTT's failure to win seats in the NCA occurred for two reasons. First, in an attempt to break from Tunisia's authoritarian past, the NCA elections were de-corporatized, meaning that no seats were reserved for identity, class, or other civil society groups (Hartshorn, 2017).[6] This created an unintentional barrier to the UGTT's success, since labor candidates would have to compete with established party

[6] The only exceptions were quotas for women, since party lists were required to alternate male and female candidates, and a special set of nineteen representatives for Tunisians living abroad.

lists for seats. While many of these parties were new, public distrust of unions' involvement in political affairs, a legacy of the suppression of political unionism under Ben Ali, placed the UGTT at a disadvantage when competing with parties led by well-known members of the political elite. Additionally, the UGTT's own desire to maintain political independence and avoid internal strife further contributed to its lack of electoral success. Fearing that endorsing a specific party list could fracture the organization, the union encouraged its members to run as independents or as members of their respective political parties (*Echaab*, 08/25/2011). While this approach preserved the UGTT's unity, it also cost the union seats, as labor-affiliated candidates struggled to gain visibility in Tunisia's fragmented political landscape.

Once the NCA was convened, a lack of defined procedures for civil society groups to access the assembly further limited the UGTT's ability to influence constitutional decision-making. According to reports, despite formal commitments to transparency and accountability, the NCA's intra-party commissions responsible for drafting constitutional proposals were reluctant to release key documents to the public or to facilitate meaningful engagement with civil society groups (The Carter Center, 2015, 58–67). These challenges were exacerbated by chronic absenteeism and constantly shifting political alliances within the NCA. Deputies frequently migrated between blocs, and new parties were formed due to routine defections, creating an unstable legislative landscape (ibid, 46–50, 53–55). As in previous periods, this made it difficult for the UGTT to build and sustain an influential coalition of legislative support.

Undeterred by its lack of official representation, the UGTT chose to work outside the NCA to influence the constitution-making process. On November 3, 2011, the UGTT, along with other excluded civil society groups created a parallel institution, the Civil National Constituent Assembly (CNCA), to develop its own constitutional framework through a more open and participatory method. While the CNCA emphasized that its efforts were intended to complement rather than compete with the NCA, its public actions subtly pressured the government to adopt a more consensual text. Leveraging the UGTT's extensive grassroots networks, the CNCA hosted conferences and roundtables to raise political awareness across the country and to provide recommendations on the constitutional proposals being drafted by the NCA (Karray, 2020). During these events, constitutional experts debated key issues, engaged with the public, and drafted policy proposals for the NCA, particularly concerning civic and individual rights. Although the NCA never officially recognized the CNCA's influence on its decision-making, widespread public opposition to the NCA's first constitutional draft – which was created without input from the CNCA – led its Constitutional Commission to initiate a nationwide consultative process similar to the one created by the CNCA. As a result, subsequent drafts included more liberal provisions (described in greater detail below), many of which had been advocated by the CNCA and the UGTT.

In addition to its lobbying efforts, the UGTT engaged in numerous protests and strikes to make its demands heard. In many ways, militant mobilization strengthened the UGTT's efforts to influence the constitution-making process from the outside. The union's ability to convince legislators of the legitimacy of its proposals depended on its credibility as representative of the working class, which necessitated continual demonstrations to showcase its ability to mobilize. Thus, at critical moments in the constitution-drafting process, the union used its organizational muscle to exert political pressure on the NCA. For example, after the release of the NCA's first draft of the constitution in August 2012, the UGTT threatened a general strike to oppose an unpopular provision that described women's role in society as "complementary" rather than "equal" to men's (Hartshorn, 2019). Although the strike never occurred, the threat underscored the extent to which the UGTT was willing to deploy its organizational resources to oppose retrogressive legislation.

The union also deployed militant tactics to advocate for new legislation regarding social and economic rights. In early drafts of the constitution, robust protections for workers' rights were lacking; for example, the first two drafts only guaranteed the right to strike as long as strikes did not "endanger the life, health and safety" of the Tunisian people (Hartshorn and Sil, 2019). However, union leaders viewed these stipulations as too restrictive and pushed for more liberal protections. In the first half of 2013, opposition to this wording led to numerous protests by the UGTT, resulting in the limitation's removal in the final draft of the constitution. The UGTT also advocated for broader social democratic ideals, including the right to decent work, health coverage, fair pay, sustainable development, and regional equality.

Ultimately, the UGTT's success in influencing the constitutional agenda was due to its strategic use of resources and tactics inherited from authoritarian rule. Despite the obstacles posed by the fragmented political environment and the exclusionary nature of the NCA, the UGTT leveraged its political autonomy and its ability to mobilize large-scale protests to shape the constitutional process from the outside. This approach, itself a legacy of unions' political exclusion under Ben Ali, enabled the UGTT to exert pressure on the NCA's decision-making despite not winning any legislative seats. Its ability to serve as an independent power-broker would also prove instrumental in concluding a pacted transition to democracy in 2014, as I discuss below.

Facilitating the National Dialogue

Finally, the UGTT played a crucial role in solidifying Tunisia's democratic transition by convening and directing the 2014 National Dialogue. By 2012, the constitutional drafting process had stalled due to deepening disagreements between the NCA and the ruling Troika coalition. One year into its mandate, the NCA had failed to deliver a new constitution, leading to widespread frustration among political parties and the general public (Portelli, 2015). Moreover, the growing influence of the Ennahda Shura Council over executive decision-making heightened tensions within the Troika government and fueled fears of an Islamist takeover of Tunisia's traditionally secular state (Portelli and Augenbaum, 2017).

Recognizing the potential for political instability, on October 16, 2012, the UGTT, in collaboration with the Tunisian League of Human Rights (LTDH) and the Bar Association (OAT), organized the first National Dialogue conference. This conference aimed to establish a broad consensus on the path forward for Tunisia's democratic transition. The meeting proposed a six-point framework for a new democratic state, highlighting key principles such as the civil nature of the state, respect for human rights, rejection of violence, and the protection of religious and economic institutions from political manipulation (M'rad, 2015). Reflecting the UGTT's influence, it also called for the adoption of a new development model to reduce social and regional disparities (ibid).

The fact that over fifty parties participated in the dialogue underscored the UGTT's organizational clout and its capacity to act as a unifying force in a deeply divided political landscape. However, despite this broad participation, the initiative ultimately faltered due to lingering tensions between key political groups. Ennahda and CPR, for instance, refused to participate in the dialogue, given the inclusion of parties that they associated with the Ben Ali regime (i.e., Nidaa Tounes). While Ennahda and CPR argued that this party's presence undermined the dialogue, others, including the UGTT, saw their inclusion as necessary for adequate representation of all political groups (M'rad, 2015).

Although these initial talks were unsuccessful, a series of political crises soon brought the Troika government in line with the UGTT's plan for reform. On October 18, 2012, Nidaa Tounes leader Lotfi Nagadh died during violent clashes with militias affiliated with the League for the Protection of the Revolution (LPR). While the LPR did not have specific ties to the Troika government, the organization had taken on an increasingly Islamist bent, implicating the Ennahda party in the spread of violence (Belghith and Patel, 2013).[7] Two months later, attacks on several UGTT regional offices – allegedly carried out by the LPR – further exacerbated tensions between the government and the UGTT. The situation reached a breaking point in February 2013, when opposition leader Chokri Belaid was assassinated. Although the perpetrators of the attack were never identified, many blamed Islamist extremists, fueling public outrage and further pressuring the government to resolve the political crisis.

In response, the UGTT organized a one-day general strike, calling for the fall of the Troika government. This strike, which attracted overwhelming support in Tunisia's capital, highlighted the UGTT's socio-political influence and significantly bolstered its negotiating position. The strike's success, combined with the mass protests that followed, pushed Prime Minister Hamadi Jebali (Ennahda) to resign, transferring power to Ali Laarayedh, another senior Ennahda member. Subsequently, President Moncef Marzouki (CPR) convened a government-sponsored National Dialogue, modeled after the UGTT's previous initiative.

[7] The perception of a connection between the LPR and the Ennahda party was aided by an attempt by Ennahda leaders to have LPR members accused of murdering Nagadh released from jail (*Tunisie Numérique*, 2/2/2013).

However, this dialogue, held between April and May 2013, failed for two main reasons. First, unlike the UGTT's initiative, it lacked the broad inclusivity necessary to lend it popular legitimacy. Key groups, including the UGTT, were excluded, which undermined its credibility in the eyes of important stakeholders. Consequently, many parties, including Nidaa Tounes, boycotted the dialogue entirely. As Samir Taïeb, head of *al-Massar*, remarked:

> We boycotted the National Dialogue because it excluded the UGTT ... We were followed by Nidaa [Tounes] who was present during the first session. Beji Caid Essebsi declared that, following the absence of the UGTT and Al-Massar, he left the dialogue. Subsequently, this dialogue made no sense, since the four parties that remained had similar positions. (Taïeb quoted in M'rad, 2015, 37)

Moreover, the government's central role in organizing the talks raised doubts about its neutrality. While the UGTT had been seen as an impartial mediator, given its lack of ties to a political party, Marzouki's initiative was perceived as a self-serving attempt to shore up the government's credibility. Opposition leaders who did participate in the dialogue questioned the government's willingness to compromise on key issues, particularly concerning the role of religion in politics and the future of the Troika coalition (M'rad, 2015, 38–39).

Sensing an opportunity to intervene, the UGTT initiated a second National Dialogue in May 2013. This dialogue, while more inclusive, was quickly beset by new challenges. Though Ennahda was initially willing to participate, tensions with members of the Popular Front, who accused Ennahda of responsibility for Belaid's assassination, led the party to temporarily withdraw from the talks (*Tunisie Numérique*, 5/16/2013). The situation deteriorated further in July 2013 when Mohamed Brahmi, another opposition member and an outspoken critic of Islamism, was assassinated.

Brahmi's assassination marked a watershed moment in Tunisia's political crisis. Like Belaid before him, Brahmi's murder galvanized opposition against the Troika government, leading dozens of leftist MPs to withdraw from the NCA. Protests erupted across the country, with demonstrators calling for the downfall of the "Muslim Brotherhood government" (*La Presse*, 7/28/2013a). At the heart of this movement was a month-long sit-in at Bardo Square (itaṣam errahil, "sit-in of departure"), which became the focal point of opposition to the Troika government. Backed by the UGTT, the sit-in sought to pressure the NCA to end the constitutional deadlock and agree to a new transitional roadmap.

Despite accusations that the UGTT was acting as a political party and unduly influencing the NCA's work, the union continued to use the political situation to its advantage. On the day of Brahmi's funeral, UGTT leaders organized a nationwide general strike, halting economic activity across the capital. In response, NCA President Mustapha Ben Jaafar suspended all parliamentary activities until a compromise could be reached between the opposition and the governing coalition. In the wake of the suspension, the UGTT convened a final round of National Dialogue, in collaboration with the LTDH, OAT, and Tunisia's employer's association, UTICA (henceforth the Quartet). On September 17, 2013, the Quartet proposed a detailed roadmap focused on three key priorities: organizing new elections, finalizing the constitution, and forming a new technocratic government. By October 5, nearly all opposition parties and two of the Troika coalition parties agreed to participate in the first official conference aimed at implementing the roadmap's provisions.

After months of intense negotiations, the National Dialogue concluded successfully in January 2014 with the adoption of a new constitution and the formation of a technocratic government headed by Mehdi Jomaa. The significance of this achievement cannot be overstated. By concluding the National Dialogue, Tunisia not only completed a successful democratic transition – one of the few to emerge from the Arab Spring – but also avoided the political violence, chaos, and counterrevolutions that plagued other neighboring countries (i.e., Libya and Egypt). This astounding success was recognized internationally in 2015 when the UGTT and its partners in the National Dialogue Quartet were awarded the Nobel Peace Prize.

The UGTT's ability to direct the political transition and secure a constitutional agreement was undoubtedly due to the skills and experience it had acquired during the authoritarian period. First, the UGTT's legacy of political autonomy allowed the union to position itself as a neutral mediator and a legitimate representative of the popular will. From the beginning of the dialogue, UGTT leaders emphasized the union's nonpartisan stance, framing its intervention as a necessary step to safeguard the democratic transition. Additionally, the union's decision to assemble a coalition built on diverse participation –

including civil society organizations representing workers, lawyers, business leaders, and human rights advocates – gave the Quartet collective legitimacy grounded in representativeness and inclusivity. Despite some criticism that it was overstepping its trade union role, the UGTT made it clear that it was not interested in governing and that the only goal of the Quartet was to ensure civil peace. As UGTT Secretary-General Houcine Abbassi stated in a televised interview with El-Wataniya:

> The UGTT has no interest in governing ... The idea and preparation of the national dialogue belong to Tunisians who have the capacity to reach an agreement ... The only pressure that the UGTT has undergone is that of the national interest. (*Tunisie Numérique*, 10/29/2013)

Second, the UGTT's deep-rooted connections with civil society and grassroots organizations enabled it to act as an effective third-party mediator when negotiations stalled. In forming the Quartet, the UGTT strategically partnered with nonpartisan civil society groups that had been part of the historical opposition to the Ben Ali regime. Originally, it created an alliance with the Tunisian League of Human Rights and Bar Association, with which it had longstanding relations due to their shared history of state repression. While the UGTT served as a refuge for LTDH activists during the organization's years of suppression under Bourguiba and Ben Ali, members of the Bar Association protested with unionists in regions throughout the country during the 2011 Arab uprisings (Appendix B: TU-37, 12/1/2013; Chihi, 2015). In August, it expanded this alliance to include representatives from Tunisia's employer's association. This unprecedented move contributed additional legitimacy to the National Dialogue, signaling the broad-based commitment of both business and workers to Tunisia's successful transition (Chihi, 2016).

To navigate the complex political landscape, union leaders relied on their extensive negotiating skills, honed over decades of bargaining with employers and the government. National Dialogue participants highlighted the UGTT's central role in resolving disputes between various political actors: "[Abbassi decided who spoke and imposed decisions ... He sometimes made participants from political parties remain in the room after the end of our sessions if no decision had been reached" (International Crisis Group, 2015). At times, resolving inter-party debates involved strategic maneuvering on the part of the UGTT:

> We kept reaching the point where someone would say to me: until here and no further, because we fear what the others will do. Of course I couldn't say that to the others. I had to keep some things to myself so that the dialogue could succeed. (Abbassi quoted in Mersch, 2015)

Most important, by concentrating on the most immediate issues facing the state – such as election dates, finalizing the constitution, and selecting a new prime minister – UGTT representatives avoided overburdening the negotiation process, thereby preventing dialogue from becoming unnecessarily derailed.

When necessary, union leaders used strong-arm tactics to force political parties back to negotiations. For instance, when Ennahda threatened to boycott the National Dialogue over disagreements on the government's resignation timeline, the UGTT mobilized its regional branches to launch strikes, pressuring the government to accept the Quartet's transition roadmap (*La Presse*, 7/28/2013b). Later, when negotiations stalled over the naming of a new prime minister, Abbassi threatened to "publicly expose those responsible for delaying the dialogue," issuing a subtle challenge to Ennahda leader Rached Ghannouchi (*Tunisie Numérique*, 11/13/2013). This assertiveness on the part of the UGTT was credited with keeping the negotiations on track at critical moments, and, particularly, in restraining Ennahda's ability to overturn a consensus agreement. As Karray (2020, 139) notes, "Ennahda never had the intention of entering into an open power struggle with the UGTT." The result was a "deep compromise" (Marzouki, 2015) – one in which all parties were able to make concessions and arrive at solutions without sacrificing their core aims.

Finally, the UGTT's historical legacy of political activism, along with its internal unity and strength, bestowed upon it an organizational weight unavailable to other political actors. Interviewees noted that because of its traditional involvement in Tunisian politics, it was "only natural" that the UGTT should assume a leading role in guiding the country's democratic transition (Appendix B: TU-5, 10/3/2013; TU-20, 10/29/2013; TU-28, 11/13/2013; TU-29, 11/17/2013). The union's credibility was reinforced by its participation in the revolution, which many believed cemented its position as an authentic representative of the people's will (Appendix B: TU-27, 11/8/2013; TU-36, 11/29/2013). Moreover, its diverse membership, extensive geographic reach, and connections to various political tendencies lent it a sort of "popular sovereignty," which enabled it to speak on behalf of Tunisian people in National Dialogue talks. Finally, its ability to mobilize its membership at key moments provided the union with organizational muscle that allowed it to serve as an effective counterweight to the Ennahda party during negotiations. Taken together, these factors made the UGTT an indispensable mediator during Tunisia's transition, cementing its role as a central player in the country's nascent democracy.

The UGTT as a Social Force: Winning Economic Gains for Workers

However, if the UGTT's organizational strength enabled it to play a central role in Tunisia's democratic transition, it also helped the union to successfully win economic concessions for its members. Although some observers worried that the union's preoccupation with political goals might compromise its ability to negotiate on behalf of workers, the UGTT was remarkably successful in securing economic gains. In addition to ending short-term contracts in the public sector, it negotiated wage increases for Tunisian workers and acquired relatively liberal protections for labor rights. Like its political successes, these gains were a consequence of the UGTT's organizational strength and its strategic use of militancy and negotiation, characteristics that can be traced back to its authoritarian past.

Job Security and Employment

One of the earliest gains won by the UGTT was the end of subcontracting labor in the public sector. Subcontracting had long been a contentious issue for Tunisian workers – during structural adjustment, Ben Ali outsourced most public sector jobs in industries such as cleaning and security services to comply with IMF recommendations for reducing public employment. While formal provisions were introduced in the labor code to protect subcontracted employees, in most cases, these workers faced harsher working conditions, lacked social benefits, and were more vulnerable to arbitrary dismissals and workplace harassment (Aliriza, 2020; King, 2017).

Thus, in the early 2000s, eliminating the practice of subcontracting labor became a cornerstone of the UGTT's socioeconomic program (*Achourouk*, 06/18/2005). In 2005, the head of the UGTT's General

Federation of Professions and Services went on a hunger strike in support of subcontracted workers, demanding that the government create a pathway for permanent employment and negotiate a collective agreement for these workers according to proposals outlined by the UGTT (King, 2017, 150). Union leaders also launched strikes and awareness campaigns to draw attention to the plight of subcontracted workers. In 2006, the UGTT organized the first Global Day of Support for Cleaning Women and Security Guards to call attention to the "slave-like conditions" of sub-contracted employees and call for the "amendment of the law to guarantee the rights of this social class" (*Le Temps*, 06/11/2010). Although the government promised to initiate a dialogue with the UGTT to eradicate subcontracting, by 2011, the practice remained widespread, with approximately 70,000 subcontracted workers in the cleaning and security sectors alone.

However, in the wake of the 2011 Arab uprisings, the call to end subcontracting and promote permanent employment became a major part of the government's agenda. Since many of the protests had been driven by a lack dignified work, officials in Tunisia's transitional government were eager to secure social stability by addressing workers' employment demands (Portelli, 2015). Capitalizing on this window of opportunity, workers and sectoral union leaders organized a wave of contentious actions – ranging from street demonstrations and strikes to sit-ins – to pressure the government to abolish precarious work, particularly subcontracting in the public sector. While many of these actions were coordinated by the UGTT, in some cases subcontracted workers independently staged wildcat protests at their workplaces, attracting media attention by inviting journalists to document their strikes and broadcast their demands (King, 2017).

In the early months of 2011, these protests overwhelmed the transitional government, forcing officials to attend to subcontracted workers' demands. In the first year of the transition, workers participated in 567 strikes, 67 percent of which were led by wildcat demonstrators (Tunisian Ministry of Social Affairs, 2014). This wave of protests caused significant damage to the Tunisian economy, contributing to the temporary closure of 281 firms and heightening fears that ongoing unrest could cripple future economic growth (ibid). To stem the tide of social unrest, interim president Fouad Mebazaa pledged to initiate social negotiations and implement a new economic program that would meet the demands of social groups. Leaders from the UGTT insisted that the eradication of subcontracting be a key component of any such program: "It is in the government's interest to quickly engage in social negotiations with [the UGTT] ... There are immediate solutions that the government can support including tenure for hundreds of thousands of [sub-contracted workers] that must be integrated into their workplaces" (*Jeune Afrique*, 02/10/2011).

On April 22, 2011, the government signed an agreement outlawing subcontracting in the public sector, converting some 31,000 workers to permanent employment (*Tunisie Numérique*, 4/23/2011).[8] This shift significantly improved the living standards of previously subcontracted employees, who gained access to secure employment, health benefits, retirement plans, and wages nearly double the amount of their prior earnings (King, 2017). While some observers have noted that this reform has only altered the nature, and not the existence of precarious work (King, 2017; Vatthauer and Weipert-Fenner, 2017), in general, the end of subcontracting in the public sector has been regarded as a historic victory. In addition to formalizing contracts for thousands of employees, this has paved the way for further elimination of informal work, including agricultural day labor and subcontracting in private industries (Han, 2023).

The UGTT's success in winning this concession was due in large part to its skills in grassroots mobilization, honed over decades of authoritarian rule. Rather than relying on negotiation to advance its demands, the UGTT applied pressure on the government through street demonstrations. The union's turn to militancy was partly due to its weak ties to political elites, which limited its ability to advance demands through conventional political channels. However, the UGTT also capitalized upon the strategic advantages of the postrevolutionary context. Indeed, the relatively freer political environment meant that unions could organize protests with less fear of repression, creating the conditions for using militancy as a deliberate tactic rather than a last-ditch response.

[8] Note that this ban was not fully implemented until January 2013 (*La Presse*, 1/04/2013).

Additionally, internal developments within the UGTT encouraged workers to continue deploying street protests. Unlike opposition parties, which struggled to recruit new members, the UGTT saw its membership increase by roughly a fourth, providing it with a broader base from which to mobilize workers and apply pressure to the regime. Part of this growth stemmed from the union's enhanced legitimacy, gained through its participation in anti-regime protests during the 2011 Arab uprisings. Additionally, the formalization of employment contracts following the end of subcontracting likely contributed to union growth, as roughly 90,000 newly regularized workers became eligible for UGTT membership (Brockmeyer et al., 2015).[9]

Structural changes within the UGTT also empowered workers to take independent collective action without interference from the union leadership. Decentralization of decision-making to the intermediate levels of the organization gave federal leaders more freedom to organize sector-wide strikes (Appendix B: TU-7, 10/6/2013; TU-22, 10/31/2013). Wildcat actions also drew upon positive experiences from the 2011 uprisings, which showcased the ability of workers to organize outside of the union framework and demonstrated what could be accomplished through disruptive actions (Appendix B: TU-24, 11/4/2013). While the UGTT leadership at times condemned these unsanctioned strikes (*Achourouk*, 01/19/2012), they frequently capitalized on the unrest to increase pressure on the transitional government. As in previous periods, the UGTT used the threat of uncontrollable social upheaval to shore up its position and force government officials to negotiate. Given the fragility of governing coalitions during the transition period, leaders were more than willing to concede to the UGTT's demands in order to maintain political stability (Portelli and Augenbaum, 2017).

Wage Increases

In addition to securing permanent employment for public sector employees, the UGTT also achieved significant wage increases for

[9] Estimates vary on the actual number of workers affected by this reform that eventually became UGTT members. While Bishara (2014) suggests that the bulk of the UGTT's membership growth from 2011 to 2014 was from the subcontracted sector, King (2017) cites a figure of about 21,500 new unionized workers from this sector based on the UGTT's own estimates.

public and private sector workers. In July 2011, the interim government reached an agreement with the UGTT to increase wages in the public sector by 4.7 percent (*La Presse*, 7/15/2011). One year later, the union successfully negotiated a minimum wage increase from TD 300 to 320, and additional wage increases in the public and private sectors of 6 and 7 percent, respectively. Finally in January 2013, the UGTT signed a historical social pact with UTICA and the government, establishing a framework for future negotiations on wage increases, social benefits, and labor-related policies. Although the pact was somewhat vague in specifics, it contained several clear commitments that benefited members of the working class: 1) a comprehensive review of the social security system, 2) an independent fund for unemployment insurance and monthly benefits of TD 200 for any redundant worker, 3) the creation of a permanent national social dialogue council to be convened after 2013.

Like the elimination of subcontracting, wage concessions were won through strategic and repeated protests. As noted in Table 7.1, wages and bonuses were central issues in labor disputes during the transition period. Although many of these actions were organized by enterprise unions to achieve specific concessions within their workplaces, the UGTT's federal and national offices occasionally coordinated sector-wide campaigns to secure more systematic wage increases. For example, in February 2012, municipal workers affiliated to the UGTT's General Federation of Municipal Agents went on a four-day strike to secure special bonuses of TD 76. During this period, essential services such as visa processing and trash collection were shuttered, leading to widespread dissatisfaction within the government and among the general public.

Table 7.1. ***Strikes in Tunisia by demand type***

Year	Number of strikes	% Work-related	% Wage-related	% Solidarity
2011	567	43	43	13
2012	505	49	35	7.5
2013	399	55	32	4
2014	451	48	33	–

Source: Tunisian Ministry of Social Affairs

Initially, the government responded to the unrest by cracking down on the UGTT, using police intervention to break up labor demonstrations. However, this repression ultimately backfired, providing the union with additional leverage to force the government to concede to its demands. Days after the crackdown, the interim government agreed to negotiations that resulted in a 6 percent wage increase for the affected municipal workers. Six months later, this increase was extended to all public sector employees, overturning the government's earlier intent to impose a salary freeze in the public sector in order to balance the 2012 budget (*La Presse*, 10/19/2012).

The UGTT's success also stemmed from its ability to balance militancy with negotiation to reach effective compromises. While strikes remained the union's primary method of pressure, union leaders complemented these actions with a robust commitment to dialogue. For instance, in December 2012, the UGTT's Administrative Commission suspended a scheduled general strike to facilitate negotiations with the government and UTICA regarding the conclusion of a long-awaited social pact. In the months that followed, strike levels declined as union leaders engaged in rigorous negotiations over specific portions of the agreement. For the UGTT, this strategic restraint was a key component of its successful pressure strategy; as UGTT spokesperson Sami Tahri explained,

> At the UGTT, we can have disagreements with our partners, but we never close the door to dialogue ... It is in the very essence of our mission as a trade union organization to have positions different from those of the government and to mobilize, within the framework of the legislation in force, in order to defend them. (Sami Tahri quoted in *La Presse*, 03/04/2012).

The union's ability to control strikes during negotiations reflected its high level of organizational capacity and its close connections with the grassroots, reinforcing its influence at the bargaining table. When UGTT leaders called for restraint, workers heeded their advice, demonstrating the union's cohesive structure and internal discipline. This strategic flexibility – combining protest with negotiation – demonstrated the UGTT's willingness to work with social partners in pursuit of the general interest of Tunisians, beyond its own parochial demands. This collaborative approach ultimately convinced business leaders to make generous concessions to workers, despite going against their traditional interests:

> We noted a tremendous surge of solidarity between business leaders, employees, and workers. Once social dialogue was initiated, we very quickly managed to find solutions to the problems that arose … We started from a simple principle: the UTICA and the UGTT – and through them, the business leaders and employees – are not enemies but they have common enemies which are unemployment, underdevelopment, foreign competition, bad governance, etc. A platform for dialogue was then created and had no other aim than social cohesion and economic development. (Wided Bouchamaoui quoted in *La Presse*, 01/16/2013)

Union Rights

Finally, the UGTT used its considerable influence over the political transition process to secure liberal protections for workers' rights. As mentioned previously, chief among the union's constitutional priorities was the safeguarding of socioeconomic rights, including the right to unionize and strike, the right to fair pay, and the right to decent work. In the UGTT's initial constitutional proposal, these rights featured prominently alongside institutional provisions for the formalization of collective bargaining and the creation of a new Socioeconomic Council to help guide Tunisia's future economic policy. In the final version of the constitution adopted by the NCA, several UGTT-backed proposals were incorporated, including protections for the freedom to organize (Article 36), the right to health and social insurance (Article 38), and the right to be employed under just and favorable conditions (Article 40). Additionally, Articles 8 and 12 included other progressive protections for labor, such as provisions mandating the state to allocate resources for addressing youth unemployment and obligations to ensure social justice and equitable development.

To win these rights, the UGTT relied on a combination of militancy and negotiation, using skills it developed during the period of authoritarian rule. At critical stages in the constitution-making process, UGTT leaders threatened protests to force the NCA to change controversial proposals or adopt their preferred revisions (Karray, 2020). Moreover, the UGTT leveraged its extensive informal connections with political actors and civil society groups to influence constitutional debates. For example, Mustapha Ben Jaafar, the speaker of the NCA, was a former syndicalist with a long history of supporting prolabor policies during his time as a leader of the Movement for Social Democrats and, later, Ettakatol. Additionally, smaller parties in the NCA began to coalesce into a left-labor bloc (Nidaa Tounes) that provided additional support for labor-friendly provisions (Hartshorn and Sil, 2019). Although members of this bloc remained formally independent from the UGTT, many of its leaders, including founder Beji Caid Essebsi, had deep ties to the union and supported its constitutional proposals.

As these groups gained strength in the NCA, the UGTT's influence over the constitution-making process grew, giving it even more space to shape Tunisia's political future. As such, the UGTT's role in securing these concessions was highly politicized, with labor unions coordinating with political parties to actively negotiate over constitutional proposals. The union also used its civil society connections to hire constitutional experts to help shape the document's provisions, ensuring that labor rights were thoroughly embedded in the final text. Finally, the UGTT organized public forums and workshops to evaluate and discuss the NCA's constitutional drafts, playing a crucial role in the amendment of several articles relating to socioeconomic and labor issues. Ultimately, this strategic use of both militancy and informal political networks enabled the union to deftly manage the constitution-making process outside of the NCA, ensuring that workers' rights remained central to Tunisia's new constitutional framework.

Summary

Despite the common perception that labor unions struggle to influence processes of political change, the UGTT took a leading role in advancing Tunisia's democratic transition. Through militant mobilization on the streets and skillful negotiation, the UGTT was able to leverage its organizational strength to shape political reforms and promote a more liberal vision for Tunisia's future. This dual strategy, combining grassroots mobilization with high-level negotiations, drew upon resources inherited from the UGTT's authoritarian. During the political transition, the UGTT was able to draw upon these legacies to strengthen linkages between its leadership and rank-and-file members through internal reforms while maintaining its autonomy from political elites. These factors enabled the union to assert itself as a powerful social actor, capable of exerting significant pressure on the government to meet its demands.

However, some unionists have voiced concerns that the UGTT's political influence has come at the expense of addressing critical social and economic priorities, such as regional development. As one union activist remarked, "Our ordinary members are tired. Yesterday we were fighting the RCD, today we are fighting Ennahda instead of addressing our own problems" (Yousfi, 2015, 197). Nevertheless, the UGTT has used its political leverage to secure significant economic concessions for workers, including permanent employment, wage increases, and liberal socioeconomic rights. The union's success in achieving both political and economic gains contrasts sharply with the lackluster outcomes of Moroccan unions, as I discuss in detail below.

Morocco

Labor Mobilization in Morocco: Union Weakness as an Obstacle to Progress

Unlike the UGTT in Tunisia, Moroccan unions entered the post-uprising era in a less turbulent political environment. After a brief period of social unrest, the monarchy quickly reconsolidated its power, introducing a series of institutional reforms meant to rehabilitate its democratic image. This wave of liberalization, while seemingly providing unions with greater freedom to organize, paradoxically limited their ability to shape the course of political and economic reforms. Combined with preexisting legacies of labor pluralism and centralized rule, this more inclusive political environment left unions weaker and less capable of mobilizing their members than ever before. Instead, unions found themselves increasingly captive to government influence, and unable to secure new concessions or protect their previous gains.

Legacies of Organizational Weakness: Union Pluralism and Centralized Rule

One of the main differences between Moroccan and Tunisian unions in the post-uprising period was the former's continued engagement with political elites. Unlike Tunisia, Morocco's labor incorporation policy was characterized by inclusionary pluralism, where the state facilitated the growth of multiple union centers and directly incorporated unions into the regime. In the pre-uprising period, this meant that Moroccan unions benefited from a host of organizational and institutional advantages, such as government subsidies, buildings for office space, and institutional representation, unavailable to unions operating in more exclusive environments. However, in the post-uprising period, this vast array of assets left a detrimental legacy by weakening labour union's role as representatives of workers' interests while simultaneously transforming them into clients of the authoritarian regime.

Indeed, the monarchy's strategy of co-opting union leaders through institutional inducements weakened their grassroots ties, reducing their capacity to effectively advocate for workers' interests. As noted in Chapter 6, by strengthening institutions like social dialogue and the Moroccan parliament, the Moroccan government more tightly incorporated labor leaders into its ruling coalition. Because of their access to political institutions, union leaders have been able to build careers as professional politicians, insulating them them from accountability to the rank-and-file. In some cases, union leaders have leveraged their political influence to build clientelist networks and secure future electoral victories within their organizations. For example, UMT leaders routinely exploit their privileged access to the Social Affairs Fund to "distribute credits to employees and executives affiliated with them, thereby securing leaders in key positions" (Ahdani and Boudarham, 2018). In other instances, such as that of Rachid El Menyari,[10] government privileges have been used as leverage to prevent union leaders from effectively representing workers' interests. As one activist close to the UMT noted:

[10] Rachid El Menyari was the former secretary-general of the UMT regional office in Rabat and head of the UMT affiliated workers' union at the regional water distribution corporation, Redal (Appendix B: MA-14, 3/31/2014). Fellow union members accused him of various improprieties at Redal including having secured his position via bribes, and deliberately restricting strikes in order to please company managers. In 2018, he was officially dismissed from the UMT on charges of corruption (Appendix B: MA-36, 1/13/2015, Ahdani and Boudarham, 2018).

> Sometimes the leader goes in and makes deals with the private sector. Instead of supporting the workers in a strike they try to calm them and convince them to go back to work and so on, promising them that they will find a solution ... But it's just talk. Just talk. They don't really do it. And they know that there are limits, because they know that they're corrupt and they know that they took public funds. Because you know if you took a lot of money for this or that that you can't mobilize for a general strike. And so [the employer] says to them well you can't go beyond this because if you do go out I'll talk about what you took. (Appendix B: MA-6, 3/12/2014)

Continued connections to parties also benefited unions politically while limiting their ability to organize. Because multiparty politics still favored the formation of large electoral coalitions, unions found it in their interest to maintain alliances with parties that could win a sizable share of parliamentary seats. However, in tandem with the monarchy's carefully managed liberalization, such alliances have deepened polarization within the labor movement, weakening unions' mobilizing potential. For instance, both the National Union of Labor in Morocco (UNTM) and FDT have suffered from internal splits due to disputes over alleged party influence over union affairs.

Within the FDT, tensions arose between two key leaders – Abderrahmane Azzouzi, who advocated for more diverse party involvement in the FDT, and Abdelhamid Fatihi, who favored informal alliances with the Socialist Union of Popular Forces. At the union's third congress, Azzouzi introduced a controversial measure to allocate seats on the FDT National Council to "political sensitivities," essentially granting center-left parties more influence over the union's direction (*Al-Bayane*, 12/10/2010). This move sparked a rift with the USFP-aligned faction led by Fatihi, who preferred to preserve the union's political independence. In 2011, the leadership contest between Fatihi and Azzouzi resulted in a split vote, with rival factions claiming to represent the legitimate voice of the union (*Aujourd'hui Le Maroc*, 1/28/2011; *Libération*, 3/31/2011).

A similar division occurred within the UNTM, where a leadership struggle between Mohamed Yatim and Abdelssalam Maâti centered on the influence of the Islamist Justice and Development Party (PJD). While Maâti formally accused Yatim of corruption, the core issue was Yatim's control of the union through his ties to the PJD and the Movement for Unity and Reform[11] (*Aujourd'hui le Maroc*, 9/29/2010; Buehler, 2015, 97). As Maâti remarked in an interview with *Aujourd'hui le Maroc*:

> we have seen that the UNTM under Mohamed Yatim was deprived of its independence and credibility as a trade union center that campaigns for workers' rights ... the Unity and Reform Movement, of which Yatim is a member, which often claimed that it was only an Islamist preaching movement and that it had no connection with politics, we have seen it interfere directly in the affairs of the union ... The PJD also got involved by discreetly supporting Yatim. (Maâti cited in *Aujourd'hui le Maroc*, 9/29/2010)

While this division did not result in a split within the UNTM, expulsions of members associated with Maâti weakened the union's organizational base and undermined its credibility with potential members.

Political liberalization following the Arab uprisings exacerbated divisions within the labor movement, as new parties sought to either align with existing unions or establish their own federations. By 2014, thirty-four labor confederations existed in Morocco, most of which had historic ties to political parties or were explicitly created by political elites. This undermined Moroccan unions' autonomy and ability to effectively represent their members; as political scientist Mohamed Darif noted, "Each party has ensured that it has an extension into the working class through its own union, distorting the very role of unions, which have become the backyards of political groupings" (Darif cited in *La Vie Éco*, 01/10/2011).

Finally, the centralization of power within Moroccan unions further subordinated rank-and-file members to the leadership, encouraging militant members to defect. Since state subsidies were funneled directly to unions' national offices,[12] they no longer depended on grassroots support for survival, further distancing them from their organizational

[11] The Movement for Unity and Reform is Morocco's largest registered Islamic social organization and has historic connections to the PJD through its founder Abdelilah Benkirane, who is the current leader of the PJD.

[12] A comprehensive review of the UMT's finances, published by Moroccan weekly *Telquel*, estimated that the union received roughly MDH 6 million in direct subsidies from the state, and MDH 50 million from mandatory dues (Ahdani and Boudarham, 2018).

base. Additionally, the institutionalization of national-level social dialogue diminished the need for unions to maintain robust organizations on the shop floor. Private sector employees repeatedly expressed frustration over the lack of union involvement in their workplaces – many workers were unfamiliar with their union representatives and reported never being notified of meetings, elections, or even receiving a union card (Appendix B: MA-6, 3/12/2014, MA-7, 3/18/2014). While official statistics suggest that 3.2 percent of the labor force – or 6 percent of wage and salary earners — are union members, personal accounts suggest that these figures are very likely inflated (Appendix B: MA-11, 3/24/2014). Tellingly, the number of elected worker delegates unaffiliated to any union (i.e., sans appartenance syndical – SAS) has increased in the post-uprising period. In 2009, the percentage of SAS delegates totaled 64.6 percent, representing some 13,000 professional offices (Meknassi and Rioux, 2010). While the percentage of SAS delegates decreased slightly in 2015, the absolute number of unaffiliated worker delegates increased to 14,828, highlighting the extent of continued defection from traditional unions (Ben Sedrine, 2017).

Thus, Moroccan unions faced a distinct set of challenges that limited their ability to influence the country's political direction in the post-uprising period. The monarchy's strategy of co-opting union leaders, coupled with authoritarian legacies of labor pluralism and centralized rule, deepened divisions within the labor movement and cultivated an environment where union leaders relied heavily on political connections to achieve their goals. While liberalization ostensibly provided unions opportunities to exert their power, their historical involvement in state-led institutions distanced union leaders from their members, limiting their capacity to mobilize. As a result, Moroccan unions found themselves marginalized in political and economic negotiations over the country's future, as I elaborate below.

Moroccan Unions and the Limits of Political Influence in a "Refolutionary" Transition

In contrast to Tunisia, the Arab uprisings in Morocco did not produce a radical break with the past. Although the February 20th movement prompted the monarchy to engage in pre-emptive reforms, these changes fell short of the broader transitions witnessed throughout much of North Africa. Rather than revolution or regime change, Morocco experienced a "refolutionary" transition (Bayat, 2020) directed by King Mohammed VI, which reconstituted the country's authoritarian political system through ostensibly democratic means. Moreover, despite their active involvement in the constitutional revision process, unions' influence over the final political order was limited. Due to their continued legacy of organizational weakness and co-optation, Moroccan unions were sidelined in the country's political transition, leaving the reform effort to be shaped by the king and his inner circle.

Revising the Constitution

Unlike Tunisia, where the pro-democracy movement played a decisive role in shaping the political transition, in Morocco, the monarchy was the principal driver of change. Although the February 20th movement initiated calls for constitutional reform, King Mohammed VI quickly seized control of the process. On March 9, 2011, he delivered a national address outlining a tentative blueprint for reform: reinforcing the separation of powers, expanding the role of the Prime Minister, enshrining civil liberties, decentralizing governance, and recognizing cultural pluralism. To implement these changes, the king established the Consultative Commission for Constitutional Revision (CCRC), appointing Abdelatif Menouni,[13] as chair. In addition to finalizing the constitution within three months, the CCRC was tasked with gathering input on its content from unions, political parties, and other key civil society actors. As part of this process, unions were invited to submit their own draft proposals for constitutional revisions, which would then be considered by the CCRC.

Despite their active participation in the consultation process, unions were largely sidelined in Morocco's political transition. Drafting of the constitution was mainly overseen by the CCRC and a secondary body appointed by the king – the Political Mechanism Accompanying the Constitutional Reform.[14] Indeed, party and union representatives

[13] Abdelatif Menouni was a respected constitutional law professor who had historic ties to the labor movement. He is the author of *Le Syndicalisme Ouvrier au Maroc* (1978).

[14] This organization was led by the king's personal advisor, Mohammed Moatassim, and reportedly was truly responsible for producing the final constitutional draft (Maghraoui, 2011).

were only informed of the constitution's content three weeks before the proposed referendum, leaving little time to review the document or substantively debate its provisions (Molina, 2011). Moreover, the monarchy quickly released the draft to the public on June 17th – a day after presenting it to union leaders – effectively preventing them from mobilizing against the constitution or advocating for further modifications(ibid).

Consequently, many of the unions' key priorities were excluded from the final constitution. Although they succeeded in achieving some of their institutional objectives (see discussion below), other labor-friendly amendments were heavily diluted or rejected altogether. For instance, the constitution failed to guarantee critical worker protections beyond superficial commitments to the right to organize. Notably absent were unconditional protections for the right to strike, leaving striking workers subject to harsh criminal penalties under the Penal Code. Additionally, robust power-sharing mechanisms that could have enabled unions to curb the monarchy's political influence were weakened by provisions that preserved the king's dominance over executive and legislative functions. Indeed, while the Prime Minister and the Council of Government were granted additional powers, these were tightly constrained by the preservation of Council of Ministers,[15] which granted the king and his political appointees exclusive control to present bills to parliament, and make critical appointments like governorships, high-ranking security offices, and leadership positions in strategic public enterprises (Benchemsi, 2012).

Unions' inability to exert greater influence over the constitution-making process can be attributed to two main factors, stemming from previous periods of authoritarian rule. First, the monarchy's successful co-optation of union leaders significantly limited their ability to push for radical reforms. Unlike the February 20th movement, which sought to abolish key articles granting the king extensive powers (i.e., Articles 19, 23, and 29), most unions' proposals were carefully aligned with the monarchy's objectives,[16] avoiding any serious challenges

[15] Note that this body was opposed by several unions and opposition groups, most prominently the *Istiqlal* and UGTM (*L'Opinion*, 04/11/2011).

[16] Only the CDT pushed for radical reforms, advocating for a democratic monarchy with a clear separation of powers between the king and the parliament (*Telquel*, 4/15/2011).

to royal prerogatives (*Aujourd'hui le Maroc*, 04/08/2011; *Telquel*, 4/15/2011). This moderate stance reflected unions' gradual political domestication, shaped by decades of institutional incorporation under inclusionary pluralist rule. As Feliu (2006) notes, the integration of civil society actors into royal commissions has been a hallmark of King Mohammed VI's reign, enabling the monarchy to co-opt civil society groups into its ruling coalition while simultaneously neutralizing them as effective political actors. Indeed, the establishment of the CCRC and the subsequent constitutional dialogue fostered an image of inclusivity while simultaneously limiting unions' influence over the new political order. Despite being confined to an advisory role in the reform process, many unions praised the monarchy for its efforts to include diverse voices in the constitution-making process:

> [We] are all pleased by the monarchy's effort to fully involve [us] in this profound and comprehensive constitutional reform, from beginning to end, within the framework of an inclusive approach based on consultation, and praise the serious and responsible dialogue that marked the work of the Political Mechanism. (*Al-Bayane*, 06/17/2011)

Another sign of unions' political domestication was their lack of opposition or substantive critique once the constitutional draft was released. In contrast to Tunisia, no public debates were held in response to the constitution, and union leaders made little effort to organize any. While this was partly due to the brief timeline between the draft's release and the constitutional referendum, central to this quiescence was union leaders' position on the second parliamentary chamber (HoC). As noted in Chapter 6, the HoC was a key instrument of regime co-optation; in addition to allowing unions to secure political representation, it also gave union leaders access to lucrative perquisites. Thus, during the reform process, union leaders made the retention of the HoC a key demand. In a televised address, UMT secretary-general Miloudi Moukharik vehemently defended the second chamber as "essential for ensuring continued representation of the working class" (*Al-Bayane*, 04/21/2011). The UGTM similarly advocated for its expansion to include more union representatives as well as those of Moroccans living abroad (*L'Opinion*, 04/11/2011).

The monarchy's decision to retain the second chamber in the new constitution signaled its continued willingness to include unions in its ruling coalition. Thus, union leaders were reluctant to oppose the document, even though it failed to meet many of their other socioeconomic and organizational demands (Appendix B: MA-9, 3/19/2014; MA-33, 5/5/2014).

Second, Moroccan unions were too fragmented and organizationally weak to present a unified challenge to the monarchy. Even if union leaders had wanted to mobilize against the constitution, decades of internal divisions and declining grassroots support left them without the organizational capacity to do so. While opposition to the constitutional process did emerge from radical unions like the CDT and reformist branches of the UMT, these efforts were quickly overshadowed by the more conciliatory approach of larger, co-opted unions like the UMT central and UGTM. As Maghraoui (2011, 686) notes, the "excessive pluralism" of Morocco's multiparty system paradoxically produced an equally "excessive consensus" over constitutional reforms, undermining any substantive opposition to the monarchy's proposals.

Finally, the dissolution of the February 20th movement during the reform process further eroded unions' bargaining power. At the height of the pro-democracy protests, union leaders used the threat of aligning with F20M to extract more substantial concessions from the regime (Buehler, 2015). However, as the reform process unfolded, F20M itself became divided, with deep divisions emerging among its various factions (Appendix B: MA-21, 4/19/2014; MA-32, 5/9/2014). Selective repression by the regime also took a toll, particularly through the targeting and radicalization of Islamist groups like the Justice and Charity Organization (Al Adl wa Ihsane) (Badran, 2022). Meanwhile, the co-optation of leftist groups, such as the unemployed graduates, further depleted unions' potential organizational support (ibid, Badimon, 2013). Without the backing of a strong protest movement, unions lost the organizational leverage needed to secure additional concessions from the regime. Consequently, most unions were forced to accept the regime's constitutional revisions, ultimately endorsing a "yes" vote in the July 1st constitutional referendum.

From Political Integration to Economic Disempowerment: The Fight for Socioeconomic Concessions

In addition to having little influence over the country's political transition, Moroccan unions also struggled to secure economic gains for workers in the post-uprising period. Despite being incorporated into the regime through the HoC, unions failed to achieve new benefits for their members or even protect the gains made in previous years. This failure stemmed from unions' organizational weakness and the channeling of labor conflict into political institutions, which domesticated union leaders and distanced them from their members' interests. As a result, unions have been unable to capitalize on the economic opportunities that emerged in the post-uprising period, as evidenced by the rollback of several labor-friendly policies, ongoing workplace abuses, and the deepening fractionalization of the Moroccan labor movement.

Job Security and Employment

As in Tunisia, unemployment and job insecurity emerged as critical concerns for Moroccan unions in the post-uprising period. The mobilization of unemployed graduates and subcontracted workers in regions like Khouribga and Rabat highlighted the crisis of informal work, which had been worsened by years of neoliberal reforms(Berman, 2019). These protests underscored the deteriorating conditions of the labor market, marked by unstable employment, poverty, and the erosion of formal labor protections. In response, the monarchy quickly promised thousands of new jobs in hopes of neutralizing dissent and preventing the unrest from spreading (Buehler, 2015).

Following the constitutional referendum, there was hope that the new government, led by PJD secretary-general Abdelilah Benkirane, would fulfill these promises. In his inaugural speech, Benkirane emphasized that job creation would be among the key pillars of his governing agenda, promising to strengthen existing employment promotion programs (ALMPs) (*L'Opinion*, 1/21/2012). Additionally, the government committed to creating a Higher Council for Youth and Associative Action, aimed at involving youth in public life and addressing their socioeconomic grievances. The passage of the 2012 Finance Law seemed to support these ambitions, allocating 1 billion dirhams to the employment promotion fund and creating more than 26,000 new positions in the civil service.

However, despite these initial efforts, the government's job creation policies ultimately fell short. While ALMPs like *Idmaj* succeeded in creating new jobs, these were often insecure and low-wage, doing little to address the deeper structural issues of underemployment and precarious work (Chatri et al., 2021, 8). Moreover, these programs largely benefited younger workers and women, highlighting the programs' limited ability to generate equitable employment outcomes (ibid). The lack of inaccessibility of these employment programs further hindered their impact, as many workers were unaware of their existence or otherwise excluded from these opportunities (Cherkaoui and Benkaraach, 2021).

The disparity in job creation across different sectors illustrates the broader limitations of the government's employment strategies. While certain groups, such as mining workers, were able to win substantial concessions – most notably through the OCP Skills program (Berman, 2019) – others were left behind. Unemployed teachers, for instance, saw minimal job concessions, and those who were offered positions were often limited to temporary and precarious work. Similarly, many workers in the textile sector faced irregular employment, securing low-wage jobs with minimal, if any, job security (Plank et al., 2014).

The reasons for these disparities lie in the organizational weakness of Moroccan labor unions. Unlike the UGTT in Tunisia, Moroccan unions did not prioritize mobilizing against informal work, with the exception of a few, smaller independent federations. Furthermore, the regime's "divide-and-rule" strategies have succeeded in keeping unionized workers, unemployed graduates, and informal workers fragmented, preventing meaningful alliances between these groups. For example, concessions are often granted to different groups at separate intervals to prevent cross-sector cooperation. In firms with both formal and informal workers, formal workers often receive preferential treatment,[17] leading to status divides that limit the possibility of joint mobilization. While formalizing informal labor could provide unions with a new base of support, many union leaders see organizing these workers as too risky and time-consuming, especially given the regime's ability to co-opt or repress labor militancy. As one union leader stated:

> [Big unions] don't have the capacity to organize these workers … they don't have connections with them and they lack the proper organization anyway. Most don't even have youth departments … Besides, organizing

[17] For example in the textile industry, regular workers are more likely to receive enhanced training, promotions, and be paid at regular intervals (Plank et al., 2014).

> with militant groups could put them in jeopardy with [the monarchy]. (Appendix B: MA-11, 3/24/2014)

Consequently, union engagement with informal labor has been inconsistent, leaving many workers to fend for themselves in negotiations with the state. The challenges faced by the National Coordination of Forcibly Contracted Teachers (NCFCT) illustrate these dynamics. While the NCFCT initially chose to operate outside of formal trade union structures, some of its members decided to join unions in hopes that such partnerships would strengthen their bargaining power. However, this decision immediately created divisions within the movement. While some members argued that union support was essential for achieving their goals, others thought that union membership would undermine the NCFCT's internal cohesion and autonomy (Zeroual and Lefnatsa, 2019).

These internal divisions ultimately weakened the movement's ability to mobilize. Union support for the movement was tepid, limiting the NCFCT's bargaining power with the state. The UNTM, in particular, faced difficulties in supporting subcontracted teachers, as their partisan affiliate was responsible for implementing the policies that the NCFCT was protesting (Appendix B: MA-7, 3/18/2014). Other unions, such as the National Union of Education (SNE-CDT) and the National Federation of Education - Democratic Tendency (FNE-TD), were too weakened by internal splits to provide meaningful support (Appendix B: MA-26, 5/7/2014). Thus, despite attempts to unionize, the rate of unionization among contract teachers remained below 5 percent, reflecting the broader organizational fragmentation of Morocco's labor movement (Zeroual and Lefnatsa, 2019).

In many cases, informal and unemployed workers fared better in negotiations when appealing directly to the state. In the mining sector, for example, workers circumvented unions in their lobbying efforts for the OCP Skills program (Berman, 2019, 144). By engaging in direct dialogue with employers, these workers were able to secure more favorable terms than they might have through union intermediation. This approach reflects the government's broader strategy of marginalizing traditional civil society actors and promoting direct consultation with aggrieved workers to demobilize protests and maintain control.

This practice, however, has only reinforced a long-term strategic weakness by entrenching the perception that passivity and cooperation yield concessions. Many Moroccan journalists note a widespread belief among labor activists that their participation in protests has led to their exclusion from job opportunities and state concessions. This perception underscores the broader challenges faced by Morocco's labor movement, which remains divided, weakened, and constrained by the state's ability to co-opt and repress dissent. As a result, unions struggle to present themselves as effective channels of worker representation in the post-uprising environment.

Wage Increases

Beyond failing to secure job protections for workers, unions in Morocco also struggled to protect wage gains in the years after the 2011 uprisings. During the 2011 round of social dialogue, unions were able to negotiate significant wage increases: 600 DH for public sector workers, 300 DH for private sector workers, and a 15 percent raise in the minimum wage. Additionally, retirement pensions increased substantially, from 600 to 1,000 dirhams per month. Although these concessions placed a heavy strain on the government's finances, they were largely effective in demobilizing unions that had previously supported the February 20th Movement.

However, the change in government following the 2012 parliamentary elections marked the beginning of a rollback of these hard-won gains. Socioeconomic concessions made in 2011 pushed the wage bill to 11.4 percent of GDP, resulting in a budget deficit of 6.8 percent (Royaume du Maroc, 2017; World Bank Group, 2019). To address the shortfall, the Benkirane government entered into a Precautionary and Liquidity Line agreement with the IMF, securing a $6.2 billion loan in exchange for implementing austerity measures. The 2013 budget reflected this shift, reversing many of the concessions granted in 2011. In addition to freezing wages in the public sector, the government reinstated mandatory exams for public administration recruitment, and rescinded consumer subsidies on fuel. By late 2013, it had also begun proposing extensive pension reforms that would raise the retirement age and increase workers' contributions.

Although Moroccan unions vigorously resisted these changes, their efforts to block these measures were largely unsuccessful. One key reason was their continued reliance on institutional strategies to levy demands. Unions initially sought to win back concessions through familiar channels of negotiation and dialogue. The 2012 round of social dialogue provided a useful opportunity for labor leaders to press the government to honor its previous commitments. However, talks quickly stalled, forcing the unions to intensify their efforts by lobbying in the House of Councillors. Though the government quickly convened the Social and Economic Council to discuss unions' proposals, these consultations failed to produce tangible results. Having strengthened its position after the demobilization of the February 20th movement, the government understood that it only needed to listen to the unions, not yield to their demands. Thus, despite being praised for willingness to "achieve social cohesion through listening, consultation, and intermediation," Benkirane postponed the 2012 social dialogue sessions, leaving workers without a clear path to address the austerity measures outlined in the 2013 Finance Law (*Al-Bayane*, 04/27/2012).

As government inaction persisted, unions shifted to more militant tactics, but these too proved ineffective due to their weakened organizational state. In 2013, labor leaders escalated their demand-making by organizing rolling strikes to protest the government's refusal to implement the 2011 agreements and boycotting the spring session of the social dialogue. This culminated in a historic move on April 14th, when three of Morocco's largest unions – the UMT, CDT, and FDT – formed a formal alliance and called for a joint general strike. The strike saw an unprecedented level of participation, with reports indicating that 84 percent of public sector workers joined the protest (*Ya-biladi*, 10/29/2014). However, despite the scale of mobilization, the strike failed to pressure the government into making any meaningful concessions.

The failure of the strike, despite its scale, can be attributed to the perceived fragility of the trade union alliance. Many observers noted that Morocco's legacy of organizational pluralism precluded genuine solidarity between Moroccan unions. As political scientist Miloud Belcadi noted, "We cannot talk about trade union unity. It is a concept that has no legal basis. We can talk about alliances or, when things are more advanced, mergers. But even if this mechanism was legally provided for, it remains a simple slogan" (*La Vie Éco*, 11/14/2014).

Indeed, for many unionists, years of division made the prospect of durable alliances improbable. Because unions were closely tied to political parties, any union merger would require corresponding party mergers, or would risk parties losing their union base (ibid). This skepticism was echoed by union members: as one UMT unionist remarked,

> The idea of a union alliance is a good one. We see from Tunisia that one powerful union is better than many ... However, I don't think it will work in the end. There is too much bad blood between the unions. At some point one of the [leaders] will remember why they separated, and there will be fights. (Appendix B: MA-27, 5/7/2014)

These internal divisions underscored the extent to which inclusionary pluralism hampered unions' ability to exert unified pressure on the state. Ironically, unions' reliance on joint strikes indicated the depth of their organizational weakness rather than their strength. With internal divisions and partisan splits hindering unions' ability to mobilize a strong base, labor militancy *required* inter-union collaboration to achieve its goals. This fragility became even more pronounced in 2015, as unions continued to push for the implementation of the concessions promised in 2011. Reflecting on the wave of joint strikes in 2015, an article in *La Vie Éco* noted, "A new walkout has been declared in the civil service, and a general strike is looming on the horizon. Abdelilah Benkirane, aware of the relatively weak mobilization of the unions, lets them do it" (*La Vie Éco*, 12/08/2015).

Union Rights

Finally, Moroccan unions faced significant hurdles in defending workers' rights in the aftermath of the 2011 uprisings. Although collective agreements promised substantial protections, including the ratification of ILO Convention 87 and the passage of a new organic law on strikes, many of these commitments have yet to be fulfilled. In large part, the government's own policies exacerbated the difficulties that unions faced in mobilizing in favor of these measures. Three policies, in particular, severely constrained unions' ability to organize and advocate for workers' interests in the post-uprising era.

First, the government's proposed organic law on strikes introduced procedural hurdles that made strikes increasingly difficult to execute. Planned regulations imposed a thirty-day notice period before a strike could legally occur, during which disputes could be subjected to compulsory arbitration (*Al-Bayane*, 03/27/2015). Additionally, a series of time-consuming steps were also required for strike approval, including convening a workplace meeting two weeks before a strike, and obtaining 75 percent attendance and 51 percent approval for it to proceed (ibid). Though these measures were presented as procedural safeguards, they increased the organizational burden on union leaders to mobilize effectively. Requirements to notify employers seven days in advance of a strike further undermined unions' strategic flexibility, giving employers time to obstruct labor actions through co-optive or coercive tactics.

Beyond procedural barriers to organizing strikes, the government also implemented more direct restrictions on unions that limited their ability to organize. In 2013, the government introduced a policy of withholding pay from striking workers, contributing to a marked decline in strike participation (*La Vie Éco*, 11/16/2012). Furthermore, the failure to pass an organic law on strikes left workers subject to penal code Article 288, which imposed lengthy prison sentences for illegal strike activity.

Proposed regulations on the freedom of association also restricted unions' organizational rights. While such measures empowered workers by providing them with the ability to appeal to courts in cases of unfair dismissal, they also tied government funding to bureaucratic reforms, including many democratic procedures to which Moroccan unions were unaccustomed.[18] These complex administrative requirements discouraged many workers from unionizing altogether:

> When I decided to create the company's union, I thought that the exercise was going to be very simple. I went to the labor inspector who gave me all the information. Once the procedure was clear in my head, I started to go around the colleagues to collect their names in order to form the office. But to my great surprise, all the people had withdrawn, leaving me alone with my piece of paper in my hands. (Anonymous Moroccan worker quoted in *Aujourd'hui Le Maroc*, 10/22/2013)

Despite their institutional representation, unions have largely been unable to resist these measures. Reports of persistent violations of trade union freedoms highlight the erosion of unions' capacity to defend their members' interests. Striking workers at Med Paper and Maghreb Steel, for example, were brutally repressed by security

[18] For example, unions would need to hold regular congresses, have turnover in their leadership, and maintain membership lists that were regularly updated (La Vie Éco, 12/09/2014).

forces who removed them from the premises at the management's request (ITUC, 2016). Additionally, police crackdowns targeted union protests in Ouarzazate, where workers rallied against the arbitrary dismissal of hundreds of employees from local hotels and mines (ITUC, 01/23/2013). In some instances, the government pursued criminal charges against union leaders, as seen in the case of Said Elhairech, who served a ten-month prison sentence for organizing a strike at the Comarit-Comanav ferry company (ITF, 2014). At the Agadir DOHA plant, management dissolved a newly formed union, dismissed fifty-one workers, and imposed punitive fines on union leader Rahmoun Abdellah, whose apartment was seized as collateral for strike damages (IUF, 2016).

However, unions' difficulties in defending workers' rights have not solely been the result of government-imposed constraints. Their own internal weaknesses have further undermined their capacity to mobilize. Many workers expressed frustration with union leaders, arguing that their alignment with political parties compromised their ability to act on behalf of workers' interests:

> Carrying out union actions is a full-time job that requires a strong moral, intellectual and physical commitment. It is necessary to defend and protect workers' rights. Except that in real life we are often disappointed by the performances of national unions. In politics as in union action, our biggest problem is trust; especially if we discover that unions and political parties are far from being real institutions with programs, but just people who have been discredited over the course of elections and experience. (Hind Jalouni quoted in *L'observateur du Maroc*, 03/06/2013)

Other workers highlighted self-serving objectives as the reason for unions' inability to advocate for their members:

> It is clear that today's unions only think about making money at the expense of employees. They enrich themselves, quarrel and reconcile and completely forget their main role: honestly defending the interests of workers. Today, trade unionism is a source of enrichment. (Ali Hanifi quoted in *L'observateur du Maroc*, 03/06/2013)

Ultimately, internal divisions and the co-optation of of union leaders by the state have severely undermined unions' credibility among Moroccan workers. Despite gaining institutional levers of power within a liberalized political system, Moroccan unions are hindered by organizational legacies that limit their effectiveness in defending workers' interests. As a result, many workers have defected from unions *en masse*, leading to a significant decline in union strength. This situation has created a vicious cycle in which formal institutions, informal practices, and a political system dominated by the monarchy work in concert to perpetuate and deepen labor's marginalization. Like labor unions in Egypt, Moroccan unions find themselves ensnared in a "paradox of effective co-optation" (Bishara, 2018), wherein their institutional incorporation provides them with a semblance of political power while simultaneously undermining their capacity to affect meaningful change.

Conclusion

Political institutions, and the organizational legacies they impart, are critical for understanding contemporary labor politics in North Africa. As I have argued in this chapter, the UGTT's strength in Tunisia and the relative weakness of labor unions in Morocco cannot be understood without appreciating how institutions inherited from the past continue to shape labor politics in the present. In Tunisia, a legacy of exclusionary corporatism provided the UGTT with two key organizational advantages – political autonomy and deep connections to the grassroots – that enabled it to effectively advocate for workers and steer the post-uprising political transition in a more democratic direction. The UGTT's independence from political parties allowed it to prioritize workers' interests and convene diverse groups to negotiate a pacted transition to democracy. Additionally, its internal cohesion allowed the union to pressure the transitional government into implementing more progressive, labor-friendly policies.

In contrast, Morocco's legacy of inclusionary pluralism bequeathed to unions a fragmented labor movement, marked by leaders who were easily co-opted by employers and the state. Many unions, structured as offshoots of political parties, were integrated into legislative institutions, giving them significant autonomy from their rank-and-file members. These unions pursued non-adversarial strategies, relying on institutional channels to exert influence; however, this dependence on formal politics has perpetuated labor weakness. With traditional unions failing to meet workers' needs, disaffiliation has become widespread, leading to low levels of organizational power. As a result, organized labor in Morocco has continued to decline despite (limited) political liberalization, evidenced by minimal legal protections for workers, persistent labor rights abuses, and the unions' weakened presence in the post-uprising era.

Given the importance of institutional legacies in shaping labor politics – both for better and for worse – it is worth asking whether, and how, these legacies might be undone. At present, both Tunisia and Morocco have reverted to authoritarian rule. Although Tunisia successfully transitioned to democracy in 2014, it abruptly returned to autocracy following the 2021 self-coup of President Kais Saied. Moreover, the UGTT, which has routinely played a key role in opposing authoritarian rule, has so far struggled to mount a vigorous opposition campaign. Resistance to Saied's authoritarian consolidation has largely been limited to public criticism of his political decisions along with sporadic protests against specific austerity measures and repressive actions. The UGTT's muted response can be attributed in part to heightened repression under Saied's tenure, as his administration has employed legal and administrative measures to curtail the union's influence. Furthermore, divisions within the union between various political groups – some of which align with Saied – have made coordinated resistance against the regime difficult (*Jeune Afrique*, 09/11/2012).

Still, the UGTT retains organizational advantages that make opposition possible, if not likely, in the future. The UGTT remains one of the largest civil society groups in Tunisia, with its membership swelling to nearly one million despite Saied's repressive attacks. Furthermore, while some signs of oligarchization are evident,[19] the union generally continues to maintain democratic procedures and strong grassroots connections, particularly at the intermediate and local levels. These levels of the union have been the primary source of opposition to Saied's regime, suggesting that broader mobilization could emerge if the UGTT's leadership remains accountable to grassroots forces. As has been true in the past, when the UGTT mobilizes, the rest of the country tends to follow. As noted by political analyst Youssef Cherif,

19 Prior to the union's 25th congress, an extraordinary nonelective congress was held to revise internal statutes that imposed term limits on members of the UGTT's executive bureau, enabling nine members of the bureau to remain in power for over ten years.

> The UGTT is by far the most powerful civilian force within the country ... It has a huge membership. Moreover, unlike the president, whose appeal rests in rhetoric, its support is institutional. People have been members of the UGTT all their lives, and they see the results every day they go to work. (Youssef Cherif quoted in Cordall, 2022)

For Moroccan unions, meaningful change in labor politics will likely require major shifts in the organizational landscape. While union alliances have yet to generate sufficient momentum for labor solidarity, renewal may come through internal reforms, such as the introduction of more democratic procedures or new leadership. Additionally, although full separation from political parties seems unlikely, increased state repression of both political and labor activism may foster militant alliances between unions and opposition groups, as seen during the early 1990s. Finally, it is possible that change could arise from workers outside the traditional union framework. If conventional labor organizations remain captive to the state, Moroccan unions may experience the "paradox of effective cooptation" (Bishara, 2018), wherein disillusioned workers form independent groups that pose a more serious challenge to the regime. The potential for such movements to effect political change will depend on the regime's ability to use "divide-and-rule" tactics to subdue these pressures. While the Moroccan state has proven adept at containing dissent thus far, its ability to fend off challenges from unaffiliated labor movements – particularly those with ties to social movements from the radical left – may weaken in the future.

Ultimately, the future of labor politics in Morocco and Tunisia will depend on the extent to which these countries' historical legacies can be transformed into meaningful resistance – or whether they will confine organized labor to the margins of political life. As unions grapple with renewed authoritarianism, organized labor may once again emerge as a pivotal agent of change, but the character and success of its efforts will likely be rooted in institutional inheritances from the past.

8 Conclusion: Implications for North Africa and Beyond

This book was motivated by a central puzzle: why do some unions in authoritarian regimes engage in political protests while others do not? Existing scholarship offers several explanations, focusing on the structure of the economy, unions' internal organization, and the nature of state–labor relations under authoritarian rule. However, in the face of economic liberalization, unions across the world have struggled to mobilize. In nearly all developing countries, austerity measures have disrupted traditional patron–client relationships between organized labor and the state, leaving unions more structurally disadvantaged and organizationally weakened than ever before.

What, then, explains divergent patterns of labor mobilization during periods of economic reform? Using a comparative analysis of Tunisia and Morocco, this book has advanced an institutionalist account of labor protest in authoritarian regimes. Despite sharing similar historical trajectories and parallel episodes of economic opening, unions in Tunisia and Morocco reacted very differently to neoliberal reforms. While Moroccan unions avoided anti-government opposition, using moderate tactics like intra-elite bargaining and negotiation to advance their demands, Tunisian unions organized vigorous protest campaigns that combined economic grievances with direct critiques of the authoritarian regime.

This difference, I argue, stems from two key factors that shape unions' willingness to mobilize protests in authoritarian regimes. First, the degree of unions' incorporation into the state affects their initial willingness to engage in political protest. Where unions are integrated into formal politics, access to official channels for demand-making and coalition-building between union officials and partisan elites moderates labor behavior by channeling workers' demands into political institutions and away from the street. In contrast, when unions are excluded from the policymaking process, the lack of access to political elites radicalizes their agendas, forcing them to rely on more confrontational tactics and recurrent mobilization to give voice to their concerns.

Second, unions' internal governance structures, and particularly the way these shape relations between union leaders and the rank-and-file, determine their capacity to sustain militant protest. When union leaders build democratic governance institutions, they strengthen their intra-organizational cohesion and mobilizing potential, creating effective barriers against elite co-optation and internal division. However, the decision to establish democratic governance is closely linked to the political conditions that unions face at their founding. Because union democracy limits labor elites' ability to pursue their personal aims, only leaders with limited access to the state and few influential allies are likely to undertake the costly, laborious work of building democratic organizations. Thus, paradoxically regimes that marginalize and depoliticize labor inadvertently empower unions by providing them with the autonomy, incentives, and capacity necessary to challenge the regime.

The cases of Tunisia and Morocco illustrate this argument and demonstrate the value of an institutional approach to understanding labor behavior in authoritarian regimes. In Tunisia, the UGTT's political militancy stemmed from its exclusion from formal politics and the absence of institutional channels to express workers' interests to the state. The exclusionary control strategies employed by Habib Bourguiba and Zine Ben Ali radicalized workers and social movements, driving these groups into alliance against the authoritarian regime. Moreover, state exclusion fostered autonomy and internal democracy within the UGTT, which at critical moments, helped to politicize Tunisia's labor elite and galvanize support for rank-and-file militancy. Consequently, labor politics in Tunisia has frequently been a confrontational process, punctuated by specific episodes of politicized opposition against the authoritarian regime.

In contrast, Morocco's selective incorporation of union and partisan elites into formal institutions divided the labor movement and moderated labor militancy. Political pluralism encouraged the formation of party-union alliances and fragmented the labor movement across ideological lines. Only during a brief period when unions and opposition parties were excluded from the government did labor politics become more militant and political. However, with the rise of King Mohammed VI and the return to inclusionary authoritarianism, these moments of activism were quickly curtailed. Renewed incorporation of labor and partisan elites reinforced divisions between rank-and-file workers, and union leaders, ushering in a new era of labor moderation and apolitical militancy.

Thus, a full understanding of labor's political behavior requires an appreciation of both unions' external political environment and their internal organization. I return to this point and its implications for contentious politics, institutionalist scholarship, and the study of authoritarian regimes in the second half of the chapter. In the next section, I explore the generalizability of my argument by demonstrating how its key variables – labor incorporation and union organization – affect labor behavior in a diverse set of cases: Bahrain, South Africa, Mexico, and Egypt. I conclude with a discussion of what my argument might reveal about the future of Tunisia and Morocco in the contemporary era.

Institutions and Labor Politics beyond North Africa

Do the institutions governing labor representation shape labor behavior beyond North Africa? Is labor opposition less likely when autocrats incorporate unions into formal institutions and link labor leaders to partisan elites? Moreover, do democratic unions emerge primarily from conditions of political exclusion, or are other organizational processes at play?

The following section extends the book's arguments across time and space. Morocco and Tunisia represent a small subset of the broader population of authoritarian regimes to which my theory is meant to apply. Testing these arguments in additional cases provides a preliminary assessment of the generalizability of my theoretical framework. Specifically, selecting cases with meaningful variation on the dependent variable – political militancy versus labor quiescence – and across explanatory variables (e.g., development strategies, labor power, union composition, and regime type) allows me to evaluate the validity of my institutional framework against competing hypotheses.

Evidence from Bahrain, South Africa, Mexico, and Egypt highlights the critical role political institutions play in shaping patterns of labor militancy. A cursory analysis of labor politics in Bahrain supports the claim that exclusionary labor control policies, foster the rise of politically militant unions. Similarly, an analysis of labor mobilization in apartheid South Africa demonstrates the positive relationship between labor exclusion, union democracy, and anti-government opposition. In contrast, the cases of Mexico and Egypt illustrate the pacifying effects of political incorporation on labor militancy. Parallelism between cases among incorporated labor federations supports the argument that institutional inclusion produces a moderate union leadership with little inclination for political mobilization. Additionally, contrast within cases between incorporated and excluded sub-national unions confirms the inverse relationship between labor incorporation, union democracy, and political militancy.

Labor Opposition in Bahrain: The Dog that Almost Barked

Historical evidence from Bahrain supports the argument that exclusionary labor control policies foster politically militant unions. During the colonial and postindependence period, state suppression of labor organizing cultivated antagonism between Bahraini unions and the al-Khalifa regime, resulting in recurrent episodes of anti-regime contention led by labor unions. In 2011, the General Federation of Bahraini Trade Unions (GFBTU) played a pivotal role in organizing anti-government protests during the "Pearl Revolution," including two general strikes that shuttered industrial production and pressured the al-Khalifa regime to adopt moderate reforms. While this mobilization was ultimately unsuccessful in overturning the regime and establishing a constitutional monarchy, the role of labor organizations in mobilizing unrest underscores the risks that labor exclusion poses to authoritarian regimes by creating potential sources of opposition.

The origins of Bahraini labor militancy can be traced to conflictual state–labor relations during the pre-independence period. As in Tunisia, labor organization in Bahrain developed under colonial rule as part of the mass mobilization sparked by industrialization in the 1930s. During this period, labor mobilization was concentrated among blue-collar workers in the Bahrain Petroleum Company (BAPCO) and focused on ending workplace discrimination that favored foreign workers over Bahraini nationals (Lawson, 1989, 70). However, as animus toward the British occupation of Bahrain grew, labor activism was increasingly oriented toward national and political issues, such as demands for Bahraini independence. In the 1950s, this shift culminated in the creation of Bahrain's first autochthonous trade union, the General Trade Union (GTU), and a universal ban on trade union organizing and political activity until 1968.

The suppression of organized labor during the colonial period brought about two significant changes in the Bahraini labor movement. First, British labor repression shifted the tenor of labor politics in Bahrain from conciliatory to highly contentious, as evidenced by the increase in labor protests following the crackdown on the GTU in 1956. As Khalaf (1985, 24) notes, "sporadic work stoppages and organized strikes were frequent reactions to the prevailing conditions of misery and lack of power" faced by Bahraini workers in the absence of legitimate representation. Second, the British ban on labor and political organizing in Bahrain strengthened organizational ties between Bahraini workers and the radical left. Although the labor movement initially developed as a response to harsh working conditions in the oil industry, during the most virulent period of labor repression (1956–1965), Bahraini unions developed strong links with underground leftist and Arab nationalist movements, such as the National Liberation Front and the Popular Front for the Liberation of Oman and the Arab Gulf. Through these connections, labor unions learned to politicize their demands, linking grievances about wages and unemployment to broader critiques of British colonial rule and the exclusion of native Bahrainis from civil administration and policing (Gengler, 2012). In addition, Bahraini unions built solidarity across Bahrain's diverse working class by highlighting the presence of a common enemy – the British state.

Even after Bahrain gained independence in 1971, unions maintained a contentious relationship with the Bahraini state. Initial hope for a return to conciliation was quickly dashed after the al-Khalifa regime delayed key labor reforms such as legalizing the right to organize and promulgating a new labor code. Furthermore, the government took deliberate steps to counter labor militancy by expanding welfare programs and establishing a system of state-organized workers' committees. As in Tunisia, the alleged purpose of these committees was to represent workers in tripartite negotiations, but the true objective was to undermine independent labor organizing by creating ersatz unions. In a 1981 communiqué, leaders of GTU (now the Bahrain Trade Union) decried state workers' committees as a "publicity stunt" designed by the al-Khalifa regime to deflect international scrutiny of

Bahrain's poor labor protections while ignoring workers' legitimate demands (BTU cited in Khalaf, 1985, 28).

On the political front, Bahraini leaders took additional steps to suppress opposition. Despite introducing a more liberal constitution and a multiparty parliament, the monarchy marginalized all political groups that might threaten its traditional prerogatives. Key ministries (also de-facto parliamentary offices) were reserved for members of the al-Khalifa family, ensuring their dominance in the National Assembly. Popular dissent was also curtailed via a 1975 executive decree which gave the government the right to detain opponents for activities that "threaten[ed] the country's internal or external security" (Stork, 1997, 34). When members of the National Assembly questioned the legality of this decree, the assembly was dissolved, ushering in a twenty-seven-year state of emergency in which the al-Khalifa regime ruled virtually unchecked. In the years that followed, the regime initiated a broad campaign of arrests, detentions, and forced exiles that decimated the country's remaining opposition, including religious movements, political parties, and trade unions (ibid).

Labor exclusion remained central to labor politics in Bahrain and was critical in driving opposition to the al-Khalifa regime during the Arab Spring. When the GFBTU called for a general strike on February 20th, its main demands were for deeper institutional representation, including the creation of a national dialogue, the establishment of a permanent Economic and Social Council, and stronger guarantees for the right to organize and assemble (AFL-CIO, 2011; ITUC, 2012). In addition, the willingness of union leaders to suspend the strike following promises of dialogue underscores the pacifying potential of inclusionary policies (Bassiouni et al., 2011, 156). Even within the GFBTU, variation in militancy across unions correlated with the level of repression faced by different sectors. For example, the Bahrain Teachers' Association and the Bahrain Nurses' Society – two of the most protest-prone unions – had long been harassed by the government for their activism around working conditions and wages, as well as for their histories of social militancy (Holmes, 2016, see also ITUC, 2013).

Importantly, the GFBTU's *political* militancy during the Pearl Revolution coincided with significant episodes of labor repression. The decision to launch a second general strike against the government, for instance, was motivated by the regime's failure to initiate a national dialogue. According to a statement released by the GFBTU on February 24, "If the government doesn't fulfill its promise of genuine dialogue then we will call for a general strike" (*Financial Times*, 3/22/2011). Additionally, the union's support for more radical demands, such as the transition to a constitutional monarchy, aligned with reports of escalating violence against protesting workers, many of whom were detained and dismissed from their jobs (Zunes, 2013). The severity of government persecution ultimately led the GFBTU to indefinitely extend its general strike on March 20, marking one of the longest episodes of anti-government opposition in Bahrain's history. Although labor unrest was eventually quelled by a Saudi-led military intervention, the state's long history of labor repression played a decisive role in driving union-led opposition against the al-Khalifa regime.

Corroboration from South Africa: Racial Exclusion and the Emergence of Democratic Unionism

Evidence from South Africa corroborates the importance of exclusionary labor control policies for shaping union's political mobilization. Until the mid-1990s, a system of rigid racial stratification – apartheid – systematically excluded the Black labor force from the political and economic privileges enjoyed by whites. In the 1970s, Black workers began to challenge this system, adopting militant tactics to combat economic discrimination on the shop floor. As the severity of repression intensified, Black unions forged alliances with community organizations and political groups, forming a "mass democratic movement" geared toward liberalizing the country's political system and ushering in a genuine transition to democratic rule (Adler and Webster, 1995, 2000; Marx, 1992).

The exclusionary politics of apartheid South Africa are well documented (Seidman, 1994, 1999; Webster, 1987). In the labor market, apartheid created a dual industrial relations system wherein white, "colored," and Indian workers enjoyed associational freedoms, while Black workers were denied the right to unionize and collectively bargain.

For most of the twentieth century, discriminatory labor laws restricted Black South Africans' mobility, confining them to low-paying, unskilled jobs were employer harassment was rampant (Halpern,

1994). Furthermore, apartheid-era political restrictions criminalized labor actions involving Black workers and limited voting rights to whites.

The immediate consequence of these exclusionary policies was the emergence of a militant labor movement among the Black working class. As Seidman notes, "the long history of racial exclusion [in South Africa] meant that Black activists were far more likely to challenge the state's very structure than to try to work within the existing framework" (1994, 23). The first major challenge to apartheid labor laws came in 1973 when workers at Coronation Tile and Brick went on strike to protest wage disparities between Black and white workers in Durban. This action triggered a wave of spontaneous strikes involving over 61,000 employees (Mhlongo, 1975, 271).

The 1973 strike wave had a profound impact on the character of labor mobilization in South Africa. The success of the Durban strikes[1] heightened worker consciousness and led to the creation of an indigenous, independent trade union movement. Between 1973 and 1978, Black workers established over a dozen labor confederations, representing roughly 30,000 members (Maree, 1985). When non-white trade unions were officially recognized in 1979, several of these united to form the Federation of South African Trade Unions (FOSATU), the country's largest independent labor organization to date (Schroeder, 1988, 54).

As a nonracial union committed to economic advancement for all workers, FOSATU grew rapidly, increasing its membership from 45,000 members in 1979 to 120,000 by 1984 (Baskin, 1991, 49; Friedman, 2011). At the same time, the country witnessed a fundamental shift in the prevalence and character of labor militancy. During a time in which protest by white workers was relatively infrequent (Adler and Webster, 1995, 79), Black workers launched broad range

[1] Following the events in Durban, the government officially sanctioned the right of indigenous (Black) workers to strike. Additionally, many companies and state officials pushed for the expansion of plant-based "works committees" and "liaison committees" to enhance communication between employers and workers and improve shop floor governance (Lichtenstein, 2019).

of protest actions including strikes, stay aways, boycotts, and factory occupations (Beittel, 1995).[2]

The aftermath of the 1973 strikes also shaped unions' organizational strategies, leading to the adoption of a distinct form of organization – trade union democracy. Facing government repression, labor activists feared that union hierarchy, which had been the dominant form of trade union organizing in the past, would expose labor leaders to state capture or risk organizational collapse (Buhlungu, 2009, 95–96). To prevent the concentration of power, new unions implemented a horizontal organizational structure known as "worker control," emphasizing direct links between members and national union leaders, regular workplace meetings, shop steward accountability,[3] and opportunities for the rank-and-file to influence local and national union agendas (Fine, 1992). Moreover, organizational structures were kept as flat as possible (to avoid the easy elimination of a small strata of leaders), with concerted efforts being placed on worker education to train future militants (Cooper, 2007).

Finally, the 1973 strikes forged new connections between workers and their communities that tangibly shifted the political character of labor militancy. Prior to the 1970s, union leaders hesitated to advance political issues, fearing that alliances with social movements would overshadow the class character of union organizing (Seidman, 1994). However, as labor and community mobilization gained momentum, rank-and-file unionists recognized that political and workplace struggles were inextricably linked. Even during the 1973 strike wave, labor mobilization displayed a "dim awareness" of the link between broader socio-political realities and workers' economic grievances (Fisher cited in Wood, 1992, 21).

The most evident link between workplace struggles and political grievances emerged in South Africa's urban townships, where workers suffered the worst indignities of apartheid. Daily manifestations of

[2] From 1973 to 1984 both "routinized" and "disruptive" protests became a regular feature of industrial relations, with the government reporting an average of 273 strikes and 160,866 working days lost per year (ILO, 2016).

[3] For example, shop stewards were required to report back to members about discussions undertaken with management before a decision could be reached and were prohibited from meeting with management alone. Further details about the role that shop stewards played in supporting union democracy are provided in Adler (1994).

racial discrimination – overcrowding, sub-standard living conditions, and lengthy and expensive commutes to work – underscored the linkages between workplace and community issues, highlighting the negative externalities of legal segregation (Seidman, 1999). Moreover, the imposition of influx control policies ("pass laws") to restrict workers' movement reinforced the connection between economic grievances and the political system. As Seidman notes, "under the migrant labor system, where even skilled workers were vulnerable to dismissal, shop-floor organization was directly affected by the country's political arrangement" (1994, 237). Consequently, by the early 1980s, labor leaders actively endorsed the idea of community-union partnerships. As one union activist put it, such alliances offered:

> the ability to assert and defend class interests, against those of other classes [in] every aspect of our lives — at work; at school; where we live; over the structures of local and national government; over the army; the police; courts and prisons; the media; the church; financial institutions and the economy as a whole. (Mayekiso cited in Jochelson, 1990, 6)

These factors, coupled with intense labor repression in the mid-1980s, positioned the labor movement as a key agent of political reform. In 1985, following the imposition of a draconian emergency law, the government increased its persecution of Black unions, deploying the army to demobilize strikes, curtail union participation in community issues, and engage in mass detention of workers for their political activities. In response, Black labor unions joined together to form a new labor confederation, the Congress of South African Trade Unions (COSATU), dedicated to protecting workers from employer harassment and state repression under apartheid. Drawing from its workerist and community foundations, the union aimed to augment workers' gains at the bargaining table by replacing white minority rule with a democratic system based on "one man, one vote."

From 1986 to 1990, growing labor politicization fueled a civil disobedience campaign that led to the end of the apartheid regime. As the severity of repression increased, rank-and-file workers urged COSATU leaders to take on a bigger role in the anti-apartheid struggle, pressuring it to align with the pro-reform United Democratic Front and adopt the basic principles of the African National Congress' (ANC) Freedom Charter (Lodge, 1983). In June 1986, COSATU organized a day-long strike on the 10th anniversary of the Soweto uprisings that involved 1.5 million Black employees, making it the biggest anti-apartheid protest in South Africa to date (*New York Times*, 1986). In the next four years, the country lost some 23 million working days to strikes – more than the previous seventy-five years combined (ILO, 2016). Ultimately, the economic impact of these strikes, over 75 percent of which were explicitly political, led business and government elites to abandon their support for apartheid and press for democratic reforms. Adler and Webster summarize this turning point,

> The range of union campaigns, protests, wildcat actions and disruptions on the shop floor demonstrated the limited effectiveness of repression in ending mobilization ... The state was faced with a choice, intensify repression towards the labor movement ... and risk alienating capital with no guarantee of eliminating mobilization from below, or turn towards more fundamental political reform. (1995, 82).

Summary

The cases of South Africa and Bahrain, support the argument that politically militant unions emerge under conditions of labor exclusion. Like the UGTT, labor movements in Bahrain and South Africa were subjected to highly repressive conditions, which forced unions to adopt confrontational tactics to assert their interests before the state. In all three cases, labor militancy displayed patterns typical of movements operating outside of formal politics: decentralized leadership, alliances with community and (banned) political groups, and revanchist political aims.

Beyond supporting my argument through parallelism, the comparison of Bahrain, South Africa, and Tunisia also helps rule out several alternative hypotheses. For example, juxtaposing labor mobilization in Tunisia and Bahrain contradicts the claim that the severity of labor militancy is determined by economic conditions or regime type. Contrary to the business cycle theories, Bahrain's labor push for democratization occurred during a period of relative economic growth, while Tunisia's labor militancy arose from escalating economic crisis. Furthermore, although both countries are authoritarian, their regimes differ significantly: Tunisia is a presidential republic, while Bahrain is a hereditary monarchy. The congruence of labor mobilization across these distinct contexts challenges the argument, that monarchies are uniquely robust to political opposition (Anderson, 1991; Herb, 1999; Menaldo, 2012). Instead, the evidence presented here suggests that the key factor determining labor militancy is not the type of regime that leaders adopt but whether labor is sufficiently incorporated into these institutions to moderate their behavior.

Additionally, a closer examination of labor mobilization in South Africa challenges path-dependent accounts of labor opposition while confirming the inverse relationship between inclusionary corporatism, union democracy, and labor militancy. The transformation of COSATU from a radical opponent of the National Party to a passive ally of the ANC in the postapartheid era underscores the importance of institutional incorporation in weakening labor activism. In 1990, COSATU formalized its alliance with the ANC and South African Communist Party to create a tripartite coalition tasked with leading a post-apartheid South Africa. For COSATU leaders, this meant deeper incorporation within the democratic regime: top union officials were granted seats on the National Economic Development and Labor Council, appeared on ANC parliamentary lists, and were appointed to ministerial offices in the national government (Buhlungu et al., 2008; McKinley, 2003). Yet following the formation of this alliance, COSATU witnessed a marked decline in labor mobilization, coinciding with its incorporation into formal politics. Fom 1994 to 1999, South Africa averaged 2,107,877 working days lost per year compared to roughly 4 million annually in the previous five years (ILO, 2016). Notably, this reduction in militancy occurred despite the implementation of economic policies that threatened labor's core interests. For instance, in 1996, the ANC-led government introduced the Growth, Employment, and Redistribution program, a business-friendly economic model that faced only moderate resistance from organized labor (Barchiesi, 1999).

Furthermore, reduction in labor militancy also coincided with notable declines in COSATU's internal governance. Mirroring the centralized organizational style of its political partners, COSATU gradually concentrated decision-making among union staff and national officials, departing from the union's previously sacrosanct democratic and collective ethos (Buhlungu et al., 2008; Buhlungu and Tshoaedi, 2013; Maree, 2013). The negative impact of these changes on union militancy was captured by Timothy Nkosi, chairperson of COSATU's Wits local shop stewards council:

> Today, the emphasis has shifted away from worker democracy, militancy and solidarity. These have been replaced by bureaucracy, moderation of workers by the political negotiations, moderation of the high expectations which the working class had on the eve of agreements between the liberation movement and the regime. (Nkosi cited in Buhlungu, 2009, 102)

In sum, available evidence suggests that focusing on institutional factors provides a better explanation for labor militancy (and moderation) than existing alternatives. The detrimental effects of institutional incorporation on labor opposition are further confirmed by the cases of Mexico and Egypt, as discussed below.

Labor Passivity in Mexico: Institutional Incorporation and Democratic Diffidence

The case of labor politics in Mexico provides compelling evidence of the moderating effect that institutional incorporation can have on labor militancy.

The historical incorporation of Mexico's chief labor union, the Confederation of Mexican Workers (CTM), into the ruling Institutional Revolutionary Party (PRI), fostered close relations between labor elites and the authoritarian state. In exchange for delivering electoral support to the PRI, the CTM received a wide array of legal, economic, and political benefits which solidified its position in the labor market and afforded union leaders a measure of influence within the postrevolutionary regime. For instance, the CTM was allocated the majority of seats on key labor boards, such as the Mexican Social Security Institute, the National Minimum Wage Commission, and the National Commission for Worker Profit Sharing (Bensusán and Middlebrook, 2012). The union also disproportionately benefited from PRI control over institutions like the National Worker Housing Unit and the Worker's Bank, which funneled special benefits to CTM-affiliated workers (ibid). Politically, the PRI used its coercive power to eliminate CTM rivals and ensure leadership hegemony over rank-and-file workers through administrative and legal controls (Burgess, 2004, 41–42; Middlebrook, 1995, 62). The CTM's inclusion on the PRI party list also granted its leaders preferential access to elected positions, creating opportunities to gain political power and (modestly) influence government policy (Middlebrook, 1995, 102; Zazueta and Peña, 1984, 382).

As in Morocco, close ties between the CTM and PRI moderated labor's response to key episodes of economic and political change. In the mid-1980s, Mexican President Miguel de la Madrid introduced an austerity program that jeopardized labor's core interests with wage restraints, cuts to social welfare programs, and increased trade liberalization. However, the CTM responded to the measures with a "business unionist" approach: although union leaders filed thousands of strike petitions and warned of future action if austerity policies were not reversed, they refrained from organizing collective action to oppose the government's economic program. Similarly, when President Carlos Salinas accelerated economic reforms in the 1990s with new liberalization and privatization measures, labor leaders did not respond with mass demonstrations. Despite a substantial decrease in average wages and a rise in unemployment, the CTM failed to stage a coordinated strike campaign against neoliberal reforms (Burgess, 2004). Instead, the union played a key role in legitimizing the government's industrial restructuring programs by ratifying the controversial anti-inflation pact and supporting the adoption of the North American Free Trade Agreement (Bensusán Areous, 1994).

The CTM's reluctance to pursue militant collective action stemmed from the integration of key labor elites into the institutional organs of the state. To secure union support for its economic program, the government granted constitutional status to worker-owned enterprises and expanded the CTM's role in wage policy decisions through its inclusion in the Economic Solidarity Pact (*Pacto*). According to Burgess (2004, 78), "The *Pacto* essentially brought the CTM's radical posturing over national wage policy to an end ... [it] made the CTM an indispensable partner in the government's economic program and gave [the union] valuable leverage in its overall relationship with the PRI."

Additionally, the de la Madrid administration granted the union generous policy concessions and subsidies to promote workers' welfare. Importantly, because these benefits were channeled through the CTM-controlled Worker's Bank, union leaders used their institutional privileges to enforce labor discipline, inhibiting rank-and-file workers from responding aggressively to harmful policies (Aguilar and Arrieta, 1990). Elite control labor opposition was further solidified union leaders' participation in the Pacto's Enforcement and Evaluation Commission which played an "extremely important" role in monitoring compliance with the state's economic policies (Burgess, 2004, 78).

Similar dynamics help explain the CTM's ambivalence toward Mexico's political opening. Throughout its sixty-year alliance with the PRI, the union remained committed to single-party rule, using its broad organizational powers to oppose electoral reforms and endorse the PRI, despite the latter's restriction of civil liberties and suppression of opposition parties. When some sectors of the party initiated democratic reforms, CTM leaders stood against party liberalization, calling for expulsion of reformist elements and throwing their weight behind the incumbent regime's preferred (Burgess, 2004, 86).

The closeness of political ties between the CTM and PRI leadership clarifies the union's resistance to political reform. As Middlebrook (1995, 291) notes "by providing pro-government union leaders with preferential opportunities for political mobility and symbolically reaffirming the labor movement's national importance, ties to the governing party have bolstered labor support for the [authoritarian] post-revolutionary order." Thus, labor leaders' fear of political power loss fueled opposition to multiparty politics, as it was suspected that stronger opposition parties might challenge the CTM's authority over its members (Murillo, 2001, 107).

The case of Mexico, therefore, supports the that labor unions with close ties to the state will substitute political mobilization with more moderate strategies like negotiation and compromise. However, labor's quiescence was not only due to its incorporation within the PRI regime. As in other countries affected by neoliberal reforms, Mexican unions also suffered from structural weaknesses that limited their capacity to mobilize. Prolonged economic crises undermined unions' bargaining power, while privatization and restrictions on labor organizing further weakened their ability to achieve their goals. Nonetheless, organizational weaknesses alone cannot explain the CTM's reluctance to oppose reforms – despite experiencing significant losses in the public sector, the union still retained a membership of 5 million workers, representing roughly 17.5 percent of Mexico's workforce (Zebadúa, 1994). Moreover, at critical moments, the CTM was able to deploy its organizational muscle to challenge key regime prerogatives, as seen in its successful effort to prevent labor's influence within the PRI from being diminished by eliminating sector organizations within the party (Middlebrook, 1995, 297–298; Samstad, 2002, 16). The fact that the union was sufficiently strong to defend its privileged position within the regime thus points to the importance of institutional incorporation, not organizational weakness, in driving patterns of labor mobilization in authoritarian regimes.

Labor Mobilization in Egypt: Variation Proves the Rule

Finally, variation in labor protest between included and excluded union federations in Egypt affirms the inverse relationship between labor incorporation and militancy while highlighting the unintended consequences of state co-option. For much of Egypt's history, close ties between the authoritarian elite and the Egyptian Trade Union Federation (ETUF) ensured quiescence and loyalty from organized labor. However, in the mid-1990s, changes in state–labor relations created new cleavages within the ETUF, leading to the emergence of independent unions that explicitly mobilized in response to the dominance of co-opted elites. These independent unions not only challenged the existing structure of state–labor bargains but also directly opposed authoritarian practices in the Mubarak regime. Thus, the historical development of the ETUF, and its close ties to the state, unintentionally induced militant political activism from autonomous, less privileged unions in a later period.

The foundation of Egypt's traditional state–labor bargain was laid in the decades following the country's 1952 revolution. Hoping to win support from the working class, the Nasser regime implemented numerous policies to co-opt and contain labor organizations. Economically, the government granted monopoly representation to the ETUF, legalized semi-closed shops, created administrative institutions to regulate worker–employer conflicts, and enacted progressive labor provisions, such as protections for social security benefits, temporary leave, and job security (Bianchi, 1989). Politically, the ETUF was integrated into the regime through sinecures that granted high-ranking labor officials positions in the cabinet, legislative assembly, and the ruling National Democratic Party (NDP) (Aidi, 2008).

Although this arrangement was highly unequal, the integration of the ETUF into the state served as a check on labor militancy, even during economic crises like the transition to a market economy during the *infitah* period (Bianchi, 1986; Posusney, 1997). Central to this strategy was the role of co-opted labor elites. The ETUF's centralized, hierarchical structure allowed upper-level leaders to control strike authorization and censure militants, enabling them to "stifle the initiative of local leaders and restrict their ability to address the day-to-day issues of workers" (Posusney, 1997, 86). On the political front, labor leaders, fearing the loss of their privileges, opposed Anwar Sadat's plans for multiparty elections until the government offered more concessions than had been provided under single-party rule (Bianchi, 1986).

In the mid-1990s, however, the implementation of a new structural adjustment program eroded the corporatist bargain struck between organized labor and the state, triggering a wave of labor militancy in the following decade. Changes to the labor code undermined the regime's key incentive for quiescence – job security – while the shift toward a more business-friendly environment threatened the ETUF's privileged position within the state (Bishara, 2018, 31). Additionally, privatization weakened union organizations in the public sector and accelerated the decay of traditional mechanisms to address labor grievances (Pratt, 2000). Most important, the Mubarak government's increasingly interventionist stance in managing the ETUF, including manipulation of union elections and repression of unauthorized strikes, further destabilized the regime-labor pact (Bishara, 2018, 33; Hartshorn, 2019; Pratt, 2000, 117).

The ultimate consequence of these changes was the creation of an independent labor movement outside of the ETUF. In the late 1980s, a grassroots effort to "liberalize" the union emerged in response to the leadership's inability to address the needs of its increasingly heterogeneous base (Bianchi, 1986, 442). By the early 2000s, calls for union pluralism gained momentum as government interference in union elections made it clear that reform-minded unionists could not change the organization from within. Following the highly fraudulent elections of 2006, hundreds of labor militants withdrew from the ETUF and formed independent unions such as the Real Estate Tax Authority Union and the Autonomous Teachers' Union (Beinin and Duboc, 2013).

The rationale behind the formation of these unions and their confrontational disposition toward the regime affirms the argument that labor exclusion breeds militant political activity. For many independent union leaders, frustration with their exclusion from Egypt's corporatist bargaining system convinced them to organize outside of the formal institutions of the state. As Dina Bishara notes, the close alignment between a co-opted union elite and a neoliberal, authoritarian regime led to a "paradox of effective cooptation" wherein excluded unionists were forced to resort to radical militancy to voice their concerns (Bishara, 2018, 36). Reflecting this dynamic, the number of labor protests tripled, rising from an average of 147 per year from 1998 to 2005 to an average of 450 from 2006 to 2010, the majority of which were organized by independent unions or workers unaffiliated with the ETUF (Land Center for Human Rights cited in Beinin, 2015).

Finally, changes in state–labor relations and the rise of independent unions shifted labor militancy in a more political direction. Decades of suppressed demands and embryonic linkages to opposition groups encouraged newer unions to link political issues with economic ones. For example, in 2010, the government's refusal to implement a proposed minimum wage increase of 400 pounds led hundreds of workers to demand the resignation of the technocratic Nazif government (Beinin, 2012). A year later, workers participated *en masse* in the movement to remove Hosni Mubarak. Responding to a call by labor activists to abandon their conventional "bread and butter" approach, thousands of workers struck in support of pro-democracy protesters' revolutionary demands.

Ultimately, this shift in labor mobilization, from willful passivity to radical political militancy, illustrates the way in which labor incorporation (or the lack thereof) affects unions' protest behavior. In states where unions are incorporated into the political system, co-optation of union elites can suppress labor activism and create a disconnect between leaders and their members. However, as the Egyptian case shows, co-optation can be a double-edged sword: when it is too effective, and limited to a few labor leaders at the top, it weakens a union's ability to contain unrest within its more restive membership. Thus, the combination of (incomplete) incorporation of the labor movement and hierarchical labor organization may undermine inclusionary corporatist arrangements by fostering reactive militancy from discontented workers. As I note in the final section of the chapter, this dynamic presents new possibilities for labor mobilization in inclusionary corporatist regimes and underscores the importance of analyzing both state–labor relations and unions' internal governance to understand their ultimate protest trajectories.

Implications: Labor Politics as Legacy and Choice

In developing an institutional theory of labor protest, this book has drawn upon insights from sociology, political economy, and political science. However, by integrating these diverse literatures, my argument nuances existing analyses, offering new theoretical implications for social movement studies and comparative politics. In the following section, I outline three key lessons from the preceding analysis that can help guide future scholarship: 1) the importance of integrating structure and agency into theories of labor politics, 2) the unintended consequences of repression for mobilization, and 3) the need to adopt more flexible models of institutional persistence and change.

One of the first lessons that can be drawn from this study is the importance of incorporating political structure and agency into explanations of contentious politics. Too often, social mobilization is seen as the product of macro-social forces exogenous to social organizations themselves (Della Porta, 2017; Eisinger, 1973; Klandermans, 1986; Kriesi, 2004; Meyer, 2004; Tarrow, 1998). My work updates this view by focusing on the role that institutions play in regulating unions' internal organization and their political relationship with the state. In doing so, I treat mobilization as a function of both inherited legacies and strategic choices. While it is true that institutional structures constructed by the state present unions with varying opportunities for collective action, the decisions unions make – particularly regarding their internal organization – can shape their behavior in extremely meaningful ways.

Integrating structure and agency into analyses of contentious politics also offers advantages to future scholarship. First, for studies of labor politics, it shifts our understanding of state–labor relations from static equilibria to much more dynamic and interactive processes. Although states define the institutional context in which unions operate, union leaders can leverage their organizational resources to transform these institutions into staging grounds for opposition. For example, as seen in Tunisia, union leaders can utilize repressive conditions to build stronger connections to their rank-and-file, enhancing their organizational capacity and positioning them to pose a more formidable challenge to the regime. Crucially, the role of union democracy in facilitating labor mobilization highlights the need to analyze the relationship between unions, their members, and the broader political environment to fully understand how labor militancy emerges. Only by grasping the tripartite relationship between states, union elites, and the people they claim to represent can we comprehend how social movements develop and why they pursue different strategies to advance their goals.

Second, attention to internal organization and individual agency illuminates "pockets of resistance" within seemingly durable authoritarian regimes. Studies of social movements often attribute collective action to the availability of political opportunities, such as major structural shifts or exceptional changes within the regime (Klandermans, 1986; Kriesi, 2004; Meyer, 2004; Tarrow, 1998). However, incorporating organizational agency into our analyses enables scholars to anticipate episodes of collective action by revealing tensions or "oppositional subcultures" within politically closed environments. This is significant because many contemporary episodes of anti-regime contention – the 1989 Eastern European revolutions, the 2011 "Arab Spring," and the recent pro-democracy protests in Algeria and Sudan – have been conceived as "occurring out of nowhere," (Kuran, 1991; Goodwin, 2011) despite early signs of movement organization prior to these uprisings. Additionally, a focus on organizations helps students of labor politics understand why unions facing similar structural conditions respond differently to crises depending on their internal politics and the types of elite-membership alliances they engender.

Another important lesson from this research is the need for scholars of contentious politics to reconsider the role that political opportunities – or the lack thereof – play in facilitating protest. The idea that the political environment shapes patterns of contention is not new (Klandermans, 1986; Kriesi, 2004; Meyer, 2004; Tarrow, 1998). Political opportunities influence how protesters assess the risks and benefits of collective action, making certain forms of contention more or less likely. However, while some scholars find that more open and democratic environments are most conducive to protest (Dalton et al., 2010; Vráblíková, 2016; Welzel and Deutsch, 2012), others suggest that semi-democratic or newly liberalizing regimes present greater opportunities for contention, as grievances in full democracies can often be managed through institutional channels (Robertson, 2010).

My research, however, challenges these assumptions by showing how repressive environments can foster protest mobilization. As seen in the case of Tunisia, political exclusion can unintentionally strengthen opposition groups, leading to heightened anti-regime contention over time. The absence of institutional avenues for demand-making can intensify labor grievances, causing unions to rely on confrontational, extra-institutional methods to relay their concerns to the state. Additionally, generalized repression can unify disaffected groups by encouraging solidarity across social divides, enabling diverse actors to identify with a shared goal of resisting authoritarian rule.

In contrast, more open political environments may coax labor movements into quiescence by enabling authoritarian elites to co-opt union leaders and distance them from the rank-and-file. Somewhat counterintuitively, I find that regimes can better manipulate and control organizations to which they grant the privilege of formal representation. Groups that are excluded from formal politics, by contrast tend to develop the autonomy and organizational resources needed to sustain opposition to authoritarian regimes. In advancing this argument, I join a newer body of research that emphasizes the ways in which political exclusion and indiscriminate repression radicalize social movements, pushing them to adopt more transgressive forms of resistance (Demirel-Pegg and Rasler, 2021; Ellefsen, 2021; Nugent, 2020).

Finally, beyond contributing to the study of contentious politics, my research also advances contemporary scholarship on authoritarian institutions, institutional persistence, and institutional change. Much of the existing literature on authoritarianism focuses on how elites strategically manipulate political institutions to sustain their rule. By deliberately designing parties and legislatures to co-opt opposition and reduce intra-regime defections, autocrats consolidate their power and foster durable regimes (Brownlee, 2007; Gandhi and Przeworski, 2007; Lust-Okar, 2004; Svolik, 2012). However, such a functionalist perspective overlooks a broad literature on the unintended consequences of institutional designs and reduces the effects of political institutions on outcomes, such as regime stability, to mere epiphenomena (Pepinsky, 2014).

In contrast, my research adopts a historical institutionalist approach, that highlights the ways in which authoritarian institutions constrain the behavior of political elites, including those who create them. While autocrats design institutions with strategic objectives in mind, contingency and reactive sequences often alter their intended effects. In Chapters 3 and 4, I demonstrate how exclusionary labor control policies in Tunisia unintentionally strengthened labor opposition by fostering union autonomy and encouraging cooperation between union members and radical leftist groups. This is because the effects of political institutions are dynamic: beyond serving their initial purposes, institutions may also provoke reactions from those they govern, producing outcomes that are far removed from their designers' original intent. Moreover, early institutional choices often lead to path-dependent coalitional arrangements, making unfavorable outcomes difficult or impossible to reverse (Mahoney, 2000).

Throughout the book, I show that understanding political coalitions is key to explaining both institutional stability and change. Many historical institutionalist works view change as the result of "critical junctures," typically emerging from exogenous shocks (Bishara, 2020; Collier and Collier, 1991; Mahoney, 2001; Pierson, 2004). Without denying the fact that such critical junctures exist, my work nuances this view by focusing on the role of coalitions in supporting institutional stability and catalyzing change. Building on the work of contemporary institutionalist scholars, I advance a power-distributional model of institutional development, arguing that the effectiveness and persistence of political institutions depend on the ability of individuals to maintain the coalitions of support that underpin them. In Chapter 5, I apply this coalitional approach to examine how two forms of institutional change – innovation and drift – affected unions' protest behavior. Using the cases of labor mobilization in Tunisia and Morocco during the 1980s, I explore how shifts in corporate institutions reshaped state–labor relations, resulting in new patterns of labor militancy. In Tunisia, unexpected changes in political leadership prompted liberal reforms to the country's bargaining and governance institutions (*institutional innovation*), temporarily aligning labor leaders and opposition parties with the Ben Ali regime. In Morocco, existing institutional frameworks interacted with broader economic shifts to generate new grievances among elites (*institutional drift*), driving unions and political parties to unite in opposition to the regime. Though the sources of change differed, in both cases, shifts in the political coalitions that undergirded existing institutions produced new patterns of labor behavior that cannot be fully explained by traditional critical juncture or path-dependent accounts. This divergence highlights the importance of analyzing coalitional politics for understanding processes of institutional innovation, evolution, and political change.

Finally, a focus on coalitions helps explain autocratic resilience in the face of political changes that might otherwise disrupt the status quo. As Chapter 6 illustrates, institutional reforms (and the effects they engender) can be fleeting if the coalitions that support them weaken or if incumbents can successfully rebuild support for previous institutional arrangements. One way that this can occur, as seen in Morocco, is when authoritarian leaders use their power to dismantle alliances borne from previous institutions to stall the process of political change. Indeed, by creating new spaces for labor and opposition parties to express their interests, the Moroccan monarchy successfully neutralized potential revolutionary coalitions between the February 20th movement and union elites, preventing the kind of cross-cutting mobilization that could have destabilized the regime.

Alternatively, support coalitions for authoritarian institutions may weaken endogenously, increasing the likelihood that seemingly "stable" autocratic regimes will break down. In Tunisia, insufficient incorporation of rank-and-file workers into Ben Ali's corporatist bargain created a new group of "institutional losers" who sought to disrupt the stability of Tunisia's labor control regime. By launching wildcat strikes, these groups reinforced the perception that repressive strategies were needed to curb labor unrest, leading Ben Ali to revert to exclusionary practices that alienated labor elites. Breakdown in the state–labor alliance was further facilitated by the democratic structure of the UGTT, itself a legacy of repression during the postindependence period. Over time, these developments eroded the space for cooperation between labor and the state, leading unions to adopt more militant behaviors. Ultimately, this led to the rapid demise of the Ben Ali regime: absent sufficient mechanisms to quiet labor unrest, the regime was overwhelmed by mass protests coordinated by radicalized workers and pro-democracy groups.

The cases of Tunisia and Morocco thus demonstrate that the resilience of authoritarian regimes hinges not only on deliberate institutional design but also on autocrats' ability to sustain the coalitions that support it. While institutional choices are often strategic, they frequently produce unanticipated responses from political actors who either consolidate opposition to the regime or reinforce authoritarian control. This underscores the need to view institutional reform as inherently political processes, shaped as much by individual agency and shifting alliances as by formal rule changes. A coalition-centered approach offers a more nuanced understanding of these dynamics, moving beyond the conventional focus on external shocks and path dependence. It also highlights how institutions designed to preserve authoritarian rule can unexpectedly generate moments of instability, opening pathways for potential political liberalization or regime breakdown.

Conclusion

Although it would be wrong to treat labor organizations as the principal agent of change in authoritarian regimes, evidence from North Africa shows that mobilization from labor unions can be of tremendous consequence. Against deepening concerns about the "end of labor," workers and unions are finding new ways to assert their relevance by engaging with nontraditional sectors and building coalitions that go beyond the workplace. In places like Tunisia, unions have not only driven key political reforms but also played a pivotal role in steering democratic transitions, demonstrating the power of organized labor during moments of political uncertainty. Additionally, in Morocco, militancy is beginning to emerge outside of the labor movement among individual workers in informal organizations, signaling a shift in how labor activism manifests.

Thus, despite the decline of traditional industrial sectors, the privatization of public enterprises, and the co-optation of traditional labor representatives by the state, unions continue to adapt, leveraging new arenas of influence and experimenting with more flexible forms of organizing. Moreover, the instabilities that these changes create generate new sources of grievances and discontent that labor unions can harness into renewed mobilization efforts. Changing economic and political conditions may undermine the organizational bases of labor unions, but these adverse circumstances present new opportunities for labor renewal and coalition-building. Labor has been, and will continue to be, significant force in authoritarian politics, posing meaningful challenges to autocratic regimes and to scholars examining the relationship between labor mobilization and political change.

Appendices

Appendix A

Labor Conflict in the Middle East and North Africa Database

Introduction and Overview

The Labor Conflict in Middle East/North Africa (MENALC) Database contains information on protests, sit-ins, strikes, and other public demonstrations perpetrated by unions and union affiliates in Tunisia and Morocco. While other protest datasets focus on social conflict more generally, the purpose of this dataset is to gather information specifically related to labor movements in order to catalog their protest activities and collective mobilization efforts.

Protest events in Tunisia and Morocco are covered beginning in 1975. Unlike other datasets, which draw from a limited number of sources, the primary information from this dataset is compiled from a comprehensive list of over 300 sources in English, French, and Arabic, as compiled by the LexisNexis Academic, Factiva, and World News Connection news sources as well as archival materials from Library of Congress, Tunisian National Archives, and Moroccan National Archives.

MENALC is directed by Ashley Anderson (University of North Carolina at Chapel Hill) and has been funded by generous grants from the National Science Foundation (NSF), Harvard University Weatherhead Center, Harvard University Institute for Quantitative Social Science (IQSS), and the Project on Middle East Political Science (POMEPS). The following is a guide to the coding of events included in the data. Each event was coded to preserve a maximum of information included in the original news report (as noted in the "EDESC" category). Characteristics of events (i.e., event type, demands) were then aggregated into sub-categories as specified below:

Dataset variables

1. CCODE
   Correlates of War numeric designation of the country

2. ID
   Event number within a given country-year. The first event recorded receives a code of 0001
3. YEAR
   Year in which the event began
4. EVENT ID
   Combination of the fields CCODE, YEAR, and ID to generate a single, unique event ID
5. STDATE
   Date on which the event began
6. STAPPROX
   Binary indicator of whether the start date was approximated (0 = No; 1 = Yes)
7. LINKEVENT
   Binary indicator of whether the event is connected to another event in the dataset (0 = No; 1 = Yes)
8. LINKID
   ID number indicating the event to which the listed event is linked
9. DUR
   Duration in minutes of the event
10. ETYPE
    Type of event, grouped into the following categories:

    Organized demonstration
    Spontaneous demonstration
    Organized violent riot
    Spontaneous violent riot
    General strike
    Limited strike
    Hunger strike
    Economic boycott
    Political boycott

11. EESCALATE
    Indicator of whether the event type changed over the course of its duration, with events grouped as above
12. EDESC
    Text description of the protest event and related circumstances.
13. APPROV
    Binary indicator of whether the event was approved by a recognized labor organization (0 = No; 1 = Yes)

14. ACTOR (1-5)
    Text description of the participants in the event (up to five actor-groups can be recorded)
15. TARGET (1-5)
    Text description of the target of the event (up to five targets can be recorded)
16. CGOVTARG
    Binary indicator of whether the central government or a national government official was the target of the protest (0 = No; 1 = Yes)
17. RGOVTARG Binary indicator of whether a regional government or a regional government official was the target of the protest (0 = No; 1 = Yes)
18. ISSUE (1-5)
19. Description of the issue/demand that precipitated the event, grouped into the following categories (up to five issues can be listed):

    Compensation (incl. payment of arrears)
    Indemnities (incl. health benefits)
    Pensions
    Working conditions
    Working hours
    Termination or layoffs (not including abusive dismissals)
    Arbitrary/abusive dismissals
    Temporary workers
    Productivity norms
    Economic reform/liberalization
    Cost of living/inflation
    Unemployment
    Organizational freedoms (i.e., right to unionize/collectively bargain)
    Resumption of negotiations
    Other reasons for industrial dispute
    Change/overthrow of regime
    Dismissal of government official
    Corruption
    Development/infrastructure
    Inequality
    Associational freedoms (not including right to unionize)

Political freedoms (i.e. freedom of press, freedom of speech, etc.)
Other reasons for political strikes

20. NPART
    Numerical estimate of the number of persons participating in the event. If multiple estimates are given, the most recent figure is used.
21. NPARTAPPROX
    Binary indicator of whether the number of participants was approximated (0 = No; 1 = Yes)
22. REPRESS
    Binary indicator of whether repressive force was used against protesters by the government or government-sponsored agents
23. NARREST
    Numerical estimate of the number of participants arrested during the event. If multiple estimates are given, the most recent figure is used.
24. NINJURE
    Numerical estimate of the number of participants injured during the event. If multiple estimates are given, the most recent figure is used.
25. NKILL
    Numerical estimate of the number of participants killed during the event. If multiple estimates are given, the most recent figure is used.
26. ELOC
    Geo-located description of the event location.
27. LOCCAT
    Categorical identifier for the event locality, grouped as follows:

    Capital city
    Other major urban area (population greater than 100,000)
    Rural (population less than 100,000)
    Multiple urban areas
    Multiple rural areas
    Province/region (exact location unknown)
    Nationwide (affects more than four major cities and/or rural areas)

28. NSOURCE
    Estimate of the number of sources used to record data for the event
29. SOURCE
    Text description of the source(s) used to record data for the event
30. DATE
    Text description of the publication date(s) for the source(s) used to record data for the event

Appendix B

Interviews

Interview Procedure

A substantial portion of the data utilized in this book was collected during 18 months of field research conducted in Tunisia and Morocco on intermittent trips taken from June 2012 to February 2015. During these field visits, I carried out semi-structured interviews based on a uniform set of questions in either English, French, Spanish, or Arabic depending on the preference of the interviewee. Each interview, except in a few exceptional cases, lasted roughly one hour. In some cases, initial interviews were supplemented with secondary interviews or email-correspondence for follow-up questions.

Depending on the preference of the interviewee, some of the interviews were recorded and later transcribed. For interviewees who declined being recorded, I took extensive notes on the conversation. In quoting the interviews in this study whether recorded or transcribed, I presented, to the best of my ability, the originality of the sentences as they were conveyed by the interviewees through the English translations of their statements.

Interview Coding

Because research on contentious politics can be sensitive in some authoritarian contexts, interviewees are cited by codes rather than their real names. Each code for an interview consists of two parts. The first part of the code denotes the interviewee's nationality, either Tunisian (TU) or Moroccan (MA). The second part of the code is a two-digit number created as part of my own reference system to keep count of the number of interviewees. The table below lists the interview codes as well as the date and location at which the interview took place.

Table B.1. *List of interviewees, Tunisia*

Code	Designation	Date	Location
TU1	Scholar	9/18/2013	Tunis, Tunisia,
TU2	Scholar	9/27/2013	Tunis, Tunisia
TU3	Federal labor leader, UGTT	9/30/2013	Tunis, Tunisia
TU4	Labor unionist	10/1/2013	Tunis, Tunisia
TU5	National labor leader, UGTT	10/3/2013	Tunis, Tunisia
TU6	Scholar	10/3/2013	Tunis, Tunisia
TU7	Federal labor leader, UGTT	10/6/2013	Tunis, Tunisia
TU8	Federal labor leader, UGTT	10/10/2013	Tunis, Tunisia
TU9	Scholar	10/12/2013	Tunis, Tunisia
TU10	Civil society leader, LTDH	10/15/2013	Tunis, Tunisia
TU11	Regional labor leader, UGTT	10/17/2013	Ariana, Tunisia
TU12	Labor activist	10/18/2013	Tunis, Tunisia
TU13	Federal labor leader, UGTT	10/22/2013	Tunis, Tunisia
TU14	Regional labor leader, UGTT	10/23/2013	Sfax, Tunisia
TU15	Labor unionist	10/23/2013	Sfax, Tunisia
TU16	Labor unionist	10/23/2013	Sfax, Tunisia
TU17	Regional labor leader, UGTT	10/23/2013	Sfax, Tunisia
TU18	Regional labor leader, UGTT	10/24/2013	Sousse, Tunisia
TU19	Federal labor leader, UGTT	10/28/2013	Tunis, Tunisia
TU20	National labor leader, UGTT	10/29/2013	Tunis, Tunisia
TU21	Federal labor leader, UGTT	10/31/2013	Tunis, Tunisia
TU22	Federal labor leader, UGTT	10/31/2013	Tunis, Tunisia
TU23	Scholar	11/4/2013	Tunis, Tunisia
TU24	Labor unionist	11/4/2013	Tunis, Tunisia
TU25	National labor leader, UGTT	11/5/2013	Tunis, Tunisia
TU26	Labor unionist	11/5/2013	Tunis, Tunisia
TU27	Labor activist	11/8/2013	Tunis, Tunisia
TU28	Federal labor leader, UGTT	11/13/2013	Tunis, Tunisia
TU29	Party official, PCOT	11/17/2013	Tunis, Tunisia
TU30	Party official, Jomhouri	11/20/2013	Tunis, Tunisia
TU31	Party official, Ettjadid	11/20/2013	Tunis, Tunisia
TU32	National labor leader, CGTT	11/21/2013	Tunis, Tunisia
TU33	Party official, Jomhouri	11/21/2013	Tunis, Tunisia
TU34	Federal labor leader, UGTT	11/22/2013	Tunis, Tunisia
TU35	Federal labor leader, UGTT	11/27/2013	Tunis, Tunisia
TU36	Civil society leader, AFTDH	11/29/2013	Tunis, Tunisia
TU37	Civil society leader, OAT	12/1/2013	Kasserine, Tunisia
TU38	Activist	12/2/2013	Sidi Bouzid, Tunisia
TU39	Activist	12/2/2013	Sidi Bouzid, Tunisia
TU40	Regional labor leader, UGTT	12/3/2013	Sidi Bouzid, Tunisia
TU41	Regional labor leader, UGTT	12/10/2013	Gafsa, Tunisia
TU42	Regional labor leader, UGTT	12/11/2013	Tozeur, Tunisia
TU43	Scholar	12/13/2013	Tunis, Tunisia
TU44	National labor leader, UGTT	1/8/2014	Tunis, Tunisia

Table B.2. *List of interviewees, Morocco*

Code	Designation	Date	Location
MA1	Labor activist	2/7/2014	Rabat, Morocco,
MA2	Bureaucrat	2/17/2014	Rabat, Morocco
MA3	National labor leader, CDT	2/19/2014	Casablanca, Morocco
MA4	Scholar	2/19/2014	Rabat, Morocco
MA5	Bureaucrat	3/11/2014	Rabat, Morocco
MA6	Civil society leader, AMDH	3/12/2014	Rabat, Morocco
MA7	Labor activist	3/18/2014	Rabat, Morocco
MA8	Business representative	3/18/2014	Rabat, Morocco
MA9	Labor activist	3/19/2014	Rabat, Morocco
MA10	Labor activist	3/19/2014	Rabat, Morocco
MA11	National labor leader, ODT	3/24/2014	Rabat, Morocco
MA12	Regional labor leader, UGTM	3/25/2014	Rabat, Morocco
MA13	Regional labor leader, CDT	3/26/2014	Marrakech, Morocco
MA14	Regional labor leader, UMT	3/31/2014	Rabat, Morocco
MA15	Labor unionist, CDT	4/2/2014	Casablanca, Morocco
MA16	Scholar	4/4/2014	Rabat, Morocco
MA17	Bureaucrat	4/7/2014	Casablanca, Morocco
MA18	Scholar	4/8/2014	Rabat, Morocco
MA19	Party official, USFP	4/9/2014	Casablanca, Morocco
MA20	Party official, Istiqlal	4/14/2014	Rabat, Morocco
MA21	Journalist	4/21/2014	Rabat, Morocco
MA22	Scholar	4/21/2014	Casablanca, Morocco
MA23	Regional labor leader, CDT	4/25/2014	Rabat, Morocco
MA24	National labor leader, UNTM	4/29/2014	Rabat, Morocco
MA25	National labor leader, UGTM	5/5/2014	Rabat, Morocco
MA26	National labor leader, FDT	5/6/2014	Casablanca, Morocco
MA27	Labor unionist, UMT	5/7/2014	Casablanca, Morocco
MA28	Labor unionist, UMT	5/7/2014	Casablanca, Morocco
MA29	Party official, PJD	5/7/2014	Rabat, Morocco
MA30	National labor leader, UNTM	5/7/2014	Rabat, Morocco
MA31	Regional labor leader, UMT	5/8/2014	Rabat, Morocco
MA32	Activist	5/9/2014	Rabat, Morocco
MA33	National labor leader, UMT	5/15/2014	Casablanca, Morocco
MA34	Bureaucrat	5/15/2014	Rabat, Morocco
MA35	National labor leader, UGTM	5/15/2014	Rabat, Morocco
MA36	Federal labor leader, UMT	1/13/2015	Rabat, Morocco

Bibliography

Cable "05TUNIS768a." Tunisian labor update: UGTT shows a more independent streak, 3/25/2005.

E. Abdeljaouad. Pauvretè et inègalités des conditions de vie au Maroc entre 2001 et 2007: Une approche multidimensionnelle, 2022.

D. Acemoglu and J. Robinson. *Economic Origins of Dictatorship and Democracy*. Cambridge University Press, Cambridge, UK, 2006.

H. Achour. *Habib Achour: Ma Vie Politique Et Syndicale, Enthousiasme Et Deceptions, 1944-1981*. Alif-Editions De La Méditerranée, Tunis, Tunisia, 1989.

Achourouk. Husayn al-ᶜabāssī li Achourouk: 80% min al-ᶜitiṣamat wa al-iḥtijājāt lā ᶜalāqat lahā bi al-niqāba, 01/19/2012.

Li-mufāwaḍāt al-ijtimaᶜiyat: mashāriᶜᶜamāl al-ḥirāsat wa al-tanẓīf wa al-mūbīliyā wa al-sīnimā wa al-tibaᶜat wa maḥaṭāt al-binzīn jāhizatan wa hadhih ᵓabraz al-matālib, 06/18/2005.

L. Achy. *Tunisia's Economic challenges*, volume 2011. JSTOR, 2011.

J. Adams. Quiescence despite privation: Explaining the absence of a farm laborers' movement in Southern Illinois. *Comparative Studies in Society and History*, 39(3): 550–571, 1997.

G. Adler and E. Webster. Challenging transition theory: The labor movement, radical reform, and transition to democracy in South Africa. *Politics & Society*, 23(1): 75–106, 1995.

Introduction: Consolidating democracy in a liberalizing world: Trade unions and democratization in South Africa. In *Trade Unions and Democratization in South Africa*, pp. 1–19. St. Martin's Press, New York, NY, 2000.

G. M. Adler. *The Factory Belongs to All Who Work in It: Race, Class, and Collective Action in the South African Motor Industry*. PhD thesis, Columbia University, New York, NY, 1994.

AFL-CIO. Concerning the Failure of the Government of Bahrain to Comply with Its Commitments under Article 15.1 of the US-Bahrain Free Trade Agreement. Technical report, The American Federation of Labor and Congress of Industrial Organizations (AFL-CIO),

2011. URL http://www.aflcio.org/issues/jobseconomy/globaleconomy/upload/bahrain_fta04212011.pdf.

Afrique-Asie. L'Explosion Sociale, 6/13/1976.

Agence de Promotion de l'Industrie. *Le FOPRODI*. Agence de Promotion de l'Industrie, Tunis, 1992.

G. J. Aguilar and L. Arrieta. En la fase más aguda de la crisis y en el inicio de la reeestructuración o modernización. In *Historia de la CTM, 1936-1990*. Facultad de Ciencias Políticas y Sociales, Instituto de Investigaciones Sociales, Facultad de Economía, Universidad Nacional Autønoma de México, 1990.

J. Ahdani and M. Boudarham. Enquête: L'Empire UMT, 2018.

J. S. Ahlquist and M. Levi. *In the Interest of Others: Organizations and Social Activism*. Princeton University Press, Princeton, NJ, 2013.

E. Ahmad. Trade unionism. In L. C. Brown, ed., *State and Society in Independent North Africa*. Middle East Institute, Washington, D.C., 1966.

Politics and Labor in Tunisia. PhD thesis, University of Michigan, Ann Arbor, Michigan, 1967.

H. Aidi. *Redeploying the State: Corporatism, Neoliberalism and Coalition Politics*. Palgrave Macmillan, New York, NY, 2008.

S. Aita. Employment and labor law in the Arab Mediterranean countries and the Euro-Mediterranean partnership. Fundación Paz Y Solidaridad Serafín Aliaga De Comisiones Obreras, 2008.

A. Akkerman. Union competition and strikes: The need for analysis at the sector level. *ILR Review*, 61(4): 445–459, 2008.

A. Akkerman, R. Wielers, and G. v. Kooten. Vakbondscoalities en stakingen. *Tijdschrift voor arbeidsvraagstukken*, 11(2): 163–172, 1995.

Al-Badil 'Ajil. Les ètincelles lumineuses des mouvements de protestation du bassin minier, 2/14/2008.

Al-Bayane. Bientôt une loi organique?, 03/27/2015.

Moukharik à l'émission "Hiwar"': "L'UMT appelle la classe ouvrière à continuer à être une force de proposition", 04/21/2011.

Le CES dévoile sa charte: "Des normes à respecter et des objectifs à contractualiser," 04/27/2012.

Veillée de référendum sur la Constitution: Partis et syndicats satisfaits du projet final, 06/17/2011.

Fédération démocratique du travail: Bataille pour la présidence, 12/10/2010.

J. H. Aldrich. *Why Parties?: The Origin and Transformation of Political Parties in America*. University of Chicago Press, 1995.

C. Alexander. *Between Accomodation and Confrontation: State, Labor, and Development in Algeria and Tunisia*. PhD thesis, Duke University, 1996a.

State, labor, and the new global economy in Tunisia. In D. Vandewalle, ed., *North Africa: Development and Reform in a Changing Global Economy*. St. Martin's, New York, NY, 1996b.

Opportunities, organizations, and ideas: Islamists and workers in Tunisia and Algeria. *International Journal of Middle East Studies*, 32(4): 465–490, 2000.

Labour code reform in Tunisia. *Mediterranean Politics*, 6(2): 104–125, 2001.

The architecture of militancy: Workers and the state in Algeria, 1970-1990. *Comparative Politics*, 34(3): 315–335, 2002a.

Enterprise Reform and Labor in North Africa. In *Privatization and Labor: Responses and Consequences in Global Perspective*. Elgar, Northampton, MA, 2002b.

Tunisia: Stability and Reform in the Modern Maghreb. Routledge, 2010.

F. Aliriza. What democracy for Tunisian workers, 2020.

J. A. Alutto and J. A. Belasco. Determinants of attitudinal militancy among nurses and teachers. *ILR Review*, 27(2): 216–227, 1974.

L. Anderson. Political pacts, liberalism, and democracy: The Tunisian national pact of 1988. *Government & Opposition*, 26(2): 244–260, 1991.

D. F. Angel-Urdinola and K. Tanabe. *Micro-determinants of informal employment in the Middle East and North Africa region*. World Bank, 2012.

O. Ashenfelter and G. E. Johnson. Bargaining theory, trade unions, and industrial strike activity. *American Economic Review*, 59(1): 35–49, 1969.

D. Ashford. Labor politics in a new nation. *The Western Political Quarterly*, 13(2): 312–331, 1960.

Attariq al Jadid. Les enseignements d'une crise qui n'est pas passagère, Témoignage d'un enfant de Redeyef qui pense sa société, 7/8/2008.

Aujourd'hui le Maroc. Ré'forme constitutionnelle: Les syndicats présentent leurs projets, 04/08/2011.

Les syndicats haussent le ton contre le gouvernement, 10/12/2010.

Etre syndiqué, pas simple au Maroc!, 10/22/2013.

Vie syndicale: Le FDT est toujours dans l'impasse, 1/28/2011.

Abdeslam Maâti: "L'UNTM a perdu sa crédibilité et son indépendance," 9/29/2010.

S. Avdagic. State-labour relations in East Central Europe: Explaining variation in union effectiveness. *Socio-Economic Review*, 3(1): 25–53, 2005.

A. Ayache. *Le Maroc: Bilan D'une Colonisation*. Éditions Sociales, 1956.

Le Mouvement Syndical Au Maroc: De 1919 à 1942 - Tome 1. L'Harmattan, 1982.

Le Mouvement Syndical Au Maroc: Vers L'Independance (1949-1956)-Tome 3. L'Harmattan, 1993.

J.-P. Azam and C. Morrison. The Political Feasibility of Adjustment in Côte D'Ivoire and Morocco. Technical report, Development Center for the Organisation for Economic Cooperation and Development, Paris, France, 1994.

T. Baccouche. Réflexions sur les relations entre l'état et le mouvement syndical. In *Syndicat et Société*. Centre d'études et de Recherches Économiques et Sociales, Tunis, TN, 1989.

M. E. Badimon. Diplômés chômeurs au Maroc: dynamiques de pérennisation d'une action collective plurielle. *L'année du Maghreb*, (III): 297–311, 2007.

Does unemployment spark collective contentious action? Evidence from a Moroccan social movement. *Journal of Contemporary African Studies*, 31(2): 194–212, 2013.

S. Z. Badran. *Killing Contention: Demobilization in Morocco during the Arab Spring*. Syracuse University Press, NY, 2022.

I. Band. Jobs and Values: Social Effects of Export-Oriented Industrialization in Tunisia, 1977.

A. Bank, T. Richter, and A. Sunik. Durable, yet different: Monarchies in the Arab Spring. *Journal of Arabian Studies*, 4(2): 163–179, 2014.

Bank al-Markazī al-Tūnisī. *Rapport annuel*. Number no. 20. Banque centrale de Tunisie, 1978.

Rapport annuel. Number no. 27. Banque centrale de Tunisie, 1985.

F. Barchiesi. Economic adjustment, political institution-alisation and social marginalisation: Cosatu and the first democratic government (1994-99). *Transformation*, (38), 1999.

R. Bashir. Al-Tafawut al-Tanmawi fī Tunis: Qabl al-Thawrah wa Baᶜdaha[Economic disparity in Tunisia: before the revolution and]. *Al-Mustaqbal al-Arabi*, (40), 2018.

J. Baskin. *Striking Back: A History of COSATU*. Verso, London, 1991.

A. Bassani. *The Political Economy of Trade Liberalization: A Comparative Study of Morocco and Tunisia*. PhD thesis, The Johns Hopkins University, Baltimore, 1993.

M. Bassiouni, N. Rodley, B. Al-Awadhi, P. Kirsch, and M. Arsanjani. Report of the Bahrain Independent Commission of Inquiry, 2011. URL www.bici.org.bh/BICIreportEN.pdf.

A. Bayat. Activism and social development in the Middle East. *International Journal of Middle East Studies*, 34(1): 1–28, 2002.

Revolution without Revolutionaries: Making Sense of the Arab Spring. Stanford University Press, Stanford, CA, 2020.

J. Beinin. Workers' Protest in Egypt: Neo-liberalism and Class Struggle in 21st Century. *Social Movement Studies*, 2009.

The Rise of Egypt's Workers. Technical report, Carnegie Endowment for Peace, 2012.

Workers and Thieves: Labor Movements and Popular Uprisings in Tunisia and Egypt. Stanford University Press, Stanford, CA, 2015.

J. Beinin and M. Duboc. A workers' social movement on the margin of the global neoliberal order, Egypt 2004–2012. In *Social Movements, Mobilization, and Contestation in the Middle East and North Africa*, pp. 205–227. Stanford University Press, Stanford, CA, 2013.

M. Beittel. Labor Unrest in South Africa, 1870–1990. *Review (Fernand Braudel Center)*, 18(1): 87–104, 1995.

S. Belghith and I. Patel. Leagues for the Protection of the Tunisian Revolution, 2013. URL https://www.opendemocracy.net/en/leagues-for-protection-of-tunisian-revolution/.

E. Bellin. Contingent Democrats: Industrialists, Labor, and Democratization in Late-Developing Countries. *World Politics*, 52(2): 175–205, 2000.

Stalled Democracy: Capital, Labor, and the Paradox of State-Sponsored Development. Cornell University Press, Ithaca, NY, 2002.

The robustness of authoritarianism in the Middle East: Exceptionalism in comparative perspective. *Comparative Politics*, 36(2): 139–157, 2004.

M. Ben Romdhane. *L'accumulation Du Capital Et Les Classes Sociales En Tunisie Depuis L'indépendance*. PhD thesis, University of Tunis, 1981.

Mutations économiques Et Sociales Et Mouvement Ouvrier En Tunisie De 1956 à 1980. In N. Sraieb, ed., *Le Mouvement Ouvrier Maghrébin*. Centre National De La Recherche Scientifique, 1985.

S. Ben Sedrine. Etat des lieux er défis à relever pour promouvoir le dialogue social au Maroc, en Jordanie, et en Tunisie. Technical report, Pilot Project for the Promotion of Social Dialogue in the Southern Mediterranean Neighbourhood, 2017.

A. Benchemsi. Morocco: Outfoxing the opposition. *Journal of Democracy*, 23(1): 57–69, 2012.

A. Benchenna, D. Ksikes, and D. Marchetti. The media in Morocco: A highly political economy, the case of the paper and on-line press since the early 1990s. *The Journal of North African Studies*, 22(3): 386–410, 2017.

R. Bendix. *Nation-Building and Citizenship*. University of California Press, Berkeley, CA, 1964.

M. Benhilal. *Annuaire de L'Afrique du Nord*, chapter Le Syndicat Comme Enjeu Politique Au Maroc 1955–1981, pp. 217–258. Centre National De La Recherche Scientifique, 1984.

Annuaire de L'Afrique du Nord, chapter Maroc – Chronique Intérieure, pp. 199–218. Centre National De La Recherche Scientifique, 1997.

M. Bennani-Chraïbi. *Partis politiques et protestations au Maroc (1934-2020)*. Presses universitaires de Rennes Rennes, 2021.

J. Benomar. *Working Class, Trade Unionism, Communism and Nationalism in Colonial Morocco*. PhD thesis, University of London, Birbeck College, 1991.

G. Bensusán and K. J. Middlebrook. *Organized Labor and Politics in Mexico: Continuities and Contradictions*. University of London Press, London, UK, 2012.

G. Bensusán Areous. The Mexican model of labor regulation and competitive strategies. *Regional integration and industrial relations in North America*, pp. 52–66, 1994.

H. Berger and M. Spoerer. Economic crises and the European revolutions of 1848. *Journal of Economic History*, 61(2): 293–326, 2001.

S. I. Bergh and D. Rossi-Doria. Plus ça change? Observing the dynamics of Morocco's 'Arab Spring' in the High Atlas. In *Arab Spring and Peripheries*, pp. 72–90. Routledge, 2018.

C. E. Berman. *Protest, Social Policy, and Political Regimes*. PhD thesis, Princeton University, Princeton, NJ, 2019.

N. Bermeo. Myths of moderation: Confrontation and conflict during democratic transitions. In *Transitions to Democracy*, pp. 120–140. Columbia University Press, New York, NY, 1999.

J. Bessis. Le mouvement ouvrier tunisien: De ses origines à l'indépendance. *Le mouvement social*, pp. 85–108, 1974.

R. Bianchi. The corporatization of the Egyptian labor movement. *Middle East Journal*, 40(3): 429–444, 1986.

Unruly Corporatism: Associational Life in Twentieth-Century Egypt. Oxford University Press, Oxford, UK, 1989.

D. Bishara. Labor movements in Tunisia and Egypt: Drivers vs. objects of change in transition from authoritarian rule. *SWP Comment*, 2014.

Contesting Authoritarianism: Labor Challenges to the State in Egypt. Cambridge University Press, Cambridge, UK, 2018.

Legacy trade unions as brokers of democratization? Lessons from Tunisia. *Comparative Politics*, 52(2): 173–195, 2020.

D. Bishara and S. Grewal. Political, not partisan: The Tunisian general labor union under democracy. *Comparative Politics*, 54(3): 453–475, 2022.

A. Blais, D. Blake, and S. Dion. Are leftist governments more generous toward public sector employees? Evidence from canada, 1967–1984. *Governance*, 6(1): 67–78, 1993.

L. Blaydes. *Elections and Distributive Politics in Mubarak's Egypt*. Cambridge University Press, Cambridge, UK, 2010.

C. Boix. *Democracy and Redistribution*. Cambridge University Press, Cambridge, UK, 2003.

C. Boix and M. Svolik. The foundations of limited authoritarian government: Institutions, commitment, and power-sharing in dictatorships. *The Journal of Politics*, 75(2): 300–316, 2013.

N. Borsali. *Bourguiba à l'epreuve de la démocratie, 1956-1963*. SAMES Editions, Sfax, 2008.

L. A. Boubaker. *Tels syndicalistes, tels syndicats: ou, les péripéties du mouvement syndical Tunisien*. S.T.E.A.G., Tunis, Tunisia, 1983.

B. Boudarbat. Unemployment, status in employment and wages in Morocco. *Applied Econometrics and International Development*, 6(1): 165–184, 2006.

A. Bouharrou. Droit du travail au maroc et flexibilité de l'emploi à l'heure du p.a.s. *Annales Marocaines d'ÉConomie*, pp. 367–373, 1993.

J. Bras. Chronique Tunisie. In *Annuaire De L'Afrique Du Nord, 1984*. Centre National De La Recherche Scientifique, Paris, FR, 1986.

Chronique Tunisie. In *Annuaire De L'Afrique Du Nord, 1985*. Centre National De La Recherche Scientifique, Paris, FR, 1987.

Chronique Marocaine. In *Annuaire de L'Afrique du Nord, 1989*. Centre National De La Recherche Scientifique, 1991.

A. Brockmeyer, M. Khatrouch, and G. Raballand. Public sector size and performance management: A case-study of post-revolution Tunisia. *World Bank Policy Research Working Paper*, (7159), 2015.

J. Brownlee. *Authoritarianism in an Age of Democratization*. Cambridge University Press, Cambridge, UK, 2007.

M. Buehler. Continuity through co-optation: Rural politics and regime resilience in Morocco and Mauritania. *Mediterranean Politics*, 20(3): 364–385, 2015.

S. Buhlungu. South Africa: The decline of labor studies and the democratic transition. *Work and Occupations*, 36(2): 145–161, 2009.

S. Buhlungu and M. Tshoaedi. A contested legacy: Organisational and political challenges facing cosatu. In *COSATU'S Contested Legacy*, pp. 1–31. Brill, 2013.

S. Buhlungu, M. Brookes, and G. Wood. Trade unions and democracy in South Africa: union organizational challenges and solidarities in a time of transformation. *British Journal of Industrial Relations*, 46(3): 439–468, 2008.

V. Bunce. Rethinking recent democratization: Lessons from the postcommunist experience. *World Politics*, 55(2): 167–192, 2003.

K. Burgess. Loyalty dilemmas and market reform: Party-union alliances under stress in Mexico, Spain, and Venezuela. *World Politics*, 52(1): 105–134, 1999.

Parties and Unions in the New Global Economy. University of Pittsburgh Press, Pittsburgh, PA, 2004.

L. Calmfors and J. Driffill. Bargaining structure, corporatism and macroeconomic performance. *Economic Policy*, 3(6): 13–61, 1988.

D. Cameron. Social democracy, corporatism, labor quiescence and the representation of economic interests in advanced industrial society. In J. H. Goldthorpe, ed., *Order and Conflict in Contemporary Capitalism*. Oxford University Press, Oxford, UK, 1984.

M. Cammett. *Globalization and Business Politics in Arab North Africa: A Comparative Perspective*. Cambridge University Press, New York, NY, 2007.

M. Cammett and I. Diwan. The roll-back of the state and the rise of crony capitalism. In *The Middle East Economies in Times of Transition*, pp. 63–98. Springer, 2016.

M. Cammett and M. P. Posusney. Labor standards and labor market flexibility in the Middle East: Free trade and freer unions? *Studies in Comparative International Development*, 45(2): 250–279, 2010.

M. Cammett, I. Diwan, A. Richards, and J. Waterbury. *A Political Economy of the Middle East*. Routledge, 4th edition, 2015.

D. T. Campbell. *Experimental and Quasi-Experimental Designs for Research*. Houghton Miller, Boston, MA, 1963.

C. Candland and R. Sil. *The Politics of Labor in a Global Age: Continuity and Change in Late-industrializing and Post-socialist Economies*. Oxford University Press, Oxford, UK, 2001.

T. L. Caraway. Freedom of association: Battering Ram or Trojan horse? *Review of International Political Economy*, 13(2): 210–232, 2006.

T. L. Caraway and M. Ford. *Labor and Politics in Indonesia*. Cambridge University Press, Cambridge, UK, 2020.

T. L. Caraway, M. Ford, and H. Nugroho. Translating membership into power at the ballot box? Trade union candidates and worker voting patterns in Indonesia's national elections. *Democratization*, 22(7): 1296–1316, 2015.

M. Catusse. Le métamorphose de la question syndicale au maroc. *Critique économique*, 2(5): 39–67, 2001.

F. Cavatorta, L. Storm, and V. Resta. *Routledge Handbook on Political Parties in the Middle East and North Africa*. Routledge Abingdon, New York, 2020.

J. Charmes. Flexibility of labor, plurality of standards, accumulation of economic capital and social capital. *Inequalities and Public Policies in Africa. Pluralités of Standards and Stakeholder Games*. Karthala, IRD, Paris, pp. 243–262, 2001.

Informal Economy and Labour Market Policies and Institutions in selected Mediterranean Countries: Turkey, Syria, Jordan, Algeria and Morocco. *ILO Report*, 2010.

A. Chatri, K. Hadef, and N. Samoudi. Micro-econometric evaluation of subsidized employment in Morocco: The case of the "Idmaj" program. *Journal for Labour Market Research*, 55(1): 17, 2021.

M. Cherkaoui and T. Benkaraach. Striving for formalisation: Gender and youth aspects of informal employment in Morocco. In *Informal Women Workers in the Global South*, pp. 137–173. Routledge, 2021.

M. Cherkaoui, A. Khellaf, and A. Nihou. The price effect of tariff liberalization in Morocco: Measuring the impact on household welfare. *Politics and economic development*, 2011.

E. Chihi. Oral history interview with lotfi azzouz, 2015.

Oral history interview with wided bouchamaoui, 2016.

L. Chouikha and E. Gobe. La Tunisie entre la «révolte du bassin minier de Gafsa» et l'échéance électorale de 2009. *L'année du Maghreb*, (V): 387–420, 2009.

L. Chouikha and H. Labidi, Kamel Jouini. État de la liberté de la presse en Tunisie de janvier 1990 à mai 1991. In *L'Information au Maghreb*. Cèrés Productions, 1992.

J. A. Clark. *Local Politics in Jordan and Morocco: Strategies of Centralization and Decentralization*. Columbia University Press, New York, NY, 2018.

H. A. Clegg. *Trade Unionism under Collective Bargaining: A Theory Based on Comparisons of Six Countries*. Basil Blackwell, London, UK, 1976.

J.-F. Clement and J. Paul. Trade unions and Moroccan politics. *MERIP Reports*, (127): 19–24, October 1984.

R. B. Collier and D. Collier. *Shaping the Political Arena: Critical Junctures, the Labor Movement, and Regime Dynamics in Latin America*. Princeton University Press, Princeton, NJ, 1991.

R. B. Collier and J. Mahoney. Adding collective actors to collective outcomes: Labor and recent democratization in South America and Southern Europe. *Comparative Politics*, 29(3): 285–303, 1997.

Conseil Economique, Social et Environnmental. Civil society and social dialogue in Morocco, 2015.

M. L. Cook. *Organizing Dissent: Unions, the State and the Democratic Teachers' Movement in Mexico*. The Pennsylvania State University Press, 1996.

L. Cooper. Workers' education and political consciousness: A case study from South Africa. *The Economic and Labour Relations Review*, 17(2): 183–198, 2007.

S. S. Cordall. Tunisia's Powerful Labor Union Is Thwarting President Saied's Ambitions, 2022.

M. Costello, J. C. Jenkins, and H. Aly. Bread, justice, or opportunity? The determinants of the Arab awakening protests. *World Development*, 67: 90–100, 2015.

C. Crouch. *Industrial Relations and European State Traditions*. Oxford University Press, Oxford, UK, 1993.

J. Currie and A. Harrison. Sharing the costs: The impact of trade reform on capital and labor in Morocco. *Journal of Labor Economics*, 15(S3): S44–S71, 1997.

M. Daadaoui. "Muslim Democrats": The rise of neo-Islamism in Tunisia and Morocco. *British Journal of Middle Eastern Studies*, 50(1): 38–49, 2023.

O. Dahi. Understanding the political economy of the Arab revolts. *Middle East Report*, 259(41): 2–6, 2011.

F. Dahmani. Tunisia: Gafsa Phosphate Company Closes Its Curtain. *Jeune Afrique*, May 7, 2015.

E. Dalmasso and F. Cavatorta. Democracy, civil liberties and the role of religion after the Arab awakening: Constitutional reforms in Tunisia and Morocco. *Mediterranean Politics*, 18(2): 225–241, 2013.

R. Dalton, A. Van Sickle, and S. Weldon. The individual–institutional nexus of protest behaviour. *British Journal of Political Science*, 40(1): 51–73, 2010.

R. Darlington. Leadership and union militancy: The case of the RMT. *Capital & Class*, 33(3): 3–32, 2009.

B. DeGorge. The modernization of education: A case study of Tunisia and Morocco. *The European Legacy*, 7(5): 579–596, 2002.

D. Della Porta. Political economy and social movement studies: The class basis of anti-austerity protests. *Anthropological Theory*, 17(4): 453–473, 2017.

T. Demirel-Pegg and K. Rasler. The effects of selective and indiscriminate repression on the 2013 gezi park nonviolent resistance campaign. *Sociological Perspectives*, 64(1): 58–81, 2021.

G. Denoeux and A. Maghraoui. King Hassan's strategy of political dualism. *Middle East Policy*, 5(4): 104–130, 1998.

G. P. Denoeux. Morocco's economic prospects: Daunting challenges ahead. *Middle East Policy*, 8(2), 2001.

F. Deyo. *Labor in the Capitalist Economy*, chapter Export manufacturing and labor: The Asian case. Sage, 1984.

I. B. Dhiaf. Chronique Politique. In *Annuaire De L'Afrique Du Nord, 1977*. Centre National De La Recherche Scientifique, Paris, FR, 1977.

B. Dillman. The political economy of structural adjustment in Tunisia and Algeria. *The Journal of North African Studies*, 3(3): 1–24, 1998.

N. Disney. The working class revolt in Tunisia. *MERIP Reports*, (67): 12–14, 1978.

S. Djankov and R. Ramalho. Employment laws in developing countries. *Journal of Comparative Economics*, 37(1): 3–13, 2009.

M. Dogan and D. Pèlassy. *Compare Nations: Strategies in Comparative Politics*. Chatham House, Chatham, NJ, 1990.

A. Duparc. Comment le groupe agroalimentaire Nestlé s'est fait racketter par le clan Ben Ali, 2011.

Echaab. Daᶜwa ᵓilā namaṭ tanmīat yurāᶜī al-hājīāt al-ᵓāsāsīa wa yaqūm ā al-āla wa al-tawāzūn bayn al-jihāt fī alhayāt al-ᵓidārīat al-wataniya lil-iḥtiḥād, 01/08/2011.

Balagh al-maktab al-tanfīdī al-waṭanī al-muᵓarakh fī 8 fīfirī 2011, 02/12/2011.

Bayān al-hayaᶜat al-ᵓidārīat al-waṭaniya al-yum 18 mars 2011, 03/19/2011.

Nadawat as-saḥāfiya, 08/25/2011.

Iḥtijājāt 'amalīyat ḥāshidat ḍid al-irhāb wa nuwayīa al-ightīāl, 11/11/1977a.

Nidā' lī al-shughalīn min al-maktab al-tanfīdī lī al-itiḥād, 11/11/1977b.

Kalimāt al-itiḥād, 11/25/1977.

H. Eckstein et al. Case study and theory in political science. *Case Study Method*, pp. 119–164, 2000.

R. C. Edwards. The social relations of production in the firm and labor market structure. *Politics & Society*, 5(1), 1975.

P. K. Eisinger. The conditions of protest behavior in American cities. *The American Political Science Review*, 67(1): 11–28, 1973.

G. Ekiert and J. Kubik. *Rebellious Civil Society: Popular Protest and Democratic Consolidation in Poland, 1989–1993*. University of Michigan Press, Ann Arbor, MI, 2001.

N. El Aoufi. L'impératif social au maroc: de l'ajustement à la régulation. *Critique économique*, (3), 2000.

N. El-Mikawy and M. P. Posusney. Labor representation in the age of globalization: Trends and issues in non-oil-based Arab Economies. In *Employment Creation & Social Protection in the Middle East and North Africa*, pp. 49–94. American University in Cairo Press, 2002.

H. El-Said and J. Harrigan. Economic reform, social welfare, and instability: Jordan, Egypt, Morocco, and Tunisia, 1983–2004. *The Middle East Journal*, 68(1): 99–121, 2014.

R. Ellefsen. The unintended consequences of escalated repression. *Mobilization*, 26(1): 87–108, 2021.

Embassy of Tunisia. TUNISIA'S TEXTILE SECTOR BOUNCES BACK, 9/24/2007.

M. Ennaceur. *Unions and Globalization: The Case of Tunisia*. ILO/International Institute for Social Studies, 2000.

M. Essaidi. Industrial relations in an emerging Morocco. *Industrial Relations in Africa*, pp. 137–146, 2007.

S. Etchemendy. Repression, exclusion, and inclusion: Government-union relations and patterns of labor reform in liberalizing economies. *Comparative Politics*, 36(3): 273–290, 2004.

Europa Publications. *The Middle East and North Africa, 1977–1978*. Europa Publications, London, UK, 1977.

L. Feliu. El movimiento de derechos humanos marroquí. In *Sociedad civil, derechos humanos y democracia en Marruecos*. Universidad, Grenada, 2006.

L. Feltrin. Labour and democracy in the Maghreb: The Moroccan and Tunisian trade unions in the 2011 Arab uprisings. *Economic and Industrial Democracy*, 40(1): 42–64, 2019.

R. Ferchiou. The social pressure on economic development in Tunsia. *Tunisia: The Political Economy of Reform*, pp. 101–108, 1991.

R. Filali-Meknassi. *Étude Sur Le Syndicalisme Marocain*. PhD thesis, Université Mohamed V, 1989.

Finances News. Réforme de la retraite: La rentrée sociale qui attend Benkirane, 04/09/2014.

Financial Times. Bahrain union suspends general strike, 3/22/2011.

A. Findlay. Tunisia: The vicissitudes of economic development. In R. Lawless and A. Findlay, eds., *North Africa*. Croom Helm, Beckenham, UK, 1984.

R. Fine. Civil society theory and the politics of transition in South Africa. *Review of African Political Economy*, 1992.

M. S. Fish. Islam and authoritarianism. *World Politics*, 55(1): 4–37, 2002.

R. D. Forst. The origins and early development of the union marocaine du tralvil. *International Journal of Middle East Studies*, 7(2): 271–287, 1976.

A. Forteza and M. Rama. Labor market 'rigidity' and the success of economic reforms across more than 100 countries. *The Journal of Policy Reform*, 9(1): 75–105, 2006.

J. B. Foster and R. W. McChesney. The global reserve army of labor and the new imperialism. *Class: The Anthology*, pp. 485–502, 2017.

I. Franceschini and E. Nesossi. State repression of chinese labor ngos: A chilling effect? *The China Journal*, 80(111–129), 2018.

R. Franzosi. One hundred years of strike statistics. *Industrial Labor Relations Review*, 42(3): 348–62, 1989.

The Puzzle of Strikes: Class and State Strategies in Postwar Italy. Cambridge University Press, Cambridge, UK, 1995.

C. Frege. Understanding union effectiveness in Central Eastern Europe: Hungary and Slovenia. *European Journal of Industrial Relations*, 8(1): 53–76, 2002.

C. Frege and J. Kelly. Union revitalization strategies in comparative perspective. *European Journal of Industrial Relations*, 9(1): 7–24, 2003.

C. Frege, E. Heery, and L. Turner. The new solidarity? trade union coalition-building in five countries. *Varieties of unionism: Strategies for union revitalization in a globalizing economy*, pp. 137–158, 2004.

M. Friedman. *"The Future Is in the Hands of the Workers": A History of FOSATU: Historical Papers Archives Project*. Mutloatse Arts Heritage Trust, 2011.

H. Frisch. Why monarchies persist: Balancing between internal and external vulnerability. *Review of International Studies*, 37(1): 167–184, 2011.

D. Fu. Fragmented control: Governing contentious labor organizations in china. *Governance*, 30(3): 445–462, 2017a.

Disguised collective action in China. *Comparative Political Studies*, 50(4): 499–527, 2017b.

Mobilizing without the Masses: Control and Contention in China. Cambridge University Press, Cambridge, UK, 2018.

W. Galenson. *Labor in Developing Economies*. University of California Press, Berkeley, CA, 2022.

C. Gall. Tunisian Discontent Reflected in Protests That Have Idled Mines. *New York Times*, May 13, 2014.

W. Gamson. *The Strategy of Social Protest*. Dorsey, Homewood, IL, 1975.

J. Gandhi. *Political Institutions under Dictatorship*. Cambridge University Press, Cambridge, UK, 2008.

J. Gandhi and A. Przeworski. Authoritarian institutions and the survival of autocrats. *Comparative Political Studies*, 40(11): 1279–1301, 2007.

J. Gandhi and O. J. Reuter. The incentives for pre-electoral coalitions in non-democratic elections. In *Comparing Autocracies in the Early Twenty-First Century*, pp. 57–79. Routledge, 2016.

M. Ganz. Leading Change: Leadership, Organization, and Social Movements. In *Handbook of Leadership Theory and Practice: A Harvard Business School Centennial Colloquium*. Harvard Business Press, Cambridge, MA, 2010.

Public narrative, collective action, and power. In *Accountability through Public Opinion: From Inertia to Public Action*, pp. 273–289. Washington, DC: The International Bank for Reconstruction and Development/The World Bank, Washington, DC, 2011.

M. L. Ganz, K. Voss, T. Sharpe, C. Somers, and G. Strauss. Against the tide: Projects and pathways of the new generation of union leaders, 1984-2001. In *Rebuilding Labor*. Cornell University Press, Ithaca, NY, 2001.

B. L. García. *Marruecos político: Cuarenta años de procesos electorales (1960-2000)*. Centro de Investigaciones Sociológicas, 2000.

J. Gengler. The (sectarian) politics of public-sector employment in bahrain. *Religion and Politics in Bahrain, May*, 27, 2012.

A. L. George and A. Bennett. *Case Studies and Theory Development in the Social Sciences*. MIT Press, Cambridge, MA, 2005.

J. Gerring. *Case Study Research: Principles and Practices*. Cambridge University Press, 2006.

J. Gerschewski. *The Two Logics of Autocratic Rule*. Cambridge University Press, New York, NY, 2023.

S. Ghali and P. Mohnen. The Tunisian path to development: 1961-2001. In *World Bank Global Conference on "Reducing Poverty, Sustaining Growth: What Works, What Doesn't, and Why,"* 2004.

M. Golden. The dynamics of trade unionism and national economic performance. *American Political Science Review*, 87(2): 439–455, 1993.

M. Golden, M. Wallerstein, and P. Lange. Post-war trade union organization and industrial relations in twelve countries. In L. P. M. G. Kitschelt, Herbert and J. D. Stephens, eds., *Continuity and Change in Contemporary Capitalism*. Cambridge University Press, Cambridge, UK, 1999.

J. Goodwin. Why we were surprised (again) by the Arab spring. *Swiss Political Science Review*, 17(4): 452–456, 2011.

M. Gordon, J. Philpot, R. Burt, C. Thompson, and W. Spiller. Commitment to the union: Development of a measure and an examination of its correlates. *Journal of Applied Psychology*, 65(4): 479, 1980.

S. Grewal. Tunisia's foiled coup of 1987: The November 8th coup. *The Middle East Journal*, 74(1): 53–71, 2020.

A. Grissa. The Tunisian State Enterprises and Privatization Policy. In *Tunisia: The Political Economy of Reform*. Lynne Rienner Publishers, Boulder, CO, 1991.

L. Guazzone and D. Pioppi. Globalisation and the restructuring of state power in the Arab world. *The International Spectator*, 42(4): 509–523, 2007.

J. Gunning and I. Z. Baron. *Why Occupy a Square: People, Protests and Movements in the Egyptian Revolution*. Oxford University Press, Oxford, UK, 2014.

T. Gurr. *Why Men Rebel*. Princeton University Press, Princeton, NJ, 1970.

B. Habib, and Tunisie Présidence de la République. 1957. Au Service de La Tunisie, *Au Service de La Paix: Discours Du Président Habib Bourguiba, Avril 1956-Avril 1957*. Edited by Tunisie Secrétariat d'état à l'information. Tunis: Secrétariat d'État à l'information.

P. Hall and R. C. Taylor. Political science and the three new institutionalisms. *Political Studies*, 44: 936–957, 1996.

R. Halpern. Organized labour, black workers and the twentieth-century South: The emerging revision. *Social History*, 19(3): 359–383, 1994.

K. Hamann, A. Johnston, and J. Kelly. Striking concessions from governments: The success of general strikes in western Europe, 1980–2009. *Comparative Politics*, 46(1): 23–41, 2013.

S. Hamzaoui. *Annuaire de L'Afrique du Nord*, chapter Champ politique et syndicalisme en Tunisie, pp. 369–380. Centre National De La Recherche Scientifique, 1999.

S. Han. Mobilizing within and beyond the labor union: A case of precarious workers' collective actions in North Africa. *ILR Review*, 76(4): 674–696, 2023.

J. Harper. *Trade Unions of the World*. International Center for Trade Union Rights, London, UK, 2006.

A. Harrison and R. Islam. Morocco private sector assessment: The labor market, 1993.

I. M. Hartshorn. Organized Interests and Constitutions Assemblies: Egypt and Tunisia in Comparison. Political Research Quarterly, 70(2): 408–420, 2017.

I. M. Hartshorn. *Labor Politics in North Africa: After the Uprising in Egypt and Tunisia*. Cambridge University Press, Cambridge, UK, 2019.

I. M. Hartshorn and R. Sil. The fate of labor after regime change: Lessons from post-communist poland and post-apartheid South Africa for Tunisia's Nobel-prize winning unions. *Economic and Industrial Democracy*, 40(1): 20–41, 2019.

E. Heintz and G. Chang. Report of informal employment for the ilo. Technical report, International Labor Organization, Geneva, 2007.

M. Herb. *All in the Family: Absolutism, Revolution and Democracy in Middle Eastern Monarchies*. State University of New York Press, Albany, New York, 1999.

A. Hermassi. *Mouvement Ouvrier En Société Coloniale: La Tunisie Entre Les Deux Guerres*. PhD thesis, École Pratiques Des Hautes Études, 1966.

D. A. Hibbs. On the political economy of long-run trends in strike activity. *British Journal of Political Science*, 8(2): 153–175, 1978.

B. Hibou. *The Force of Obedience: The Political Economy of Repression in Tunisia*. Polity, Cambridge, UK, 2011.

R. Hinnebusch. Toward a historical sociology of state formation in the Middle East. *Middle East Critique*, 19(3): 201–216, 2010.

A. O. Hirschman. *Exit, Voice, and Loyalty: Responses to Decline in Firms, Organizations, and States*, vol. 25. Harvard University Press, Cambridge, MA, 1970.

P. Hirschsohn. Union democracy and shopfloor mobilization: Social movement unionism in South African auto and clothing plants. *Economic and Industrial Democracy*, 28(1): 6–48, 2007.

A. A. Holmes. Working on the revolution in Bahrain: From the mass strike to everyday forms of medical provision. *Social Movement Studies*, 15(1): 105–114, 2016.

B. Horton. Morocco: Analysis and Reform of Economic Policy. Technical report, World Bank, Washington, D.C., 1990.

S. Huntington. How countries democratize. *Political Science Quarterly*, 106(4): 579–616, 1991.

ICFTU. *Annual Survey of Violations of Trade Union Rights*. ICFTU Press, 1990-1996.

Annual Survey of Violations of Trade Union Rights. ICFTU Press, 1991.

Annual Survey of Violations of Trade Union Rights. ICFTU Press, 1995.

Annual Survey of Violations of Trade Union Rights. ICFTU Press, 2005.

ILO. *Yearbook of Labor Statistics*. International Labour Office, Geneva, Switzerland, 1960.

Yearbook of Labor Statistics. International Labour Office, Geneva, Switzerland, 1970.

Yearbook of Labor Statistics. International Labour Office, Geneva, Switzerland, 1983.

Global wage report: Minimum wages and collective bargaining towards policy coherence. Technical report, International Labor Organization, Geneva, 2008.

Unemployment rate (%), 2016. Data retrieved from ILOSTAT Database, https://ilostat.ilo.org/data/arab-states/.

Institut Nationale de la Statistique. Statisques par thémes, 2013. https://ins.tn/statistiques/81.

International Crisis Group. *Popular Protest in North Africa and the Middle East (IV): Tunisia's Way*. International Crisis Group, 2011.

Tunisia's National Dialogue Quartet Set a Powerful Example, 2015. URL https://www.crisisgroup.org/middle-east-north-africa/north-africa/tunisia/tunisia-s-national-dialogue-quartet-set-powerful-example.

B. Isitt. *Militant Minority: British Columbia Workers and the Rise of a New Left, 1948-1972*. University of Toronto Press, 2011.

ITF. ITF condemns Moroccan court decision, 2014. URL https://www.itfseafarers.org/en/news/itf-condemns-moroccan-court-decision.

ITUC. Morocco: Trade Unionists Brutally Attacked, 01/23/2013. URL https://www.ituc-csi.org/morocco-trade-unionists-brutally.

Spotlight interview with Salman Jaffar Al Mahfoodh (Bahrain - GFBTU), 2012. URL https://www.ituc-csi.org/spotlight-interview-with-salman-10736.

2013 Annual Survey of Violations of Trade Union Rights: Countries at Risk - Bahrain, 2013. URL https://www.refworld.org/reference/annualreport/ituc/2013/en/46050.

The 2016 Global Rights Index: The World's Worst Countries for Workers. ITUC-CSI-IGB, 2016.

IUF. Morocco: DOHA workers continue campaign to support Abdullah Rakhmoun, demand jobs and union rights, 2016. URL https://www.iuf.org/news/morocco-doha-workers-continue-campaign-to-support-abdullah-rakhmoun-demand-jobs-and-union-rights/.

P. Jarley, J. Fiorito, and J. T. Delaney. National union governance: An empirically-grounded systems approach. *Journal of Labor Research*, 21(2): 227, 2000.

J. C. Jenkins. *The Politics of Insurgency. The Farm Worker Movement in the 1960s*. Columbia University Press, New York, NY, 1985.

Jeune Afrique. Tunisie: Le principal syndicat veut des négociations sociales "rapides," 02/10/2011.

En Tunisie, l'UGTT menace d'une grève générale sur fond de discorde interne, 09/11/2012.

Tout pour eliminer Achour, 11/13/1985.

M. Jibril. Les évenements et les problèmes de fond. *Lamalif*, 127: 28–31, July–August 1981.

K. Jochelson. Reform, repression and resistance in South Africa: A case study of Alexandra township, 1979–1989. *Journal of Southern African Studies*, 16(1): 1–32, 1990.

A. E. Jones. Investigating the local-global paradox: Corporate strategy, union local autonomy, and community action in chicago. In *Organizing the Landscape: Geographical Perspectives on Labor Unionism*. University of Minnesota Press, Minneapolis, MN, 1998.

R. J. Jonna and J. B. Foster. Marx's theory of working-class precariousness – and its relevance today. *Alternate Routes: A Journal of Critical Social Research* 27, 27, 2016.

Journal Officiel du Republique de la Tunisie. Décret n ° 95-30 du 9 janvier 1995, relatif à la composition et au fonctionnement de la commission consultative d'entreprise et aux modalités d'élection, 1/20/1995.

Portant approbation de la convention collective-cadre, 5/25/1973.

S. Karam. Trade unions lend weight to Morocco reform movement, May 1, 2011. URL https://www.reuters.com/article/idUSROB151320/.

H. Karoui and M. Messaoudi. Le discours syndical en tunisie à la veille du 26 janvier 1978: l'élan suspendu. *Annuaire de l'Afrique du Nord*, pp. 285–304, 1982.

B. Karray. Proposals, intermediation, and pressure: The three roles of the UGTT in Tunisia's post-revolutionary constitutional process. In *Socioeconomic Protests in MENA and Latin America: Egypt and Tunisia in Interregional Comparison*, pp. 123–144. Springer, 2020.

B. E. Kaufman. Bargaining theory, inflation, and cyclical strike activity in manufacturing. *ILR Review*, 34(3): 333–355, 1981.

R. R. Kaufman. Corporatism, clientelism, and partisan conflict. In J. M. Malloy, ed., *Authoritarianism and Corporatism in Latin America*. University of Pittsburgh Press, Pittsburgh, PA, 1977.

J. Kelly. *Rethinking Industrial Relations: Mobilisation, Collectivism and Long Waves*. Routledge, 1998.

J. Kerrissey and E. Schofer. Labor unions and political participation in comparative perspective. *Social Forces*, 97(1), 427–464 2018.

N. Ketchley. *Egypt in a Time of Revolution*. Cambridge University Press, Cambridge, UK, 2017.

A. a.-H. Khalaf. Labor Movements in Bahrain. *MERIP Reports*, 132, 1985.

C. Khosrowshahi. Privatization in Morocco: The politics of development. *The Middle East Journal*, 51(2): 242–255, 1997.

W. Kim and J. Gandhi. Coopting workers under dictatorship. *Journal of Politics*, 72(3): 646–658, 2010.

S. J. King. Informalized government workers in Tunisia: Reinstatement as formal workers with collective bargaining rights. In *Informal Workers and Collective Action: A Global Perspective*. ILR Press, 2017.

B. Klandermans. Psychology and trade union participation: Joining, acting, quitting. *Journal of Occupational Psychology*, 1986.

T. A. Kochan. How American workers view labor unions. *Monthly Labor Review*, 102(4): 23–31, 1979.

K. Kopinak. *Desert Capitalism: Maquiladoras in North America's Western Industrial Corridor*. University of Arizona Press, Tuscon, 1996.

J. Kopstein. Chipping away at the state: Workers' resistance and the demise of east Germany. *World Politics*, 48(3): 391–423, 1996.

U. Korkut. Entrenched elitism in trade unions in Poland and Romania: An explanation for the lack of union strength and success? *Economic and Industrial Democracy*, 27(1): 67–104, 2006.

W. Korpi and M. Shalev. Strikes, industrial relations and class conflict in industrial societies. *British Journal of Sociology*, 30(2): 164–187, 1979.

M. Kraïem. *État Et Société Dans La Tunisie Bourguibienne*. MIP Livre, Tunis, TN, 2011.

H. Kriesi. Political context and opportunity. *The Blackwell companion to social movements*, pp. 67–90, 2004.

T. Kuran. Now out of never: The element of surprise in the east European revolution of 1989. *World Politics*, 44(1): 7–48, 1991.

C. Kurzman. Can understanding undermine explanation? The confused experience of revolution. *Philosophy of the Social Sciences*, 34(3): 328–351, 2004.

S.-H. Kwon and M. O'Donnell. Repression and struggle: The state, the chaebol and independent trade unions in South Korea. *The Journal of Industrial Relations*, 41(2): 272–293, 1999.

S. Lakoff. Debate: The reality of muslim exceptionalism. *Journal of Democracy*, 15(4): 133–139, 2004.

R. Lambert and E. Webster. The re-emergence of political unionism in contemporary South Africa? In *Popular Struggles in South Africa*, pp. 20–41. Routledge, 1988.

E. Lanchovichina. *Eruptions of popular anger: The economics of the Arab Spring and Its aftermath*. The World Bank, 2017.

J. Lane, G. Hakim, and J. Miranda. Labor market analysis and public policy: The case of Morocco. *The World Bank Economic Review*, 13(3): 561–578, 1999.

V. Langohr. Labor movements and organizations. In *The Arab Uprisings Explained: New Contentious Politics in the Middle East*, pp. 180–200. Columbia University Press, New York, NY, 2014.

La Presse. Tunisie: Entretien avec – Wided Bouchammaoui (présidente de l'UTICA) – Cent commandements pour relancer croissance et emploi, 01/16/2013.

Sahbani appelle le gouvernement à respecter le pluralisme syndical, 02/16/2014.

Condamnés au dialogue et à l'entente: UGTT - gouvernement, 03/04/2012.

Ouverture lundi à Sousse du Congrès de la réconciliation, 04/15/1989.

Une croissance attendue de 3,1

Vers une régularisation de situation pour 30.000 employés, 1/04/2013.

Congrès de l'UGTT 16-17-18 décembre: Chassé-croisé et tractations, 12/15/1993.

Les conventions seront signées dans les prochains jours: Augmentation des salaires dans les secteurs public et privé, 7/15/2011.

Du gaz lacrymogène à l'encontre des sit-inneurss: Aux alentours de l'ANC, 7/28/2013a.

"La Tunisie ne supporte plus l'ambiguïté'!": Interview — Houcine Abassi, SG de l'UGTT, 7/28/2013b.

La Vie Éco. Maroc : les partis finiront-ils par tuer les syndicats, 01/10/2011.

80% des ménages au Maroc ont un revenu inférieur à 6650 DH par mois, 07/06/2009.

67 Md de DH de masse salariale, 132 Md de recettes fiscales, 11/02/2007.

Pourquoi l'unité syndical est une leurre , 11/14/2014.

Prélèvement sur les salaires des grévistes : le gouvernement passe à l'acte, 11/16/2012.

Gouvernement et syndicat, vers une guerre d'usure?, 12/08/2015.

Loi sur les associations: une réforme qui risque d'être houleuse, 12/09/2014.

Faut-il supprimer la Chambre des conseillers, 12/30/2005.

F. H. Lawson. *Bahrain: The Modernization of Autocracy*. Routledge, 1989.

A. Layachi. Reform and the Politics of Inclusion in the Maghrib. *The Journal of North African Studies*, 5(3):15–42, 1999.

A. LeBas. *From Protest to Parties: Party-Building and Democratization in Africa*. Oxford University Press, Oxford UK, 2011.

L'Économiste. Dialogue social: L'offre du gouvernement, 04/04/2008.

Dialogue social: Les syndicats rejettent l'offre du gouvernement, 04/22/2008.

L'UGTM en rangs serrés derrière l'Istiqlal, 05/12/2008.

Dialogue social: La riposte des syndicats, 05/13/2008.

Séminaire de l'UMT: Les syndicats africains récusent la politique néo-libérale, 10/13/1994.

Vieux démons, 11/12/2007.

L'emploi augmente mais le chômage va plus vite, 12/11/1998.

Un monde fou, 12/20/2006.

Y. Lee. *Militants or Partisans: Labor Unions and Democratic Politics in Korea and Taiwan*. Stanford University Press, Stanford, CA, 2011.

Le Maghreb. L'UGTT et le Mouvement, 4/25/1981.

Le Monde. 'Dans un pétition addresse au gouvernement: Deux cents intellectuels s'élèvent contre les mesures visant à "liquider le secteur agricole dominal,"' 12/1/1976.

Les fraudes électorales continuent à susciter des remous, 6/24/1983.

V. I. Lenin. *What Is to Be Done?* Wellred Books, 1935.

Les Éco. Le dialogue social chauffe le 1er-Mai, 04/30/2011.

Dialogue social: El Fassi dos au mur, 4/11/2011.

Le Temps. Appel à un dialogue constructif qui rétablit la confiance et consolide la paix sociale: Réunion extraordinaire de la commission administrative de l'UGTT, 01/06/2011.

Report de la réunion du Conseil National UGTT, 01/12/2011.

Congrès extraordinaire de l'UGTT: Pour l'unité, contre l'extrémisme, 04/22/1989.

Harcèlement, tentative de viol, absence de couverture sociale, licenciement abusif...: Corps de mé'tier : Le calvaire des femmes de ménage, 06/11/2010.

C. Lévesque, G. Murray, and S. L. Queux. Union disaffection and social identity: Democracy as a source of union revitalization. *Work and Occupations*, 32(4): 400–422, 2005.

M. Levi. *Consent, Dissent, and Patriotism*. Cambridge University Press, New York, NY, 1997.

M. Levi, D. Olson, J. Agnone, and D. Kelly. Union democracy reexamined. *Politics & Society*, 37(2): 203–228, 2009.

S. Levitsky and S. Mainwaring. Organized labor and democracy in Latin America. *Comparative Politics*, 39(1): 21–42, 2006.

S. Levitsky and L. A. Way. Between a shock and a hard place: The dynamics of labor-backed adjustment in Poland and Argentina. *Comparative Politics*, 30(2): 171–192, 1998.

T. Levitt. Prosperity versus strikes. *Industrial and Labor Relations Review*, pp. 221–226, 1953.

Libération. Communiqué Syndicat National des Cheminots, 01/26/1978a.

L'UMT ordonne et ne pas discute, 01/26/1978b.

Communiqué du Conseil Nationale de la CDT, 02/11/1993.

La Guerre des Dates, 02/18/1994.

Lutte ouvrière... lutte démocratique, 05/01/1993.

Aujourd'hui, option grève nationale: Débrayage tous azimutss, 11/03/2010.

Noubir Amaoui: Nous somme contraintes à la grève, 11/12/1990.

La grève pour défendre le pain et la dignité, 11/30/1990.

FDT: Les militants du PSU denoncent les complots, 3/31/2011.

A. Lichtenstein. "We feel that our strength is on the factory floor"': Dualism, shop-floor power, and labor law reform in late apartheid South Africa. *Labor History*, 60(6): 606–625, 2019.

J. Lindvall. Union density and political strikes. *World Politics*, 65(3): 539–569, 2013.

S. M. Lipset. Democracy and working-class authoritarianism. *American Sociological Review*, 24(4):482–501, 1959.

Radicalism or reformism: The sources of working-class politics. *American Political Science Review*, 77(1): 1–18, 1983.

S. M. Lipset, M. A. Trow, and J. S. Coleman. *Union Democracy*. The Free Press, Glencoe, IL, 1956.

L'observateur du Maroc. Entretien avec Miloudi Moukharik: "Nous sommes maintenant dans la logique de la négociation avant de passer à la protestation," 02/17/2014.

Ce qu'ils pensent des syndicats, 03/06/2013.

T. Lodge. The African national congress in South Africa, 1976–1983: Guerrilla War and armed propaganda. *Journal of Contemporary African Studies*, 3(1-2): 153–180, 1983.

L'Opinion. Appel à manifester le 20 février: L'UGTM boycotte tout appel à des manifestations illégales "La patrie d'abord, la patrie toujours," 02/18/2011.

Réforme constitutionnelle: L'UGTM plaide pour le renforcement du rôle des partis politiques et des syndicats, 04/11/2011.

Le peuple marocain rejette les résultat du scrutin du 10 juin compte tenu des irrégularités qui l'ont entaché et de la falsification de la volonté des électeurs, 06/23/1983.

Bonne gouvernance économique et mesures sociales au menu du gouvernement: Lier la responsabilité à la reddition des comptes, 1/21/2012.

Le gouvernement rejette en bloc les amendments istiqlaliens sans daigner les discuter, 12/7/1989.

Le gouvernement est responable de la crise sociale, 2/23/1989.

Les abus et le mécontentement s'amplifiant, 3/9/1991.

Les multiples violations de la loi dont sont victimes les travailleurs, 4/29/1990.

Pourqoui le gouvernment n'a-t-il pas demandé un vote de confiance, 5/5/1990.

Communiqué de l'UGTM à propos de dernières hausses des prix des produits de basse, 6/19/1981a.

Le prix: Annuler les dernières hausses, 6/19/1981b.

Echec de la grève opportuniste, grâce à la conscience et à la vigilance de la classe ouvrière, 6/22/1981.

R. E. Lucas. Monarchical authoritarianism: Survival and political liberalization in a Middle Eastern regime type. *International Journal of Middle East Studies*, 36(1): 103–119, 2004.

E. Lust-Okar. Divided they rule: The management and manipulation of political opposition. *Comparative Politics*, 36(2):159–179, 2004.

Structuring Conflict in the Arab World: Incumbents, Opponents, and Institutions. Cambridge University Press, Cambridge, UK, 2005.

D. Maghraoui. Constitutional reforms in Morocco: Between consensus and subaltern politics. *The Journal of North African Studies*, 16(4): 679–699, 2011.

J. Mahoney. Path dependence in historical sociology. *Theory and Society*, 29(4): 507–548, 2000.

Path-dependent explanations of regime change: Central america in comparative perspective. *Studies in comparative international development*, 36: 111–141, 2001.

K. Mannheim. *Essays on the Sociology of Culture*. Routledge & Kegan Paul, London, 1956.

C. L. Maranto and J. Fiorito. The effect of union characteristics on the outcome of NLRB certification elections. *ILR Review*, 40(2): 225–240, 1987.

J. Maree. The emergence, struggles and achievements of black trade unions in South Africa from 1973 to 1984. *Labour, Capital and Society*, 18(2):278–303, 1985.

Cosatu, oligarchy and the consolidation of democracy in an african context. In *COSATU's Contested Legacy*, pp. 56–89. Brill, 2013.

G. Marks. *Unions in Politics: Britain, Germany, and the United States in the Nineteenth and Early Twentieth Centuries*. Princeton University Press, Princeton, NJ, 1989.

T. Marshall. *Citizenship and Social Class*. Cambridge University Press, Cambridge, UK, 1950.

G. Martin-Muñoz. Political reform and social change in the Maghreb. *Mediterranean Politics*, 5(1): 96–130, 2000.

A. W. Marx. *Lessons of Struggle: South African Internal Opposition, 1960–1990*. Oxford University Press, New York, NY, 1992.

K. Marx. *Das Kapital*. Penguin Books, New York, NY, 1976.

N. Marzouki. Tunisia's Rotten Compromise. *Middle East Report Online*, 2015.

D. McAdam. *Political Process and the Development of Black Insurgency, 1930-1970*. University of Chicago Press, Chicago, IL, 1st edition, 1982.

Political Process and the Development of Black Insurgency, 1930-1970. University of Chicago Press, Chicago, IL, 2nd edition, 1999.

J. McAlevey. The crisis of new labor and Alinsky's legacy: Revisiting the role of the organic grassroots leaders in building powerful organizations and movements. *Politics & Society*, 43(3): 415–441, 2015.

T. J. McKeown. Case studies and the limits of the quantitative worldview. *Rethinking social inquiry: Tools, Shared Standards*, 139: 153, 2004.

D. T. McKinley. Cosatu and the tripartite alliance since 1994. In *Rethinking the Labour Movement in the 'New South Africa'*, pp. 43–61. Routledge, 2003.

R. F. Meknassi and C. Rioux. Relations professionnelles et négociation collective au Maroc. Technical report, International Labour Organization, 2010.

V. Menaldo. The Middle East and North Africa's resilient monarchs. *The Journal of Politics*, 74(3): 707–722, 2012.

A. Menouni. *Le Syndicalism Ouvrier Au Maroc*. Les Éditions Maghrebines, 1979.

S. Mersch. The intermediary, 2015. URL https://qantara.de/en/article/tunisias-union-leader-houcine-abbassi-intermediary.

D. S. Meyer. Protest and political opportunities. *Annual Review of Sociology*, 30(1): 125–145, 2004.

S. Mhlongo. An analysis of the classes in South Africa. *Race & Class*, 16(3): 259–294, 1975.

K. J. Middlebrook. *The Paradox of Revolution: Labor, The State, and Authoritarianism in Mexico*. The Johns Hopkins University Press, Baltimore, 1995.

S. G. Miller. *A History of Modern Morocco*. Cambridge University Press, New York, NY, 2013.

I. F. Molina. The Monarchy vs. the February 20th Movement: Who Holds the Reins of Political Change in Morocco. *Mediterranean Politics* 16(3): 435–441, 2011.

M. Monjib. *La monarchie marocaine et la lutte pour le pouvoir: Hassan II face à l'opposition nationale*. L'Harmattan, 1992.

K. Moody. *Workers in a Lean World: Unions in the International Economy*. Verso Books, New York, NY, 1997.

C. H. Moore. *Tunisia since Independence: The Dynamics of One-party Government*. University of California Press, Berkeley, CA, 1965.

Politics in North Africa: Algeria, Morocco, and Tunisia. Little, Brown, 1970.

A. Moutadayene. Economic crises and democratisation in Morocco. *The Journal of North African Studies*, 6(3): 70–82, 2001.

H. M'rad. *Le Dialogue National en Tunisie*. Éditions Nirvana, 2015.

M. V. Murillo. *Labor Unions, Partisan Coalitions and Market Reforms in Latin America*. Cambridge University Press, New York, NY, 2001.

C. Murphy. Fear and leadership in union organizing campaigns: An examination of workplace activist behavior. *SAGE Open*, 6(1): 2158244015623932, 2016.

E. Murphy. *Economic and Political Change in Tunisia: From Bourguiba to Ben Ali*. St. Martin's, New York, NY, 1999.

S. Naccache. The political economy of trade policy in Tunisia. *Middle East Development Journal*, 1(1): 31–58, 2009.

T. Nam. Rough days in democracies: Comparing protests in democracies. *European Journal of Political Research*, 46: 97–120, 2007.

H. B. Nassif. Generals and autocrats: How coup-proofing predetermined the military elite's behavior in the Arab spring. *Political Science Quarterly*, 130(2): 245–275, 2015.

J. M. Nelson. Organized labor, politics, and labor market flexibility in developing countries. *The World Bank Research Observer*, 6(1): 37–56, 1991.

y. *New York Times*, "News Summary," 5/2/1986.

B. Nissen. Living wage campaigns from a "social movement" perspective: The Miami case. *Labor Studies Journal*, 25(3): 29–50, 2000.

Alternative strategic directions for the US labor movement: Recent scholarship. *Labor Studies Journal*, 28(1): 133–155, 2003.

The effectiveness and limits of labor-community coalitions: Evidence from South Florida. *Labor Studies Journal*, 29(1): 67–88, 2004.

D. C. North. Institutions and credible commitment. *Journal of Institutional and Theoretical Economics (JITE)*, pp. 11–23, 1993.

D. C. North and B. R. Weingast. Public choice in seventeenth-century England. *The Journal of Economic History*, 49(4), 1989.

S. M. Nsouli, S. Eken, P. Duran, G. Bell, and M. Yucelik. The Path to Convertibility and Growth. Technical report, International Monetary Fund, Washington, D.C., 1993.

S. M. Nsouli, J. Decressin, S. Eken, K.-S. Enders, V. C. Thai, and F. Cartiglia. *Resilience and Growth through Sustained Adjustment: The Moroccan Experience*. International Monetary Fund, 1995.

E. R. Nugent. *After Repression: How Polarization Derails Democratic Transition*, Princeton University Press, Princeton, NJ, 2020.

A. Oberschall. *Social Conflict and Social Movements*. Prentice-Hall, Englewood Cliffs, NJ, 1973.

G. O'Donnell and P. C. Schmitter. *Transitions from Authoritarian Rule: Tentative Conclusions about Uncertain Democracies*. Johns Hopkins University Press, Baltimore, 1986.

M. Olson. *The Logic of Collective Action: Public Goods and the Theory of Groups*. Harvard University Press, Cambridge, MA, 1965.

M. Oubenal and A. Zeroual. Les transformations de la structure financière du capitalisme marocain. *Revue Marocaine Des Sciences Politiques et Sociales*, pp. 137–160, 2017.

J. Page. Getting ready for globalization: A new privatization strategy for the MENA region. In M. Celasun, ed., *State-Owned Enterprises in the Middle East and North Africa*. Routledge, New York, NY, 2001.

H. S. Parnes. *Union Strike Votes: Current Practice and Proposed Controls*. Princeton University Press, Princeton, NJ, 1995.

Parti Socialiste Destourien. *La Politique Contractuelle et les Événements de Janvier, 1978*. Dar al-Amal, Tunis, TN, 1978.

M. Parvin. Economic determinants of political unrest: An econometric approach. *Journal of Conflict Resolution*, 17(2): 271–296, 1973.

C. Pennell. *Morocco since 1830: A History*. New York University Press, New York, NY, 2000.

T. Pepinsky. The institutional turn in comparative authoritarianism. *British Journal of Political Science*, 44(3): 631–653, 2014.

K. J. Perkins. *A History of Modern Tunisia*. Cambridge University Press, New York, NY, 2004.

A History of Modern Tunisia. Cambridge University Press, 2nd edition, 2014.

T. Persson and G. Tabellini, eds.. *Monetary and Fiscal Policy*. MIT Press, Cambridge, MA, 1994.

K. Pfeifer. Between Rocks and Hard Choices: International Finance and Economic Adjustment in North Africa. In D. Vandewalle, ed., *North Africa: Development and Reform in a Changing Global Economy*. St. Martin's, New York, NY, 1996.

How Tunisia, Morocco, Jordan and even Egypt became IMF "Success Stories"' in the 1990s. *Middle East Report*, (210): 23–27, 1999.

J. A. Piazza. Globalizing Quiescence: Globalization, Union Density and Strikes in 15 Industrialized Countries. *Economic and Industrial Democracy*, 26(2): 289–314, 2005.

P. Pierson. *Politics in Time: History, Institutions and Social Analysis*. Princeton University Press, Princeton, NJ, 2004.

L. Plank, A. Rossi, and C. Staritz. What does 'fast fashion'mean for workers? apparel production in Morocco and Romania. In *Towards Better Work: Understanding Labour in Apparel Global Value Chains*, pp. 127–147. Springer, 2014.

K. Polanyi. *The Great Transformation*. Beacon Press, Boston, MA, 1957.

The Livelihood of Man. Academic Press, Inc., New York, NY, 1977.

F. Polletta and J. M. Jasper. Collective identity and social movements. *Annual Review of Sociology*, 27(1): 283–305, 2001.

S. Portelli. Oral history interview with Mustapha Ben Jafar, 2015, https://clio.columbia.edu/catalog/13791567.

S. Portelli and A. Augenbaum. Oral history interview with Moncef Marzouki, 2017. URL https://clio.columbia.edu/catalog/13793743.

M. P. Posusney. Irrational workers: The moral economy of labor protest in Egypt. *World Politics*, 46(1): 83–120, 1993.

Labor and the State in Egypt: Workers, Unions, and Economic Restructuring, 1952–1996. Columbia University Press, New York, NY, 1997.

Globalization and labor protection in oil-poor Arab countries: Racing to the bottom? *Global Social Policy*, 3(3): 267–297, 2003.

M. P. Posusney and L. J. Cook. *Privatization and Labor*. Edward Elgar Publishing, 2002.

N. Pratt. Maintaining the moral economy: Egyptian state – labor relations in an era of economic liberalization. *The Arab Studies Journal*, 8(2/1): 111–129, 2000.

A. Przeworski. Some problems in the study of the transition to democracy. In *Transitions from Authoritarian Rule: Comparative Perspectives*. The Johns Hopkins University Press, Baltimore, 1986.

Democracy and the Market: Political and Economic Reforms in Eastern Europe and Latin America. Cambridge University Press, 1991.

M. Rama. How bad is unemployment in Tunisia? Assessing labor market efficiency in a developing country. *The World Bank Research Observer*, 13(1): 59–77, 1998.

S. Rassouni. Al-itihād al-maghribi lil-shugl: andamā yaʿīsh alniḍāl wa al-ikhtilāl, 2012.

Réalités. Le salaires du mérite, 02/11/1993.

Le Plan de bataille de l'UGTT, 03/25/1993.

Mohamed Trabelsi S.G.A. de l'UGTT: "L'autonomie de l'UGTT est mieux acceptée aujourd'hui"', 04/13/1995.

L'UGTT: la deuxième vitesse, 04/19/1985.

Dialogue Social: Partage, vérité, et avenir, 04/29/1993.

Qui a gagnè, 04/30/1993.

Le dit, le non dit, et l'attendu, 05/13/1993.

A. Rees. Industrial conflict and business fluctuations. *Journal of Political Economy*, 60(5): 371–382, 1952.

A. Report. Ben ali tackles reforms in post-bourguiba Tunisia. *Africa Report*, January-February 1988.

A. Rhazaoui. Recent Economic Trends: Managing the Indebtedness. In W. Zartman, ed., *The Political Economy of Morocco*. Praeger, New York, NY, 1987.

A. Richards and J. Waterbury. *A Political Economy of the Middle East: State, Class, and Economic Development*. Westview, Boulder, 1990.

J. Riddell. *Free Trade Unions in the Fight for African Freedom*. International Confederation of Free Trade Unions and its African Regional... 1961.

B. Rijkers, C. Freund, and A. Nucifora. The perils of industrial policy: Evidence from Tunisia. *Technical Report, Mimeo, The World Bank.*, 2014.

C. Rist. La progression des greves en france et sa valeur symptomatique. *Revue d'Economie Politique*, 21: 161–193, 1907.

G. Robertson. Leading labor: Unions, politics and protest in new democracies. *Comparative Politics*, 36(3): 253–272, 2004.

The Politics of Protest in Hybrid Regimes: Managing Dissent in Post-Communist Russia. Cambridge University Press, Cambridge, UK, 2010.

M. Roomkin. Union structure, internal control, and strike activity. *ILR Review*, 29(2): 198–217, 1976.

A. M. Ross and D. Irwin. Strike experience in five countries, 1927–1947: An interpretation. *ILR Review*, 4(3): 323–342, 1951.

Royaume du Maroc. 2006. 50 ans de développement humain et perspectives 2025. Technical report Royaume du Maroc. URL: http://www.amb-maroc.fr/Dossiers/rdh-doc.pdf

Royaume du Maroc. Système de la fonction publique, 2017.

N. Rudra. Are workers in the developing world winners or losers in the current era of globalization. *Studies in Comparative International Development*, 40(3): 29–64, 2005.

D. Ruschemeyer, E. H. Stephens, and J. D. Stephens. *Capitalist Development and Democracy*. University of Chicago Press, Chicago, IL, 1992.

C. Sabel. *Work and Politics: The Division of Labor in Industry*. Cambridge University Press, Cambridge, UK, 1982.

L. Sadiki and L. Saleh. *Revolution and Democracy in Tunisia: A Century of Protestscapes*. Oxford University Press, Oxford, UK, 2024.

A. Safi. Les moyens d'exercer le droit syndical dans l'entreprise. In *Syndicat et Société*. Centre d'études et de Recherches Économiques et Sociales, Tunis, TN, 1989.

J. Saghir. Privatization in Tunisia. CFS Discussion Paper Series, 1993.

A. Salah-Bey. Trade unions and economic and social development in the Maghreb. *International Labour Review*, 94: 375–397, 1965.

M. M. Salih. *Economic development and political action in the Arab World*. Routledge, 2014.

J. G. Samstad. Corporatism and democratic transition: State and labor during the Salinas and Zedillo administrations. *Latin American Politics and Society*, 44(4): 1–28, 2002.

S. Sandoval. *Social change and labor unrest in Brazil since 1945*. Routledge, 1995.

J. Santucci. Les Élections Législatives Marocaines de Juin 1977. In *Annuaire de L'Afrique du Nord, 1977*. Centre National De La Recherche Scientifique, 1979.

Chronique Marocaine. In *Annuaire de L'Afrique du Nord, 1984*. Centre National De La Recherche Scientifique, 1986.

Chronique Marocaine. In *Annuaire de L'Afrique du Nord, 1986*. Centre National De La Recherche Scientifique, 1988.

A. H. Saulniers. Privatization in Morocco. In *Constraints and Impacts of Privatization*, pp. 210–225. Routledge, London, UK, 1993a.

Privatization in Morocco. In V. V. Ramanadham, ed., *Privatization: A Global Perspective*. Routledge, New York, NY, 1993b.

A. Sayer. Approaching moral economy. In H. C. Stehr, Nico and B. Weiler, eds., *The Moralization of the Markets*. Transaction Books, New Brunswick, 2006.

S. Schaar and E. Ahmad. M'hamed ali and the Tunisian labour movement. *Race & Class*, 19(3): 253–276, 1978.

A. Schipani. Left behind: Labor unions and redistributive policy under the Brazilian workers' party. *Comparative Politics*, 54(3): 405–428, 2022.

O. Schlumberger. Opening old bottles in search of new wine: On non-democratic legitimacy in the Middle East. *Middle East Critique*, 19(3): 233–250, 2010.

R. Schroeder. Trade Unions, Politics and the Working Class Struggle: The Food and Canning Workers Union, 1975 to 1986. Unpublished honours thesis.

K. Scopes. Understanding the new labor movements in the "third world": The emergence of social movement unionism. *Critical Sociology*, 19(2): 81–101, 1992.

J. Scott. *The Moral Economy of the Peasant*. Yale University Press, New Haven, CT, 1976.

D. Seddon. Winter of discontent: Economic crisis in Tunisia and Morocco. *MERIP Reports*, 127, 1984.

Riot and rebellion: Political responses to economic crisis in North Africa (Tunisia, Morocco and Sudan), 1986.

Morocco and the Western Sahara. *Review of African Political Economy*, 14(38): 24–47, 1987.

The politics of "adjustment" in Morocco. In *Structural Adjustment in Africa*, pp. 234–265. Springer, 1989.

G. Seidman. *Manufacturing Militance: Workers' Movements in Brazil and South Africa, 1970-1985*. University of California Press, Berkeley, CA, 1994.

Is South Africa different? Sociological comparisons and theoretical contributions from the land of apartheid. *Annual Review of Sociology*, 25(1): 419–440, 1999.

B. Selwyn. Strike waves and wage explosions, 1968–1970: An economic interpretation. *Journal of Agrarian Change*, 7(4): 526–553, 2007.

Workers in global commodity chains: The organization of labour in export grape production. In A. Bonanno and J. S. B. Cavalcanti, eds., *Globalization and the Time-Space Reorganization: Capital Mobility in Agriculture and Food in the Americas*, volume 17 of *Research in Rural Sociology and Development*. Emerald Group Publishing Ltd, 2011.

M. Shalev. Strikes and the crisis: Industrial conflict and unemployment in the western nations. *Economic and Industrial Democracy*, 4: 417–460, 1983.

The Future of Labour Movements, chapter The resurgence of labour quiescence. In *The Future of Labour Movements*, Sage Publications, London, UK, 1992.

E. Shorter and C. Tilly. *Strikes in France, 1830-1968*. Cambridge University Press, Cambridge, UK, 1974.

D. Soskice. Strike waves and wage explosions, 1968–1970: An economic interpretation. In C. Crouch and A. Pizzorno, eds., *The Resurgence of Class Conflict in Western Europe since 1968*, pp. 221–246. Palgrave Macmillan, New York, NY, 1978.

D. Soskice, R. Bates, and D. Epstein. Ambition and constraint: The ambition and constraint: The stabilizing role of institutions. *Journal of Law, Economics, and Organization*, 8(3): 547–560, 1992.

K. W. Stein. The intifada and the 1936-39 uprising: A comparison. *Journal of Palestine Studies*, 19(4): 64–85, 1990.

A. C. Stepan. *The State and Society: Peru in Comparative Perspective*. Princeton University Press, Princeton, NJ, 1978.

A. C. Stepan and G. Robertson. An "arab" more than a "muslim" democracy gap. *Journal of Democracy*, 14(3): 30–42, 2003.

Debate: Arab, not muslim exceptionalism. *Journal of Democracy*, 15(4): 140–146, 2004.

J. Stepan-Norris and M. Zeitlin. Union democracy, radical leadership, and the hegemony of capital. *American Sociological Review*, pp. 829–850, 1995.

J. Stork. Bahrain's Crisis Worsens. *Middle East Report*, 207, 1997.

L. Storm. *Democratization in Morocco: The Political Elite and Struggles for Power in the Post-independence State*. Routledge, London, UK, 2007.

G. Strauss. Union democracy. In G. Strauss, D. G. Gallagher, and J. Fiorito, eds., *The State of the Unions*. Industrial Relations Research Association, Madison, WI, 1991.

M. Svolik. *The Politics of Authoritarian Rule*. Cambridge University Press, Cambridge UK, 2012.

P. Swenson. *Fair Shares: Unions, Pay and Politics in Sweden and West Germany*. Cornell University Press, Ithaca, NY, 1989.

S. Tarrow. *Power in Movement*. Cambridge University Press, New York, NY, 1998.

A. Tattersall. There is power in coalition: A framework for assessing how and when union-community coalitions are effective and enhance union power. *Labour & Industry: A Journal of the Social and Economic Relations of Work*, 16(2): 97–112, 2005.

Power in Coalition: Strategies for Strong Unions and Social Change. Routledge, 2020.

C. Taylor et al. *Sources of the Self: The Making of the Modern Identity*, Harvard University Press, Cambridge, MA, 1989.

Telquel. Ils n'ont rien compris!, 4/15/2011.

Tout sur l'argent des partis politiques marocains, 5/15/2012.

O. Tesquet. Ben ali: les Compromissions d'orange en tunisie, 2011. URL http://owni.fr/2011/03/03/ben-ali-les-compromission-dorange-en-tunisie/.

Agence France Presse. Compensation deal for Tunisian textile workers. 12/12/2002.

Réalités. Que veut la patronat?, 3/11/1996.

Mohamed trabelsi s.g.a. de l'ugtt: "l'autonomie de l'ugtt est mieux acceptée aujourd'hui", 4/13/1995.

Quand les chiffres s'en mêlent, 4/22/1993.

Les négociations sociales piétinent: Mohamed trabelsi s'explique, 4/9/2008.

Négociations sociales: L'impasse, 5/12/2008.

Remous à l'ugtt, 9/2/1998.

The Carter Center. The constitution-making process in Tunisia: Final Report, 2011-2014., 2015.

The World Bank. World bank privatization database, 2008.

Human capital index, 2016. URL https://data.worldbank.org/indicator/HD.HCI.OVRL. data retrieved from World Development Indicators.

K. Thelen. Historical institutionalism in comparative politics. *Annual Review of Political Science*, 2(1): 369–404, 1999.

K. A. Thelen. *How Institutions Evolve: The Political Economy of Skills in Germany, Britain, the United States, and Japan*. Cambridge University Press, New York, NY, 2004.

G. Therborn. The rule of capital and the rise of democracy. *New Left Review*, 103, 1977.

E. Thompson. The moral economy of the english crowd in the eighteenth century. *Past and Present*, 50(1): 76–136, 1971.

C. Tilly. *From Mobilization to Revolution*. Addison-Wesley Publishing Corporation, Reading, Massachusetts, 1978.

Contention and Democracy in Europe, 1650–2000. Cambridge University Press, New York, NY, 2004.

M. Toumi. *La Tunisie De Bourguiba à Ben Ali*. Presses Universitaires De France, Paris, France, 1989.

A. Tounsi. Les enseignants du supérieur et le pouvoir politique en Tunisie: portée et signification de la grève administrative. *L'Année du Maghreb*, (II): 415–418, 2007.

Transparency International. Corruption Perceptions Index - Morocco, 2010. data retrieved from the Corruption Perceptions Index, https://www.transparency.org/en/cpi/2010.

G. Trejo. Religious competition and ethnic mobilization in Latin America. *American Political Science Review*, 103(3): 323–342, 2009.

G. Tsbelis and P. Lange. Strikes around the world: A game theoretic approach. In S. M. Jacoby, ed., *The Workers of Nations: Industrial Relations in a Global Economy*. Oxford University Press, Oxford, UK, 1995.

Tunis Afrique Presse. L'UGTT reconnaît avoir commis une faute en appelant à la candidature du président déchu, 12/28/2011.

Tunisia Ministry of Plan. Troisième plan de développement, 1968.

Tunisian External Communication Agency. *Tunisie: le pacte national: 7 novembre 1988*. Agence tunisienne de communication extérieure, 1994.

Tunisian Ministry of Social Affairs. *Taṭawar al-waḍaʿal-ijtimāʿī khilāl sina 2010 muqārina bi-sina 1998*. Tunisian Ministry of Social Affairs and Foreign Relations, 2010.

Taṭawar al-waḍaʿal-ijtimāʿī khilāl sina 2011 muqārina bi-sina 2010. Tunisian Ministry of Social Affairs and Foreign Relations, 2012.

Taṭawar al-waḍaʿal-ijtimāʿī khilāl sina 2013 muqārina bi-sina 2012. Tunisian Ministry of Social Affairs and Foreign Relations, 2014.

Tunisie Numérique. Tunisie – Houcine Abassi: "Le pouvoir ne nous intéresse pas," 10/29/2013.

Tunisie: Houcine Abassi: "Le Quartet désignera les responsables si le dialogue venait à échouer," 11/13/2013.

Tunisie: Un communiqué d'Ennahdha suscite la colère à Al massar et au PR, 2/2/2013.

Un accord met fin aux difficultés de 31.000 ouvriers de nettoyage et de gardiennage, 4/23/2011.

Tunisie: Ennahdha se retire du dialogue national après le mot de Ziad Lakdhar, 5/16/2013.

UGTT. *Développement plus Rapide, Distribution plus équitable*. UGTT Press, Tunis, 1977.

Pour un société démocratique et juste. UGTT Press, Tunis, 1984.

Al-taḍamun ḍaman al-mustaqbal. UGTT Press, Tunis, 1995.

Vers un Renouveau Syndical: Diagnostic Quantitatif de l'UGTT par ses Cadres, 2006.

Al-Tanmiyah al-Jihawiyyah bi Wilayat Sidi Bouzid: Baina Al-Waqiʿal-Mukabbal wa Al-Imkanat Al-Waʿidah [Regional Development in Sidi Bouzid: Between the Limitations of Reality and Promising Capacities]. UGTT Press, Tunis, 2010.

UGTT. Union Générale Tunisien du Travail. *Social and Economic Report*. UGTT Press, Tunis, 2001.

United States Bureau of Labor Statistics. Labor conditions in the kingdom of Morocco. In *Labor Digests on Countries in Africa*. United States Department of Labor, 1966.

Summary of the Labor Situation in Tunisia. Bureau of Labor Statistics, 1958. URL https://books.google.com/books?id=AiPClPkPvxUC.

United States Department of Labor. *Foreign Labor Trends: Tunisia*. U.S. Dept. of Labor, Bureau of International Labor Affairs, 1989.

Foreign Labor Trends: Tunisia. U.S. Dept. of Labor, Bureau of International Labor Affairs, 1991.

Moroccan Human Rights Practices, 1993. Government Printing Office, 1994.

J. Upham. *Trade Unions in the World*. Harlow, Essex, UK, 1993.

J. S. Valenzuela. Labor movements in transitions to democracy: A framework for analysis. *Comparative Politics*, 21(4): 445–472, 1989.

Labour Movements and Political Systems: Some Variations. In M. Regini, ed., *The Future of Labour Movements*. Sage Publications, New York, NY, 1992.

J.-P. Vatthauer and I. Weipert-Fenner. The quest for social justice in Tunisia: Socioeconomic protest and political democratization post 2011. *PRIF Reports*, 143, 2017.

P. Vermeren. *Histoire du Maroc depuis l'indépendance*. La Découverte, 2002.

K. Voss and R. Sherman. Breaking the iron law of oligarchy: Union revitalization in the American labor movement. *American Journal of Sociology*, 106(2): 303–349, 2000.

K. Vráblíková. *What Kind of Democracy?: Participation, Inclusiveness and Contestation*. Routledge, 2016.

D. Waldner. *State Building and Late Development*. Cornell University Press, Ithaca, NY, 1999.

M. Wallerstein. Union organization in advanced industrial democracies. *American Political Science Review*, 83(2): 481–501, 1989.

J. Walton and D. Seddon. Food riots past and present. In J. Walton and D. Seddon, eds., *Free Markets and Food Riots: The Politics of Global Adjustment*. Blackwell, Oxford, UK, 1994.

S. E. Waltz. The Islamist challenge in Tunisia. *Journal of Arab Affairs*, 3(1): 99, 1984.

J. Waterbury. The coup manqué. In E. Gellner and C. A. Micaud, eds., *Arabs and Berbers*, pp. 397–424. Duckworth, London, UK, 1972.

E. Webster. The two faces of the black trade union movement in South Africa. *Review of African Political Economy*, 14(39): 33–41, 1987.

C. Welzel and F. Deutsch. Emancipative values and non-violent protest: The importance of "ecological" effects. *British Journal of Political Science*, 42(2): 465–479, 2012.

B. Western. A comparative study of corporatist development. *American Sociological Review*, pp. 283–294, 1991.

G. White. *A Comparative Political Economy of Tunisia and Morocco: On the Outside of Europe Looking In*. State University of New York Press, Albany, New York, 2001.

M. J. Willis. *Politics and Power in the Maghreb Algeria, Tunisia and Morocco from Independence to the Arab Spring*. C Hurst & Company, 2012.

J. D. Wolfe. Corporatism and union democracy: The British miners and incomes policy, 1973-74. *Comparative Politics*, 17(4): 421–436, 1985.

E. J. Wood. An insurgent path to democracy: Popular mobilization, economic interests, and regime transition in South Africa and El Salvador. *Comparative Political Studies*, 34(8): 862–888, 2001.

G. Wood. The 1973 Durban strikes: Of local and international significance. *Contree*, 31, 1992.

World Bank Group. Creating markets in Morocco: A second generation of reforms: Boosting private sector growth, job creation and skills upgrading, 2019.

Ya-biladi. Maroc: 83,7% de participation à la grève générale, selon les syndicats, 10/29/2014.

Maroc: Les partis politiques très divisés sur les manifestations du 20 février, 12/18/2011.

D. J. Yashar. *Contesting Citizenship in Latin America: The Rise of Indigenous Movements and the Postliberal Challenge*. Cambridge University Press, New York, NY, 2005.

C. Yates. The internal dynamics of union power: Explaining canadian auto workers' militancy in the 1980s. *Studies in Political Economy*, 31(1): 73–105, 1990.

S. Yom. Civil society and democratization in the Arab world. *Middle East*, 9(4): 15–32, 2005.

S. Yom and F. G. Gause III. Resilient royals: How Arab monarchies hang on. *Journal of Democracy*, 23(4): 74–88, 2012.

H. Yousfi. *L'UGTT, Une Passion Tunisienne Enquête Sur Les Syndicalistes En Révolution, 2011-2014*. Med Ali Édition, Sfax, TN, 2015.

M. Zaanouni. Les Chantiers de Travail: L'Experience Tunisienne de 1958 à 1963. *L'Action*, 27, 29, 31 October 1963.

W. Zartman and R. A. Duga. The monarchy and the constitution in Morocco. *Il Politico*, 30(1): 126–143, 1965.

C. Zazueta and R. d. l. Peña. *La estructura del Congreso del Trabajo: estado, trabajo y capital en México, un acercamiento al tema*. Centro Nacional de Información y Estadísticas del Trabajo: Fondo de Cultura Económica, 1984.

E. Zebadúa. The heralded revolution: The project of modernization in Mexico. *International Journal of Political Economy*, 24(3): 71–85, 1994.

S. Zeghidi. Les mutations du mouvement syndical tunisien au cours des 15 dernieres années. In *Syndicat et Société*. Centre d'études et de Recherches Économiques et Sociales, Tunis, TN, 1989.

S. Zemni. The extraordinary politics of the Tunisian revolution: The process of constitution making. *Mediterranean Politics*, 20(1): 1–17, 2015.

S. Zemni and K. Bogaert. Urban renewal and social development in Morocco in an age of neoliberal government. *Review of African Political Economy*, 38(129): 403–417, 2011.

A. Zeroual and A. Lefnatsa. The new forms of organization of wage-related resistance in Morocco. *Confluences Mediterranee*, 111(4): 105–118, 2019.

R. Zghal. Mouvement Ouvrier et Mouvement Syndical, Le Vécu du Syndicalisme à Travers Deux Enquêtes en Milieu Industriel. In *Syndicat et Société*. Centre d'études et de Recherches Économiques et Sociales, Tunis, TN, 1989.

A. Zouari. Collective action and governance structure in Tunisia's Labor Organization. In M. K. Nabli and J. B. Nugent, eds., *The New Institutional Economics and Development: Theory and Applications to Tunisia*. Elsevier Science Publishers, New York, NY, 1989.

S. Zunes. Bahrain's arrested revolution. *Arab Studies Quarterly*, 35(2): 149–164, 2013.

Index

www.ingramcontent.com/pod-product-compliance
Lightning Source LLC
LaVergne TN
LVHW011701200926
848484LV00004B/1028
* 9 7 8 1 0 0 9 6 3 4 9 3 9 *